The First World War and the Nationality Question in Europe

National Cultivation of Culture

Edited by

Joep Leerssen (*University of Amsterdam*)

Editorial Board

John Breuilly (*The London School of Economics and Political Science*)
Katharine Ellis (*University of Cambridge*)
Ina Ferris (*University of Ottawa*)
Patrick J. Geary (*Institute for Advanced Study, Princeton*)
Tom Shippey (*Saint Louis University*)
Anne-Marie Thiesse (*CNRS, National Center for Scientific Research*)

VOLUME 23

The titles published in this series are listed at *brill.com/ncc*

The First World War and the Nationality Question in Europe

Global Impact and Local Dynamics

Edited by

Xosé M. Núñez Seixas

BRILL

LEIDEN | BOSTON

The conference that gave origin to this book, as well as translation and language edition costs, have been covered by the *Consello da Cultura Galega* (Council of Galician Culture), Santiago de Compostela (consellodacultura.gal).

Cover illustration: Local members of the Language Brotherhood of Betanzos (Galicia), 1918. ©Arquivo Municipal de Betanzos.

Library of Congress Cataloging-in-Publication Data

Names: International Context of the Galician Language Brotherhoods and the Nationality Question in Interwar Europe (2016 : Santiago de Compostela) | Núñez Seixas, Xosé M. (Xosé Manoel), 1966- editor.
Title: The First World War and the nationality question in Europe : global impact and local dynamics / edited by Xosé M. Núñez Seixas.
Description: Leiden ; Boston : Brill, [2021] | Series: National cultivation of culture, 1876-5645 ; vol. 23 | Includes bibliographical references and index.
Identifiers: LCCN 2020037614 (print) | LCCN 2020037615 (ebook) | ISBN 9789004437951 (hardback) | ISBN 9789004442245 (ebook)
Subjects: LCSH: Europe--Politics and government--1918-1945--Congresses. | Imperialism--Europe--History--20th century--Congresses. | Nationalism--Europe--History--20th century--Congresses. | World War, 1914-1918--Political aspects--Congresses.
Classification: LCC D727 .I565 2021 (print) | LCC D727 (ebook) | DDC 940.3/1--dc23
LC record available at https://lccn.loc.gov/2020037614
LC ebook record available at https://lccn.loc.gov/2020037615

Typeface for the Latin, Greek, and Cyrillic scripts: "Brill". See and download: brill.com/brill-typeface.

ISSN 1876-5645
ISBN 978-90-04-43795-1 (hardback)
ISBN 978-90-04-44224-5 (e-book)

Copyright 2021 by Koninklijke Brill NV, Leiden, The Netherlands.
Koninklijke Brill NV incorporates the imprints Brill, Brill Hes & De Graaf, Brill Nijhoff, Brill Rodopi, Brill Sense, Hotei Publishing, mentis Verlag, Verlag Ferdinand Schöningh and Wilhelm Fink Verlag.
All rights reserved. No part of this publication may be reproduced, translated, stored in a retrieval system, or transmitted in any form or by any means, electronic, mechanical, photocopying, recording or otherwise, without prior written permission from the publisher. Requests for re-use and/or translations must be addressed to Koninklijke Brill NV via brill.com or copyright.com.

This book is printed on acid-free paper and produced in a sustainable manner.

Contents

List of Figures   VII

1   Introduction. The First World War and the Nationality Question: From Local to Glocal Perspectives   1
    Xosé M. Núñez Seixas

PART 1
The First World War, Transnational Action and the Principle of Nationality

2   Cultural Mobility and Political Mobilization: Transnational Dynamics, National Action   17
    Joep Leerssen

3   Wilson's Unexpected Friends: The Transnational Impact of the First World War on Western European Nationalist Movements   37
    Xosé M. Núñez Seixas

4   Nationalizing an Empire: The Bolsheviks, the Nationality Question, and Policies of Indigenization in the Soviet Union (1917–1927)   65
    Malte Rolf

5   Federalism in Multinational States: Otto Bauer's Theory   87
    Ramón Máiz

6   New Worlds Tackling on Side-tracks: The National Concepts of T.G. Masaryk and Oszkár Jászi during the First World War (1914–1919)   115
    Bence Bari

PART 2
Local Dynamics

7   Micro-Nationalisms in Western Europe in the Wake of the First World War   145
    Francesca Zantedeschi

8   The Language Brotherhoods: European Echoes in the Development of Galician Nationalism (1916–1923)   170
    Ramón Villares

9   The Galician Language Brotherhoods and Minority Languages in Europe during the First World War   199
    Johannes Kabatek

PART 3
The Legacy of the First World War and the Nationality Question

10   The Impact of the First World War on the (Re-)Shaping of National Histories on Europe   223
    Stefan Berger

11   From Nationalities to Minorities? The Transnational Debate on the Minority Protection System of the League of Nations, and Its Predecessors   245
    Stefan Dyroff

12   Agrarian Movements, the National Question, and Democracy in Europe, 1880–1945   266
    Lourenzo Fernández-Prieto and Miguel Cabo

    Index   291

Figures

2.1	Concert tours of Franz Liszt	22
2.2	Art academies mapped against the birthplace of their pupils, 1823–1848	23
2.3	Reticulation of Floral Game-style festivals	23
2.4 & 2.5	Correspondence networks of Jacob Grimm and (juxtaposed) of E.M. Arndt and Prosper Mérimée	24, 25
2.6	The intensifying degrees of the Cultivation of Culture harmonized with a cumulative (rather than serial) view of Hroch's phase model, and mapped as a function of sequentiality-in-time vs. spatial locatedness	35
3.1	"The great democratic harvest" *L'Esquella de la Torratxa*, 15 November 1918	56
9.1	Mutual relationship between linguistic facts and metalinguistic discourse	204
9.2	The triangle of language planning	205
9.3	Discursive transversality	206

Introduction

The First World War and the Nationality Question: From Local to Glocal Perspectives

Xosé M. Núñez Seixas

This volume assembles most of the papers presented at the international conference *From Empires to Nations: The International Context of the Galician Language Brotherhoods and the Nationality Question in Interwar Europe,* convened by the Galician Culture Council (*Consello da Cultura Galega*) in Santiago de Compostela on 6–7 October, 2016. The primary objective of the conference was to commemorate the centenary of the foundation of the first organization that embraced the creed of Galician ethnonationalism, the Language Brotherhoods or *Irmandades da Fala*. This marked the transition from the regionalist to the nationalist stage of the Galician movement, and heralded its later evolution during the 1920s and 1930s, as the Galicianist Party (*Partido Galeguista*) became a significant actor in Galician politics until the outbreak of the Spanish Civil War. This was a result of an endogeneous evolution, conditioned by the previous existence of a cultural renaissance in Galician language since the mid-nineteenth century, as well as by the intellectual agency of historians, writers and regionalist activitists who crafted the main symbols and narratives of modern Galician identity.[1] However, the emergence of the Language Brotherhoods was also, as similar developments in Wales, Frisia, Occitania, Corsica and other European regions displayed, a 'local' byproduct of a transnational phenomenon: the wave of national self-determination that accompanied the course of the Great War. Therefore, the second aim of the Santiago conference was to bridge new perspectives on the European and global context in which the modern Galician movement emerged and developed, playing interchangeably with different historiographic scales.[2]

Certainly, Spain was a non-belligerent country, and Galician activists had no direct experience of the war at the trenches of at the rear, unlike Flemish, Breton and Sardinian regionalists who returned home and processed their war

---

1 For a complete overview of the history of the Galician movement, see Beramendi (2007). See also in English Beramendi and Núñez Seixas (1995), as well as Núñez Seixas and Iglesias Amorín (2020).
2 See Revel (1996).

experience into new doctrines and ways of understanding territorial politics.[3] The first Galician ethnonationalists were men forged by the previous regionalist tradition, as well as journalists and intellectuals who had migrated to Latin America in the preceding decades. They were influenced by the development of the Catalan movement, as well as by Portuguese republicans. They were also extremely receptive towards the new echoes of the nationality question beyond the Pyrenees, from the activity of Polish and Yugoslav émigrés in London, Geneva and Paris to the meetings of the *Union des Nationalités*, the diffusion of the principle of nationality as a propaganda weapon by the contending sides in the war, the news arriving from the Easter Rising in Dublin in April 1916, and later on by the spread of Wilson's fourteen points and the Russian revolutionaries' manifestos in favour of national self-determination.

What happened in Galicia was another expression of a global phenomenon, the new *wave* of national self-determination fostered by the specific moment of the Great War, and which extended throughout Europe, Africa and Asia with particular intensity from 1916 onwards. What has been called the *Wilsonian moment* also had a previous impact on West and East European peripheries, and developed at a parallel pace to the diffusion of the principle of national self-determination at the imperial periphery in Asia and Africa.[4] This was further proof of the apparent paradox pointed out by Anne-Marie Thiesse: *rien de plus international que le nationalisme*.[5] Indeed, from Moldavia to Galicia, it is possible to encounter similar theoretical principles, which inspired the doctrines, symbols and political cultures that have shaped the various nationalist movements since the long nineteenth century.[6]

In fact, all nationalists and patriots around the globe consider their beliefs to be genuine. Yet, they are also convinced that they are a part of wider phenomenon: the re-organization of the world into national categories, following the fall of the Ancien Regime and the breakup of pre-modern multi-ethnic empires. Nevertheless, the discursive tools and the narrative strategies used by nationalists in Europe and beyond are comparable, and to some extent they are also the outcome of transnational transfers of narratives, symbols and models. In all nationalist movements across Europe, similar frames of writing national history may be found, as well as comparable narratives of the ethnic distinctiveness, dynamics of standardization of minority languages, and appeals to people's sovereignty rooted in ancient traditions. They all have recourse

---

3   See Carney (2015); Secchi (1976); Shelby (2014).
4   Dunn and Fraser (1996); Manela (2007).
5   Thiesse (2001: 11).
6   Leerssen (2006).

to myth-making.[7] This is a result of the circulation of a set of theoretical writings initially conceived as cornerstones of the national theory of the nation itself, which inspire intellectuals, activists and politicians in other territories.

There was an intense transnational circulation of national theories and historical narratives from the mid-nineteenth century. The transfer and appropriation of images and models inspired local nationalists to think about their own nations. At some critical moments, something similar to a "domino effect" took place in Europe, such as during the "spring of peoples" in 1848. Similar moments, which also extended towards the periphery of European colonial empires, took place in 1918/19, as well as from the mid-1950s. The last wave restricted itself to East-Central Europe, the Caucasus and Central Asia, and spread between 1988(89 and 1992. The "contagion" exerted by the example of successful national movements on other, less developed (or not yet successful) sub-state nationalisms, was not an irrelevant factor in the spread of nationalism.[8]

The Great War involved the geo-strategic appropriation of the 'principle of nationality' by both warring sides, the Entente and the Central Empires. Both were interested to different degrees in fostering nationalist demands in the enemy's backyard, and in some cases in gaining a broader support from the home front by appealing to irredenta territories (such as Alsace-Lorraine, Trieste and Dalmatia, etc.). This gave rise to a new wave of diffussion of nationalism, which in the end would lead to new processes of nation-state formation usually accompanied by forced border rearrangements and ethnic violence, which in practice extended the war until 1923.[9] This was certainly not an entirely new phenomenon in European history. Thus, the nationality principle had also been invoked by some of the contending sides from the Greek independence war of 1830 and Napoleon Third's support for Italian nationalists against the Austrian empire, to the Balkan wars of 1912–13. Now, however, the appeal to the nationality principle as a moral legitimization of the war effort could serve a twofold objective. Beyond the strategic interests of the belligerent powers, the defence of the 'oppressed nations' also provided left-wing and liberal factions that endorsed the war effort of their countries with a legitimate cause: either that of the freedom of small nations smashed by the German boot, or that of the subject nationalities of the Tsarist Empire.[10]

---

7   Berger (2015).
8   See Núñez Seixas (2019); Kernalegenn, Belliveau and Roy (2020).
9   See Prott (2016).
10 See an updated overview of the ethno-national dimensions of the Great War in Chernev (2017).

The new international visibility of the principle of nationalities during the Great War was also aided by a third factor. Some nationalist movements directly involved in the war, from the Czechs to the Yugoslavs and the Irish, launched a highly intensive propaganda campaign through the activity of émigrés in several European cities, as well as the support provided by the migrant diasporas in the US, which was particularly relevant in the Polish, Czech, and Irish cases. This contributed to making nationalist claims visible on the international stage, and had a secondary effect in triggering variegated nationalist movements in Europe during and after the conflict. Since mid-1917, a new concept, national self-determination, entered the stage of world politics. The endorsement given by the first Russian revolutionary government and then by the Bolsheviks to the right of self-determination of peoples and nationalities led to the first statements made by US president Woodrow Wilson in favour of Poland's right to achieve statehood, some form of autonomy for the nationalities of the Austro-Hungarian empire, and the preference of clear-cut state borders based on geographic, ethnic and historic arguments. This materialized in the Fourteen Points.

International stability, the pursuit of geo-strategic interests and balance of power were for state elites more important than great principles. Until November 1918, they feared that *Kleinstaaterei,* the fragmentation of multi-national States into minuscule successor states, might prove fertile ground for the expansion of revolutionary doctrines. Until November 1918, the utmost priority of the Entente's diplomacy was not supporting the dissolution of the Ottoman empire and Austria-Hungary. However, the course of events led to the dissolution of the Habsburg empire, followed by the Ottoman. In the last months of 1918 and during 1919, proclamations of independence from Prague to Riga went alongside revolutionary episodes, riots and armed conflicts. In the turmoil of the war and its aftermath, some nationalist elites achieved their paramount objectives, while others, like the Ukrainians, did not. This related to macro-political events, such as the development of the Russian civil war.[11]

Spurred on by propaganda to acknowledge internationally the claims of Central and Eastern European nationalities, the political and intellectual elites of several nationalist movements in Western Europe had strong motivations to advance in their demands, which seemed legitimized by the great powers. For many of these movements, the external stimulus of the First World War played a significant role in the evolution and maturing of their political projects. Several even became full-fledged nationalisms after a regionalist phase, from the

---

11   For an overview on some of these border conflicts and civil war in the aftermath of the Great War, see Gerwarth and Horne (2012), as well as Gerwarth and Manela (2014).

Galicians to the Corsicans and the Welsh. Becoming 'nationalists' in the upcoming 1920s meant for many ethnic activists being in line with modern times.

During the war years, the theoretical development of the nationality principle in the Western world had been updated, though it had not yet hybridized with the concept of self-determination that was proper to the liberal current and North American religious tradition. Its meaning was linked to the liberty of the governed to choose their government democratically, and became more extensively incorporated into European political vocabulary after 1917. The democratic principles of the *consent of the governed* and of *self-governing decisions* were only gradually incorporated into the nationalities principle. This was also supported by pacifist activists who favoured international cooperation for the future as a means of avoiding war.

Yet the outcome of the war did not meet these optimistic expectations. The border rearrangements imposed by the winners at the Peace Conference of Versailles, alongside the several conflicts that broke out in several European regions, meant just a partial fulfilment of the right of national self-determination. While this was a reality just for some, such as people from Upper Silesia or Northern Schleswig, many Europeans, from Magyars from Transilvania to Bohemian Germans, were denied it. Self-determination created many satisfied nationalists, but also many dissatisfied and irredentist nationalists. The genie was now out of the bottle, and would continue to be for the ensuing decades.[12]

The different contributions to this volume attempt to shed new light on the development of the question of nationalities in Europe during the First World War and its aftermath from different perspectives, blending the global outlook with the view from below, the telescope with the microscope, from the local contexts, with particular (but not exclusive) attention to Galicia, whilst East European and West European nationalities are dealt with on an equal footing.

The first section deals with global and theoretical issues. Joep Leerssen (Universiteit van Amsterdam) opens the volume with a fascinating account of the modalities of diffusion of nationalism in Europe by paying particular attention to the "cultivation of culture", the cultural practices and theoretical issues associated with nationalism and their adoption in different parts of the continent. He relies on his previous work, especially on the conclusions of the far-reaching research project (*Spin network*) led by himself for the last decade, which has successfully mapped the diffusion of practices and theories for the cultivation of national culture in Europe since the Enlightenment.[13] Leerssen's

---

12 See Sharp (1996).
13 See Leerssen (2018).

chapter touches on a crucial aspect dealt with in this volume such as cultural transfer and its concrete modalities, from elite culture to symbols and popular myths. He also focuses on the importance of transnational transfers to explain the almost simultaneous emergence of national claims, which may also be explained by the "diffusion by impact", a good example of this being the immediate echo that the Easter Rising of 1916 had on such culturally distant places as the Basque Country and Galicia.

Chapter 3, penned by Xosé M. Núñez Seixas (Universidade de Santiago de Compostela) also deals with the ways and modalities through which the principle of nationalities, firstly, and the newly-coined principle of national self-determination from 1917, spread through some nationalist movements in Western Europe, with particular focus on the case of Catalonia and the Basque Country, as well as the theoretical issues related with both principles which were at stake during the war. These notions —how to define the nation, one the one hand, and how to implement the principle of nationality in practice, on the other— were embedded in a more general framework that ethnonationalist activists could not escape: the geostrategic interests involved in the possible application of the nationality principle in Europe as a precondition for an enduring peace settlements. In fact, what began as a propaganda weapon deployed by both contending sides in the war, was reframed as a new principle for extending the revolution by the Russian bolsheviks, as well as an alternative liberal doctrine to attract the unsatisfied nationalities from the Central and Ottoman empires to the side of the Entente, as US president Woodrow Wilson entered the stage with his Fourteen Points. In the end, Wilson's principles were optimistically and opportunitiscally interpreted as a new international legitimacy for nationalist claims all over Europe, including its Western part.

In Chapter 4, Malte Rolf (Carl von Ossietzky Universität Oldenburg) deals in detail with the origins and evolution of the Bolshevik doctrine of national self-determination, the theoretical issues linked to its emergence and conceptualization, as well as the concrete meaning ascribed to it by the revolutionary leaders. Once in power, the modalities of the internal transformation of the multinational Tsarist empire into a multiethnic and multinational federation of Soviet republics was first determined by the necessity of winning the civil war by identifying "Great Russian chauvinism" as their main enemy, and promising peripheral territories of the empire a stronger degree of autonomy within the framework of a socialist federation. After the Bolsheviks' definitive victory, the higher objective came on to be extending the new socialist faith through a policy that combined stick and carrots. This became evident in the Soviet nationality policy of the early Stalinist period: "nativization", aimed at spreading socialism framed in national and local cultural codes: or to use Stalin's words, "national in form, socialist in content". The emergence of the Soviet Union as a "paradise of nationalities" was a colateral result of this policy, which was also exploited as a strategy to spread the appeal of communist parties in the ethnic peripheries of Europe and the colonized peoples of Africa and Asia.[14]

In Chapter 5, Ramón Máiz (Universidade de Santiago de Compostela) addresses a different aspect of the theoretical development of the question of nationalities around the First World War: the doctrines that aimed at overcoming the national state, and crafted innovative solutions for the long-term survival of multinational states. This was particularly relevant in areas such as the former Habsburg empire, where the entangled modalities of mixed ethnic settlement in several territories made it barely possible to implement the nation-state model imported from Western Europe. Máiz analyses in depth the thinking of the Austrian Social-democrat Otto Bauer, and highlights the pre-war theoretical developments of his theory for the solution of the nationality question, as well as the influence of the imperial crisis of Austria-Hungary on his post-war reflections. Bauer did not only undertake a critique of the Marxist theory of the nation, but he also emphasized the voluntaristic nature of the nation, as a community shaped by the free consent of its members: therefore, his idea of the nation was democratic and progressive. However, he expressed no contempt for smaller, "ahistorical" ethnic groups, and recognized the fact that cultural rights had to find recognition within a multi-national federal state, based on an eclectic mixture of personality principle —the individual's free ascription to a national community— and territorial autonomy, where possible.

In Chapter 6, Bence Bari (Central European University, Budapest) also addresses some of the crucial theoretical issues at stake regarding the principle of nationality and national self-determination, but he does so from a different perspective. On the one hand, he focuses on the political debates that took place among nationalist émigrés and West European champions of nationalities, taking the prominent example of the Czech nationalist leader and philosopher Tomáš G. Masaryk, and on the oher hand he examines the federalist proposals craftet by the Hungarian Sociologist Oszkár Jászi. Both displayed evolving positions towards the key concepts nationality, national minority and national self-determination in the course of the conflict, and proved to be pragmatic opportunists, particularly from 1916 onwards. Masaryk soon realized that national self-determination and full statehood for a Czech(oslovak) nation was attainable, and successfully adapted his political vocabulary to the

---

14 See Mevius (2010).

new concepts en vogue, trying to claim nationhood for Czechs and Slovaks, and the status of ethnic minorities for the rest of the nationalities present in the future territory of Czechoslovakia. On the contrary, Jászi remained skeptical towards the possibility of implementing national self-determination in Central Europe, but was open towards the possibilities offered by multinational federations and interregional cooperation. However, the end of the conflict and Hungary's defeat forced him, as a short-lived Minister of Nationalities of the postwar Károlyi government (November-December 1918) to "salvage" as much of Hungarian territory as possible. Yet, he failed in his attempts to keep other ethnic groups within the borders of Hungary by offering them home-rule. In the end, the transnational dynamics imposed by the wave of national self-determination imposed their logic: while Masaryk was a winner, Jászi was a loser.

Section II, *Local dynamics*, centers on the concrete reception of transnational debates and principles in local contexts, with particular attention to Western Europe. In Chapter 7, authored by Francesca Zantedeschi (Gerda Henkel researcher / Universidade de Santiago de Compostela, Hispona research group), an illuminating and well-informed comparative overview is offered of the impact of the First World War on several "micro-nationalisms" in France (focusing on Brittany, Occitania and the Catalan Roussillon) and elsewhere, namely in the Aosta Valley and Wallonia. She reconstructs in depth the local reception of the principle of nationality and later of Wilsonian ideas by local regionalists and cultural activists, who only in some cases had crossed the theoretical line and gone to define their territories as "nationalities", and concludes how important this external stimulus was to influence their evolution. Thus, almost all groupings embraced ethnonationalism or, at least, attempted to present their cause in the new vocabulary also coined by the emergence of the question of national minorities after the Paris Peace Conference. Yet this did not preclude that those political and cultural factions continued to have a weak social echo in the national audiences they addressed. The fact that the war had also contributed to reinforcing national states in Italy or France also displayed the twofold sides of the consequences of the conflict for national minorities and nationalities alike.

In Chapter 8, penned by Ramón Villares (Universidade de Santiago de Compostela), a detailed account is offered for an international audience of the emergence of the Language Brotherhoods in Galicia, founded in 1916 as the first political organization of the emergent Galician nationalism. Although there were theoretical and cultural forerunners that went back to the 1840s, in form of a cultural renaissance and various political groups that advocated some form of decentralization or Galician home-rule, the wartime context was not irrelevant for the emergence of the *Irmandades*. As Villares shows, endogeneous factors, such as the growing relevance of the land-reform movement since the previous decade and the consolidation of a new intellectual middle-class partly shaped by return migrants, contributed to this evolution. However, exogenous factors, such as the impact of the Portuguese revolution (1910), the political offensive of the Catalan movement —also determined, as shown in Chapter 3, by the war context— in search for allies outside Catalonia, and the reception of Wilsonian echoes also played a role. This included the impact of the Dublin events of Easter 1916 and the evolution of Irish nationalism, which, as in other cases, exerted great fascination on local activists. As the author concludes, the Brotherhoods remained a minority group, yet the seeds of the later development of Galician nationalism as a relevant political movement for twentieth-century Galician history are inseparable from the circumstances that surrounded the Great War.

In Chapter 9, Johannes Kabatek (Universität Zürich) concentrates on a particular aspect of the diffusion of the nationality principle, that of the language revivals and cultural renaissances around the First World War. From the angle of comparative linguistics, the author explains the transformation of a "dialect" or linguistic variant into a full-fledged "language" as an act depending on the will of the speakers. The success and failure of language revivals are also dependent on the way in which intellectual and political elites establish what a language is, and how and why it should be resurrected, by means of a linguistic policy in case nationalists acthieve statehood or some form of territorial self-government for their nation. Kabatek points out the influence exerted on some national movements, such as those of Catalonia and Galicia, by the wartime and postwar context, marked by the officialization as state languages of hitherto minority languages and the international recognition, at least in theory, of the linguistic rights of ethnic minorities in multiethnic states. He concludes that language policies and cultural nationalisms followed very different strategies, and language uses were far more complex. In some cases, vernaculars only played a symbolic role for national movements. Whereas all attempts to reenact the decaying Gaelic as the national language of the emerging Irish new state were met by failure, Swiss German dialects retained their strength at the level of daily and private interaction, and *Hochdeutsch* remained as the written and formal language for Swiss Germans, who did not feel the necessity to reverse this situation of stable diglossia.

The third section of the volume addresses some issues related to the legacy of the nationality question after the First World War through the ensuing decades. In Chapter 10, Stefan Berger (Ruhr-Universität Bochum) analyses in a comparative way the impact of the First World War in the writing of national histories across the continents, including both old-established states whose historians reacted to losses of territory or regime changes, and new "nationalizing states" which were anxious to consolidate new national narratives and to spread them to their population. The author deals in depth with two major transnational debates: that of war guilt and that of the justification or rejection of the postwar settlement imposed by the Peace Treaties. Next, he also analyzes the weakening of the nineteenth-century tradition of liberal and national historiography, as well as the tension between professionalization of the historical profession and the requirements to legitimize the existence of the new and surviving nation-states. Finally, Berger also examines a new relevant issue for historians in the whole continent: national borders and borderlands, and therefore national minorities. As the author concludes, historians were once again put in the service of either legitimizing the new state borders, or claiming lost territories.

Chapter 11, authored by Stefan Dyroff, explores the continuities in terminology and theoretical conception between the nationality question during the Great War and the interwar period. He illustrates these continuities through the analysis of the transnational debates that took place amongst intellectuals, pacifist and liberal activists and nationalist émigrés and representatives around the Lausanne-based Union des Nationalités and the Central Organization for a Durable Pleace. He then compares these debates whith those that took place in the 1920s in other transnational organizations which followed a similar path, such as the International Federation of League of Nations Societies and the Congress of European Nationalities. However, after 1919, the new issue which was subject to transnational discussion was the "problem" of national minorities, officially labelled as "ethnic, religious and linguistic" minorities, which remained within the borders of the new nationalizing states sanctioned by the Peace Treaties imposed on them by the peacemakers, and placed under the protection of the emerging League of Nations.[15] While state elites expected the Treaties to favour a smooth assimilation of ethnic minorities, minority activists, including political émigrés, scholars and intellectuals, developed a set of initiatives in conjunction with liberal internationalists and pacifists in order to grant minorities the treatment previously deserved by nationalities. In this respect, the transnational discussion on the minority issue, though based on a different vocabulary (the "minority rights"), owed much to the theoretical developments on the nationality question in 1914–18, and was often fostered by the same protagonists.

Finally, in Chapter 12, Lourenzo Fernández Prieto and Miguel Cabo Villaverde (Universidade de Santiago de Compostela) analyze in broad comparative

---

15   Brubaker (1996).

terms the complexities of the relationship between the agrarian and nationality questions before, during and after the First World War. As the authors underline, ruralism was a frequent element of nationalist ideologies, and agrarian collective action (from land-reform movements to peasant parties) often went hand in hand with nationalist mobilization in West and particularly East-Central Europe. Moreover, some of the more conflictive issues related to the nationality and/or minority question beyond 1918, such as the access of different ethnic groups to land property, were inextricably intertwined with the agrarian question and the spread of democracy to rural regions. Galicia constitutes a good case in point for this, as was also the case with Brittany, Croatia, Serbia or the Czech lands. As the authors conclude, ruralism was a manifold and polyvalent phenomenon, which interacted with political and cultural nationalisms in several ways, and was not only understood as the nostalgia for premodern social hierarchies.

The different, though convergent approaches to the development of the nationality question during and after the First World War which are presented in this volume constitute a caleidospic view of a particular *moment*, which from the angle of transnational history can also be regarded as the beginning of a new era in the history of nationalism: that of the triumph of the national(izing) state and of the principle of self-determination, as some contemporary scholars noted in the 1930s.[16] From 1918, old imperial models based on the preservation of diversity within unity through the coexistence of diverse and flexible patterns of home-rule began to decline. If the British empire constituted to some extent the exception to the rule, it cannot be overlooked that the Irish Free State born in 1921 behaved in many ways as a new national state before its definitive break with the British crown in 1939, while Welsh and Scottish nationalist parties also emerged and developed since the early 1920s, and nationalist agitation grew in India and other parts of the empire. The anticolonial outburst of 1945–47, seen as the first stage of the process of decolonization, had clear forerunners in the years following the First World War.

The spread of the Bolshevik doctrines of self-determination to the imperial peripheries also determined that anticolonial activists, communists and ethnonationalists interacted in the old imperial metropoles during the 1920s, from Paris to Amsterdam and London. Tunisian, Moroccan, Vietnamese and Indonesian anticolonial nationalists learned some useful lessons from European ethnonationalists and communists, which were to bear fruits thirty years later.[17] Similarly, ethnic minority parties and sub-state nationalist parties alike

---

16   See Macartney (1934) and Carr (1939).
17   Goebel (2015); Basch, Glick-Schiller and Szanton Blanc (1994); Hargreaves (1993).

were politically reinforced, or ideologically renewed, by the impact of the First World War, from the Galician Language Brotherhoods to the first Sicilian and Sardinian autonomist groups. In some cases, such as in Sardinia and Flanders, demobilized soldiers marked by their war experience were among the main supporters of new nationalist and autonomist parties, such as the Flemish *Frontpartij* and the Sardinian *Partito Sardo d'Azione*.

As suggested by recent research, the social and cultural consequences of the Great War were polyvalent and multifaceted. While in some countries war veterans and angry civilians offered a fertile ground for fascism, in other areas they constituted a firm basis for the reinforcement of state-led nationalisms and the definitive erosion of local and regional cultures. There was not a one-sided and homogeneous impact of the First World War on the development of the question of nationality in Europe and outside Europe. Moreover, the wartime period should be regarded as a crossroad of different dynamics. Eric J. Hobsbawm has suggested that the period after 1918 was a turning point in the history of nationalism that marked its apogee.[18] However, in this collection this period is regarded as a watershed: from that point, the political vocabulary framed during the war, that of national self-determination, nationality and minority rights, was to become overwhelming for the following decades, at least until the 1960s.

Bibliography

Basch, L.G., N. Glick-Schiller & Ch. Szanton Blanc (1994), *Nations Unbound: Transnational Projects, Postcolonial Predicaments, and Deterritorialized Nation-States*, n. p.: Gordon and Breach.

Beramendi, J.G. (2007) *Galicia, de provincia a nación. Historia do galeguismo político, 1840–2000*, Vigo: Edicións Xerais.

Beramendi, J.G. & X.M. Núñez Seixas (1995), "The Historical Background of Galician Nationalism (1840–1950)", *Canadian Review of Studies in Nationalism*, XXII:1–2, pp. 33–51.

Berger, S. (2015), *The past as History. National identity and historical consciousness in modern Europe*, Basingstoke: Palgrave.

Brubaker, R. (1996), *Nationalism reframed. Nationhood and the national question in the new Europe*, Cambridge: Cambridge UP.

Carney, S. (2015), *Breiz Atao! Mordrel, Delaporte, Lainé, Fouéré: une mystique nationale (1901–1948)*, Rennes: Presses Universitaires de Rennes.

---

18   Hobsbawm (1990: 132-36). See also Storm & Van Ginderachter (2019).

Carr. E.H., ed. (1939), *Nationalism: A report by a Study Group of the members of the Royal Institute of International Affairs,* London: Royal Institute of International Affairs.

Chernev, B. (2017), "Shifts and Tensions in Ethnic/National Groups", in: *1914–1918-online. International Encyclopedia of the First World War,* ed. by Ute Daniel et al., DOI: 10.15463/ie1418.10210.

Dunn, S., & T.G. Fraser, eds. (1996), *Europe and Ethnicity. World War I and Contemporary Ethnic Conflict,* London: Routledge.

Gerwarth, R., & J. Horne, eds. (2012), *War in Peace. Paramilitary Violence in Europe after the Great War,* Oxford: Oxford UP.

Gerwarth, R., & E. Manela, eds. (2014), *Empires at War. 1911–1923,* Oxford: Oxford UP.

Goebel, M. (2015), *Anti-Imperial Metropolis: Interwar Paris and the Seeds of Third World Nationalism,* Cambridge: Cambridge UP.

Hargreaves, J.D. (1993), "The Comintern and Anticolonialism: New Research Opportunities", *African Affairs,* 92, pp. 255–261.

Hobsbawm, E.J. (1990), *Nations and Nationalism since 1789: Programme, Myth, Reality,* Cambridge: Cambridge UP.

Kernalegenn, T., J. Belliveau, & J.-O. Roy, eds. (2020), *La vague nationale des années 1968. Une comparaison internationale,* Ottawa: University of Ottawa Press.

Leerssen, J. (2006), *National Thought in Europe: A Cultural History,* Amsterdam: Amsterdam UP.

Leerssen, J. ed. (2018), *Encyclopedia of Romantic Nationalism in Europe,* Amsterdam: Amsterdam UP, 2 vols.

Macartney, C.A. (1934), *National States and National Minorities,* Oxford: Oxford UP.

Manela, E. (2007), *The Wilsonian Moment: Self-determination and the Origins of Anticolonial Nationalism,* Oxford: Oxford UP.

Mevius, M., ed. (2010), *The Communist Quest for National Legitimacy in Europe, 1918–1989,* London: Routledge.

Núñez Seixas, X.M. (2019), *Patriotas transnacionales. Ensayos sobre nacionalismos y transferencias culturales en la Europa del siglo XX,* Madrid: Cátedra.

Núñez Seixas, X.M. & A. Iglesias Amorín (2020), "Language, Cultural Associations, and the Origins of Galician Nationalism (1840–1950)", in K. Lajosi & A. Stynen (eds.), *The Matica and Beyond. Cultural Associations and Nationalism in Europe,* Leiden/Boston: Brill, pp. 162–180.

Prott, V. (2016), *The Politics of Self-Determination. Remaking Territories and National Identities in Europe, 1917–1923,* Oxford: Oxford UP.

Revel, J., ed. (1996), *Jeux d'échelles. La micro-analyse à l'expérience,* Paris: Gallimard/Le Seuil.

Secchi, S. (1976), *Dopoguerra e fascismo in Sardegna. Il movimento autonomistico nella crisi dello stato liberale,* Torino: Einaudi.

Sharp, A. (1996), "The genie that would not go back into the bottle. National self-determination and the legacy of the First World War and the Peace Settlement", in Dunn & Fraser (eds.), *Europe and Ethnicity*, pp. 10–29.

Shelby, S.D. (2014), *Flemish Nationalism and the Great War: The Politics of Memory, Visual Culture and Commemoration*, Basingstoke: Palgrave Macmillan.

Storm, E., & M. Van Ginderachter (2019). "Questioning the Wilsonian moment: The role of ethnicity and nationalism in the dissolution of European empires from the Belle Époque through the First World War", *European Review of History/ Revue Européenne d'histoire*, 26:5, pp. 747–756.

Thiesse, A.-M. (2001), *La création des identités nationales. Europe XVIIIe – XXe siècle*, Paris: Éditions du Seuil.

PART 1

The First World War, Transnational Action and the Principle of Nationality

CHAPTER 2

Cultural Mobility and Political Mobilization: Transnational Dynamics, National Action

Joep Leerssen

> *wie es eigentlich gewesen: wahnsinnig kompliziert*
> (after Ranke)

∴

1   Transnational Nationalism and Methodological Nationalism (Somme, Dublin, A Coruña)

The year 1916 is commemorated in Ireland for two different reasons by two different mnemonic communities. Ulster Protestants remember the Battle of the Somme, which inflicted enormous casualties amongst, specifically, Ulster regiments. For the history of Irish nationalism, the date evokes the Easter Rising, when a group of radicalized cultural activists from the Gaelic League and the Irish Volunteers occupied strategic points in the capital, Dublin, and proclaimed an independent Irish Republic. In a wholly different part of Europe, A Coruña, a formative event took place in that self-same year: the foundation of the *Irmandades da Fala* or "Language Fraternities".

The simultaneity and correlations between these three disparate and dissimilar events is intriguing in a number of respects. None of them can be understood except in immediate relation to one other, and therefore in intermediate relation to the third one. Ulster volunteers in the British Army had in many cases enlisted to demonstrate their Unionism, that is to say: their refusal to be part of a Home Rule plan for Ireland which would have come into effect but for the outbreak of the Great War; the Irish insurrectionists obtained weapons from Germany and acted on the established principle that "England's difficulty is Ireland's opportunity"; and the contributions to this book all make abundantly clear to which extent the Gaelic League and Irish revivalism provided an inspiration and a template for action to the *Irmandades da Fala*.

Conversely, the synchronicity and mutual entanglements between Ulster Unionism, Irish nationalism, and Galician regionalism highlight the disparities which must be factored into any comparative treatment. How does war, waged by imperial states, interact with language revivalism in the empires' provincial peripheries? How does imperialism interact with something, or some things (without in many cases being quite clear as to the precise ideological meaning of those terms) that can be called either regionalism or nationalism? Why is language activism such an important proxy or mobilizer for an autonomist or separatist political agenda? Most importantly, to what degree do local, socially circumscribed actions relate to their translocal motivations and effects – in other words: how does entanglement come about?

These questions are to some extent rhetorical and to some extent heuristic. Without claiming to give an exhaustive answer to each of them, I hope in the following pages to tease out some of their implications and to present a possible model for a significant challenge that emerges clearly from them: the need for a properly comparative, transnational history of national (and regional) movements. In doing so I draw on the data and insights gathered into a comparative scope by the many contributors to the *Encyclopaedia of Romantic Nationalism in Europe*.[1]

The gravest obstacle to such a transnational history of nationalism is our own tunnel vision: our propensity to methodological nationalism. In accounting for social and political movements as they manifest themselves in a given country, by default we tend to look for its underlying causes and infrastructures within that country. That tunnel vision is ingrained and understandable, and derives from three causes: one is that the archives which historians work from are usually institutionalized, ordered and repertoried on a national basis and indeed often curated by the state; the other is the problem of language, which makes us gravitate to the sources we understand and sidelines those written in foreign languages; and the third (least excusable) is an ingrained gravitation among historians to explain historical phenomena from "underlying" causes (i.e. infrastructural, social, institutional or political, i.e. locally or socially specific). All these factors tend to marginalize (in my view wrongly so) the causative factors which are communicated over longer distances, from other countries or in other languages. We invariably explain the growth of a plant from its roots, rarely from its pollination. A transnational approach is needed to account for the long-distance diffusion of ideologies and movements, for their entanglements and transfer, and will therefore need to bring out the communicative and intellectual exchanges from under the shadow of the local (social and political) activities.

---

1 See Leerssen (2018); digital version online at ernie.uva.nl. The network visualizations given in the following pages are from that website.

Empires, to begin with, provide an ambience for such transnational entanglements: those between the various regional and colonial dependencies of Madrid are well known and do not need to be revised within the scope of this article; further afield, the Russian empire provided a trait d'union between the Baltic and the Caucasus: the father of modern Armenian literature, Xačatur Abovyan, was intellectually formed by his studies in Tartu/Dorpat; and the Polish Uprising of 1831 inspired a Georgian conspiracy in 1832. The wars that were waged between those empires are the crucible in which the national movements were forged into statehood: the Great War that was begun by two multi-ethnic empires (Austro-Hungary and Russia) ended in the national dismemberment of both; the Somme made the Easter Rising possible.

2 Direct Transnationalism: Knock-on Effects

These examples already indicate various modalities of what we may call "knock-on" or "direct-impact" nationalisms: In a shared imperial framework, a national movement in one place may provoke another one somewhere else. We can, I think, distinguish various modalities in which these interactions take shape.

1. One is that of **hostile imitation**.[2] The relationship between Irish nationalism and Ulster Unionism is one case. Ulster Protestants apprehended the effects of Home Rule (the main, autonomist objective of Irish nationalism) and as a result started a counter-movement of their own, vindicating the non-Irishness of Ulster much as Irish nationalists vindicated the non-Britishness of Ireland. A similar process took place between the Flemish and Walloon movements in Belgium, and between Greek and Turkish nationalists in Cyprus.

2. Secondly, nationalisms proliferate through activist solidarity, when activists from different communities join forces and strategies. This model is predicated on the transnational mobility of important activists, impelled by exile or emigration: Giuseppe Mazzini, Adam Mickiewicz, Fan Noli, etc. This "roaming activists" model has particular relevance for diaspora nationalisms in the New World and anticolonial activists from different colonial peripheries of the European empires.[3]

---

[2] I have seen some colleagues credit the notion of "hostile imitation" to Ernest Gellner, but have been unable to locate the phrase in his writings.
[3] Cf. Anderson (2005), as well as Stutje (2019).

3. Thirdly, generic "**organizational templates**" may inspire different national movements from one to another: from the early-nineteenth-century format of the secret society (*Tugendbund, Philarets/Philomaths, Carbonari, Filiki Etairia, Frăţia*) to the late-twentieth-century adoption of the "liberation front" template (Palestinian Liberation Organization, *Euskadi Ta Askatasura*, Irish Republican Army...).
4. Fourthly, there may be cooperation between various minorities with a **shared grievance** against a jointly repudiated imperial centre (as in the provincial peripheries of Spain, or the Slavic borderlands of the Habsburg Empire). Indeed, the crumbling of multi-ethnic imperial states, especially following the loss of colonies or under the strains of the First World War, presents a veritable cascade of knock-on nationalisms.
5. In crumbling empires, a fifth sub-type of knock-on nationalism can be observed in the imperial heartlands facing the peeling off of their subaltern peripheries (Castilian Spain, Austria, England). Loss of Empire is not just an eighteenth-century phenomenon: it takes place in successive waves well into the twentieth century. In each crisis, a type of "**rump nationalism**", a nostalgic, regionalistically-inflected sense of post-imperial identity emerges in the heartland (Little Englandism; the Spanish post-1898 reform movement or *regeneracionismo*; the late-Habsburg Vienna-Tyrolean cult of the Viennese chocolate cake *Sachertorte*, Johann Strauss waltzes, Alpine sentiment and operetta irony; Dutch and Danish introspective nationalism after 1839 and 1864) which is often fixated on monarch and traditions, and may be a belated survival of that extinct spectral ideology called *Reichspatriotismus*.

These ideal-typical rubrics can, of course, overlap or intersect. Ulster Unionism and the Walloon movement can be both a form of anti-Irish/anti-Flemish hostile imitation and a form of British/Belgian rump nationalism; the transfers linked to "organizational templates" and/or "roaming activists" are often seen in conjunction with other transfer models. But between them, the five rubrics appear to me to cover most forms of "knock-on" national activism.

3 Undirected Transnationalism: Diffusion, Profusion, Condensation

My main point, however, is that these modalities of direct knock-on effects do not cover the entirety of the historically documented proliferation of nationalism across the European continent. In many cases, national thought is diffused, i.e. spread over a wide and unfocused area, before undergoing a process of condensation (and taking effect) in another context. Many, many copies and translations of Walter Scott's novels were diffused across Europe for a limited number of authors to start applying the genre to their own national past. Typically, such diffusion processes do not have a specific directionality; they are not a targeted "marketing campaign" with an individually identified aim; and their effects are not necessarily intentional or premeditated.

This fact may obscure the causality that was at work. The condensation end of a diffusion process is often not traceable in a linear one-on-one cause-to-effect trail, and as a result the influence from one case to another may not be obvious to the historian. As in the biblical parable, many handfuls of grain need to be sown, and wasted, for some to shoot up as a new crop; but no new crop will shoot up except out of a sown seed. In many instances, it will seem as if things are just "in the air", part of a given *Zeitgeist* or ambient condition. As if the growth of mushrooms is just a result of humid weather at a certain turn of the season; or as if the emergence of national movements is just due to a rising middle class or a stage of modernity. However, the mushrooms grow where they grow because of their mycelium and their spores, and the emergence of a national movement is always due to the intentionality of the actors involved. They "got the idea" and they did not get it out of thin air: ideas circulated in profusion as well as in diffusion.

In many cases, this diffusion-and-condensation therefore relies on the profuse communication of ideas over longer, and in many cases transnational distances, and in many cases that communication was a cultural as much as a political one. At least two of the modalities outlined above also had their cultural manifestations:

– the "organizational templates" that spread from one national movement to another involved, not just modes of joining political activists, but also modes of cultural sociability: reading societies and book clubs; choral societies; sports clubs.
– The "roaming activists" in some salient cases were artists and intellectuals rather than political organizers: performing composers like Franz Liszt and Richard Wagner, vagabond writers like Byron, Madame de Staël and Washington Irving.

In addition, there appear to be some modalities of transfer that are specific to the pattern of cultural diffusion/condensation. I list the following:

1. **Institutional exchange.** Art academies, conservatoires, universities and salons provide meeting grounds for intellectuals and artists who are travelling beyond their place of origin, typically at an early, formative stage of their career. It is in these paces that ideas can spread from one originating ambience to another one. St Sava's, the Princely Academy in Bucharest, forerunner of the present-day university there, was an important meeting-place for budding

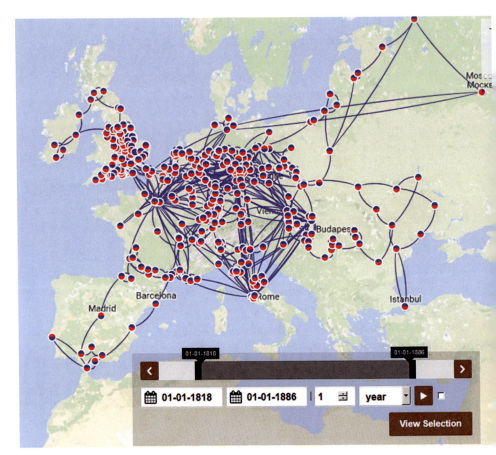

FIGURE 2.1 Concert tours of Franz Liszt

intellectuals who would later take the lead in Greek, Albanian, Romanian and other national movements. The art academies of Paris, Antwerp and Düsseldorf taught national history-painting to new generations of artists from Norway to Poland and Romania, to say nothing of the studios and coteries of Rome or the universities of Vienna, Vilnius or St. Petersburg. The life stories of virtually all artists and intellectuals that were influential in the articulation of national ideals shows that they formed their ideas during sojourns abroad and from contacts, in those places, with like-minded people from other countries.

2. **Associational reticulation.** Many cultural forms of sociability and conviviality, while conceived in a certain place, inspired analogous initiatives elsewhere. The spread of the "Floral Games" format from Toulouse to Barcelona and thence to Valencia, San Sebastián, and various cities in Galicia and the Provence is a case in point; another example is the spread of sports clubs and

CULTURAL MOBILITY AND POLITICAL MOBILIZATION   23

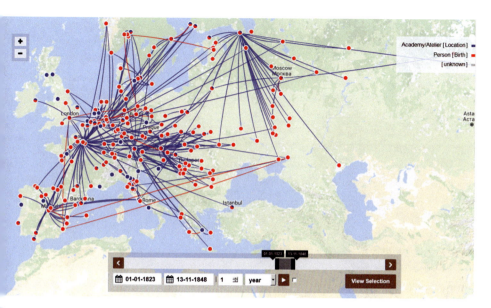

FIGURE 2.2 Art Academies Mapped against the Birthplace of Their Pupils, 1823–1848

FIGURE 2.3 Reticulation of Floral Game-style Festivals

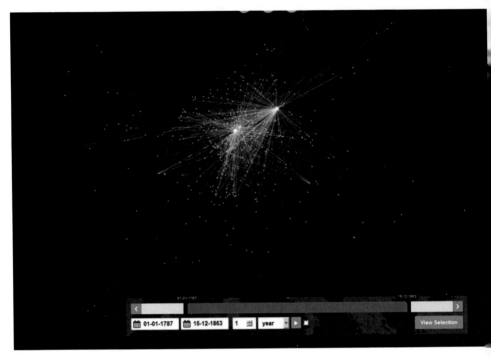

FIGURE 2.4 Correspondence network of Jacob Grimm

of choral societies. These were urban-based initiatives and often crossed political or linguistic borders, linking the cities concerned in an ad-hoc web or network rather than locking them into a common identity or territory. The format of the choral society, for instance, spread from German sociability to the emerging Baltic nations. Whatever regionalist or nationalist community-building resulted from this seems to have taken place in each city's *hinterland* or surrounding region; only in small countries with low urbanization (Wales, Estonia) does the *hinterland* appear more or less territorially congruous with an emerging nation. In the German case, the nation-building effect of choral societies resulted from their federative concatenation, common transregional festivals and shared repertoire.[4]

3. The **shared repertoire** of cultural products and activities was not necessarily bounded by the single society or cultural community. Music travelled far and wide; different groups in different parts of Europe felt that the *Marseillaise*, the "Va pensiero" chorus from Verdi's *Nabucco* and the "Amour sacrée de la patrie" aria from Auger's *La muette de Portici* applied to their plight and

---

[4] See Leerssen (2015), as well as Lajosi & Stynen (2015).

CULTURAL MOBILITY AND POLITICAL MOBILIZATION

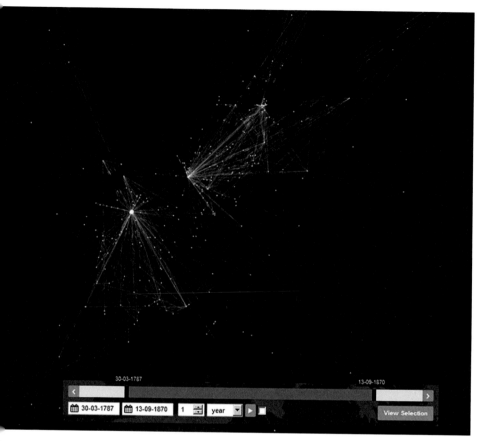

FIGURE 2.5 Correspondence networks (juxtaposed) of E.M. Arndt and Prosper Mérimée

aspirations. The poems of Lord Byron, the novels of Walter Scott, Friedrich Schiller's *Don Carlos* and *Wilhelm Tell*, were as influential in translation (and among multilingually adept readers) as within their own language-area of origin. The Edda and Beowulf inspired German, English and Scandinavian audiences alike; Jan Kollár and Vuk Karadžić resonated across the entire Slavic world.

4. The intense **communication of ideas** between Romantic-Nationalist intellectuals disseminated, in a virally contagious mode, the ideas generated by the new, nationally-framed modes of knowledge production, especially among philologists and historians. Although they saw their task increasingly in national terms (Jacob Grimm being as fervent a German patriot as Michelet was a French one), they corresponded, reviewed each other's works, and enlisted each other in their local learned societies, in a network whose density is remarkable. On the basis of a sample of some 40,000 letters, involving key

"nodal" figures like Jacob Grimm and Walter Scott, it may be safely asserted that no two Romantic intellectuals, from Reykjavík to Odessa, were further than two "degrees of separation" removed from each other. Two intermediary correspondents suffice to link the Breton ballad-collector Théodore Hersart de La Villemarqué to the Finnish president of the Imperial Russian Academy of Sciences in Saint Petersburg, Anders Sjögren. Yet at the same time these networks have a specific distribution that indicates the sympathies and antipathies of key cultural actors. The cleavage between the non-French network of Ernst Moritz Arndt and the non-German network of Prosper Mérimée (two near-contemporaries with a roughly comparable cultural status and a roughly equal quantity of repertoried letters, c. 4000 each) is a striking illustration of growing French-German estrangement; spatially mapped, this communicative "dead zone" uncannily foretells the frontlines of the First World War.

4 Embracing Complexity

To study these exchanges means that multiple paper trails and diffuse bodies of documentary evidence need to be traced in many different directions, almost like mapping the mycelium that links the mushrooms in a forest, or the diffusion of their multitudinous spores on the varying winds. The processes are nothing if not complicated, and any linear cause/here-to-effect/there narrative will foreground a certain strand to the neglect of many different other ones in the tangled skein. The dynamics of national movements, once liberated from the artificial simplification of a mono-national, monodisciplinary tunnel vision, are the very definition of "non-linearity" and must be mapped and visualized by the means suited to that condition: the study of complex systems, involving complexity-reducing instruments like multidimensional matrix-mapping and network analysis. The *Encyclopedia of Romantic Nationalism is Europe* was devised as a "proof of concept" for such an approach: it employs a three-dimensional matrix, setting off fields and media of **cultural production** (philology, visual arts, folklore, music etc.) against self-defining **cultural communities** (Albanians to Welsh), with, for a third dimension, the **chronology of cultural events** from 1780 to 1920.

It is this last aspect, the insistence on diachronicity and on the datability of cultural practices (for, as Hugo von Hoffmannsthal put it, *Jedes Wort ist doch auch ein Ereignis*), which sets this approach apart from the social-scientific ways of matrix mapping and network analysis. Diachronicity is all the more important since the regionalist and national movements of Europe, while often following a similar developmental sequentiality roughly within the Very Long Nineteenth Century (as per Miroslav Hroch's phase model, for instance, to which I shall return further on), some started earlier than others, and some moved through certain stages faster than others; yet all shared the same formative crisis-dates such as 1813–15, 1848, the Crimean War.

With those three dimensions (fields, communities, chronology), the European system can be mapped more or less like a "Rubik's Cube", and although the various twists and turns of such an articulated cube can be bewilderingly complicated (as real life is, and was), the system itself reduces those complications to complexity: something neither linear not chaotic, an unlimited number of permutations fitting within a limited number of descriptive parameters.

In line with Bruno Latour's actor-network theory,[5] such a view of European national movements will look, not only at the human personalities involved (or at that metaphysical Primum Movens of the twentieth century, "society"), but also at cultural products such as books, musical compositions, statues, and associations. They too have a connective power and causal agency. At the same time, the approach is not sociological but culture-historical, hermeneutic rather than cybernetic, in that the importance of each actor is determined, not by mere presence, but by the importance attached to it by other actors, with human actors being indispensable links in the arbitration of importance. Thus, the absence or presence of language difference, as such, is not in and of itself decisive: some highly "different" languages like Saami were only belatedly and hesitantly instrumentalized in national consciousness-raising, which the comparatively minor differences between Ukrainian and Russian, or Bulgarian and Macedonian, were taken very seriously indeed. It is, rather, the importance attached to language difference, by people at the time, that mattered. Hence the notion of "culture", as used here, is always an experiential and reflected one (the experience of culture, cultural reflection), and folded into the recursive notion of a "cultivation of culture". Not culture, but its cultivation and valorization marks the shift from anthropological behaviour to political ideology. It also allows us to map "culture" (as a set of practices and fields) against modalities of cultivation, and degrees of intensity in doing so, resulting in the following matrix:[6]

The methodology briefly sketched here cannot claim to be the only way of approaching a properly transnational, comparatist study of national/regional movements in Europe; but it does attempt to face the fundamental challenge for any properly transnational approach to nationalism and regionalism: the need to factor in the agency of cross-border communication, and the fact that in such cross-border communications, cultural diffusions are no less important than direct political knock-on effects.

---

5   See Latour(2005).
6   Cf. Leerssen (2006).

TABLE 2.1 The cultivation of culture: a matrix

	SALVAGE, RETRIEVAL, INVENTORY	FRESH CULTURAL PRODUCTION	PROPAGATION, PROCLAMATION IN THE PUBLIC SPHERE
LANGUAGE	dictionaries grammars [L1]	orthography standardization/ dialect debates languages purism [L2]	language activism language planning language education [L3]
DISCOURSE	editions of older – literary texts – historical documents – legal sources [D1]	[a] translations/ adaptations: Bible, world clasics [b] national/ historical drama, novel, poetry [c] national history-writing [d] literary history, literary/ cultural criticism [D2]	history education historical pageants commemorations literary events/festivals/awards [D3]
ARTEFACTS, MATERIAL CULTURE	archeography monumental remains symbolically invested sites [A1]	monument protection policy, restorations design, decorative arts historicist painting, museums [A2]	monuments, dedications of public spaces official use of historicist architecture/ decorative arts/design [A3]
PERFORMANCES, CULTURAL PRACTICES	editions of oral literature proverbs, superstitions, pastimes manners and customs, folklore folk dances, folk music [P1]	rustic-realist literature traditional sports/ pastimes, national music composed [P2]	revived or invented traditions events/ festivals / awards: (folklore, sports, music) [P3]
SOCIAL AMBIENCE		[a] associations, city academies, reading societies [b] periodicals, publishing ventures [S]	
INSTITUTIONAL INFRASTRUCTURE		[a] state academics, universities, chairs [b] libraries, archives [c] museums, government agencies [I]	

5 Back to Dublin and A Coruña: Nationalism, Regionalism, and Multiscalarity

All these cultural and communicative factors see Europe, Latour-style, as a network of exchanges. That view runs counter to the ingrained habit of seeing it as a jig-saw puzzle of discrete, self-enclosed nation-states, or as nesting gravitational system of centres and peripheries, shot through with sub-centres and sub-peripheries. A communicative network view releases the *Irmandades da Fala*, despite its peripheral position within Spain and (doubly so) within Europe, from its perceived marginality; it will also locate Galicia both as a participant in the regionalist revival of the subaltern Iberian/Romance-language communities, and as a stepping-stone between Ireland and Cuba or Argentina (where the influence of the Galician communities during these years is comparable to the activities of Irish, Polish, Slovak and Croatian diasporas in the United States).

From the outset, parallels and divergences between the Galician and Irish cases leap to the eye. In both cases, the social and political mobilization is conducted under the invocation of the native language. The ostensible primary aim of the *Irmandade dos Amigos da Fala*, established in A Coruña one month after the Easter Rising, was one of language preservation and language revivalism – if the name is anything to go by. (And even if that name was a euphemistic "dog whistle" code for more political autonomism, in the style of *Tugendbund* or *Filiki Eteria* associations, the choice of the euphemism is still meaningful.) Similarly, in Dublin, half the signatories of the 1916 Declaration of Independence had found their way to armed separatism by way of a language-revivalist association, founded in 1893: the Gaelic League. Dedicated to a programme of nativist-cultural revivalism called "de-Anglicization", the Gaelic League had organized music and dance competitions, amateur theatricals, tourist excursions to the Gaelic-speaking West of Ireland, and, most of all, language classes in which the people of Ireland could reconnect with their fast-disappearing language. In a classical confirmation of Miroslav Hroch's phase model,[7] these cultural consciousness-raising activities soon gave rise to clashing social demands, notably over education and the use of Gaelic on postal addresses and shop signs. Between 1905 and 1910 the organization radicalized, converging with separatist political parties such as Sinn Féin, and being infiltrated by the terrorist activists of the American-based Irish Republican Brotherhood. In the process of this radicalization, the aim of language revival

---
7 Of the many writings, I mention Hroch (2005).

became one of mere symbol politics, and the nationalist agenda shifted its emphasis away from cultural revivalism to social and political separatism.[8]

Was the Dublin-to-Coruña connection a direct knock-on transfer or a cultural diffusion? My (admittedly limited) acquaintance with the sources leads me to suspect the latter: the two movements had no common goals, shared grievances or direct intermediaries; the respective languages hoisted as rallying flags in Dublin and A Coruña had no familiarity or rivalry. Instead, there is a well-documented history of Galician intellectuals internalizing the inspiring parallel with the other Atlantic peripheries, using the common appellation of "Celts" to invoke a shared ambience of rain and bagpipes. Galician Celticism goes all the way back to the mid-nineteenth century, when historians like Benito Vicetto and Manuel Murguía wrote the region's early history in the light of Gaelic migration myths, going as far as invoking the Irish-Gaelic mythological figure Breogán as a national ancestor. Furthermore, in 1935, Antón Villar Ponte, founding father of the Language Brotherhoods, translated W.B. Yeats's nationally Irish plays *Cathleen Ní Houlihan* and *The Land of Heart's Desire*, together with Plácido R. Castro, into Galician.[9] Between the mythography/history of the 1880s and Villar Ponte's translations, the documentation suggests that Galician nationalists did look to Ireland as a cultural point of reference. The contacts between the two countries were of a cultural rather than social-activist nature; typically for cultural connections, they were also indirect. Two intermediary stepping-stones link Galician intellectuals to Irish mythology: one is the Celtic philologist Henri d'Arbois de Jubainville, professor at the Collège de France, whose mythological studies were consulted by Murguía; the other is Joaquín de Villanueva (1757–1837), an exiled Liberal priest and former member of the Cortes of Cádiz, who had taken refuge in Dublin, and developed an interest there in Irish-Gaelic antiquarianism —his Gaelic-antiquarian writings were extensively drawn upon by Vicetto.

All the same, both the Gaelic League and the Irmandades de Fala present an instrumentalization of culture for purposes of social and political activism. Their common cultural inspiration is diffuse and pan-European; but their sphere of action is strictly local, aimed at their own country. That is in itself a conclusion to keep in mind: the cultivation of culture is often communicated transnationally, whereas political action is mainly intra-national.

---

8 More details and sources can be consulted in Leerssen (2016a).

9 Antón Villar Ponte has already translated *Cathleen Ní Houlihan* into Galician in 18921 (*Nós*, 8, 5 December 1921). See also http://www.fundacionplacidocastro.com/reflexions-arredor/irene-romero-iturralde/historia-dunha-traducion-placido-castro-anton-villar-ponte-e-dous-folc-dramas-de-w-b-yeats; also Leerssen (2016b), which for the Galician part is indebted to the work of Fernando Pereira.

There is, however, one more inference I would like to tease out from the comparison between the League and Irmandades. Language activism in Ireland was never regionalist; in Galicia it hardly ever dared to call itself nationalist. Unlike the development of Gaelic language activism, Galician language cultivation never led to armed, separatist rebellion in the streets of A Coruña or Santiago de Compostela, or to short-term proclamations of an independent Galician Republic.

Where does regionalism end and nationalism begin? The question is vexed and much debated, and addled by the fact that the word has quite different connotations in different languages and in the differing ideological self-perception of the various movements that called themselves "regionalist". A common-sense base-line may be that regionalism involves the cultivation of cultural differences that are not considered so fundamental as to preclude the participation of a cultural community within the nation-state; in other words, regionalism is the self-positioning of a "self-differentiating ethnic group" (to quote Walker Connor's definition of the nation[10]) which does not involve separatism. If regionalism involves claims to "autonomy", that autonomy is conceived of as a subsidiary self-governance within the state and subject to the state's sovereignty.

The distinction is notoriously problematic. For one thing, it is not stable in time: what may be regionalism at one moment will develop into separatism later on; conversely, what at one point counts as national distinctness may erode over time into mere regional variation. Furthermore, given the fact that in cultural life the afterlife of the past may overlap with the emergence of the future (Reinhart Koselleck's *Gleichzeitigkeit des Ungleichzeitigen*), it may well be that we see both trends represented in a single society side by side at any given moment. The political spectrum will usually include various gradations of mild regionalism alongside radical nationalism. The case of Valencia is an example in point, with the added complication that the Other against which Valencian regionalism positions itself may be, fluidly, either Madrid or Barcelona, or both.

These anomalies (for such they must seem in an analytical frame where regionalism and nationalism are separate categories, one more or less represented by the Galician *Consello da Cultura Galega*, the other by the Irish IRA) reduce, I believe to a more manageable format if we consider them transnationally. For the transnational approach involves more than cumulating discrete national cases into a multinational "Champion's League"; it also means that the discrete unitary nature of the national level is queried and seen in its inner differentiations as much as in its outer connections.

---

10   Connor (1994).

Cross-national entanglements and cross-pollinations demonstrate that nations are not, like pebbles, smooth, hard, and distinct; and as much as their outside is not smooth and impenetrable, their inside is not homogeneous, crystalline and undifferentiated. International connections often run between provincial cities and their respective regions, as the reticulations of the Floral Games show.

The insight that the cross-cultural entanglements take place between cities and between regions as well as between nations, all at the same time, is now known as "multi-scalarity". It means that cultural self-positionings and a "cultivation of culture" may take place at the urban/municipal level, at the regional level, or at the national level – an often these levels interact. Prague can be Bohemian/Czech, Habsburg, Pan-Slavic, or the urban environment of (as it may be) Franz Kafka, the Golem, Bedřich Smetana or Jaroslav Hašek. How much of the Catalan *Renaixença* was a matter of Barcelona city culture rather than regionalism? How much of Dutch cultural nationalism is an upscaling of Amsterdam city culture to the level of national importance? Cultivations of culture and self-assertions may at any point slide from municipalism to regionalism to nationalism – and back, as the history of cities like Florence, Munich and Edinburgh shows.

In other words, whether or not a national movement reaches a Hrochian Phase C of mass agitation depends both on the intensification of its demands and its anti-state antagonism, and on the scale of its catchment area. Both are contingent upon the actions and circumstances of the given moment.

6 Conclusions: Directionality and Diachronicity

So what have I outlined here, an amorphous mess? To some extent, yes: and the messiness is the message. National movements in Europe are transnational and highly fluid, in their cultural self-definitions, self-positionings and transnational entanglements. That in itself should be a salutary caution against anyone who wants to catch this tangled complexity in a neat, deterministic typology; against unreflected presentism or anachronistic finalism that projects the contemporary ethnolinguistic and national-ideological landscape of Europe back onto the past, naively using the world as we know it as a meaningful map of what the world used to look like; against methodological nationalism that unthinkingly applies the state as a fixed parameter by which these dynamics can be systematized. The state may have ordered our archives and research institutions, structuring the conditions under which we approach the past; but the organization of our archives is no reliable reflection of the historical developments themselves.

Even so, to conclude that the past was a transnationally entangled mess is not meant to foreclose the issue. Once the complexity has been acknowledged and to some extent mapped, can we say anything about possible patterns, structural features, or developmental sequences in this complexity?

Historically, a few general lines of development are becoming visible from the complex data-analyses and mappings in the *Encyclopaedia of Romantic Nationalism in Europe*. I outline a few large-scale trends that affect a variety of cultural fields/media and a variety of national communities across Europe.

- A shift from "past to peasant": early national cultivations of culture are strongly historicist, with a particular gravitation to the chivalric Middle Ages; later on, there is a turn to the contemporary peasantry and the people inhabiting the countryside as the true repository of the nation's identity. This is mirrored in the visual arts from the monumental to rustic genre-painting and the rise of (often vernacular-inspired) decorative arts; in literature and opera we see the shift from historicist themes to rustic idylls and peasant drama; in architecture, a shifting preference from historicist neo-styles or eclecticism to vernacular elements.
- In knowledge production (history, philology, folklore) we note a shift from amateur interest to professionalization and factualism, linked to institutional developments around the universities and the rise of positivism. At the same time, the Romantic-amateur tradition of the early generation remains influential in popular culture and cultural production.
- The development, by the end of the century, of avant-garde nationalism, often carried by *Arts-and-Crafts*-inspired utopian progressives, aiming to vindicate the nation as fully-fledged part of a progressive European modernity. This wave often stands at odds with the lingering afterlife of an older, nostalgic and nativist nationalism.
- At the same time, a hardening of the discourse of ethnicity, whereby notions of blood and ancestry are used less and less as metaphors for the transgenerational inheritance of culture, and more and more as literal, physical invocations of biological descent.
- A communicative dissemination which in the course of the century upscales from the local (solitary/private/convivial) to the collective or public. In literary media, this involves a shift from poetry to the novel and periodical, opera and theatre; in associational culture, a shift from private entertainments and extended family networks and salons to urban associations,

museums, theatres/opera houses, and middle-class sociability with translocal activities.

These large-scale currents allow for more specific comparatist research questions. Why were revivals of folk dress, and its adoption by urban middle classes, more important or successful in certain countries (Tyrol, Scotland, Latvia, Norway) than in others? What was the mobilizing impact of sports clubs (*Turnverein, Sokol*), or *excursionista*-style activities (Catalonia, Slovak lands), or amateur theatre (Norway, Ireland, Iceland), in different countries? How do we account for the differences in national music culture in Wales (where choral singing was important) and Ireland (where convivial informal singing, instrumental music and dancing were more important)? What role did standard songbooks play for a national song repertoire in Germany, Denmark or other countries? What schools, styles and lines of diffusion did the spread of national styles in architecture follow across Europe, and through what professional training-networks?

Most importantly, of course, given also the present topic, is what role was played by language mobilization in different countries. In almost each national movement we see a tension between historicist language cultivations and demotic ones: those who prefer a formal language in continuance of the prestigious, literary tradition of a great past, and those who prefer a less formal language that addresses the full popular community of present-day speakers. (Generally, the European trend is towards an ascendancy of the modern-popular forms as the century wears on.) To which extent was linguistic activism a real issue in its own right, or else a launching platform for other nationalistic aims and issues? How did state intolerance (evinced in different degrees in different European countries, from indifference to active repression) affect the mobilization of minority languages?[11]

I have at various points in this contribution referred to processes of intensification, radicalization, instrumentalization, often in the context of Miroslav Hroch's phase model. I would like it to be understood that these vectors cannot be unambiguously mapped in time, or given specific period-datings. Some

---

11   I bypass in this context the intriguing but very complex question of to what extent regionalism relates to nationalism as "dialect" relates to language. At the ideological level, that correlation is certainly made: many national movements in the nineteenth century were at pains to prove that they communicated in an idiom that qualified as a "language", not a mere *patois*; but in articulating that fluid, highly debatable, yet categorical distinction, many vague and heterogeneous considerations played a part: the phylogenetic or cladistic place of the local idiom vis-à-vis the state's official language (Slovenian playing the trump card of its dualis as a distinguishing feature), the history of literacy or literature in the local idiom (Ukrainian and Macedonian tracing an independent descent from Old Church Slavonic, Catalan and Occitan from Latin), and its usage in a modern-day public sphere (print media, cultural production).

movements are earlier than others, and when or after how much time a certain case moves from this phase to that, cannot be standardized. In addition, the cultivation of culture is at work within any of the Hrochian phases, which should, I think, not be seen as distinct successive units, like different wagons in a train, but rather as increasing wind speed and precipitation in a weather system. If, within the "cultivation of culture", I trace a process of intensification from salvage to productivity to propagandistic instrumentalization, this too should be seen as gradations in a fluid, intensifying process rather than as a neatly demarcated "one-two-three" succession.

Waves of more intense types of culture assertion may come and go while a more anodyne form of cultural preoccupations continues unabated; but although the intensification process is not irreversible, its emergent directionality is invariant: developing movements tend to overlay the initial, blandly cultural phase with a more assertively political one. They never emerge by intensifying a blandly political beginning with an assertively cultural radicalization. That directional, stadial logic is, I submit, fundamental, ubiquitous and highly meaningful in nineteenth-century Europe. It also means that culturally communicated transfers are comparatively more important in the culturalist Phase A of national movements, or indeed in regionalism, and that knock-on nationalism and impact diffusion becomes more important in more activist stages (Phases B and C). This may help to explain the gradual divergence

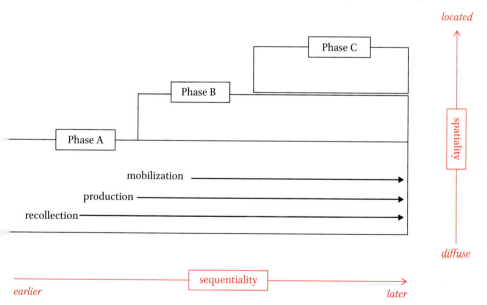

FIGURE 2.6 The intensifying degrees of the Cultivation of Culture harmonized with a cumulative (rather than serial) view of Hroch's phase model, and mapped as a function of sequentiality-in-time vs. spatial locatedness.

between the Catalan and Provençal movements after their initial enmeshed simultaneity. It may also help to situate the foundation of the *Irmandades da Fala* within the dynamics of Galician regionalism/nationalism and within the chronology of developing regionalism and nationalism in Europe.[12]

Bibliography

Anderson, B. (2005), *Under three flags: Anarchism and the anti-colonial imagination*, London: Verso.

Connor, W. (1994), *Ethnonationalism: The quest for understanding*, Princeton, NJ: Princeton UP.

Hroch, M. (2005), *Das Europa der Nationen. Die moderne Nationsbildung im europäischen Vergleich*, Göttingen: Vandenhoeck and Ruprecht.

Lajosi, K., & A. Stynen, eds. (2015), *Choral Societies and Nationalism in Europe*, Leiden: Brill.

Latour, B. (2005), *Reassembling the social: An introduction to actor-network-theory*, Oxford: Oxford UP, 2005.

Leerssen, J. (2006), "Nationalism and the cultivation of culture", *Nations and nationalism* 12:4, pp. 559–578.

Leerssen, J. (2015), "The nation and the city: urban festivals and cultural mobilization", *Nations and nationalism* 21:1, pp. 2–20.

Leerssen, J. (2016a), "Cúchulain in the General Post Office: Gaelic Revival, Irish Rising", *Journal of the British Academy*, 4, pp. 138–167.

Leerssen, J. (2016b), "Gods, heroes and mythologists: Romantic scholars and the pagan roots of Europe's nations", *History of Humanities* 1, 71–100.

Leerssen, J., ed. (2018), *Encyclopedia of Romantic Nationalism in Europe*, Amsterdam: Amsterdam UP.

Stutje, K. (2019), *Campaigning in Europe for a free Indonesia: Indonesian nationalists and the worldwide anticolonial movement, 1917–1931*, Copenhagen: NIAS Press.

---

12 With thanks to the student assistants of the Study Platform on Interlocking Nationalisms (SPIN, www.spinnet.eu) whose laborious data entry has resulted in all the lines on the maps reproduced here and on http://ernie.uva.nl.

CHAPTER 3

Wilson's Unexpected Friends: The Transnational Impact of the First World War on Western European Nationalist Movements

Xosé M. Núñez Seixas

This essay attempts to provide a transnational view of the positions held by several ethno-nationalist movements in Western Europe regarding autonomy, self-government, sovereignty and independence during the Great War and its immediate aftermath. It argues that there was a greater similarity between Western and East-Central Europe than has been generally sustained. Indeed, since the mid-nineteenth century, from Finland to Galicia, and from Ireland to Macedonia, there was an intense circulation of models, doctrines and stimuli amongst different nationalist movements. The history of nationalist movements in Europe is also a good case for entangled history. Although all national claims are the specific outcome of endogenous circumstances, their framing and development also respond to international stimuli, as well as to transfers and the appropriation of ideas referring to the *nation* as a new political. Paradoxically, nationalism is in itself a typically transnational phenomenon.[1]

All nationalist activists or "patriots", both state-led and stateless, consider their doctrine and narrative to be genuine expressions, rooted in their own history. However, the more they are convinced of their uniqueness in comparison to others, the more similar they are to each other. This is not only because the discursive tools and the narrative strategies they use are comparable; but is also a result of the circulation of a set of theoretical writings initially conceived as cornerstones of the theory of their own nation, which inspire activists in other territories.

Explicitly, the liberal writings diffused since the end of the eighteenth century, from America and France, added to the previous diffusion of the Enlightenment; they combined their concern with their respective political community defined as a nation, with emphasis on a set of values that should serve as a basis for the creation of new communities of citizens, whose main basis for

---

[1] Werner & Zimmermann (2006). See also Thiesse (2011: 11).

legitimacy was not dynastic loyalty but the nation. However, even the ethnocentric theory of the nation developed by the German *Aufklärung* and then developed by authors such as Johann-G. Fichte (*Reden an die deutsche Nation*, 1808) also implicitly contained elements that could be applied elsewhere. Firstly, it was tempting to adopt the idea of *Volksgeist* and History as a founding element of the nation for all those new nationalists who did not share any enthusiasm towards liberalism. Secondly, this theory was extremely useful, as it served to claim the existence of a nation wherever the citizens' will encountered difficulties in expressing itself, or where national consciousness was simply shared by a handful of patriots. Thirdly, all nationalists came to believe that it was natural that the world was divided into different nations. Thus, the models used by the neighbouring nations to stress their authenticity could also serve, as a mirror effect, to stress one's distinctiveness.

Although a history of the cross-references made by national historians, antiquarians and writers all over Europe still remains to be written, some good examples of transnational circulation of national models can be traced back.[2] Thus, the writings of Mazzini and Mancini, the main thinkers of the Italian Risorgimento's liberal nationalism, experienced a noteworthy diffusion in Western and Central Europe during the ensuing decades. Galician and Scottish historians alike quoted Mazzini's writings enthusiastically, and something similar occurred from Norway to Romania. The synthesis of objective and subjective criteria for the definition of what a nationality is was seen as a particularly interesting contribution to the reawakening of "small nations" all over Europe and America.

In the decades before the outbreak of the First World War, there was already an intense transnational circulation of national theories. This diffusion of images and models inspired local nationalists to think about their own homelands. They merely changed the ingredients of the recipe: instead of foreign heroes and places of memory, one just added his own national motives. However, the pattern of diffusion did not always follow one direction: it is not a model from above, from "large" (e. g. Germany, France, Italy) to "small" or "latecoming" nations (e. g. Romania, Flanders or Corsica). Certainly, the circulation of national doctrines has always been heavily conditioned by the overarching pattern of the geographical diffusion of ideas. Paris was the centre of intellectual life in Europe; Italians were more exposed to the French influence than the German, while Germans were much more intellectually influential in Northern and East-Central Europe. But there was also a circulation of theories

---

2   Leerssen (2006).

and models amongst "small nations" themselves, or amongst European peripheries.³

Some authors have stressed the relevance of the "demonstration effect" or "transnational contagion" exerted by the example of successful national movements on other, less developed (or not yet successful) substate nationalisms.⁴ These models may refer to the use of similar labels and principles, but they also may include the imitation of symbolic and cultural practices (such as literary contests in the mid-nineteenth century and "Celtic" festivals in some areas), as well as the participation of nationalist activists in the fight for the liberation of other nations. Nevertheless, those models do not necessarily give rise to the emergence of new nationalist claims where appropriate social and cultural conditions are not present.

The circulation of models, ideological stimuli and cultural practices amongst ethnic or national peripheries prior to 1914 combined with the emergence of a liberal internationalist movement, flanked by pacifism. Ethnonationalist activists joined liberal champions of the rights of nationalities, ethnic and religious minorities, and colonized peoples at international conferences, and exploited the window of opportunity that these platforms offered to give audibility to their cause.⁵ Paradoxically, the emergence of liberal and pacifist internationalism from the end of the nineteenth century was flanked by the first attempts to combine that current with the increasing ehnonationalist demands from "subject" nationalities in Eastern and Western Europe, as well as from some imperial peripheries, from South Africa to India, alongside the agitation promoted by Anti-Slavery committees, suffragist and pacifist groupings.⁶ A good example of this were the two Conferences on Nationalities and Subject Races held in London in June 1910 and, again, in February 1914.⁷ The First World War offered a huge opportunity for ethnonationalist activists to gain audibility for their cause, as the nationality question was exploited as an useful propaganda tool by both sides, thus gaining an unexpected global audience and a decisive influence on war aims and peacemaking.

---

3 See Nygard and Strång (2016).
4 See Conversi (1993). Some authors refer to that contagion as one factor explaining the recurrent correlation between nationalism and war since the early nineteenth century: see Wimmer (2013).
5 See Guieu (2008); Cortright (2008), and Davies (2014).
6 Sluga (2013).
7 See *Nationalities and Subject Races. Report of a Conference held in Caxton Hall, Westminster, June 28–30, 1910*, London: P.S. King, 1911, as well as Ucelay-Da Cal (2020a: 54–64).

1   Nationalities, Minorities, Regions: A Plural Landscape

What was the transnational landscape of substate nationalist claims in Europe like in the years before the outbreak of World War I? In 1913, the French historian, Charles Seignobos, published his book *Les aspirations autonomistes en Europe*, based on his interest in the nationality question in Central-Eastern and Western Europe. He placed the developments in Alsace-Loraine, Catalonia, Bohemia, Ireland, Lithuania and others on the same plane.[8] In February that year, the transnational journal *Les Annales des Nationalités* published a report on the demands of European *autonomist* movements in Catalonia, Bohemia, Lithuania, Latvia and Ukraine. In French public opinion –which epitomized European public opinion– the 1907 Catalan home-rule project, and the position of the conservative regionalist party *Lliga Regionalista* [Regionalist League], were on a par with the hopes of John Redmond and his Irish Parliamentary Party, the radical political fraction of the Young Czechs and the Lithuanian nationalists in exile.[9] Both Seignobos and the editors of *Les Annales des Nationalités* distinguished between what they called nationalities in the proper sense of the term (those of the East-Central multinational empires) and the 'annexes of old States in which the desire for autonomy has been revived: Ireland and Catalonia'.[10]

However, and despite these endeavours by some intellectuals and émigrés to craft a transnational agenda of nationality claims, no common programme existed before 1914 to accommodate all their aspirations. In fact, five models for managing ethno-national diversity operated prior to the First World War:[11]

1) Pre-modern territorial self-government within the multinational composite monarchies of the *Ancien Regime*, by becoming one more *body* or aggregated territory within a multi-ethnic monarchy. This was the paradigmatic case of Hungary after the *Ausgleich* or Compromise of 1867, as the Habsburg monarchy was in practice divided into two autonomous parts. Such a model also encompassed the aspirations of many Irish nationalists in the early twentieth century, including the *Sinn Féin* party, founded by Arthur Griffith, who had been influenced by Boer nationalism after his stay in South Africa years before, in 1903. In his later book, *The Resurrection of Hungary* (1904), Griffith's stated objective was to

---

[8] Seignobos (1913).
[9] See Ucelay-Da Cal (2003).
[10] *Annales des Nationalités*, II: 7–10 (1913).
[11] For much of the following section, see Núñez Seixas (2019). For an integrated perspective, see M. Hroch (2000, 2005). A suggestive overview in Ucelay-Da Cal (2020b).

become one more political body of the British Empire, adopting the form of a pre-modern dynastic union, or under a dominion regime such as that which had ruled Canada since 1867, and would become the case for Australia and New Zealand after 1907, and the South African Union after 1910.[12] In fact, most Czech nationalists before 1914 also strove for a similar objective within the Austro-Hungarian empire, aiming at constituting an autonomous part of the empire similar to Hungary. Something similar was intended by autonomist Icelanders and Faroe Islanders farther to the north, within the composite State of the Danish Oldenburg dynasty, also known at that time as the 'state conglomerate'.[13]

2) Becoming a body (organic or not) or a federated State within a multinational federation. This sort of approach incorporated the influence of federalist theories ranging from the Americans, Alexander Hamilton and James Madison, to the nineteenth-century Catalan Republican, Francesc Pi i Margall, which reverberated through the writings of the Republican Catalanist, Antoni Rovira i Virgili, from 1905, and several of the broad left-wing *Félibrige rouge* formulations of late nineteenth-century Occitanists. These all invoked the example of an idealized and often poorly understood Helvetic Confederation.

3) Variants of decentralization in the form of regional self-government or autonomy. These included the concession of a political and/or administrative autonomy statute to territories exhibiting the cultural, institutional or geographic singularities that justified it. This model was supported by several segments of Sardinian public opinion in the late nineteenth century, as well as in Sicily and in Italian *meridionalist* theories. In the French case, Jean-Charles Brun and the *Fédération Régionaliste Française* called for an overall 'decentralization from above' to be implemented in the whole territory of France. Its design responded mainly to functionalist and administrative rationalization criteria but was open to cultural recognition policies, thanks to the influence of Breton and Occitan regionalists (and some ethnonationalists) within the organization.[14]

4) Setting up a new national State. There were scarce examples of state secession without the intervention of a foreign power or as a result of an international conflict between 1878 and 1914. Amongst them stand out the case of Norway's achievement of statehood in 1905, after holding a referendum that obtained an overwhelming majority of affirmative votes,

---

12 See Griffith (1904). For an interpretation, see Maume (1995).
13 See Østergård (2015).
14 See Wright (2003).

and which resulted in a peaceful separation from Sweden. Yet, instead of opting to constitute a Republic, the Norwegians preferred to invite a Danish prince to found a constitutional monarchy.

The Norwegian model exerted thereafter a considerable degree of fascination on different national movements, and also had some influence on the evolution of Catalan nationalism. However, several newly-formed ethnonationalist parties in Western Europe chose to defend a position of independence *tout court*, though with variation and nuance Examples include the early years of the Basque Nationalist Party (*Partido Nacionalista Vasco*, PNV), founded in 1895, or the *Parti National Bréton* (1911), which split from the more moderate *Union Régionaliste Bretonne*. The claims put forward by these small groups fluctuated from the pre-modern, pacifist, *Ancien Regime* composite State model (such as the PNV, which from 1903–05 on sought a return to the 'ancient laws' or *fueros* that were in effect prior to 1833), to the confederal model promoted by Breton nationalists. Some others also advocated the achievement of independence through violence, such as the Macedonian movement from 1903 onwards.

5) Local autonomy, non-territorial or corporative ethnic models. An example of this were the Hungarian or German communities in several parts of Transleithania (such as Transylvania), or the corporative self-organization of German minorities in the Baltics under the Tsarist empire. Common to all of them was loyalty to the empire or the state they belonged to, based on dynastic and confessional principles,[15] combined with administrative self-government and full autonomy to manage their cultural institutions and enjoy their linguistic rights.

Autonomist and/or national demands prior to 1914 were overwelmingly over-represented in East-Central Europe. However, they were not limited to that area of the continent, and not even to Europe. Other cases close at hand included Catalonia, the Basque Country, Ireland and Flanders, along with regionalist and emerging nationalist demands in France and even Italy. It could even be argued in a counterfactual manner that had the First World War not been unleashed, discussion and establishment of a Home Rule model for Ireland would probably have occurred in 1914–15, and 'Home Rule all around' might have extended to Scotland. Parallel to these developments were advances in the Flemish movement and the success of political Catalanism in December of 1913, with the latter's achievement an early form of limited self-government (the *Mancomunitat*) encompassing all four Catalan provinces.[16]

---

15   See Osterkamp and Schulze-Wessel (2017).
16   See Clough (1930); Balcells, Pujol and Sabater (2006).

2 Exiles and Transnational Agents in Search of Audibility

The global confrontation that began in August 1914 involved the large-scale, geo-strategic appropriation of the 'nationality principle' by both warring sides, and gave rise to a new wave of diffussion of nationalism. In the end, this would lead to new processes of nation-state formation usually accompanied by forced border rearrangements, armed conflicts and ethnic violence, which in practice extended the war until 1923.[17] This was certainly not an entirely new phenomenon: the principle of nationality had also been invoked by some of the contending sides from the Greek independence war of 1830 to the Balkan wars of 1912–13. Now, however, it could both serve strategic ends and provide left- and liberal left-wing movements with a legitimate cause.

First, the depiction of rivals as oppressors of small nationalities, especially in the multinational Russian, Austro-Hungarian and Ottoman empires, overlapped with the ongoing dispute between French *Civilisation* and German *Kultur*. After 1917, the principle of nationalities achieved an overwhelming echo in the international public sphere. It became a mobilizing motto for both sides, but particularly for the *Entente*. This had an important demonstrative effect in the impetus given to several European nationalist movements during and after the conflict.[18]

Presenting the war as an idealistic crusade in favour of the rights of the peoples became necessary too for legitimizing the multiple sacrifices required of civilians in the belligerent countries (particularly the *Entente*), as well as maintaining the most liberal and left-wing sectors of public opinion —who were drawn to a just cause— within the *union sacrée* that fuelled the war effort. However, international stability and the balance of power were for state elites more important than adhering to great principles. Prior to the autumn of 1918, very few European or North American statesmen supported the disaggregation of the multi-ethnic empires they fought against. This would have complicated the European geopolitical map and possibly spread to overseas colonial territories. Likewise, since November 1917, there was real concern that political fragmentation and social unrest might prove fertile ground for the expansion of the Soviet Revolution.

The Central Empires used the nationality principle as a propaganda weapon to a lesser extent, as it involved great contradictions for Austria-Hungary. Nevertheless, they supported the demands of Polish and Ukrainian nationalists in Russia, as well as the claims for self-determination put forward by several

---

17 See Wimmer (2013) and Bianchini (2013). A recent reappraisal in Prott (2016: 21–53).
18 For further details, see Núñez Seixas (2001: 33–73).

movements in the Caucasus region. The Berlin government also supported the activities of several emigré groups which acted in Switzerland and other neutral countries, and fostered the recognition of Flemish as a co-official language in occupied Flanders, supporting the cultural demands of Flemish nationalists who opted for collaboration (the so-called *activists*).[19] Similarly, the German military authorities implemented a relatively benign occupation policy in the Baltic States and the Western borderlands of the Russian empire that favoured the autonomy of the non-Russian ethnic groups, including the Jewish communities. They also maintained some contact with Irish nationalists, and provided logistic support to the Easter Rising of April 1916, which ended in failure.[20]

The contending sides sought diplomatic advice from journalists, historians and geographers who were acquainted with the nationality question in East-Central Europe. This was a reflection of the increasing influence of transnational 'experts' on international politics, who were connected to a wide network of colleagues in several countries and helped transforming international relations.[21] Experts such as the Scottish historian, Robert W. Seton-Watson, the English historian, Edward H. Carr, and the English journalist, Wickham Steed, became useful intermediaries between the circles of exiled Central European nationalists in London, Paris or Rome and the foreign offices and chancelleries of the victorious States. They also published several journals, with the support of pacifist and internationalist organizations such as the Union of Democratic Control, where an open discussion was launched on the principle of nationality and the idea of self-determination, as well as its possible implications for the future of democracy on the European continent. This was of capital importance when the *Entente* accepted as an unavoidable fact the break-up of the Austro-Hungarian Empire; yet they never accepted anything beyond the limited application of the nationality principle whenever it was compatible with their own geopolitical interests.[22]

Spurred on by propaganda to acknowledge at an international level the claims of Central and Eastern European nationalities, the political elites of several national and regional movements in Western Europe found strong motivation to advance in their demands, which seemed justified and legitimized by the great powers. For many of these movements, the external stimulus of the Great War, now depicted as a war waged in favour of subject nationalities,

---

19 See Zetterberg (1978) and Wils (1974).
20 See Pott (2011).
21 See, for example, Rodogno, Struck and Vogel (2015).
22 See Calder (1976); Seton-Watson and Seton-Watson (1981), Sluga (2006: 37–60). On the interaction between Anglo-American diplomats and Czech exiles, see Hadler (1995).

played a significant role in the evolution and maturing of their political projects. Several even became full-fledged nationalisms after a previous regionalist stage, such as the Galicians, Bretons, Corsicans, Frisians and the Welsh. All of them came to adopt 'nationalist' agendas, and imagined their territories as nationalities aiming at achieving self-determination in the future.[23] The same occurred with the autonomist *Ligue Valdôtaine,* founded in 1909 to represent the interests of the French-speaking minority of the Aosta Valley in Italy.[24] Following Wilson's statements, even the Romansh language activists in Switzerland also embraced in February 1919 the vocabulary of self-determination, and labelled the terrritories where the different varieties of Romansh and Ladin languages were spoken as *Rhaeto-Romance nation.*[25] On the contrary, other territorial movements, such as that of Sardinia, did not experience a similar evolution and largely remained confined within the limits of regionalism.[26]

During the war years, the theoretical reflection on the nationality principle in the Western world had been updated, though it had not yet hybridized with the concept of self-determination that was more typical in the liberal current and North American Anglophone religious tradition.[27] The latter's meaning was linked to the liberty of the governed to choose their government democratically and became more extensively incorporated into European political vocabulary after 1917. The nationality principle expressed that national communities based on organic-objective criteria and/or voluntary association, and which existed within multi-ethnic monarchies or multinational empires, should aspire to full self-government, although not necessarily to freely dispose of themselves through the practical exercise of sovereignty. However, the deeply democratic principles of the *consent of the governed* and of *self-governing decisions,* that is, the right of all to help direct their society's public affairs, were only gradually incorporated into the nationalities principle. They also acquired a pacifist sense based on the Herderian paradigm of international relations. Accordingly, if the world was meant to be naturally composed of different nations, only when all nations were supposed to be free, would the

---

23 On the transition from Welsh linguistic demands to a nationalist agenda, see Morgan (1981: 203–08); Davies (1985) and Diekmann (1998). For the Bretons, see Déniel (1976) and Carney (2015). On the Corsicans, see Yvia-Croce (1979). On the Frisians, see Zondergeld (1978).
24 See Cell (2017), as well as Zantedeschi's contribution to this volume.
25 See Valár (2013: 208–10).
26 On the peculiar case of the strong Sardinian movement, which did not embrace a minority nationalist agenda until the 1960s, see Secchi (1976), Cubeddu (1993).
27 See, for example, Hauser (1916) and Tchernoff (1918).

long-term causes of conflict disappear.[28] Therefore, universal peace and the progress of mankind would come about through a national harmonization of distinct tonalities. This principle was susceptible to be adopted by very diverse political actors, including those removed from any explicit nationalist caprice: pacifists, Liberal and Christian internationalists, Fabian socialists and many others. In fact, this tendency met with some success during and just after the Great War, holding that world peace could only be guaranteed if 'national oppression' was eradicated as a source of conflict.[29]

All these theoretical endeavours failed to solve the basic problem: Ethnos or Polis? What is, and what defines, a nation? Who (what territory or human collective) was entitled to the right to self-determination and could aspire to legitimately invoke the nationality principle? There was one organic-historicist nationality principle of mainly German origin, another of liberal-voluntarist flavour, and also a number of intermediate positions. The variations could be adapted to fit the situation and strategic interests of specific actors, powers, movements or nationalist groups. During the conflict, French, Italian and German intellectuals published several contributions on that issue. However, their interpretations of the nationality principle largely responded to the strategic interests of the great powers. Thus the French, Italians, Germans, and later the Czech and Polish nationalist leaders appealed alternatively to the subjective will of the citizens or to historical tradition, culture and language, depending on their short-term territorial dilemmas: from the issues voted on in the referendums held in Upper Silesia and Schleswig-Holstein after the war, to defining borders in Transylvania, Pomerania or South Tyrol at the Peace Conference.[30]

However, at that point in the twentieth century, 'colonial' nationalities or peoples seldom appeared on any nationalist agendas of Europe. They had not yet achieved 'civilization' status (in the eyes of Europeans) but were nonetheless beginning to take note of the strategies and theories set in motion by European irredentist nationalisms. Examples include the young Vietnamese student Hò-Chi-Minh in Paris, Indian nationalists residing in London who were inspired by Irish revolutionaries, and Irish who learned from Indians and Boers.[31]

---

28 See, for example, Toynbee (1915) and Seton-Watson (1915: 70).
29 See *The New Europe*, 1 (19 October 1916); Macartney (1934: 215–17); Organisation Centrale por une Paix Durable (1917); Séailles (1918).
30 See Wambaugh (1933); Kaltenbach (1938); Prott (2016: 113–47).
31 See Manela (2007); Goebel (2015); Roberts (2013) and Stutje (2019).

3 The Union des Nationalités

The global solutions to the national question that were put forward during the War by several transnational organizations, in search for a solid base for world peace, were extremely variegated. The Belgian pacifist thinker Paul Otlet, who inspired the *Declaration of the Rights of Nationalities* (1914, 1916), established that the diverse range of solutions encompassed full independence, federative autonomy and asymmetrical decentralization (in current phraseology), or what he labelled as 'personal statute regimes', i. e. cultural autonomy based on individual adscription.[32] Occasionally, some innovative proposals suggested that nationalities become subjects of international law regardless of whether they had a State or not. However, they found little echo in the main European chancelleries.

The evolution of the Union des Nationalités illustrates the ambiguous use of the nationality principle during the Great War and its aftermath. This organization had been founded in Paris in 1912 by representatives of ethnonationalist parties, French intellectuals and pacifist leaders who intended it to act as a sort of intermediary for the *European autonomist movement* vis-à-vis French and global public opinion. With the outbreak of World War I, French diplomacy took an interest in taking control of the *Union des Nationalités*, exploiting the nationality principle in France's own benefit. One of its champions, a journalist from Provence called Jean Pélissier, worked for the French information services in the Balkans for two years. However, the German war propaganda machine also became interested through the exiled Lithuanian, Jean Gabrys (Juozas Parzaitis), who had founded the organization. He was now working to gain German support for the independence of Lithuania, which had been subjugated under the Tsarist empire. Accordingly, the first two Conferences of Nationalities (1913, 1915) took place in Paris with the enthusiastic support of the French liberal left, while the third one took place in Lausanne in June 1916 under the auspices of German diplomacy. The Germans had also financed the participation of several nationalist delegates from the Caucasus, Poland, Ukraine, Finland and the Baltics, and had set up a League of Allophone Peoples of Russia a few days earlier. In spite of its noteworthy media presence and attendance by Basque and Catalan representatives, the third Conference of Nationalities was essentially an anti-Russian propagandistic event.[33]

---

32 See Otlet (1914: 64–70). On Otlet's relevance, see also Laqua (2013: 26–37).
33 The Spanish ambassador in Switzerland remarked with good reason that "it is generally held that the meeting [...] was promoted by the central empires for political ends regarding the matters of Poland and the Baltic countries and in it there were only a few

When Jean Pélissier returned to Switzerland in 1917, he focused on relocating the Union des Nationalités within the French sphere of influence, particularly through his relationship with Paul Painlevé, the War Minister in Paris from March of that year (and Prime Minister from September to November). In exchange, the Quai d'Orsay would support the demands of the non-Russian nationalities in the unstable context created in the Tsarist empire after February revolution, and the growing threat of a separate peace being signed by the Petrograd government with the Central Empires. This involved diplomatic recognition of the Ukrainian *Rada* or parliament, as well as the support for the independence activists in the Baltic countries, Armenia and Georgia. In spite of Pélissier's efforts to place the Union des Nationalités within the network of para-official committees dependent on the Paris government, his opportunities for politically influencing the delineation of the new European borders diminished in late 1917. Painlevé's government was replaced by that of Georges Clemenceau, who argued for the restrictive application of the principle of nationalities. Meanwhile, Gabrys continued a double game of seeking German support while maintaining contacts with French diplomacy.[34]

The irruption of Woodrow Wilson on the European stage provided a new ideological mantle to throw over the programme of the Union des Nationalités, and seemed to cover all internal contradictions by endorsing the principle of a peace without victory based on a generous recognition of the claims of nationalities all accross the continent. The organization went on to uphold a general statute of the rights of nationalities and minorities in the new Europe after the Peace Conference. In late 1919 the Union des Nationalités disappeared.[35]

4   The Wilsonian Wishful Thinking

Certainly, the most decisive factors in opening windows of opportunity for substate nationalist demands all over Europe after 1917 were three: a) the immense geopolitical vacuum caused by the upcoming end of the European multi-national empires; b) the geo-strategic interests of the *Entente* powers,

---

ideologues or stray individuals strolling about to fill in the picture". Report of the Spanish embassy in Berne, 17 August 1916 (Archives of the Spanish Ministry of Foreign Affairs, Madrid, H-2824).

[34]   See Soutou (1995), as well as the German edition of the memoirs of Jean Gabrys in Gabrys (2013).

[35]   See, for example, J. Pélissier, 'Le futur Congrés de la Paix et les idées du Président Wilson', *Les Annales des Nationalités*, VI:5 (1917); 'La Question des Nationalités et les messages du Président Wilson', *Les Annales des Nationalités*, VI: 11–12 (1917).

and c), the proximity of these territories to the emerging Soviet state. However, the Great War also meant a global diplomatic upheaval, and gave international mediators and non-official representatives new chances in the chancelleries of the contending powers. Capitalizing on international uncertainty, several nationalist activists and groups accessed diplomatic circles and exerted some influence on the diverse foreign ministries. A good example is that of Czech émigrés. From 1916 onwards, Tomáš G. Masaryk and Edvard Beneš substantially influenced the British Foreign Office (and even US president, Woodrow Wilson) in framing their attitudes towards the future of Central Europe.

The definitive impulse for the international diffusion of the principle of national self-determination came from revolutionary Russia. The Bolsheviks made intelligent and pragmatic use of that slogan since the beginning of 1917, though always subordinating it to their primordial interest in the expansion of socialism. The Russian revolutionaries probably maintained the most influential and extensive discussion of self-determination at that time, using it as a tool for propaganda and ideological or territorial expansion, which heavily influenced the stance on that issue by almost all European left-wing organizations. The first provisional government established in Petrograd after the February revolution in 1917 proclaimed its commitment to national self-determination in April that same year, in a way that no other government did.[36]

Short after the Bolshevik takeover of power in Russia, US president Woodrow Wilson entered the global stage of the discussion on the nationality principle, as he addressed the US Congress and voiced for the first time his programme of Fourteen Points in December 1917, made public on January of the following year. Far more important than the points themselves, which were largely improvised and full of uncertainties, was its enthusiastic reception across the world. The so-called 'Wilsonianism' in Europe consisted of a sympathetic liberal and left-wing interpretation of Wilson' programme. However, the Fourteen Points included no general recognition of the nationality principle, nor of national self-determination. For strategic reasons, he guaranteed territory to Poland, demanded that Alsace-Lorraine be returned to France, called for the re-tracing of Italian borders along more or less clear ethnographic lines, and merely incorporated possibilities of self-government for the Austro-Hungarian nationalities. Indeed, Wilson was not particularly committed to the nationality principle, and was even less acquainted with the ethnographic complexity of Europe. Based on his profound religious belief, he advocated a liberal interpretation of self-determination as the search for the

---

[36] See Chernev (2011), as well as Throntveit (2011).

consent of the governed. However, the reception of this principle in Europe added to it a new element: the nationality principle. The German notion of *Selbstbestimmung* contributed to transform individual self-determination into collective self-determination: this entitled a territorial community, a nationality, to become its subject.[37]

Certainly, Woodrow Wilson did not only react to the Bolsheviks, but also attempted to give the concept of self-determination his own imprint, based on the Anglophone liberal tradition of John S. Mill, and detaching it from purely ethnic and Marxist revolutionary perspectives. The British premier, Lloyd George, who also made some statements in favour of national self-determination short before Wilson did, also adhered to that civic notion of the consent of the governed.[38] Not even the lesser known four points of president Wilson's address to the US Congress on February 11, 1918 made any explicit reference to the recognition of national self-determination, but merely proclaimed that "well-defined national aspirations shall be accorded the utmost satisfaction that can be accorded them without introducing new or perpetuating old elements of discord and antagonism" that would threaten peace. The necessity to come up with Italy's war aims forced Wilson and his adjutant Colonel House to refer explicitly to the Adriatic towns of Fiume and Trieste, while the reference to the imperial colonies was restricted to the German ones. By September 1918, the original fourteen points had become twenty-seven.[39]

There also were some additional reasons that explained the unexpected popularity of Wilson and his fourteen Points in Europe. The American president offered a reformist moral programme that vindicated the sacrifices of those who sustained the war effort. He promised a future based on international cooperation and an alternative to the Bolshevik model. This generated the Wilsonian myth around the US president as the champion of just causes: a "double illusion" of pacifist and reformist content alike.[40] Moreover, an unexpected consequence of Wilson's statements was the diffusion of the principle that ethnically defined nationalities were to become subjects of sovereignty, as nations (communities) and not explicitly individuals (citizens) became those who had to consent to be governed.[41] As Basil Thompson, a member of the British War Cabinet, summarized with irony in December of 1918:

---

37 See Weitz (2015). Some contemporary authors, mainly experts on International Law, also reflected on Wilson's concepts of self-determination, such as Mandelstam (1919), and Gibbons (1918).
38 See Lloyd George (1928: 1512–13).
39 See Smith (2002), and Heater (1994).
40 See Miquel (1971: 37–213).
41 See Gerson (1956); Mamatey (1957), Brecht (1992) and Sanborn (2014).

It is a remarkable fact that the extremists of all nations appear to have adopted President Wilson as their protagonist. He is to find himself, it would seem, the champion of British Bolsheviks, of Catalan separatists, of French majoritarian Socialists, of Irish sinnfeiners, of Indian anarchists, in short, of everyone who has a real or imaginary grievance.[42]

Therefore, President Wilson became identified as the highest moral expression of the war, as the apostle for the restoration of a just peace. His generic positions spread and were simplified in the public sphere from Britain to the vanquished powers, becoming general principles that anyone who adhered to democratic values would support: self-determination (whatever this could mean), disarmament, 'peace without victory' and the future creation of a League of Nations to guarantee peace.[43]

5 The Wilsonian Dream: A View from Below (Basque Country and Catalonia)

How was the diffusion of the nationality principle during the conflict perceived from below, from the outlook of ethnonational activists in Europe? Most of them simply interpreted what was going on in the war as a further confirmation of their intuition: the guidelines for the near future were to be marked by the overall implementation of the nationality principle as a sign of modernity, and the constitution of a League of Nations as a guarantee of the freedom of the small nations and the 'oppressed nationalities', as well as the end of imperial hegemony in Europe. This was not particularly different from what the spokesmen of the victorious national movements of East-Central Europe voiced in their organs by 1917–18.[44]

Western European ethnonationalists invoked similar principles, and expected that their ideas, legitimized by the success of the Czechs or the Poles, would also find acceptance in the international public sphere and the new global order. A good example of this was offered by Guillem Forteza, the first president of the small Catalanist association *Nostra Parla*. He admirably summarized in November of 1918 his perception of the inter-connectedness between external stimuli and domestic politics:

---

42 Quoted by Swartz (1971: 219).
43 See, for example, Tobia (1974); Martin (1958) and Fraenkel (1960). See also Pérez Casanova (2012).
44 See, for example, J. Banjanin, "Les nationalités opprimées et les Alliés", *La Nation Tchèque*, IV:1–2 (1918), as well as Seton-Watson (1991).

> Can our undeniable regionalist sentiment receive greater external stimuli? I think not. Even a cursory view of the characteristics of the sentimental tide that has swept the world since the waning of the armed tempest will reveal that in some points the social ebb is exorbitant and thus also the revolutionary flow. In other points, this spirit of rebellion is more moderate. In some, it is almost imperceptible. However, if we gave serious attention to the nationalist movement that pulls all of humanity, we would be incapable of establishing a scale of intensity. Everywhere, in all latitudes and all civilized dominions, the most radical nationalism triumphs. There will be strong and angry discussions on other political matters when nations gather to compose the Articles of Peace, but not regarding the matter of nationalism.
>
> [...] Be sure of this: not a minute will be lost arguing over what is understood by 'nation'. The world knows that a nation is all integrated groupings of men who give homage to a certain spirit born legitimately out of cooperation [...] from that 'integrated grouping of men' with the 'land' that Providence has assigned them.[45]

The spreading of the new vocabulary on national self-determination was much more intense in territories with more developed nationalist movements, such as the Basque Country and particularly in Catalonia, which had become a mass movement since the first decade of the twentieth century. The period of 1914–19 constituted a time of upheaval for the entire Catalanist political scene as the internal balance shifted significantly, giving rise to major political and strategic transformations within the movement. Cleavages and realignments occurred at several levels, especially in the political and strategic arena, generated by dual influences. In the Catalan case, there was firstly the political instability of the Regime of the Spanish Restoration monarchy in its later years (1914–23), which created a window of opportunity for launching a political offensive in pursuit of a more extensive self-government regime for Catalonia —either as an Autonomy Statute, or as a member state of a Spanish/Iberian multinational federation. Secondly, a process of steady 'Catalanization of external influences' also took place.[46]

While Republican and radical Catalan nationalists were vehemently sympathetic towards the Allies, and displayed an intense francophile stance, moderate right-wing Catalanists opted for neutrality; yet some of the conservative

---

[45] G. Forteza, 'Triunfo del nacionalismo' (*La Almudaina*, 23 November 1918), reproduced in Mir (1990: 318–21).
[46] Extensively on this, see Núñez Seixas (2010: 31–90; 2018).

Lliga's leaders also felt sympathy towards Germany, while many others expressed their preference for the victory of France and its allies. Left-wing, Republican-oriented and radical Catalanists expected to break the hegemony of the Lliga within the Catalan movement by exploiting the upcoming victory of the Entente in their favour. They even launched an active propaganda campaign in favour of the several hundreds of Catalan volunteers who had joined the French Army and the French Foreign Legion, presenting them as Catalonia's contribution to the victory of democracy and the nationality principle. Although only a few dozen volunteers were really Catalanists (many of them were immigrants in France, as well as adventurers, Republican idealists alongside Spanish volunteers, and mercenaries), some Catalanist groups dreamed of making them become a properly Catalan legion, comparable to the Polish and the Czech one, which would win the sympathy of the Entente towards the Catalan cause. Therefore, Catalanist representatives would be entitled to put on the table their claims for autonomy, federalism and even statehood at the moment when peace was discussed.[47]

As the war was nearing its end, even the conservative *Lliga* hoisted up the banner of the nationality principle and the dream of the Entente's intervention in Spanish politics, expecting that this would accelerate the achievement of Home-Rule for Catalonia. This was a parallel and complementing strategy to the party's political offensive to reform and decentralize the Spanish political system. Basque nationalists also attempted to endorse their autonomy campaign in 1918 with some Wilsonian appeals, which would legitimize the modernity of nationality claims. However, the strong Catholicism and conservative leaning of most Basque leaders prevented them from being further influenced by the left-wing and Republican interpretation of Wilsonian thought.[48] Moreover, the echoes from Wilson's Fourteen points also reached the weaker Galician movement. A new generation of activists had made the ideological step of adopting nationalism as an inspiring doctrine since late 1916, and claimed that the nationality principle also opened the path towards a new concept of Europe, within which Galicia would be able to develop its self-government.[49] With differing nuances, similar expectations were also raised in Ireland, where much hope was placed on the influential Irish-American lobby in the United States. In fact, the Sinn Féin leaders embraced Wilsonianism as a strategy of

---

47   Martínez Fiol (1991), Esculies & Martínez Fiol (2014).
48   See, for example, 'Al Pueblo Vasco', *Euzkadi*, 25 October 1918; 'Por qué estamos con Wilson', *Euzkadi*, 31 October 1918, and J. Villalonga Ybarra, 'La Sociedad de las Naciones', *Hermes*, 27 (November 1918). See also Ugalde (1996: 257–63).
49   See Núñez Seixas (1991), as well as Ramón Villares' contribution to this volume.

external pressure on the British empire, which legitimized their political claims on the international stage and would cloak them with a left-wing liberal rhetoric.[50]

A new wave of enthusiasm spread amongst Catalanist supporters of the Allies when the US entered the war in March of 1917, and especially after Wilson's Fourteen Points were made public. Within the radical wing of the Catalan movement, Wilson's principles were interpreted as support for Catalonia's self-determination, though the final result of that remained vague. Moreover, the social reformist leaning of Wilsonianism made it possible to radical Catalanists to keep on dreaming of a middle-class patriotic revolution, detached from the Bolshevik model. Several Catalanist groups, including some from the American diaspora, sent messages to the US President; they also revived the claim for independence through a variety of publications. Within left-wing, republican and federalist Catalanism, Wilson was seen as an idealistic defender of the freedom of persons and peoples. In July 1918, Antoni Rovira i Virgili summarized this view:

> The essence of Wilsonian thinking is contained in two basic principles: those of democracy and nationalities. Mr Wilson wants the world to be dominated by the freedom of men and of peoples [...] His famous formula of the right of peoples to govern themselves contains both the democratic and the nationalities principles.[51]

The impact of the October Revolution had forced the Catalanist left to choose between Wilson and Lenin. Many felt sympathy for the Bolsheviks, who were regarded as radical Republicans; but most left-wing Catalanists and radical nationalists opted for the path of social reformism with a humanist imprint, which they associated with the credo of the US president. This seemed to better fit with the aspiration of radical Catalanists to unleash a peaceful revolution that would take Catalonia sooner or later to a vaguely defined stage of "national freedom". As the Catalanist republican deputy José M. España stated in February 1919, the "Wilsonian right" consisted of "the recognition of the collective freedom of the peoples", thus culminating "the work of the French Revolution". What Catalonia demanded was "a natural political right according to the Wilsonian theories", which would led to an overall restructuring of Spain, in line with the "new trends of our times in the bigger states of Europe and America".[52]

---

50 See Brindley (1988).
51 A. Rovira i Virgili, "Mr. Wilson president de l'Entente", *La Veu de Catalunya*, 31 July 1918.
52 See España Sirat (1919: 76–79), as well as Duarte (2015).

The armistice of November 1918 and the subsequent dissolution of the Austro-Hungarian and Ottoman empires generated a new wave of optimism among Catalan Republicans and radical nationalists. They predicted an upcoming domino effect by which all the oppressed nationalities in Europe would achieve their freedom under the auspices of the League of Nations. Aside from the rhetorical hopes placed in the US president, Wilsonian enthusiasm turned into a tangible wave of popular support and homage throughout Catalonia in late 1918. Several town-councils held banquets in honour of Wilson, and christened streets with his name. Barcelona City Council approved the appointment of the US president as honorary citizen of the town, as a "shield of justice, champion of the principle of nationalities, and representative of the universal tenets of peaceful and human internationalism". In December 1918, the Catalan regional council (*Mancomunitat*) also agreed to rebuild the devastated village in an area of the French front where Catalan volunteers had been deployed. Some days later, several republican deputies from Catalonia presented in the Madrid parliament a draft for Catalan home-rule, which stated that "the current circumstances of the world" required that the structured of the Spanish polity should be reformed to accommodate itself "to the concert of peoples".[53]

In the end, what most Catalanists wanted was to exploit a moral endorsement of their short-term autonomist, more moderate principles. As the trench journal of the Catalanist volunteers stated in December 1918, the sacrifice of Catalan soldiers on the front would bring about President Wilson's intervention, as a cartoon portrayed the American president breaking the chains of Catalonia in the presence of Alsace, Bohemia and other territories liberated by the Allied powers.[54] Another cartoon, published by a satirical Catalan weekly (fig. 3.1.), portrayed president Wilson as reaping the harvest of his doctrines of self-determination in Europe: alongside the wheat spikes of Bohemia, Alsace and Poland, two spikes with a Basque beret and a Catalan cap were waiting to be croped, while the Catalan nineteenth-century federalist thinker Francesc Pi i Margall was thanked by Wilson himself for having taught him the doctrines of federation and the nationality principle.[55]

However, the impact of Wilsonianism also influenced the emergence of new political factions within the Catalan movement, which were more oriented

---

53   Balcells, Pujol and Sabater (2006: 110–11); *La Vanguardia*, 13 November and 4 December 1918.
54   "Recorda't", *La Trinxera Catalana*, 19 December 1918.
55   'La gran collita democràtica', *L'Esquella de la Torratxa*, 15 November 1918.

FIGURE 3.1 "The great democratic harvest", *L'Esquella de la Torratxa*, 15 November 1918
"Wilson: we owe everything to you, don Francisco. You have planted well and abundantly; we harvest a good yield".

towards the liberal left and pro-independence leaning, and harboured the "new" principle of national self-determination as an alternative to "old-fashioned" models of home-rule within a composite monarchy, as well as to bolshevik self-determination. What really fascinated Catalan nationalists was the success of the Republican form of government in the new postwar Europe. In absence of border changes and geopolitic turmoil, most nationalist of Western Europe attempted to link themseles, at least rhetorically, to what was regarded as the first step towards the success of the nationality principle as a new guideline of modern international relations.

6 Expectations and Reality after Versailles

To a large extent, Wilsonian expectations by minority nationalists all over Western Europe came to naught. Although Wilson somehow "miraculously managed to give the concept of national self-determination international status", the US president was a figure who aroused many more nationalist expectations than he satisfied or was even willing to satisfy, partly because, as US State secretary Robert Lansing lamented, Wilson had no clear idea of what he meant by being the subject of self-determination.[56] At the Versailles Peace Conference, the nationality principle was only applied strategically and made compatible with the most impending geopolitical interests of the victorious powers.

The new Nation-States in East-Central Europe sought to implement a homogenizing policy imposing in the short- and mid-term a single national consciousness and a homogenous culture. Certainly, something similar had occurred in Western Europe fifty years earlier, when the Flemish of Northern France or the Occitans of the Italian Piedmont were assimilated into the ethnic majorities of their respective national States in the name of progress and civilization. However, by 1918/19, the social awareness of belonging to an ethnic minority or a distinct nationality had gained a foothold in many ethnically mixed areas now under the aegis of new nationalizing States.[57] After 1918–19, identification with irredentist minorities and support for 'our oppressed brothers beyond our borders' became a demand associated with radical State nationalism in the Weimar Republic, Hungary and Poland. The solution offered was partially inspired by the British example of multi-ethnic governance,

---

56   See Hoff (2007: 47); Lansing (1921: 97–98).
57   See Mayer (1959), as well as the reappraisal by Macmillan (2002).

which recognized the individual rights of the members of a minority not be discriminated against by the State in matters of language, religion or beliefs.[58]

The nationality principle did not become the guiding criterion for restructuring the political map of Europe, as heralded by Wilson's admirers in Catalonia or Flanders. On the contrary, the underlying philosophy of the minority protection system implemented by the League of Nations became one of guaranteeing respect for the individual rights of people belonging to minorities of 'race, language and religion', within a long-range perspective of peaceful and steady assimilation into the ethnic majority. Although this basic concept differed from that inspiring the nationality principle, a certain continuity can be traced between the international discussion on nationality rights and national self-determination during the war, and the emerging transnational debate on minority rights and protection of national minorities since the early 1920s.

A further legacy of nationality politics during the conflict was that the elites of nationalist movements in Europe came to regard proto-diplomatic agitation in times of global turmoil as an important element for attaining their objectives.[59] However, not all émigrés enjoyed similar opportunities to those enjoyed in wartime by Masaryk and Beneš. Irish and Indian nationalists sent delegations to Paris but were not allowed to present their claims at the Peace Conference. Something similar happened with some political groupings from Catalonia, Brittany or Scotland, all of whom tempted to present documents and memoranda to various state delegations at the Peace Conference.[60] Even so, the example of ethno-nationalists who succeeded in achieving their objectives after 1918 —owing in part to proto-diplomacy—influenced the strategies of those who sought to follow in their footsteps. They learned the compulsory nature of setting up propaganda bureaus in the greatest European capitals, and presented their claims in multilingual brochures and journals in order to influence the new actor that supposedly became relevant after 1918: international public opinion. They also sought to gain the support of intellectuals, journalists and influential elites in London, Vienna, Paris, Berlin or Geneva and launched political campaigns to influence the decision-making process of the

---

58 See Brubaker (1996).
59 See, for example, the contemporary reflection by A. Rovira i Virgili, "Necessitat de que tot nacionalisme tingui una política internacional", *Revista Anyal*, 1915, reproduced in Martínez Fiol (1988: 79–85).
60 See examples in Macardle (1965: 207–82); Bonsal (1969); Gasquet (1995); Y. Kerberio, 'Les représentants de la minorité bretonne chez le Président Wilson en 1919', *Minorité-La Voix des Peuples*, 15 January 1938.

League of Nations in matters related to the minority protection.[61] Transnational minority agitation in Europe during the 1920s and 1930s had learnt many lessons from émigrés and the internationalization of nationalist mobilization during the First World War.

Bibliography

Balcells, A., E. Pujol & J. Sabater (2006), *La Mancomunitat de Catalunya i l'autonomia*, Barcelona: Proa/IEC.

Beer, M., & S. Dyroff, eds. (2014), *Politische Strategien nationaler Minderheiten in der Zwischenkriegszeit*, Munich: Oldenbourg.

Bianchini, S., ed. (2013), *Self-Determination and Sovereignty in Europe. From Historical Legacies to the EU External Role*, Ravenna: Longo.

Bonsal, S. (1969), *Suitors and Suppliants. The Little Nations at Versailles*, Port Washington, NY: Kemikat Press.

Brecht, W. (1992), *Selbstbestimmung und imperiale Herrschaft: Zur Haltung Woodrow Wilsons gegenüber der aussereuropäischen Welt*, Münster: Lit.

Brindley, R. (1988), 'Woodrow Wilson, Self-Determination and Ireland 1918–1919: A View from the Irish Newspapers', *Eire-Ireland*, Winter issue, pp. 62–80.

Brubaker, R. (1996), *Nationalism Reframed. Nationhood and the National Question in the New Europe*, Cambridge: Cambridge UP.

Calder, K.R. (1976), *Britain and the Origins of the New Europe, 1914–1918*, Cambridge: Cambridge UP.

Carney, S. (2015), *Breiz Atao! Mordrel, Delaporte, Lainé, Fouéré: une mystique nationale (1901–1948)*, Rennes: Presses Universitaires de Rennes.

Celi, A. (2017), "La Grande Guerra e le origini dell'autonomismo valdostano", in G. Zanibelli (ed.), *La Grande Guerra in Provincia. Comunità locali e fronte interno: fonti e studi su società e conflitto*, Siena: Nuova Immagine Editrice, pp. 325–337.

Chernev, B. (2011), "The Brest-Litovsk Moment: Self-Determination Discourse in Eastern Europe before Wilsonianism", *Diplomacy & Statecraft*, 22:3, pp. 369–87.

Clough, S.B. (1930), *A History of the Flemish Movement in Belgium. A Study of Nationalism*, New York: Richard R. Smith.

Conversi, D. (1993), "Domino effect or international developments? The influences of international events and political ideologies on Catalan and Basque nationalism", *West European Politics*, 16:1, pp. 245–70.

---

61 See Beer and Dyroff (2014), as well as Núñez Seixas (2016), and Ucelay-Da Cal, Núñez Seixas & Gonzàlez Vilalta (2020).

Cortright, D. (2008), *Peace. A History of Movements and Ideas*, Cambridge: Cambridge UP.

Cubeddu, S. (1993), *Sardisti. Viaggio nel Partito Sardo d'Azione tra cronaca e storia. Volume I (1919–1948)*, Sassari: Edes.

Davies, D.H. (1985), *The Welsh Nationalist Party 1925–1945. A Call to Nationhood*. Cardiff: Univ. of Wales Press.

Davies, Th. (2014), *NGOs: A New History of Transnational Civil Society*, Oxford: Oxford UP.

Déniel, A. (1976), *Le mouvement bréton, 1919–1945*, Paris: Maspero.

Diekmann, K. (1998), *Die nationalistische Bewegung in Wales*, Paderborn: Schöningh.

Duarte, A. (2015) "Visiones de un mañana aleatorio. Notas sobre el intelectual republicano-catalanista ante la Gran Guerra", *Historia y Política*, 33, pp. 99–122.

Esculies, J., & D. Martínez Fiol (2014), *12.000! Els Catalans a la Primera Guerra Mundial*, Barcelona: Ara llibres.

España Sirat, J.M. (1919), *Las corrientes autonomistas en el mundo y el pleito de Cataluña*, Lleida: Sol y Benet.

Fraenkel, E. (1960), "Das deutsche Wilsonsbild", *Jahrbuch für Amerikastudien*, 5, pp. 66–120.

Gabrys, J. (E. Demm, ed.) (2013), *Auf Wache für die Nation – Erinnerungen*, Frankfurt a. M.: PL Academic Research.

Gasquet, S. de (1995), "La France et les mouvements nationaux ukrainiens", in G.-H. Soutou (ed.), *Recherches sur la France et le problème des nationalités pendant la premiére guerre mondiale (Pologne, Ukraine, Lithuanie)*, Paris: Presses de l'Université de Paris-Sorbonne, pp. 172–183.

Gerson, L.L. (1956), *Woodrow Wilson und die Wiedergeburt Polens 1914–1920*, Würzburg: Holzner.

Gibbons, H.A. (1918), *Le point de vue américain sur la question des nationalités et la Société des Nations*, Paris: n. ed.

Goebel, M. (2015), *Anti-Imperial Metropolis: Interwar Paris and the Seeds of Third World Nationalism*, Cambrige: Cambridge UP.

Griffith, A. (1904), *The Resurrection of Hungary: A Parallel for Ireland*, Dublin: Whelan and Son.

Guieu, J. (2008), *Le rameau et le glaive. Les militants français pour la SDN*, Paris: Presses de Sciences Po.

Hadler, F., ed. (1995), *Weg von Österreich! Das Weltkriegsexil von Masaryk und Benes im Spiegel ihrer Briefe und Aufzeichnungen aus den Jahren 1914–1918. Eine Quellensammlung*, Berlin: AkademieVerlag.

Hauser, H (1916), *Le principe des nationalités. Ses origines historiques*, Paris: Alcan.

Heater, D. (1994), *National Self-Determination: Woodrow Wilson and his Legacy*, New York: St. Martin's Press.

Hoff, J. (2007), *A Faustian Foreign Policy from Woodrow Wilson to George W. Bush: Dreams of Perfectibility*, New York: Cambridge UP.

Hroch, M. (2000), In the National Interest. Demands and Goals of European National Movements of the Nineteenth Century: a Comparative Perspectie, Praga: Charles University.—(2005), Das Europa der Nationen: Die moderne Nationsbildung im europäischen Vergleich, Göttingen: Vandenhoeck & Ruprecht.

Kaltenbach, F.W. (1938), *Self-Determination 1919. A Study in Frontier-making between Germany and Poland*, London: Jawolds.

Lansing, R. (1921), *The Peace Negotiations: A Personal Narrative*, Boston/New York: Houghton Mifflin Co.

Laqua, D. (2013), *The Age of Internationalism and Belgium, 1880–1930. Peace, Progress and Prestige*, Manchester: Manchester UP.

Leerssen, J. (2006), *National Thought in Europe: A Cultural History*, Amsterdam: Amsterdam UP.

Lloyd George, D. (1928), *War Memoirs*, London: Odhams, vol. 2.

Macardle, D. (1965), *The Irish Republic*, New York: Fawar, Straus & Giroux.

Macartney, C.A. (1934), *National States and National Minorities*, London: Oxford UP.

Macmillan, M. (2002), *Paris, 1919: Six Months That Changed the World*, New York: Random House.

Mamatey, V.S. (1967), *The United States and East Central Europe 1914–1918: A Study in Wilsonian diplomacy and propaganda*, Princeton, NJ: Princeton UP.

Mandelstan, A.N. (1919), *Mémoire sur la delimitation des droits de l'homme et de la nation d'après la doctrine du president Wilson*, Paris: Hugonis.

Manela, E. (2007), *The Wilsonian Moment: Self-determination and the Origins of Anticolonial Nationalism*, Oxford: Oxford UP.

Martin, L.W. (1958), *Peace without Victory: Woodrow Wilson and the British Liberals*, New Haven: Yale UP.

Martínez Fiol, D., ed. (1988), *El catalanisme i la Gran Guerra (1914–1918). Antologia*, Barcelona: La Magrana/Diputació de Barcelona.

Martínez Fiol, D. (1991), *Els 'voluntaris catalans' a la Gran Guerra, 1914–1918*, Barcelona: PAB.

Maume, P. (1995), "The Ancient Constitution: Arthur Griffith and his intellectual legacy to Sinn Féin", *Irish Political Studies*, 10:1, pp. 125–37.

Mayer, A.J. (1959), *Wilson vs. Lenin: Political Origins of the New Diplomacy 1917–1918*, New Haven: Yale UP.

Miquel, P. (1971), *La Paix de Versailles et l'opinion publique française*, Paris: Flammarion.

Mir, G. (1990), *El mallorquinisme polític 1840–1936*, Palma de Mallorca: Moll, vol. I.

Morgan, K.O. (1981), *Rebirth of a Nation. Wales, 1880–1980*, Oxford: Clarendon/Univ. of Wales Press.

Núñez Seixas, X.M. (1991), "Galicia no espello europeu. As relacións internacionais do nacionalismo galego, 1916–1936", *A Trabe de Ouro*, 8, pp. 507–20.

Núñez Seixas, X.M. (2001), *Entre Ginebra y Berlín. La cuestión de las minorías nacionales y la política internacional en Europa, 1914–1939*, Madrid: Akal.

Núñez Seixas, X.M. (2010), *Internacionalitzant el nacionalisme. El catalanisme polític i la qüestió de les minories nacionals a Europa (1914–1936)*, Valencia: Afers / Universitat de València.

Núñez Seixas, X.M. (2016), "Unholy Alliances? Nationalist Exiles, Minorities and Antifascism in interwar Europe", *Contemporary European History*, 25:4, pp. 597–617.

Núñez Seixas, X.M. (2018), "Catalonia and the 'War of Nations': Catalan Nationalism and the First World War", *Journal of Modern European History*, 16:3, pp. 379–98.

Núñez Seixas, X.M. (2019), *Patriotas transnacionales. Estudios sobre nacionalismos y transferencias culturales en la Europa del siglo XX*, Madrid: Cátedra.

Nygard, S., & J. Strång (2016), "Facing Asimmetry. Nordic Intellectuals and Center-Periphery Dynamics in European Cultural Space", *Journal of the History of Ideas*, 77:1, pp. 75–98.

Organisation Centrale por une Paix Durable (1917), *Avant-Projet d'un Traité général rélatif aux Droits des Minorités Nationales*, Stockholm: Oskar Eklund.

Østergård, U. (2015), "Nation-Building and Nationalism in the Oldenburg Empire", in A. Miller and S. Berger (eds.), *Nationalizing Empires*, Budapest/New York: CEU Press, pp. 461–509.

Osterkamp, J., & M. Schulze-Wessel, eds. (2017), *Exploring Loyalty*, Göttingen: V&R.

Otlet, P. (1914), *La fin de la guerre. Traité de paix générale basé sur une charte mondiale déclarant les droits de l'humanité et organisant la confédération des états*, Brussels: Oscar Lamberty.

Pérez Casanova, G.J. (2012), "¡Sálvanos, Wilson! El remedio americano para la decadencia europea", in C. Navajas & D. Iturriaga (eds.), *Coetánea. Actas del III Congreso Internacional de Historia de nuestro Tiempo*, Logroño: IER, pp. 187–196.

Pott, W. (2011), *Auf der Suche nach Unterstützung für Irland: Roger Casements Wirken in Deutschland und die deutsche Unterstützung des Osteraufstandes*, Munich: AVM.

Prott, V. (2016), *The Politics of Self-Determination. Remaking Territories and National Identities in Europe, 1917–1923*, Oxford: Oxford UP.

Roberts, P. (2013), "Wilson, Europe's Colonial Empires, and the Issue of Imperialism", in R.A. Kennedy (ed.), *A Companion to Woodrow Wilson*, Chichester: Wiley-Blackwell, pp. 492–517.

Rodogno, D., B. Struck and B. Vogel, eds. (2015), *Shaping the Transnational Sphere: Experts, Networks, and Issues from the 1840s to the 1930s*, New York/Oxford: Berghahn.

Sanborn, J.A. (2014), *Imperial Apocalypse: The Great War and the Destruction of the Russian Empire*, Oxford: Oxford UP.

Séailles, G. (1918), *Le principe des nationalités et ses applications,* Paris: P. Levé.

Secchi, S. (1976), *Dopoguerra e fascismo in Sardegna. Il movimento autonomistico nella crisi dello stato liberale,* Torino: Einaudi.

Seignobos, Ch. (1913), *Les aspirations autonomistes en Europe,* Paris: Alcan.

Seton-Watson, H. (1991), "Czechs, Poles and Yugoslavs in London, 1914–1918", in *L'Émigration politique en Europe aux XIXème et XXème siècles,* Rome: École Française de Rome, pp. 277–93.

Seton-Watson, H., & Ch. Seton-Watson (1981), *The Making of a New Europe. Robert W. Seton-Watson and the Last Days of Austria Hungary,* London: Methuen.

Seton-Watson, R.W. (1915), *What is at Stake at the War,* London: Oxford UP.

Sluga, G. (2006), *Nation, Psychology and International Politics 1870–1919,* Basingstoke: Palgrave Macmillan.

Sluga, G. (2013), *Internationalism in the Age of Nationalism,* Philadelphia: Univ. of Pennsylvania Press.

Smith, D.M. (2002) "The Fourteen Points", in A. DeConde (ed.), *Encyclopedia of American Foreign Policy,* New York: Scribner, vol. II, pp. 380–86.

Soutou, G.H. (1995), "Jean Pélissier et l'Office Central des Nationalités, 1911–1918: Un agent du gouvernement français auprés des nationalités", in id. (ed.), *Recherches,* pp. 13–38.

Stutje, K. (2019), *Campaigning in Europe for a Free Indonesia: Indonesian Nationalists and the Worldwide Anticolonial Movement, 1917–1931,* Copenhaguen: NIAS Press.

Swartz, M. (1971), *The Union of Democratic Control in British Politics during the First World War,* Oxford: Clarendon Press.

Tchernoff, J. (1918), *Le principe des nationalités d'après la tradition républicaine,* Paris: L'Action Nationale.

Thiesse, A.-M. (2011), *La creation des identités nationales. Europe XVIIIe-XXe siècle,* Paris: Éditions du Seuil.

Throntveit, T. (2011), "The Fable of the Fourteen Points: Woodrow Wilson and National Self-Determination", *Diplomatic History,* 35:3, pp. 445–81.

Tobia, B. (1974), "Il partito socialista italiano e la politica di Wilson (1916–1919)", *Storia Contemporanea,* V:2, pp. 274–303.

Toynbee, A.J. (1915), *Nationality and the War,* London: Dent.

Ucelay-Da Cal, E. (2003), *El imperialismo catalán. Prat de la Riba, Cambó, D'Ors y la conquista moral de España,* Barcelona: Edhasa.

Ucelay-Da Cal, E. (2020a), "Cómo surgieron las internacionales de nacionalistas. La coincidencia de iniciativas sociales muy diversas, 1864–1914", in Ucelay-Da Cal, Núñez Seixas & Gonzàlez Vilalta (eds.), *Patrias diversas,* pp. 25–66.

Ucelay-Da Cal, E. (2020b), "How to Become Independent in Europe (and America) Before 1931: Upholding the Monarchy or Proclaiming a Republic", in A. González i

Vilalta (ed.), *The Illusion of Statehood: Perceptions of Catalan Independence up to the End of the Spanish Civil War*, Brighton/Eastbourne: Sussex Academic Press, pp. 1–55.

Ucelay-Da Cal, E., Núñez Seixas, X.M., & Gonzàlez Vilalta, A., eds. (2020), *Patrias diversas, ¿misma lucha? Alianzas transnacionalistas en el mundo de entreguerras (1912–1939)*, Barcelona: Eds. Bellaterra.

Ugalde, A. (1996), *La acción exterior del nacionalismo vasco (1890–1939): Historia, pensamiento y relaciones internacionales*, Oñati: IVAP.

Valár, R. (2013), *Weder Italiener noch Deutsche! Die rätoromanische Heimatbewegung 1863–1938*, Baden: Verlag für Kultur und Geschichte.

Wambaugh, S. (1933), *Plebiscites since the World War*, Washington: Carnegie Foundation, 2 vols.

Weitz, E.D. (2015), "Self-Determination: How a German Enlightenment Idea Became the Slogan of National Liberation and a Human Right", *American Historical Review*, 120:2, pp. 462–96.

Werner, M., & J. Zimmermann (2006), "Beyond Comparison: *Histoire Croisée* and the Challenge of Reflexivity", *History and Theory*, 45, pp. 30–50.

Wils, W. (1974), *Flamenpolitik en aktivisme. Vlaanderen tegenover Belgie in de eerste Wereldoorlog*, Leuven: Davidsfonds.

Wimmer, A. (2013), *Waves of war: Nationalism, state formation, and ethnic exclusion in the modern world*, Cambridge et al.: Cambridge UP.

Wright, J. (2003), *The Regionalist Movement in France: Jean Charles-Brun and French Political Thought*, Oxford: Oxford UP.

Yvia-Croce, H. (1979), *Vingt années de corsisme, 1920–1939. Chronique corse de l'entre-deux-guerres*, Ajaccio: Cyrnos et Mediterranée.

Zetterberg, S. (1978), *Die Liga der Fremdvölker Russlands 1916-1918. Ein Beitrag zu Deutschlands antirussischem Propagandakrieg unter den Fremdvölkern Russlands im Ersten Weltkrieg*, Helsinki: Akateeminen Kirjakauppa.

Zondergeld, G. (1978), *De Friese Beweging in het Tijdvak der beide Wereldoorlogen*, Leeuwarden/Ljouvert: De Tille.

CHAPTER 4

Nationalizing an Empire: The Bolsheviks, the Nationality Question, and Policies of Indigenization in the Soviet Union (1917–1927)

Malte Rolf

The Soviet Union was a multinational empire. In this it had much in common with many other empires, but it was unique in its attempt to be the first explicit anti-imperialist empire that was built on the notions of political federation and internal nation-building as part and parcel of the official agenda. The Soviet "Empire of nations", as Francine Hirsch once coined it, was to present nothing else but the complete opposite to Tsarist Russia that had been overcome by the revolutions of 1917.[1]

This contribution deals with the Bolsheviks' nationality policies as a very distinct approach towards the nationality question in interwar Europe. It portrays the guiding principle of Lenin's and other Communists' "answer" to the nationality issue they inherited from the *ancien régime*. The article analyses how the Bolsheviks interpreted the fall of the Romanov-monarchy and the conclusions they drew from their interpretation. Moving on in chronology, it discusses how these underlying assumptions of national policies underwent fundamental changes during the Civil War that raged in Russia from 1917 to 1921. In the end, Lenin and other party leaders constructed a unique state they called the "USSR" and imposed specific policies of indigenization (*korenizatsiia*). This study will try to demonstrate how such attempts of "rooting in" came into conflict with simultaneous strategies to Sovietize the culture and people of the Empire and why such inherent tensions contributed to the totalitarian dictatorship of Joseph Stalin. In conclusion, the Soviet Union as a multi-ethnic empire will be placed in historical perspective, and the particular nature of this "empire of nations" that may have imploded in 1991, but that proved to be persistent for more than seventy years, will be discussed.

---

1 See Hirsch (2005).

1   "Prison of the people"? Late Imperial Russia, Autocracy and the
     "national question(s)"

During the second half of the 19th century and in particular after the revolution of 1905, contemporaries who were critical towards the Tsar's autocratic rule quite often referred to Imperial Russia as the "Prison of the people" – both addressing the repressive nature of autocracy in political terms as well as the supposed heavy burden of Russification and oppression in non-Russian peripheries. Although it might not be difficult to dismiss this kind of polemic as somewhat exaggerated or even as national-revolutionary propaganda, it is still important to keep in mind that within the political discourse of that time, the perception of the Tsarist Empire as being a Russificatory oppressive power was quite common. As we shall see, this perception was of the greatest importance to the Bolshevik re-approach to the national question.[2]

But how did the Romanov Empire earn this reputation? The Russian Empire was an extremely complex entity. It was a vast multi-ethnic and poly-confessional composite monarchy that incorporated various historical districts with very distinct ways of governing and different forms of indirect rule through local (non-Russian) elites. The national census of 1897 gives an idea of this heterogeneity: of the 125 million people living in Russia, only 44 % were ethnic Russians, another 18 % Ukrainians, followed by 7 % Poles and 4 % Jews. Ethnographers of that time intensely disputed the number of nationalities (*narodnosti*) within the Empire, but figures around 100 nationalities as well as a vast number of beliefs, languages and confessional groups were frequently mentioned. Even the imperial elite was a composite one: according to the 1897 census, Russian was the mother tongue of only 53 % of the noble elite, and non-Russians figured prominently in the higher echelons of the Tsarist state administration.[3]

St. Petersburg tried hard to manage this diversity. Traditionally, the peripheries of the Empire had been governed by forms of indirect rule and by co-opting the local elite into the Russian nobility, while leaving the social and administrative structures of the incorporated entities mostly untouched.[4] However, this traditional mode of a composite monarchy changed dramatically with the great reforms under Alexander II. After having lost the Crimean War, St. Petersburg strove to unify the administration of the various provinces

---

2 See Martin (2001b:71).
3 See figures of the 1897-census in Bauer, Kappeler and Roth (1991). See also Cadiot (2005), Geyer (1996: 100–05); Kappeler (1992: 233–67), Lieven (1989), and Rolf (2014c).
4 See, for example, Baberowski (1999); Kappeler (2000); Kappeler (1992: 134–38).

and, in general, to make the Empire more homogenous. The Tsar and his reformer were inspired by various international role models. Among them Napoleon III. figured prominently in his seemingly successful effort to modernize France and to establish a homogenous administrating state.

This was in particular true for regions that, like Poland or the Caucasus, had seen local rebellions before. Here, administrative Russification – in the sense of imposing new Empire-wide structures and an external imperial bureaucracy – was pushed very far, including a linguistic Russification of all state affairs.[5] But even in less unruly borderlands – like the Baltic provinces – a tendency to further homogenize the administrative structures let to policies that were seen as Russificatory by many contemporaries in those peripheries.[6] In the long term, St. Petersburg's attempt to overcome the Empire's diversity unleashed considerable discomfort, critics and even upheaval in the borderlands – forms of reluctance that were more and more seen as a form of national resistance against the centre's Russificatory policies. In this process, the transnational flow of ideas played a key role. In particular, Polish intellectuals were incited by European national movements and hoped to follow the path of Garibaldi and the Risorgimento. Lithuanian, Latvian, Estonian and Finish activists intensively read Herder's praise of folk culture and copied many of the rituals and practices that had characterized the German pre-march national movement.[7]

Starting with the 1890s, "national questions" – as contemporaries referred to it – were increasingly dominating the political discourse on the future and nature of the Empire, with radicalizations on both sides. While the Imperial government and its local representatives (who were, in fact, often non-Russians) were rather careful with *divide-et-impera*-policies and always denied the Russificatory impetus of imperial administration, a growing number of voices within Russian civil society called for further privileges for Russians. "Russia for Russians" was the slogan not only of far-right nationalists, but also of moderate conservatives and marked a sort of consensus among Russian political actors in the Duma and the government. Again, a transnational horizon of reference points was of crucial importance, since contemporaries were closely following the privileging policies towards the "state nation" in other dynastical Empires. It seemed as if the German Kaiserreich and even the Habsburg monarchy were

---

5   See Dolbilov (2004); Dolbilov (2004); Rodkiewicz (2012); Rolf (2012, 2015, 2017, 2021); Staliūnas (2007a, 2007b); Weeks (2004).
6   See Haltzel 1981; Thaden (1981, 1984); Waldron (1985).
7   See, for example, Baberowski (2000); Haltzel 1977; Suny and Martin (2001). See also the thematic issue "Nationalismus und nationale Bewegungen in den nichtslawischen Regionen Rußlands und der Sowjetunion", *Jahrbücher für Geschichte Osteuropas* 47:4 (1999).

gradually turning "national".[8] On the other hand, a growing number of opinion leaders of the non-Russian nationalities saw St. Petersburg as a Russificatory and repressive power that seemed to endanger further national development. Although the secessionists' camps within the non-Russian elites (even among the Poles) remained rather small and radical revolutionaries managed to threaten the autocracy only during the turmoil of the revolution of 1905, there was a growing feeling of alienation among national elites during the last decade before the war. To escalate matters even further, national intellectuals were well informed about the inner structure of the Austro-Hungarian monarchy that served as a role model for many claims for "national" or "cultural autonomy". Just across the border, the Habsburg Empire bore witness that an imperial order could integrate forms of national self-determination.[9] In Russia, little legitimacy was granted to the Romanov Empire or the Tsar, and few contemporaries believed that Petersburg's autocracy could ever leave behind the present cauldron of "national questions" and interethnic hatred and violence. By 1914, a broad spectrum of contemporaries shared the notion that the Empire as a composite state would sooner or later come to an end.

2   Bolshevik Debates on the "National Question" and National Self-determination

When the Bolsheviks took power in 1917, they were confronted with the task of manoeuvring their own revolutionary state through the turmoil of revolution and civil war. Soon, this state became an Empire of its own – and the Bolsheviks were faced with the challenge to give answers to the many national questions. By doing so, Lenin and other party leaders referred to their set of knowledge and perceptions of the ills of Tsarist Russia before the war. To understand why they created a radical alternative to the *ancien régime*, we must take a closer look at the underlying assumptions and set of believes that guided the Bolsheviks during the chaotic years following the October Revolution.

In the Bolsheviks' analysis of the failures of the Tsarist Empire, Great Russian chauvinism ranked prominently as a destabilizing factor. In addition to class struggle, the political repressive system and police and military domestic violence, the Bolsheviks saw supposed Russificatory policies as one of the

---

[8] See Golczewski and Pickhan (1998); Martiny (1992); Hagen (1964); Miller (2008); Rolf (2014a, 2015, 2017, 2021); Weeks (1996: 172–91).

[9] See Aoshima, Werth and Staliunas (2021); Blobaum (1995); Rolf (2013a, 2018, 2021); Weeks (2006); Staliunas (2014); Buchen and Rolf (2015).

main reasons for the people's rejection of the monarchy and the implosion of the Empire in 1917. "Great Russian chauvinism" seemed to have offended national sentiments everywhere in the peripheries, thus destabilizing the whole Empire.[10] There were good reasons for this argument – the revolution of 1905 proved to be most violent in the Empire's borderlands (like Poland, the Ukraine, the Caucasus or the Baltic provinces), where social and national agendas of local political actors overlapped or even merged. We should also keep in mind that many of the younger Bolshevik leaders (like Joseph Stalin, Lasar Kaganovich or Grigori Ordzhonikidze) came from these fringes and shatter-zones of the Empire and therefore knew the enormous potential of national mobilization and upheaval from first-hand experience.[11]

Soon after 1917, Bolsheviks coined the term of the "greater danger principle" – identifying Great Russian chauvinism as the main source of turmoil and local rejection of the Imperial capital.[12] In this perspective, bourgeois nationalism was viewed as a historical anachronism that needed to be overcome, but some forms of national resistance against Imperial rule were acknowledged to be "progressive" and even necessary in the Bolsheviks' grand historical narration. National self-determination therefore became a claim which in the Bolsheviks' view was positively connoted, although there always remained the danger of a "bourgeois degeneration" of this concept. Of course, it was a matter of debate when good, "non-bourgeois" national policies might turn into bad "bourgeois" nationalism.[13]

In any case, slogans like "freedom of the people" and "the right of national self-determination" figured prominently among the Bolsheviks' promises for a better future in 1917, and this, no doubt, was only partly political masquerade. In fact, having witnessed the endless national quarrels in Late Imperial Russia, many Bolshevik leaders (and Lenin was one of them) were aware of the destabilizing effect a strong centrist and pro-Russian agenda would have on a complex multi-ethnic Empire.[14]

Shortly after their seizure of power, the Bolsheviks started radically rebuilding the fundaments of "their" revolutionary state. Already the proclamations they initiated in the Second All-Russian Congress of Workers' and Soldiers'

---

10 See, for example, *Joseph V. Stalin:* "The National Question in Russia", in *Joseph V. Stalin: Marxism and the National Question*, first published in *Prosveshcheniye*, No. 3–5 (March-May 1913). On this debate, see in greater detail Martin (2001b); Meissner (1996).

11 See Ascher (1988), Altstadt Mirhadi (1986); Baberowski (2001, 2003a: 77–83); Benecke (2007); Rolf (2013b); Weinberg (1993).

12 See Martin (2001b: 71).

13 See Kappeler (1992: 300–06); Simon (1986: 34–106). See also in translation Simon (1991).

14 See Smith (1999); Suny and Martin (2001).

Deputies' Soviets to legitimize the armed toppling of the Provisional Government include the explicit promise of future national self-determination. In January 1918, they proclaimed the *Russian Soviet Republic* to be the nucleus of a new entity that – in their theological expectation of the world revolution – would shortly be extended by other revolutionary governments. Extension might have been the future perspective; the bitter reality was in fact a dramatic loss of territories under Bolshevik control. In many peripheries of the former Empire, national leaders declared secession after Lenin had dispersed the All Russian Constituent Assembly in January 1918. In March 1918, the Germans forced the Bolsheviks to sign the Treaty of Brest-Litovsk, including massive territorial partitions, and with the evolving Civil War even further inner-Russian provinces were lost to anti-Bolshevik forces. Ignoring their political isolation and facing military disaster, Lenin and his comrades-in-arms still rushed to give their new state a constitutional form. In July 1918, the constitution of the *Russian Soviet Federative Socialist Republic* (RSFSR) was issued, that in many ways would serve as the role model for the Soviet constitution in 1923. The new state structure was a radical break with the past in many dimensions. Now, the organs of *Soviets* were declared the institutions to represent the peoples' will. According to the constitution, the All-Russian Congress of Soviets, with its Central Executive Committee, held supreme power and would formally elect the government: the Council of People's Commissars. The constitution was just as ground-breaking with regard to the state's inner structure: it characterized the RSFSR as a "Federation of soviet national republics" (Article One, chapter one) and thus declared the principle of nationality to be the basic paradigm for its internal administration. Moscow now promised to grant a large degree of autonomy to the regions and nationally defined territories, and the non-Russian peripheries of the *ancien regime* should even be considered as formally independent republics, only loosely tied to Russia by international treaties. With this constitution, the Bolsheviks hoped to achieve an institutional containment of the explosive powers inherent to centrifugal national movements.[15]

By doing so, Moscow's new rulers relied heavily on many political concepts that their direct socialist opponents, the Social revolutionaries, had developed in recent years. But the constitution was also remarkably inspired by a transnational import of ideas. Already during his years of exile, Lenin had followed closely the debates that socialists in Austro-Hungary had waged over the national question. He had commented on the political notions of Karl *Kautsky*, Karl Renner or Otto Bauer, although he had rejected most of their ideas on

---

15   See Meissner (1996: 44–49); Smith (1999: 29–31).

forms of national self-determination. However, in 1918, the prospect of overcoming national differences in a cosmopolitan socialist identity seemed rather utopian and had little to offer to the concrete task of managing and governing the seized state. Thus, when writing the constitution, the Bolsheviks were more open to the concepts of the Habsburg socialists. While Renner's vision of personalized national identity detached from territory was declined, Otto Bauer's concept of territorialized "cultural autonomy" turned out to be crucial for the Bolsheviks' debates in 1918 and their national policies that followed. Territorialization nationalities seemed to be the key in the task to leave behind the cauldron of constant inter-ethnic tensions.[16]

In an intensive international transfer of ideas, the Bolsheviks also adopted other basic assumptions of the Austro-Marxists. They began to imagine the nation as a cohesive community of destiny and thus as an essential entity that would not simply "wither away" in the socialist order to be established. Moscow's leaders now subscribed to a notion of nationality as an essential need of men's self-determination. In consequence, nationality needed to be incorporated in the building structure of the new state. Establishing socialism now meant empowering national culture (in a given territory) and seeking "national forms" for "socialist content". Although Stalin coined this phrase only several years later, already in 1918, many aspects of Bauer's idea of territorialized national-cultural autonomy were promoted to the guiding principle of the RSFSR.[17]

These key underlying assumptions underwent some changes during the raging civil war that followed the revolution and that ended in 1921 with the "red Reconquista"[18] of almost all the territories that had belonged to Imperial Russia.

3   Civil War, "Red Reconquista" and the Making of a "Union of Soviet Socialist Republics": Adopting Bolshevik National Policies to Complex Realities (1917–1923)

Hardly anyone believed that the Bolsheviks, a marginal group of revolutionaries with little or no connection to the Empire's peripheries, would be able to

---

16   Kappeler (1992: 298–302); Smith (1999: 29–34).
17   Iosif Stalin, *Marksizm i natsional'no-kolonial'nyi vopros: Sbornik izbrannykh statei i rechei* (Moscow: Partizdat TsK VKP(b), 1935).
18   Geyer (1997: 271).

withstand the siege of a multi-facetted coalition of anti-Bolshevik forces.[19] In the end, the Bolsheviks won the civil war and even managed to extend the limits of their new red Empire almost to the former borders of Tsarist Russia. Amongst many other decisive factors, the Bolsheviks' ability to cooperate with a great variety of local warlords and to build coalitions with indigenous "national" military leaders surely played a key role. Although soon after 1917 the slogan of national self-determination did not imply a regions' right to secession (which last had been accepted by the new revolutionary government in the case of Finland), red propaganda still operated with the "national cause" during and after the civil war. When conquering territories on the peripheries, the Red army and the new Soviet power were not represented as an import of revolution so much as a liberation of nationalities.[20]

In fact, the sheer existence of the RSFSR gave some credibility to such bold statements. The Bolsheviks rushed to demonstrate that this new guiding principle of a much-decentralized federation was more than paper work. Already during the civil war, when the Red Army overran their "White" enemies in the imperial peripheries, Bolshevik cultural propaganda focused much on the "blossoming of nations" in the cultural sphere. Even before the term "indigenization" was coined, Moscow tried hard to create a self-image of a new form of power that was explicitly anti-imperialist and that merely helped the many non-Russian nationalities in the course of their further cultural development. They also made intensive use of indigenous cultural brokers and translators in the local settings, although the Bolshevik had little doubt that many of them were rather "false friends" in terms of Marxist purity.[21] This new sort of pragmatism displayed by Moscow's agents in the borderlands was, of course, enforced by the bitter struggles of the Civil War and the Bolsheviks' relative weakness. But it gave some credential to their claims of presenting a new form of power that would do more justice to local-national interest. At least the Bolsheviks had more to offer than many of the commanders of the "Whites", who promised the return of the much hated *ancien régime*.[22]

The civil war gave birth to another guiding principle that would characterize power relations in the Soviet Union until its very end. With the Communist Party, the Bolsheviks created a parallel structure of power that would compensate for the rather loose organization of federal state institutions and that

---

19 On this, see Katzer (1999).
20 See Baberowski (2016); Fedtke (2006); Hirsch (2005); Northrop (2001a).
21 See, for example, See, for example, Fedtke (2006); Simon (1986: 34–82).
22 Smith (1999: 29–64).

would counter-balance the granting of (formal) authority to local soviet organs. The Communist Party, on the contrary, was organized on a strict hierarchical basis and decision-making was monopolized by a small power-clique in the Kremlin. Lenin thus intended to tame the centrifugal forces inscribed in the constitutional arrangements of the RSFSR. The "Red commissars" that operated in every regular army unit and partisan group demonstrate well how much the Kremlin trusted only local communist cadres. During the bitter struggle of Civil War and partisan warfare, the Bolsheviks were scarcely selective when it came to finding local and national allies in the fight with "white" forces. But it was one of the "formative experiences" of the Civil War for Moscow's leaders that in the long run only a narrow circle of Communist functionaries could be ultimately trusted. In later period of crises, the Bolsheviks tended to enforce policies that rested on this "lesson learned" during the founding years of the Soviet Union.[23]

How much Bolshevik national policies had to adopt to the complex and often bitter realities of the Civil War and the vastness of the new red Empire is clearly shown in the founding constitution of the Soviet Union, which was drafted shortly after the war in December 1922 and which in 1923 finally founded a unique state. The Bolsheviks remained faithful to the idea of a federal state structure and also granted many institutions of national representations at a local republican and all-state level. The constitution of the USSR inherited many of the guiding principles of the RSFSR's basic law. Like the latter, the 1923 constitution was the result of a crossover of trans-national concepts of "solving" the national question and inner-soviet factors of influence. Since the underlying principle of the constitution stayed untouched until the very end of the Soviet Union in 1991, it is worth highlighting some of its key features with regard to institutions of national representation.[24]

The Union of Soviet Socialist Republics constituted a complex hierarchy of autonomous districts and republics, the latter being formally close to independent states. First 4, soon 11 and later 15 republics made up the USSR as equal partners. All the republics had their own de jure government, parliaments and state departments. The republics were clearly defined as "national", with a privileged titular nation running the state affairs. To shelter the other nationalities from all sort of "chauvinistic" policies by the republic's capital autonomous regions, districts and even smallest village entities were created where the respective national majority had the right of political representation and cultural activity. The guiding principle here was to territorialize nationality: each

---

23   Fitzpatrick (1985: 57–76); Joravsky (1985: 93–113).
24   See on the following and in greater detail Martin (2001a: 1–28); Meissner (1996: 50–52).

nation should have a territory and all territories needed to be nationally labelled. The Soviet Union was administrated according to this principle; it turned into a patchwork consisting of a vast number of nationally defined sub-units.[25]

In addition, certain central union-wide institutions were also established that would further allow the articulation of national interests in Moscow. For example, one of the chambers that constituted the Central Executive Committee of the USSR was the Council of Nationalities. Thus, the constitution presented a federal model to an extreme that even some Bolshevik contemporaries criticized for overdoing the case and for creating a dangerous fragmentation of a revolutionary state which, at least in some minds, still strove for world revolution. Lenin argued for this kind of federalist state structure, although due to his worsening health he contributed only little to the general debates on the constitution. He probably realized that the Bolshevik party would be the key power structure within the union of nation. And indeed, it was the strictly centrist and hierarchical organization of the *(All-)Russian Communist Party (Bolsheviks)* that in the long run enabled Moscow to manage the constitution's complexity and to maintain control of the peripheries. Although the Bolshevik party also displayed an image of a liberator of nations, no structures of national representations were ever institutionalized within the Communist Party. On the contrary, the guiding principles of a "socialist democracy" ensured the unquestioned authority of the highest executive bodies, like the Politburo in the Kremlin. In the following decades, the party served as the stabilizing moment within the federal state structure. Together with the union-wide networks of a growing secret police, the party enabled Moscow's leader to make unquestioned decisions at the top of the power hierarchy and to enforce them even in the peripheries. In particular, under Stalin, state institutions played a subordinated role within the balance of power.[26]

Many historians have therefore neglected the importance and potential of the federal state structure. It is thanks to American historian Terry Martin that only a decade ago historiography started to reconsider the role of national representation in the Soviet Union.[27] He and others have also directed our attention to the unique Bolshevik concept of indigenization and "nativization" (*korenizatsiia*) that was empowered by the constitution and that opened up

---

25   See on this Martin (1998: 824–27).
26   See Simon (1986: 46–56).
27   See on one of his earlier publications: Martin 1999. His groundbreaking monograph was published two years later: Martin (2001a).

much room for national cultural policies in the inter-war period and again after Stalin's death in 1953.

4 "*korenizatsiia*" and "Sovietization": Soviet Approaches to the "national question" in the Inter-war Period

The concept of *korenizatsiia* literally means "rooting-in". This indicates its basic notion: the Bolsheviks firmly believed that only by using the local "national" languages and cultural codes could they bring the larger message of Marxism and revolution to the indigenous people. They had learned during the Civil War that they needed local brokers and translators to reach out to the people in the vast peripheries. To spread some socialist ideas, they used a national coding or – as Joseph Stalin put it – culture, education, and propaganda should be "national in form, socialist in content".[28] Thus, *korenizatsiia* aimed at indigenizing Soviet rule by integrating some parts of the local ethnic elite into the new power structure, hoping that in the long term they would be surpassed by new local elites more loyal to the Kremlin.[29]

For this objective, Moscow was willing to invest large resources in the spreading of the indigenous cultures of many ethnic groups. Books were published in their native languages, mother-tongued schools opened and, generally speaking, native ethnic culture was given the highest esteem in the 1920s. Within an affirmative action empire, non-Russians were explicitly privileged. The Kremlin stayed faithful to the idea of an "anti-imperialist empire", with the experience of the disastrous results of Tsarist Great Russian chauvinism in mind. The titular nations of the Soviet republics or the autonomous districts were especially entitled to proceed with forms of "nation-building": that is, promoting their own ethnic-national culture – without touching, of course, Moscow's basic political domination. It was the fundamental assumption of the Soviet "Empire of Nations" that a person belonged firmly to his or her ethnic group and could not change this cultural heritage. It was accompanied by the guiding principle that each national group should live separately in its own territory, its own republic or autonomous district.[30]

As long as the Kremlin maintained ultimate power, the Soviet Empire of nations seemed to work well. In those times, the central party leaders hardly

---

28 Iosif Stalin, *Marksizm i natsional'no-kolonial'nyi vopros: Sbornik izbrannykh statei i rechei* (Moscow: Partizdat TsK VKP(b), 1935).
29 Geyer (1997: 280–89).
30 Martin (2001b: 73–76); Smith (1999: 144–71).

realized that their policy strongly promoted a nationalization of the USSR and that it produced nationalized elites that later on could turn against Moscow. Critical voices within the Communist Party (such as Nikolai Bukharin) that pointed to the problematic aspects of nation-building within a Socialist state were marginalized by the argument that "rusotiapstvo" – all forms of displays of Russian superiority and chauvinism – would only lead to national resistance. The "greater danger principle" functioned so well that Moscow was even willing to tolerate traditional features of national culture (as religious practices) in order not to offend local elites. National cultural development was interpreted as a necessary historical phase that only in the long run would lead towards common classless socialist society.[31] All of this opened up much room for a blossoming of small nations during the 1920s. The national census of 1926 counted 176 officially acknowledged nationalities that all in one form or another had the right to develop and spread their national culture.[32] All of this amounted to a unique experiment of an "Empire of Nations" that radically altered the fundamental governmental principles that the pre-1917 composite monarchies had developed in order to cope with the challenges of governing a multi-ethnic state. It is worth noting that this truly revolutionary dimension of Soviet rule remained much neglected during the 1920s. While international awareness of the Bolshevik's endeavour to reconstruct society as a whole and to build a socialist state ran high, only few contemporaries showed interest in Moscow's nationality policies and the making of an "affirmative action empire".[33]

However, during the last years of the post-revolutionary decade tensions already grew. A younger generation of revolutionaries felt alienated within their own state, that by acclamation was supposed to be socialist, while in fact traditional social structures were still dominant not only in the peripheries. Reports of local communists actively participating in traditional or religious rituals poured oil into the flames of revolutionary radicalism. Obviously, the goal of Sovietizing the people in the USSR had produced very little success.[34]

Stalin made use of this discomfort of younger communists and historians rightly identify the time period of the so-called "cultural revolution" between 1929 and 1933 as the foundation of his later personal dictatorship. It was a time when the whole idea of state sponsored nation-building came under attack

---

31 See Martin (2001b: 71).
32 Hirsch (1997).
33 One of the few exceptions to this was Joseph Roth, who visited the Soviet Union in 1926–27 and who travelled to the Caucasus. See Roth (1995: Chap. VII). On the "affirmative action empire", see Martin (2001b).
34 Baberowski (2003a: 553–86; 2004: 18–24).

and the established national elites in the peripheries were suspected of being disloyal or, even worse, bourgeois-counter-revolutionary. Many of the local national communists were purged during these days and Moscow tried to intensify its control over the republics in general.[35]

Still, all of this should not be misinterpreted as a clear sign of the shrinking importance of the category of "nationality" during Stalinism. Some institutional continuity may help to demonstrate this: for example, the Soviet of Nationalities formally remained one of the highest state organs even in the constitution of 1935.[36] As Terry Martin, Yuri Slezkine or Jörg Baberowski have shown with their research, national categories, as fixed officially ascribed classifications, became even more relevant in the 1930s. First of all, the basic notion of an Empire of nations remained untouched. Slezkine, reciting the Lithuanian communist Joseph (Juozas) Vareikis, once called the Soviet Union a "communal apartment" in which strictly defined and differentiated nationalities lived in separate rooms.[37] There is much truth to this image: even in the 1930s, the "rhetoric of ethnic diversity and the practice of ethnic quotas remained obligatory".[38] In the Stalinist USSR, nationality turned into a strict identifier of each individual that was "objectively" defined, ascribed, and that could not be changed. Later, nationality even became a fixed category printed – as the infamous "fifth point" – on the passport of every Soviet citizen.[39]

As a result, propaganda in Stalin's times celebrated the colourful panorama of the large "Soviet family of the people" and respected their "friendship". Thus, the basic notion of an Empire of nations remained the guiding principle even during Stalinism – although, no doubt, the general framework of an overarching "Soviet culture" was much more emphasized during these years. Numerous propaganda displays depicted the "new Soviet man" and "Soviet culture" as a kind of transnational cement of the USSR as a multinational Empire.[40] During the 1930s, the party-state invested increasing resources to further Sovietize the national cultures, integrating them into Soviet high culture. Using Russian as the imperial lingua franca, this also meant pushing Russian language schooling in the peripheries. Starting with the Second World War, Russians in general

---

35 See Baberowski (2003b: 94–134; 2004; 1998); Grünewald (2006); Kindler (2014: 109–78); Northrop (2001b, 2001c): Martin (19998); Teichmann (2016).
36 Meissner (1996); Simon (1986: 157–71).
37 See Dulluruwski (2006, 2007), Martin (2000a; Slezkine (2000a).
38 Slezkine (2000b: 330).
39 See Baberowski (2006: 203–08); Martin (2000a: 34957 2000b); Simon (1986: 153–79); Slezkine (2000a); Edgar (2004); Hagen (2004); Payne (2001); Roy (2000).
40 See Castillo (1995); Plamper (2004); Petrone (2000: 23–45); Rolf (2009, 2013c: 64–93).

became privileged as "first among equal".[41] But even with more emphasize on such a Russian-based Soviet high culture, the underlying notion that the USSR was a multinational Empire based on the diversity of separate and official sponsored nationalities was never abandoned. The Soviet Union remained an Empire of nations until its very end.

5 "An Empire of Nations" and the "End of Empires": The Soviet Union as a Multi-Ethnic Empire in Historical Perspective

The dissolution of the USSR in 1991 had many founding fathers. The national movements played a key role in the quick demise of the former super power. Separatists in the Caucasus or the Baltic regions strove to break away from what they considered as Moscow's occupation. In the last years of the USSR, demonstrations filled the streets in Tbilisi, Yerevan or Riga. Their participants first demanded regional autonomy but soon waved national flags and called for independence. No doubt, these forces interacted with other factors undermining the Kremlin's authority and its will to suppress such manifestations. However, within a general crisis situation, the national movements on the peripheries contributed heavily to the decay of the one-party system and, in the end, to the collapse of the USSR.[42]

This is hardly disputed in the research on Gorbachev's transformation period, but literature tends to portray the national movements as the ultimate "other" of the Soviet system. In this perspective it seems as if the separatists marked the most extreme opposition to the regime and had nothing in common with the state they aimed to crush.[43] Having the Soviet affirmative action Empire in mind, one could instead see such national movements as part and parcel of the Soviet nationality policy implemented by the Kremlin for more than 70 years.[44] It were exactly the regime's own guidelines of Soviet nation-building that first facilitated the rise of the Empire, but in the end contributed to the implosion of the USSR. Such an interpretation has important implications

---

41 See Blitstein (2001); Bandenberger (2001, 2002); Kappeler (1992: 171–79).
42 See Brown (1996); Halbach (1992): 66–92; Lapidus, Zaslavsky and Goldman (1992); Lapidus (1992a, 1992b); Misiunas (1990); Vardys (1992); Zaslavsky (1992).
43 See, for example, the self-styled image of contemporary national activists such as Landsbergis (2000).
44 See on the continuities of Soviet nationality policies after Stalin's death Lehmann (2012: 196–203); Smith (2006); Fowkes (2002); Suny (1993: 110–22).

for the broader context of understanding the interplay of national politics/nationalism and communism in general. National emphasis should not merely be seen as a functional strategy of communist elites to gain legitimacy but as a system of communication where communists and parts of society equally participated. A shared horizon of a strongly nationalized worldview existed that was accepted as the cultural norm by very different and sometimes conflicting political actors. No clear boundary can be drawn between what was defined as "socialist" and what was "national". Quite on the contrary, these categories widely overlapped for contemporaries, including communists, and therefore opened space for different and competing forms of fusing and crosscutting "national" and "socialist" elements. Nationalizing socialism was a contested field of debates and practices – but it was also a common denominator of communication between the regime and society.[45]

From a historical perspective, the Soviet "Empire of nations" was a unique experiment: it was supposed to be a modern, multi-ethnic and "anti-imperialist" empire based on the acknowledgment and even open promotion of national differences and manifold state-sponsored nation-building. Visions of overarching "Soviet culture" or a later fusion of all citizens into a new form of "Soviet mankind" remained rather vague and never questioned the dominance of national categories as identifiers and signifiers in the public discourse. As long as the authoritarian rule of a centrist Kremlin-orientated party ensured the citizen's discipline and obedience, the whole system proved to be stable. In a moment of crisis – like Gorbachev's perestroika – and an easing of censorship and the authority's control over public discourse, the centrifugal potential of national mobilization prevailed.

During the late 1980s, the inherent paradoxes of the Soviet Empire of nations became apparent. A nationalized worldview had been promoted by the regime for decades. It could easily turn "nationalist" and anti-centrist in the end. Thus, although Soviet nationality policy did contribute to the rise of the USSR, it also had a lion's share in the final demise of the Empire.

Bibliography

Altstadt-Mirhadi, A. (1986), "Baku. Transformation of a Muslim Town", in M.F. Hamm (ed.), *The City in Late Imperial Russia*, Bloomington: Indiana UP, pp. 289–318.

---

45 See Rolf (2014b) and Weeks (2010).

Aoshima, Y., Werth, P. & Staliunas, D., eds. (2021), *Protecting the Empire: Imperial Government and Russian Nationalist Alliance in the Western Borderlands in the Late Imperial Period*, Budapest: CEU Press.

Ascher, A. (1988), *The Revolution of 1905. Russia in Disarray,* Stanford: Stanford UP.

Baberowski, J. (1998), „Stalinismus an der Peripherie. Das Beispiel Azerbajdzan 1920–1941", in M. Hildermeier & E. Müller-Luckner (eds.), *Stalinismus vor dem Zweiten Weltkrieg. Neue Wege der Forschung/ Stalinism before the Second World War. New Avenues of Research,* Munich: Oldenbourg, pp. 307–336.

Baberowski, J. (1999), "Auf der Suche nach Eindeutigkeit. Kolonialismus und zivilisatorische Mission im Zarenreich und der Sowjetunion", *Jahrbücher für Geschichte Osteuropas,* 47, pp. 482–503.

Baberowski, J. (2000), "Nationalismus aus dem Geist der Inferiorität. Autokratische Modernisierung und die Anfänge muslimischer Selbstvergewisserung im östlichen Transkaukasien 1828–1914", *Geschichte und Gesellschaft,* 26, pp. 371–406.

Baberowski, J. (2001), "Die Entdeckung des Unbekannten. Rußland und das Ende Osteuropas", in J. Baberowski et al. (eds.), *Geschichte ist immer Gegenwart. Vier Thesen zur Zeitgeschichte,* Stuttgart: Deutsche Verlags-Anstalt, pp. 9–42.

Baberowski, J. (2003a), *Der Feind ist überall. Stalinismus im Kaukasus,* Munich: Deutsche Verlags-Anstalt.

Baberowski, J. (2003b), *Der rote Terror. Die Geschichte des Stalinismus,* Munich: Deutsche Verlags-Anstalt.

Baberowski, J. (2004) "Verschleierte Feinde. Stalinismus im sowjetischen Orient", *Geschichte und Gesellschaft,* 30, pp. 10–36.

Baberowski, J. (2006) "Stalinismus und Nation. Die Sowjetunion als Vielvölkerreich 1917–1953", *Zeitschrift für Geschichtswissenschaft,* 54, pp. 199–213.

Baberowski, J. (2016), "Gewalt als Machttechnik. Revolution und Staatswerdung an der asiatischen Peripherie der Sowjetunion 1917–1941", in E. Frie & U. Planert (eds.), *Revolution, Krieg und die Geburt von Staat und Nation. Staatsbildung in Europa und den Amerikas 1770–1930,* Tübingen: Mohr Siebeck, pp. 213–243.

Bauer, H., Kappeler, A. & Roth, B., eds. (1991), *Die Nationalitäten des Russischen Reiches in der Volkszählung von 1897,* Stuttgart: Franz Steiner.

Benecke, W. (2007), "Die Revolution des Jahres 1905 in der Geschichte Polens", in M. Aust & L. Steindorff (eds.), *Russland 1905. Perspektiven auf die erste Russische Revolution.* Frankfurt a. M.: Peter Lang, pp. 9–22.

Blitstein, P.A. (2001), "Nation-Building or Russification? Obligatory Russian Instruction in the Soviet non-Russian Schools, 1938–1953", in R.G. Suny & T. Martin (eds.), *A State of Nations. Empire and Nation-Making in the Age of Lenin and Stalin,* Oxford: Oxford UP, pp. 253–274.

Blobaum, R.E. (1995), *Rewolucja. Russian Poland, 1904–1907,* Ithaca: Cornell UP.

Brandenberger, D. (2001), "'It is Imperative to Advance Russian Nationalism as the First Priority'. Debates within the Stalinist Ideological Establishment, 1941–1945", in Suny & Martin (eds.), *A State of Nations*, pp. 275–299.

Brandenberger, D. (2002), *National Bolshevism. Stalinist Mass Culture and the Formation of Modern Russian National Identity, 1931–1956*, Cambridge: Cambridge UP.

Brown, A. (1996), *The Gorbachev Factor*, Oxford, Oxford UP.

Buchen, T. & Rolf, M. (2015), "Elites and Their Imperial Biographies. Introduction", in T. Buchen & M. Rolf (eds.), *Eliten im Vielvölkerreich. Imperiale Biographien in Russland und Österreich-Ungarn (1850–1918) / Elites and Empire. Imperial Biographies in Russia and Austria-Hungary (1850–1918)*, Berlin: De Gruyter, pp. 33–37.

Cadiot, J. (2005), "Searching for Nationality. Statistics and National Categories at the End of the Russian Empire (1897–1917)". *Russian Review*, 64, pp. 440–455.

Castillo, G. (1995), "Peoples at an Exhibition. Soviet Architecture and the National Question", *South Atlantic Quarterly*, 94, pp. 715–746.

Dolbilov, M. (2004), "Russification and the Bureaucratic Mind in the Russian Empire's Northwestern Region in the 1860s", *Kritika: Explorations in Russian and Eurasian History*, 5, pp. 245–272.

Edgar, A.L. (2004), *Tribal Nation. The Making of Soviet Turkmenistan*, Princeton, NJ: Princeton UP.

Fedtke, G. (2006), "Wie aus Bucharern Usbeken und Tadschiken wurden. Sowjetische Nationalitätenpolitik im Lichte einer persönlichen Rivalität", *Zeitschrift für Geschichtswissenschaft*, 54, pp. 214–231.

Fitzpatrick, S. (1985), "The Civil War as a Formative Experience", in A. Gleason, P. Kenez & R. Stites (eds.), *Bolshevik Culture. Experiment and Order in the Russian Revolution*, Bloomington, Indiana UP, pp. 57–76.

Fowkes, B. (2002), "The National Question in the Soviet Union under Leonid Brezhnev. Policy and Response", in E. Bacon & M. Sandle (eds.), *Brezhnev Reconsidered*, Houndmills: Palgrave Macmillan, pp. 68–89.

Geyer, D. (1996), "Nation und Nationalismus in Rußland", in M. Hettling & P. Nolte (eds.), *Nation und Gesellschaft in Deutschland*, Munich: C.H. Beck, pp. 100–113.

Geyer, D. (1997), "Russland in den Epochen des zwanzigsten Jahrhunderts. Eine zeitgenössische Problemskizze", *Geschichte und Gesellschaft*, 23, pp. 258–294.

Golczewski, F. & Pickhan, G. (1998), *Russischer Nationalismus. Die russische Idee im 19. und 20. Jahrhundert. Darstellung und Texte*, Göttingen: Vandenhoeck & Ruprecht.

Grünewald, J. (2006), "Der Kaukasus und die Ursprünge stalinistischer Gewalt", *Zeitschrift für Geschichtswissenschaft*, 54, pp. 232–250.

Hagen, M. (1964), "Das Nationalitätenproblem Russlands in den Verhandlungen der III. Duma 1907–1911", Ph. D. Dissertation, University of Göttingen.

Halbach, U. (1992), *Das sowjetische Vielvölkerimperium. Nationalitätenpolitik und nationale Frage*, Mannheim: Bibliographisches Institut.

Haltzel, M.H. (1977), *Der Abbau der deutschen ständischen Selbstverwaltung in den Ostseeprovinzen Russlands. Ein Beitrag zur Geschichte der russischen Unifizierungspolitik 1855–1905*, Marburg a. Lahn: Herder-Institut.

Haltzel, M.H. (1981), "Triumphs and Frustrations of Administrative Russification, 1881–1914", in E.C. Thaden (ed.), *Russification in the Baltic Provinces and Finland, 1855–1914*, Princeton: Princeton UP, pp. 150–160.

Haugen, A. (2004), *The Establishment of National Republics in Central Asia*, Houndmills: Palgrave Macmillan.

Hirsch, F. (1997), "The Soviet Union as a Work-in-Progress. Ethnographers and the Category Nationality in the 1926, 1937, and 1939 Censuses", *Slavic Review*, 56, pp. 251–279.

Hirsch, F. (2005), *Empire of Nations. Ethnographic Knowledge and the Making of the Soviet Union*, Ithaca: Cornell UP.

Joravsky, D. (1985), "Cultural Revolution and the Fortress Mentality", in A. Gleason, P. Kenez & R. Stites (eds.), *Bolshevik Culture. Experiment and Order in the Russian Revolution*, Bloomington: Indiana UP, pp. 93–113.

Kappeler, A. (1992), *Rußland als Vielvölkerreich. Entstehung, Geschichte, Zerfall*, Munich: C.H. Beck.

Kappeler, A. (2000), "Nationsbildung und Nationalbewegungen im Russländischen Reich", *Archiv für Sozialgeschichte*, 40, pp. 67–90.

Katzer, N. (1999), *Die weiße Bewegung in Russland. Herrschaftsbildung, praktische Politik und politische Programmatik im Bürgerkrieg*, Cologne/Weimar/Vienna: Böhlau.

Kindler, R. (2014), *Stalins Nomaden. Herrschaft und Hunger in Kasachstan*, Hamburg: Hamburger Edition.

Korros, A. (2002), *A Reluctant Parliament. Stolypin, Nationalism, and the Politics of the Russian Imperial State Council, 1906–1911*, Lanham: Rowman & Littlefield.

Landsbergis, V. (2000), *Lithuania Independent Again. The Autobiography of Vytautas Landsbergis*, Seattle: University of Washington Press.

Lapidus, G.W. (1992a), "From Democratization to Disintegration. The Impact of Perestroika on the National Question", in Lapidus, Zaslavsky & Goldman (eds.), *From Union to Commonwealth*, pp. 45–70.

Lapidus, G.W. ed. (1992b), *The "Nationality Question" in the Soviet Union*, New York: Garland.

Lapidus, G.W., Zaslavsky, V. & Goldman, P., eds. (1992), *From Union to Commonwealth. Nationalism and Separatism in the Soviet Republics*, Cambridge: Cambridge UP.

Lehmann, M. (2012), *Eine sowjetische Nation. Nationale Sozialismusinterpretationen in Armenien seit 1945*, Frankfurt a. M.: Campus

Lieven, D. (1989), *Russia's Rulers Under the Old Regime,* New Haven: Yale UP.
Martin, T. (1998), "The Origins of Soviet Ethnic Cleansing", *Journal of Modern History,* 70, pp. 813–861.
Martin, T. (1999), "Interpreting the new archival signals. Nationalities policy and the nature of the Soviet bureaucracy", *Cahiers du Monde Russe,* 40, pp. 113–124.
Martin, T. (2000a), "Modernization or neo-traditionalism? Ascribed nationality and Soviet primordialism", in S. Fitzpatrick (ed.), *Stalinism. New Directions,* London: Routledge, pp. 348–367.
Martin, T. (2000b), "Terror gegen Nationen in der Sowjetunion", *Osteuropa,* 50, pp. 606–16.
Martin, T. (2001a), *The Affirmative Action Empire. Nations and Nationalism in the Soviet Union, 1923–1939,* Ithaca: Cornell UP.
Martin, T. (2001b), "An Affirmative Action Empire. The Soviet Union as the Highest Form of Imperialism", in Suny & Martin (eds.), *A State of Nations,* pp. 67–90.
Martiny, A. (1992), "Nationalitäten und Nationalitätenpolitik", in G. Schramm (ed.), *Handbuch der Geschichte Russlands. Band 3, II: 1856 – 1945. Von den autokratischen Reformen zum Sowjetstaat,* Stuttgart: Anton Hiersemann, pp. 1743–1778.
Meissner, B. (1996), "Sowjetföderalismus und staatsrechtliche Stellung der Nationalitäten der RSFSR bis 1991", in A. Kappeler (ed.), *Regionalismus und Nationalismus in Russland.* Baden-Baden: Nomos, pp. 41–55.
Miller, A. (2008), *The Romanov Empire and Nationalism. Essay in the Methodology of Historical Research,* Budapest/New York: Central European UP.
Misiunas, R.J. (1990), "Baltic Nationalism and Soviet Language Policy. From Russification to Constitutional Amendment", in H.R. Huttenbach (ed.), *Soviet Nationality Policies. Ruling Ethnic Groups in the USSR,* London: Cassell, pp. 206–220.
Northrop, D. (2001a), "Nationalizing Backwardness. Gender, Empire, and Uzbek Identity", in Suny & Martin (eds.), *A State of Nations,* pp. 191–220.
Northrop, D. (2001b), "Hujum. Unveiling Campaigns and Local Responses in Uzbekistan, 1927", in D.J. Raleigh (ed.), *Provincial Landscapes. Local Dimensions of Soviet Power 1917–1953,* Pittsburgh: University of Pittsburgh Press, pp. 125–145.
Northrop, D. (2001c), "Subaltern Dialogues. Subversion and Resistance in Soviet Uzbek Family Law", *Slavic Review,* 60, pp. 115–139.
Payne, M.J. (2001), *Stalin's Railroad. Turksib and the Building of Socialism,* Pittsburgh, Pittsburgh UP.
Petrone, K. (2000), *"Life has become more joyous, comrades". Celebrations in the Time of Stalin,* Bloomington: Indiana UP.
Plamper, J. (2004), "Georgian Koba or Soviet "Father of Peoples"? The Stalin Cult and Ethnicity", in P. Aport, J.C. Behrends, P. Jones & E.A. Rees (eds.), *The Leader Cult in Communist Dictatorships: Stalin and the Eastern Bloc.* Houndmills: Palgrave Macmillan, pp. 123–140.

Rodkiewicz, W. (1998), *Russian Nationality Policy in the Western Provinces of the Empire (1863–1905)*, Lublin: Scientific Society of Lublin.

Rolf, M. (2009), "A Hall of Mirrors. Sovietizing Culture under Stalinism", *Slavic Review*, 68, pp. 601–630.

Rolf, M. (2012), "Russifizierung, Depolonisierung oder innerer Staatsaufbau? Konzepte imperialer Herrschaft im Königreich Polen (1863–1915)", in Z. Gasimov (ed.), *Kampf um Wort und Schrift: Russifizierung in Osteuropa im 19.-20. Jahrhundert*. Göttingen: Vandenhoeck und Ruprecht, pp. 51–88.

Rolf, M. (2013a), "A Continuum of Crisis? The Kingdom of Poland in the Shadow of Revolution (1905–1915)", in V. Fischer et al. (eds.), *The Russian Revolution of 1905 in Transcultural Perspective. Identities, Peripheries, and the Flow of Ideas*. Bloomington: Slavica Publishers, pp. 159–174.

Rolf, M. 2013b, „Metropolen im Ausnahmezustand? Gewaltakteure und Gewalträume in den Städten des späten Zarenreichs", in F. Lenger (ed.), *Kollektive Gewalt in der Stadt. Europa 1890–1939*, Munich: Oldenbourg, pp. 25–49.

Rolf, M. (2013c), *Soviet Mass Festivals, 1917–1991*, Pittsburgh: Pittsburgh UP.

Rolf, M. (2014a), "'Approved by the Censor': Tsarist Censorship and the Public Sphere in Imperial Russia and the Kingdom of Poland (1860–1914)", in J.C. Behrends & T. Lindenberger (eds.), *Underground Publishing and the Public Sphere. Transnational Perspectives*. Vienna: LIT, pp. 31–74.

Rolf, M. (2014b), "Die Nationalisierung der Sowjetunion. Indigenisierungspolitik, nationale Kader und die Entstehung von Dissens in der Litauischen Sowjetrepublik der Ära Brežnev", in B. Belge & M. Deuerlein (eds.), *Goldenes Zeitalter der Stagnation? Perspektiven auf die sowjetische Ordnung der Brežnev-Ära*, Tübingen: Mohr Siebeck, pp. 203–230.

Rolf, M. (2014c), "Imperiale Biographien. Lebenswege imperialer Akteure in Groß- und Kolonialreichen (1850–1918) – zur Einleitung", *Geschichte und Gesellschaft*, 40, pp. 5–21.

Rolf, M. (2015), *Imperiale Herrschaft im Weichselland. Das Königreich Polen im Russischen Imperium (1864–1915)*, Munich: Oldenbourg.

Rolf, M. (2018), "Between State-Building and Local Cooperation: Russian Rule in the Kingdom of Poland (1864–1915)", *Kritika. Explorations in Russian and Eurasian History*, 19:2, pp. 385–416.

Rolf, M. (2021), „"What is the "Russian Cause" and whom does it serve? Russian Nationalists and Imperial Bureaucracy in the Kingdom of Poland", in Y. Aoshima, P. Werth & D. Staliunas (eds.), *Protecting the Empire*.

Roth, J. (1995), *Reise nach Rußland. Feuilletons, Reportagen, Tagebuchnotizen 1919–1930*, Cologne: Kiepenheuer & Witsch.

Roy, O. (2000), *The New Central Asia. The Creation of Nations*, New York: NYU Press.

Simon, G. (1986), *Nationalismus und Nationalitätenpolitik in der Sowjetunion. Von der totalitären Diktatur zur nachstalinschen Gesellschaft*, Baden-Baden: Nomos.

Simon, G. (1991) *Nationalism and Policy Toward the Nationalities in the Soviet Union. From Totalitarian Dictatorship to Post-Stalinist Society*, Boulder, Co: Westview Press.

Slezkine, Y. (2000a), "Imperialism as the Highest Stage of Socialism", *Russian Review*, 59, 227–234.

Slezkine, Y. (2000b), "The Soviet Union as a communal apartment, or how a socialist state promoted ethnic particularism", in Fitzpatrick (ed.), *Stalinism*, pp. 313–347.

Smith, J. (2006), "Non-Russians in the Soviet Union and after", in R.G. Suny (ed.), *The Cambridge History of Russia*. Cambridge: Cambridge UP, pp. 495–521.

Smith, J.R. (1999), *The Bolsheviks and the National Question, 1917–1923*, Houndmills, Palgrave Macmillan.

Staliunas, D. (2007a), "Between Russification and Divide and Rule. Russian Nationality Policy in the Western Borderlands in the mid-19th Century", *Jahrbücher für Geschichte Osteuropas*, 55, pp. 357–373.

Staliunas, D. (2007b), *Making Russians. Meaning and Practices of Russification in Lithuania and Belarus after 1863*, Amsterdam: Rodopi.

Staliunas, D. (2014), "Making a National Capital out of a Multiethnic City: Lithuanians and Vilnius in Late Imperial Russia", *Ab Imperio*, 1, pp. 157–175.

Suny, R.G. (1993), *The Revenge of the Past. Nationalism, Revolution, and the Collapse of the Soviet Union*, Stanford, Stanford UP.

Suny, R.G. & T. Martin (2001), "The Empire Strikes Out. Imperial Russia, "National" Identity, and Theories of Empire", in Suny & Martin (eds.), *A State of Nations. Empire and Nation-Making in the Age of Lenin and Stalin*. Oxford: Oxford UP, pp. 23–66.

Teichmann, C. (2016), *Macht der Unordnung. Stalins Herrschaft in Zentralasien 1920–1950*, Hamburg: Hamburger Edition.

Thaden, E.C. (1981), "The Russian Government", in E.C. Thaden (ed.), *Russification in the Baltic Provinces and Finland, 1855–1914*. Princeton: Princeton UP, pp. 15–110.

Thaden, E.C. (1984), *Russia's Western Borderlands, 1710–1870*, Princeton: Princeton UP.

Vardys, V.S. (1992), "Lithuanian National Politics", in R. Denber (ed.), *The Soviet Nationality Reader. The Disintegration in Context*. Boulder/Co: Westview, pp. 441–484.

Waldron, P. (1985), "Stolypin and Finland", *The Slavonic and East European Review*, 63, pp. 41–55.

Weeks, T.R. (1996), *Nation and State in Late Imperial Russia. Nationalism and Russification on the Western Frontier, 1863–1914*, DeKalb: Northern Illinois UP.

Weeks, T.R. (2004), "Russification. Word and Practice 1863–1914", *Proceedings of the American Philosophical Society*, 148, pp. 471–489.

Weeks, T.R. (2006), "Managing empire. Tsarist nationalities policy", in D. Lieven (ed.), *The Cambridge History of Russia. Vol. 2: Imperial Russia, 1689–1917*, Cambridge: Cambridge UP, pp. 7–44.

Weeks, T.R. (2010), "Remembering and Forgetting. Creating a Soviet Lithuanian Capital. Vilnius 1944–1949", in J. Hackmann & M. Lehti (eds.), *Contested and Shared Places of Memory. History and Politics in North Eastern Europe,* London: Routledge, pp. 134–150.

Weinberg, R. (1993), *The Revolution of 1905 in Odessa. Blood on the Steps,* Bloomington: Indiana UP.

Zaslavsky, V. (1992), "The Evolution of Separatism in Soviet Society under Gorbachev", in G. Lapidus, Zaslavsky & Goldman (eds.), *From Union to Commonwealth,* pp. 71–97.

CHAPTER 5

Federalism in Multinational States: Otto Bauer's Theory

Ramón Máiz

1 Introduction*

The work of the Austrian Social-Democratic leader, Otto Bauer, develops a sophisticated theory of the nation far removed from the hegemonic postulates of state nationalism that triumphed in the military, economic and political context of the final crisis of the Austro-Hungarian Empire and the pre-war period, like that of nationalisms against the state that were postulated in the emerging struggle of nationalities.[1] His work analysed with extreme lucidity what Michael Mann has called "the dark side of democracy",[2] the theoretical and political roots of the different varieties of the oppression of minorities and ethnic cleansing. We also find in it the first observation that the principle of national self-determination, in its self-evident "democratic" transparency, is extremely dangerous for minorities, since "it has the proclivity for the sacrifice of cultural minorities on the altar of national construction, homogenizing cultural communities through the conflation of ethnos with demos".[3] The fate of his work, however, in the confrontation between the two major tendencies of the nationalist conflict-stateless nations vs. nations with states-exacerbated by the Great War, the October Revolution and the rise of fascism, oscillated between oblivion and manipulation. Distorted and rejected by the communist movement of the time, from the internationalism of Rosa Luxemburg[4] to the instrumentalism of Lenin or Stalin, it would also be forgotten by the social-democratic tradition itself which, following Karl Kautsky own incomprehension,[5] would uncritically assume the monist and centralist theses of the national state. The final failure of

---

* An expanded version of this chapter was published at the Non Territorial Autonomy special issue of the journal *Philosophy and Society*. The author thanks the journal's editors for their permission.
1   Hanisch (2011).
2   Mann (2005).
3   Nimni (2015: 63).
4   Luxemburg (1979).
5   Kautsky (1978).

the reconfiguration of the Austro-Hungarian Empire as a plurinational federal system, as well as the impossible unity of the working class within a multi-ethnic state, would forever dictate the contributions of a work to be dispatched in future with the labels of "Culturalist theory" of the nation and "cultural autonomy".[6]

Paradoxically, Bauer's theory of the nation would be termed "economistic" by much later thinking about nationalism, which considered it to be indebted to the Marxian paradigm of ultimate determination by the relations of production and social classes: "The nation as a result of the conditions of production of the life of a people". For others, on the other hand, especially in the Marxist tradition, it was always excessively "culturalist", lost in esoteric concepts such as "character" or "destiny": "The nation as a set of human beings linked by a community of destiny in a community of character". In contrast to each other, however, what surprises the eventual reader today is the sophistication of a vision of the national question from the "sociological method" and the "social sciences", which translates into scientific-complex social phenomena and complex situations, from the multiplicity of factors that shape the national collective identity,[7] against the temptation of any materialistic or idealistic reductionism. In this article, I argue the substantive *political* nature of a theory that tries to articulate at all times an explanatory diagnosis of the national phenomenon from the social sciences, with a consequent normative prognosis of plurinational accommodation in heterogeneous and plural societies. Thus, the interest of Bauer's work, as I shall try to demonstrate, goes far beyond the field of study of the history of political ideas and the innovative contributions of Austro-Marxism, and is prolonged in very illuminating analyses which, indebted to a political and intellectual context that is exceptional for many reasons (that *Finis Austriae*), have little use for the current debates on the complexities of cultural, ethnic and national accommodation in the multinational states in the context of globalization. In the forthcoming pages, I shall first analyse the main fundamental components of his explanatory theory of the nation as an inessential community, and then give an account of the normative and institutional consequences in the democratic redesign of multinational States.

2   The Transit from Kant to Marx

The first matter that draws attention in Bauers work, *The Question of Nationalities and Social Democracy*,[8] is concerned precisely with the connection of the

---

6 Czerwínska (2005: 137).
7 Blum & Smaldone (2016: XI).
8 Bauer (2000).

empirical-explanatory theory with the normative theory of the nation. In his analysis, he perceived a desire for rigour that would allow the *parti pris*, the summary apriorisms of the socialist tradition on nationalism as "bourgeois ideology", "the end of nations", "peoples without history", etc., to be abandoned, in order to *understand the national question as a complex social problem*. From this perspective, any theoretical normative elaboration on the national phenomenon (the collective identity of the "we", the opposition between ourselves and others, the design of the federal institutional arrangements) must be based on a solid systematic investigation of the national question through the social sciences. That is, it is not only a matter of the Austro-Marxist tradition, to recover the central role of "theory" for socialism,[9] but to work from a double perspective: an empirical analysis of the construction of nations (the emergence and adaptive evolution of culture communities based on the relations of production and class conflicts) that serves as adequate support for a theoretical alternative orientation (the federal State of nationalities). It is necessary to emphasize, from the beginning, this original perspective in the context of the time,[10] the double dimension of his non-reductionist theory of the nation (empirical and normative), in order to provide a full account of a contribution that is no longer the metaphysical verbiage of the *Volksgeist*, but of the positivist historiography of nationalism, the feverish search for the antecedents (historical, linguistic, anthropological) of the nation. It is an analysis that also shines in the face of the entire socialist and communist tradition, plagued by reductionism and instrumentalism, and even stands out against Austro-Marxist authors like Renner, with whom Bauer possesses, as we shall see, undeniable disagreements[11] and theoretical debts, such as the introduction of the non-territorial principle of personality.[12]

As occurs throughout Austro-Marxism, analyses of the work of Otto Bauer have emphasized his youthful Kantianism. And indeed, as he himself acknowledged in the 1924 prologue to *Die Nationalitätenfrage und die Sozialdemokratie*, at that time "he was fascinated by the critical philosophy of Immanuel Kant". The Kantian imprint can be traced, for example, to the concept of *Community*, through Max Adler's interpretation of it and its reformulation by Ferdinand Tönnies in *Gemeinschaft und Gesellschaft*: the community as the original source of all social relations. Thus, in his work on *Die Nationalitätenfrage*, a peculiar "communitarianism", as an a priori socialization that unifies individuals

---

9   Marramao (1977: 53).
10 See Haupt et al. (1974: 47).
11 See Nagel (2016: 17).
12 See Arzoz (2015: LXXX).

through social ties and a sort of transcendental deduction of the community, is posited as the ontological dimension that bestows affective bonds upon groups of individuals in a given context, forming a national collective identity. From here on, Bauer takes the principle of individuality of nations and proceeds to a reading of self-determination ("Selbstbestimmung") as self-government, as Autonomy,[13] collective *sapere aude* that democratically cement each community in its specific difference and its historical permanence.

This a priori socialization of human nature in the various nations must not deceive us regarding its supposed metaphysical nature. Next, Bauer postulates the Nation as a concrete articulation, at a given time and place, of the community of nature and the community of culture. This "community of nature" has nothing to do, however, with the biological theories of social Darwinism of the time, which preached the nation as a community of origin based on race. By "nature", Bauer understands, from Marx and historical materialism, the material conditions of the reproduction of social life in a given country and historical moment. However, in his view, the struggle for the survival of human beings is translated not only in the field of material production and reproduction, but in the space of culture, in the creation of a community of culture that, in the tradition of German Romanticism, constitutes for Bauer a sphere of creative transmission – and not mere passive socialization – of tradition, a key factor in the construction of a nation. There is a fundamental difference in the concept of *Kulturnation* as used by Bauer and by the social-democracy of the time, which should not be confused. Taking into account the interaction between the three dimensions of the nation already mentioned (economic, cultural and political), the "cultural nation" does not enlighten in Bauer a right to purely cultural, but, as we shall see, properly political autonomy. Here lies one of the greatest misunderstandings, which are reiterated uncritically again and again, regarding the scope of Bauer's self-government, as if it were an autonomy for purely cultural and linguistic matters. On the contrary, the concept of "cultural nation" in Bauer has two noteworthy consequences: 1) Bauer did not subscribe until 1918 to the principle of self-determination of nations as a prelude to secession, and even then he did so with many nuances and reduced to specific cases, being in favour to the end of the democratic accommodation of several nations in multinational States; and (2) he defends "political autonomy" with broad economic, administrative, cultural and even military powers for the Federal States. No trace, then, of "Austro-Hungarian monarchist centralism".[14]

---

13 See Bauer (1980: 278).
14 See Czerwínska (2005: 128).

This is the reason why it is mandatory to avoid from the beginning the misunderstandings regarding the supposed apriorism that this argument, the confessed "childish Kantian sickness", would operate in the work of Bauer under the influence of Max Adler, because these are reduced to the normative dimension of his theory, rather than to that of the empirical. In the latter, which is dominant in the whole of the author's work —which is repeatedly interpreted as "sociological"— the explanatory paradigm is none other than that of historical materialism: "Here we try to test Marx's method of social research in a new field of work".[15] His purpose is to "understand modern nations through the Marxist conception of history", as derived from the development of productive forces and the capitalist mode of production, as well as from changes in social structure and class articulation and conflict social in presence.

A non-reductionist historical materialism guides the entire explanatory analysis of the national question: nations are "precipitates of history" ("Niederschlag seiner Geschichte"),[16] "frozen history" ("erstarrte Geschichte"), "products of history" ("Erzeugnis der Geschichte"),[17] etc. But what kind of historicity produces nations? Not that of historicism, of course. Bauer discards, above all, the nationalist *spiritualism* of the "national spirit" or "the national soul" ("Volksgeist", "Volksseele"), and he explicitly departs from the attempt by German post-Kantian idealism, from Hegel to Fichte, to develop a *Metaphysik der Nation*, that is, to replace "an empirical phenomenon, scientific and correctly determined, with a form of manifestation of a supposed metaphysical essentiality".[18] In his view, the problem posed by the *Volksgeist* concept lies not only in the fact that it is ultimately a polysemic term, without rigorous conceptual content; on the contrary, and more importantly, he considers what must be explained as having been explained tautologically, taking as a cause what is but a mere idealized abstraction of the effect —the construction of a specific nation— that he wishes to explain. The 1907 critique of nationalist spiritualism in Germany, a country whose cultural and scientific achievements Bauer admired to the extreme of openly subscribing to the intellectual superiority of the German, was the reason why Mommsen could be regarded to all intents and purposes as a confessed German nationalist.[19] In fact, traditional German nationalism, that is, before the conservative revolution and the work of Ernst Jünger after 1918, postulated a spiritual concept of national

---

15 Bauer (2007: V).
16 Bauer (1907: 16).
17 Bauer (1907: 18).
18 Bauer (1907: 6).
19 See Mommsen (1979: 212).

community or national destiny ("Volksgemeinschaft", "gemeinsames Schicksal"), of a clearly irredentist influence and which encompassed Germans from abroad and especially from Austria. It should be remembered that in a key text written in his nationalist young years —*Betrachtungen eines Unpolistischen* (1918)—, Thomas Mann defended the thesis that the politicization and democratization of Germany was in direct opposition to the "structure of the German spirit" and therefore politics and democracy became non-German, even "anti-German".[20]

On the other hand, Bauer, in proposing an idea of nation as "social practice", the result of complex interactions, also openly confronted rudimentary nationalistic material with a biological and racist root, from an evolutionary and adaptive point of view (with explicit and repeated references to Darwin, completely alien to the prevailing "social Darwinism" versions). In this order, he acidly criticized the explanations of the national empirical fact from a kind of *germplasm* ("Keimplasma") transferred from one generation to another; the Nation, in short, conceived as a *Naturgemeisnchaft*, a natural community founded on a genetic material substrate that constitutes its ultimate origin.[21] Bauer mercilessly attacks the idea of conceived nations as the inevitable product of the shared genetic inheritance of a people, springing from a plasma constituent, an essential carrier of one or other innate physical or spiritual qualities. Here, too, Bauer points out, not only is it erroneous regarding the factors that operate in the genesis of nations, but the causal relation is reversed: the alleged causes are merely effects of the political and social construction process of the nation, selected from the conditions in which peoples produce their livelihoods in specific contexts. They are therefore the contingent and ever-changing product "of determinations and interactions of production and exchange of ancestors, of their struggle for existence".[22] Hence a non-deterministic application of historical materialism to the processes of national construction: changes in the mode of production are translated into very profound mutations not only in the development of productive forces, but in the nature of the relations of production and, as consequence, in the social structure and the specific class struggle that condition the access to and the contents of each national culture. In his view, far from any spiritual or biological essentialism, it is necessary to explain the interaction of this motley and elusive set of factors – economic, cultural and political – in their heterogeneity and mutual historical dependence on the struggle for existence. In Bauer, we

---

20 Mann (1983: 262).
21 See Bauer (1907: 11).
22 See Bauer (1907: 39).

also find an original articulation of Marxism and Darwinism, already suggested by Marx himself in *Das Kapital*[23] by incorporating the "fruitful Darwinian idea of natural selection".[24] García-Pelayo already pointed out in his day that Darwin's influence "not only allows Bauer to conceive of history as a struggle for existence, but also to reject substantialism and, therefore, the immutability of the biological fact".[25] (The logical corollary of this Darwinism shall be seen later when analysing the concept of "National evolutionist policy".

In this order, it is necessary to emphasize the *modernism* of Bauer's argument about the processes of national construction. In fact, the nation is not an original community that goes back to the night of the times, but a modern process that, based on materials from other times, is built with the advent of capitalism and its political struggles. This is one of Bauer's few agreements with Kautsky on nationalisms: the existence of a turning point, with the propagation of the capitalist mode of production, in the construction of nations. The generalization of capitalism, the world of commodities and industrial production, are factors that generate an unknown national integration, overcoming the fragmentation characteristic of feudalism, not only with the creation of (national) markets, but also through the emergence of the (national) state in its modern sense and its work of nationalization (linguistic standardization, educational system, universal suffrage, political rights, parliamentary democracy, etc.). But this process of nationalization that accompanies capitalism and the construction of national states should not lead to deceit, as it continues to illuminate an exclusionary nation that raises material barriers and policies to the full integration of the popular classes into national education, the exclusive patrimony of the ruling classes and their organic intellectuals: "National culture is the culture of the ruling classes".[26] Thus, under the "superb building of national culture" of modernity lies exploitation and class domination.

3 Critique of the Classical Marxist Theory of the Progressive Disappearance of Nations

Analysing the national question from non-economistic historical materialism has far-reaching critical effects for classical Marxist theory and some of its fundamental assumptions and postulates. Bauer uses a non-deterministic

---

23 See Marx, Book I, Chapter 23, Note 89 (MEW 23: 392).
24 See Bauer (1907: 24).
25 See García-Pelayo (1979:20).
26 See Bauer (1907: 44).

historical materialism to question the basic Marxist theses of Marx and Engels, and also of his contemporaries, such as Kautsky, Rosa Luxemburg, or Lenin, on the nature and future of nations.[27] The radical novelty that modern capitalism represents for the emergence of the nation has therefore been demonstrated, contrary to the nationalist myth of the origins: "Nations are communities that link their members during a certain time, but not at all to the nation of our time with their ancestors three or four centuries ago".[28]

Moreover, Bauer submits to systematic criticism the thesis of the gradual disappearance of nations, considered by classical Marxism as mere residual atavism, ruins of a process that entails the primacy of class struggle and the universal and inevitable triumph of the working class which, strictly speaking, "has no country". This is an idea derived, in turn, from the Marxian hypothesis that national struggles, from the National State or against the national State —whilst the overcoming of the State ("Aufhebung des Staates") will render them increasingly "idealistic" and "illusory"— will be replaced with the real "real struggles" around class interests.[29]

On the one hand, Bauer's analysis shows, on the one hand, the *deep social roots of national struggles*, in which the national dimension is configured as a central element of the political scenario of modernity, superimposed on the class dimension; at the same time, the foundational exclusion of the nation from the working classes, expelled from the cultural community of the nation, is highlighted. The latter entails that that class conflicts are often hidden in the form of national struggles. Nevertheless, Bauer underlines, to a lesser extent, a fundamental extreme that escapes the classical and contemporary Marxists; namely: "the national content of the class struggle".[30] This was translated, above all, into the national specificity of class struggles, which cannot be interpreted from the simplifications of naive internationalism and cosmopolitanism. Every labour movement has its own roots, its interests, its biography of social struggles, among which its demands for full inclusion in the cultural community, destiny and character that constitutes "its" specific nation should not be forgotten. It is a belonging that is expropriated by the dominant elites, since private ownership of the means of production is at the base not only of the relations of capitalist exploitation, but also of its political domination, and

---

27   See Haupt et al. (1947: 49) and Herod (1976: 39 and ff.).
28   Bauer (1907: 3).
29   Máiz (2010: 147).
30   Bauer (1907: 495).

of the exclusion of the working classes from its active participation in the cultural community of the nation.

But even more so, only in the progress towards socialism, with the irruption of the popular classes at the level of the nation, will the latter cease to constitute the restricted property of the classes that own the means of production, an exclusive and elitist "Cultural community of the cults". Thus, far from blurring the value of the nation on the horizon of class politics, Bauer argues against the whole Marxist tradition that the true inclusive realization of a national community of culture worthy of such a name will only take place in socialism.[31] Therefore, as progress towards socialism progresses, nations will not be a mere "residue of history", which fades away in the framework of teleological holism that would lead according to Marx to "overcoming power in general".[32] Quite the contrary, there will be a "growing differentiation of the spiritual culture of nations".[33] Moreover, only "with democratic socialism can the entire people be included in the national cultural community".[34] With regard to the national question, Bauer postulates, in short, that socialism translates into three fundamental achievements: 1) Incorporation of all the people in the national community of culture; 2) Achievement of the full self-government of the nation; and (3) Increasing and free cultural differentiation of nations.[35]

Therefore, in response to the ingenuous cosmopolitanism inherited from the "bourgeois prejudice" towards the nation, Bauer proposes a critical Marxist re-appropriation of the nation. The latter, however, moves radically away from all "naive nationalism",[36] in the arms of which the workers movement is repeatedly shed, despite the usual internationalist rhetoric, when it sees its precarious hard-won working conditions threatened. Hence the need for a "clearly conscious internationalist policy",[37] on the basis of the complete reformulation of the concept of nation inherited from the nineteenth century. This new internationalism will be translated, as shall be seen, into the field of institutional designs in a simultaneous rejection of the centralism of the national state and its inverse mimesis in the principle of nationalities and the right to secession.

---

31 Bauer (1907: 61).
32 See Marx (MEW III 901).
33 Bauer (1907: 94).
34 Bauer (1907: 88).
35 Bauer (1907: 94).
36 Bauer (1907: 264).
37 Bauer (1907: 266, 499).

4 Critique of the Theory of "Nations without History"

Bauer's second farewell to the postulates of classical Marxism on the national question lies in his critique of the theory of peoples and "nations without history", that is, without a state, first introduced by Hegel and formulated later by Engels ("geschichtslose Nationen"), in response to the Revolutions of 1848. Faced with this thesis, Bauer presents an elaborate and complex theory of the *awakening of nations without history*,[38] which refutes the fundamental thesis of a debtor theory, once again from the teleological holism of the Marxist scheme. We can systematically reconstruct these alternative arguments, which operate on several planes:

1. The supposed "nations without history" were by no means completely incapable of developing a historical life of their own, despite the failure, which must be explained by the concurrence of very precise economic, political and cultural factors – in the construction of one's own independent State.

2. Neither are they by nature incapable of developing a more autonomous history of self-government in the future. It may be able to transpose *historical nations* if the conditions are right: economic (transition from manufacturing to industry), social (liberation of the peasantry) and politics (bourgeois revolution).

3. The capital error that underpins in his understanding, in the thesis of "nations without history" (and in this Bauer agrees, despite their differences in other issues,[39] what Karl Renner pointed out in his 1899 book, *Staat und Nation*, was no other than the equivalence of Nation and State (National State), inherited from the French Revolution, and which translates into the undisputed thesis that each State must correspond to one, and only one nation: "Staat und Nation müssen sich decken".[40] From this assumption, there could be only one Austrian nation, and the Germans, Czechs, Poles and Slavs would not only be subjects (in conflicting transit to "citizens") of the Austro-Hungarian Empire, but also compatriots of the Austrian community.[41] In the other part of the dual *kaiserlich und königlich* empire, the Hungarians would be Magyar in

---

38 Bauer (1907: 187).
39 Nagel (2016: 17–19).
40 Renner (1899; 1994: 26).
41 Bauer (1907: 93).

nationality, and there would be no place for Serbian or Romanian national identities.

4. Hence the double problem derived from the underlying monist-nation-state equation in its double version: a) that of the *National state*, that is, each state should house a single nation (compulsively assimilating internal national minorities); b) that of the *Principle of Nationalities*: each nation must own its own independent State, placing secession as the sole objective of the demands of self-government and creating a nationalizing state, in turn an oppressor of its own minorities.

5. The reformulation of the concept of nation that Bauer undertakes is at the foundation of his concept of a *multinational State* or *State of nationalities* ("Nationalitätenstaat"), which, more precisely, as an institutional design, is configured as *plurinational federalism* as ("Nationalitätenbundesstaat"), designed to accommodate several nations with the same respect, rights and capacity for self-government, avoiding the domination of some by others.

Of great interest is Bauer's analysis of the case of the Czech lands via his theory of the awakening of "nations without history". In his view, capitalist modernity has brought with it essential economic, social, cultural and political changes which overthrow the diagnosis and prognosis that condemned the Czech people to the mere "residue" of history. Very revealing of Bauer's original and complex analysis of the national question, and unheard of in the Marxist tradition, its main features can be systematized as follows:

1) The development of a capitalism with its own bases and dynamics in Bohemia and Moravia resulted in the development of an autochthonous bourgeois class and the correlative displacement of the hegemony of the German bourgeoisie in the country. The transition from the world of small peasant production and manufacturing to the world of industrial production, urbanization and factories, provided the basis for a national revolution.

2) This Czech bourgeoisie assumed the ideals of the Enlightenment and Liberalism, proceeding to a national interpretation of the legacy of the French Revolution.

3) The development of new cultural, linguistic and educational attitudes and policies resulted in the creation of a national education system that popularized and dignified the history, language and culture of the Czech people

4) The class struggle resulting from the generalization of capitalism resulted in an increase in the consciousness of the working class that was built,

not in spite of it, but in close connection with the national consciousness of the Czech people.

5) In turn, economic, cultural and educational development strengthened the emergence of a new and qualified generation of intellectuals who, faced with German hegemony, developed a new Czech national narrative through their activities related to history, language, music, literature, etc.

6) As result of all these economic, social, cultural and political processes, a new national class block or alliance was forged, which made the Czech Republic into a historic nation with widely popular claims of self-government and its own state.

7) Finally, Bauer adds one more factor to his analysis. Emigration from capitalist crises of the time became a factor of reactionary nationalization in Austria and Germany. Given that the gradual rise of the organic composition of capital, the result of the transition from small peasant production to the industrialized capitalist world in the Empire as a whole, generated large surplus population movements in search of new factory centres, a growing German and Austrian xenophobia towards the Czech people (who were accused of stealing work and reducing the wages of national citizens), began to develop. Thus, the development of industrialization and migratory flows encouraged nationalist hatred to rise as the driving force of national struggles. To the Czech intellectuals' hatred of German domination would be added, conversely, the German workers' hatred of Czech emigrants who competed with lower wages and presented an image of "strike-breakers".[42] Then came, in Bauer's view, the birth of a new and complex phenomenon, which defied a vulgar materialistic interpretation: 1) political interaction between *class* and *nationalist* spaces, and 2) the enhancement of material *interests* and *emotions* in the presence of class hatred was reinforced by national hatred and xenophobia.[43]

5 The Concept of Nation as a Non-Essential Community

Once the commonplaces of nationalist and Marxist traditions of the time had been abandoned, what was Bauer's alternative concept of nation? His idea of "nation as a community of destiny that generates a community of character" ("Die Nation aus Schicksalsgemeinschaften wachesende Charaktergemeinschaft")[44]

---

42 Bauer (1907: 231).
43 Bauer (1907: 229).
44 Bauer (1907: 98–99).

has been the source of innumerable misunderstandings and partial readings ("culturalism", "psychologism", "Hegelianism", etc.), and so this study will now systematically address its scope and nature. Given the importance of this concept in the formulation of the concept of *community*, both in terms of character and destiny, it is necessary to clarify with some precision its formulation by Bauer. First of all, it should be underlined that there are three concepts involved in the explanation of the processes of national construction by Bauer: 1) Cultural community, 2) National destiny, 3) National character. As shall be shown presently, far from culturalist reductionism, the factors involved in the processes of national construction are, in his view, the three mentioned above: economic, cultural and political.

As has already been pointed out, the nation, for Bauer, does not constitute a *natural* community; instead, a specific cultural community (*Kulturgemeinschaft*) arises from the processes of continuous social differentiation,[45] from the evolution of the conditions in which human beings produce their vital sustenance and unequally distribute the result of their work. On the other hand, the transmission of cultural goods between generations gives rise to a shared destiny of the nation which translates into a relative community of character or *Charaktergemeinschaft*.[46] The material substratum of the nation ceases to constitute a kind of obscure natural background, which in Europe at the beginning of the century began to acquire unmistakable racist tones. For Bauer, the development of a national community is not explained by the alleged "natural hereditary transmission of physical qualities", but by the creative transmission of "cultural goods", both material and immaterial. Thus, in the explanation of the processes of national construction, two moments are articulated in a very novel way for the time:

a) the evolution of the materialist dimension of the production and reproduction of existence (development of productive forces, relations of production, mode of production), with the qualitative changes implied by generalization and the incipient transformations of industrial capitalism. It should be emphasized that, for the first time, the process of constructing the national consciousness is derived not from a differentiated ethnicity that stretches back into the depths of time, but from the relations of production and class conflicts of the period;

b) the cultural dimension, that is, the specific cultural property of each nation, its intergenerational transmission, and the political struggles for inclusion and participation in its elaboration by the working classes.

---

45   Agnelli (1969: 132).
46   Bauer (1907: 22).

Every national cultural community is always formed by *reciprocal action* between individuals and social classes, and not as an effect of an immaterial or universal essence or substance that passively unifies them ("Volksgeist", "Seele", "Schicksal", "Geist", etc.). There is, therefore, no "firm ground" on which to stand (that "Das feste Land" that Herder longed for in the community), nor an ontological foundation to grasp, from which the political presence of the nation can be deduced. We are now, for all intents and purposes, in the world of modernity, the one Marx characterized lucidly in the Communist Manifesto as that where "All that is solid melts in the air". Certainly, for Bauer, following the footsteps of Ferdinand Tönnies, the *Gemeinschaft* cannot be reduced to *Geseellschaft*, and the collective identity of peoples should not be considered the mere sum of competitive individualities. Similarly, the double meaning of *Gemeinschaft*, as elaborated by Kant in his *Kritik der reinen Vernunft*, was namely, a *communio*, a substantial static community, and a *commercium*, the reciprocal social interaction associated with the freedom of modernity, Bauer clearly opts for the latter, but in terms of historical materialism and class struggle. Community is, for him, a reciprocal action constitutive, and not merely expressive, of a prior community essence occurring previously in history, and in modernity, this community dimension is indebted to the new relations of production of capitalism and its specific political conflicts. These are the limits of Bauer's *communitarianism*. This is undoubtedly one of the most interesting contributions of his theory of the nation: from the capitalist relations of production that translate into class struggle, from the construction of a state that monopolizes political power to ends previously unsuspected and of the creation of a differentiated culture, although exclusive to the emerging classes, the nation is conceived not as a crystallized empirical fact, but as a *contingent and indeterminate historical process*. This is the permanently incomplete result of the interaction between the three factors already mentioned: economic-social, cultural and political. A process, therefore, which has nothing to do with the "immanent development of the national consciousness", but as a random, complex and multi-causal production of a "shifting national being".[47]

Precisely contrary to what one might think, nowhere is this processual, open, non-teleological character of the Nation better observed than in the very concept of *national character*. The latter is postulated as a bridge between the cultural and linguistic dimension and the relations of production. Bauer elaborates his concept independently on the spiritualism of *Volksgeist* (Hegel, Herder) and on the idea of nation as a totality and metaphysical essentiality that inevitably unfolds in history (as Fichte did in his *Reden an die deutsche Nation*).

---

47   Bauer (1907: 43).

His perspective is that of the nation as a set of shared and disputed characteristics (values, attitudes, myths and symbols), created by a cultural community of historical destiny in its particular material struggle for existence, yet devoid of any hint of "substantial appearance", of all "fetishism of the national character".[48]

In this way, the national character assumes very precise features:

1) *It constitutes the result of a process of national construction*, and therefore an *explanandum* not an *explanans*,[49] that is, a factor that must be explained, since it is not a causal dimension of the national phenomenon.[50]
2) It is always partial: the community of character is relative, not absolute, competes and interacts in each individual with other possible identifications, such as class or religion.
3) *It is not permanent*, but modifiable and changeable ("veränderlich") in the course of history, and is shaped in modernity, rather than on "common ancestry" from time immemorial, through a "new culture".
4) *It is not homogeneous*: the community of character does not imply homogeneity at all, but permanent interaction, pluralism and struggle for the inclusion of the working classes. The distance with the concept of nation as a unanimous *organic totality* of Fichte, constructed by ablating what is heterogeneous from the bosom of the people and from the exclusive tracing of "inneren Grenzen" or "internal frontiers",[51] is clear here in unmistakable terms.
5) *It articulates interests and emotions:* Bauer insists, in the face of the theoretical body of classical Marxism, and the advances of psychology and Viennese psychoanalysis of the time, on the need to introduce into the explanation of nationalisms not only the material preferences of citizens, but also their affections and feelings. The study of *national hatred* amongst majorities and minorities is a good example of this.

Thus, for Bauer, the nation is not an empirical fact crystallized once and for all in history, but is configured as a complex open political process, contingent on the creation of a community that, devoid of metaphysical, cultural or racial substance, becomes, strictly speaking, a *non-essentialist community*: "From this perspective, the nation is not for us a frozen thing in time, but a process that is

---

48 Bauer (1907: 112).
49 Leisse (2012: 238).
50 Bauer (1907: 27).
51 Máiz (2012: 37).

becoming". Or equally, "the nation as the product of an always unfinished process that is continuously developing".[52]

Hence, for Bauer, "the history of a nation cannot be closed at any moment", nor can pluralism and internal antagonisms be extirpated from it. The community of destiny, does not only 1) not constitute a "homogeneity of destiny", but is also merely a common and conflicting experience of it.[53] In this case, it is not only a question of the social and political changes that accompany them, but also of the national character. No trace may be observed in Bauer of that disdain for politics as an "artificial" and volatile sphere before the rocky naturalness of the nation, which Friedrich Meinecke already noticed in his day in the classic idea of a German nation, that *Deutsche Grösse*, by Goethe, Schiller or Humboldt.[54] Nor can any trace of the decisionism and warmongering that characterized the German nationalist mutation after the war, starting with Ernst Jünger and the conservative revolution, be detected.

In short, Bauer explains the nation as the contingent result of a process of national construction in which various features interact, and which must be evaluated empirically in each concrete context and conjuncture: 1) *economic factors* (the conditions of human beings in their struggle for the existence, the transformations of the relations of production and productive forces, modifications of labour relations in capitalism); (2) *cultural factors* (the intergenerational transmission of cultural goods and their changes through the contributions of emerging new social classes); and (3) *political factors* (the configuration of the centralist state based on the "atomistic-centralist vision",[55] and overlapping class and national conflicts). As we have already pointed out, this argument is politically decisive, since the history of nations is the history of the ruling classes, and national culture is nothing but the culture of elites, excluding the popular classes. Indeed, Bauer goes a step further: in fact, "what unifies the nation is neither the unity of blood nor the unity of culture, but the unity of the culture of the ruling classes".[56] For this reason, the history of nations is, above all, the political history of the struggles for the expansion and transformation of the national cultural community. Only with progressive enlargement, with the ever-incomplete realization of the cultural community,[57] by including the totality of the working classes by means of their conversion into

---

52 Bauer (1907: 105–06).
53 Bauer (1907: 107).
54 Meinecke (1963: 76).
55 See Renner (1899; 1994).
56 Bauer (1907: 104).
57 Bauer (1907: 115).

a national class and through access to participation in the production of cultural goods, may a genuine national community one day be reached.

However, this expansion of the national cultural community is by no means the inevitable product of economic evolution, or of intergenerational cultural transmission, but of the political mobilization of the working class and its radical reformulation of traditional national struggles. Thus, in contrast to the policy of conservative nationalism, Bauer postulates an entirely new national evolutionary policy, whose aim is not the nationalist closure on the borders of an own State, under the tutelage of the ruling classes, but the struggle for the "development of the entirety of the people into a nation".[58] From this perspective, the relative enlargement of the national cultural community, undertaken by the proprietary classes in the wake of the bourgeois revolutions, will further the expansion of the nation towards the working classes through the triumph of democratic socialism. That is why this national evolutionist policy is the policy of the modern working class and not the naive internationalism of workers supposedly deprived of their country, nor the embrace of naive nationalism directed by the bourgeoisie, its interests and its values. Bauer argues that socialism cannot abandon the realm of the nation, in which the struggle for the hegemony of a country is solved, to nationalists, thereby postulating a strictly labour-focussed policy. But to penetrate this strategic field implies, in turn, the need for a radical liquidation of the essentialist concept of a nation inherited from the nineteenth century and its normative derivatives, the monist thesis equally shared, beneath its rhetorical antagonism, by the Principle of Nationalities ("one nation, one state") and the Principle of the national state ("one State, one nation").[59]

6 The Nation as a Plural and Heterogeneous Community

It must be emphasized that, as a result of its non-essentialist character, the shared national cultural community does not translate into the pathological obsession with the homogeneity of the national field, even though it gives rise to "a community of destiny that generates a community of character". On the one hand, for Bauer, "Community does not mean mere homogeneity";[60] on the other, the community of destiny does not suppose blind "subjection to the same destiny". Social and especially class differences are important and imply

---

58   Bauer (1907: 139).
59   Bauer (1907: 149).
60   Bauer (1907: 97).

different levels of cultural appropriation and the "shared" national destiny, as well as very different versions and interpretations of the national culture.

However, in addition, Bauer gives an additional twist in his critique of the idea of nation as a holistic and homogeneous totality: in his view, the humanity of modern times is not divided into discrete nations, and therefore: 1) every individual belongs unquestionably to a single nation, and 2) each territory or state to a single nation. In this respect, it is necessary to remember that in the Austro-Hungarian Empire, the national groups in each part of the empire constituted a minority in the area which they controlled politically: the Germans, for example, represented only 36% of the population of Cisleithania and the Magyars did not reach 50% in Hungary. On the other hand, the Czechs (the majority in Bohemia and Moravia), Poles, Ukrainians and Slovenians aspired to influence politically Cisleithania itself.[61]

One of Bauer's most relevant contributions of the analysis of the national question, with the normative and institutional consequences that shall be assessed presently, lies precisely in the rejection of the ethnic homogeneity of territories, that is, in the questioning of the classical monist equation of the nationalisms of the nation state or against the nation state: one state = one territory = one nation = one culture. Bauer analyses the social scientific analysis and the normative consequences for the first time (preceded in it, within the legal field, by Karl Renner) of an empirical fact that put an end to the illusive assumption of ethnic-territorial homogeneity. In his understanding, it is necessary to account for phenomena that in modernity would only become more accentuated and widespread. First of all, the existence of many border areas in which human beings of different cultures and nationalities mix and have two or more national identities. Or rather, the presence of countries in which massive migrations, caused by the economic crisis or the unequal transition from primitive to industrial capitalism, if not the arrival of numerous refugees from the wars, ethnic cleansing or genocide, creates in the Europe of the end of the Austro-Hungarian Empire a cultural, national and identity landscape much more variegated and complex than the one foreseen by State nationalisms, or the nationalisms that aspire to construct their own State in the service of a single nation, its culture and interests. These cases, which in their time Bauer considered significant ("non-meagre"), acquire capital political importance because they question from a new angle (the ensuing population and cultural movements) the aforementioned major equation of nationalist monism: one territory = one nation = one language. The presence of individuals whose nationality and culture are minority within the territory in which they reside,

---

61   Nimni (2005: 3).

who belong to two or more nations, or who even do not belong fully and totally to any, gives rise to a "totally novel" phenomenon of minority or overlapping national identities.

From the primary establishment of the national state, but also from the beginning of nationalities, the civic status of these human beings (the product of diaspora, migration, and the artificiality of the drawing up of borders) becomes an intractable problem: they are highly numerous in Europe, blur the national homogeneity of territories and, consequently, become "unwanted and distrustful", or worse, "in times of national struggles, subjected to assimilationist domination, when not despised as "traitors and turncoats".[62] Thus, minorities and cultural mixed-race people constitute a challenge without a democratic response from the classic nationalist territorial assumptions. The national cultural community presents here a doubly inessential nature, not only as a contingent result of a process of political construction, but also as a plural matrix of diverse cultural interpretations and overlapping of identities, rendering illusory any attempt at resolution through the application of the *pure territorial principle*, without engaging openly in the domination and oppression of minorities. Moreover, the *territorial principle*, by implying that each territory is owned by a national majority and, where it is the case that the majority and national minorities inhabit the territory, leads to the inevitable oppression of minorities by the majority: "The pure territorial principle everywhere subjects these minorities to the majority".[63] In Renner's words, the territorial principle states that "if you live in my territory you are subject to my legislation and my language".[64] Thus, the construction of territorial and sovereign national states, old or new, involves declaring all foreigners who cross borders as being outside and beyond the rule of law. For this reason, the issue of minorities is a priority for Bauer, who devotes many pages to his quantitative and qualitative study within the Empire, noting that an increasingly smaller part of the population lives in communities where various nationalities and cultures do not co-exist. The strict application of the territorial principle in a time of mass migration implies the endemic inequality of rights and the domination of majorities over minorities and, ultimately, owners of the means of production over working migrants, as Karl Renner liked to specify: "The domination of the sedentary minority over the emigrant majority".[65]

---

62   Bauer (1907: 102).
63   Bauer (1907: 295).
64   Renner (1899, 1994: 30).
65   See Renner (1899, 1994: 43).

7 The Critique of the Principle of Nationalities and the Proposal of Plurinational Federalism

The explanatory theory of the nation from the "sociological method", "social sciences" and "historical materialism" in Bauer has profound consequences for his normative political theory and the institutional redesign of the State from the point of view of the territorial organization of power. The first is, of course, a radical double criticism of the centralist territorial state, the model of the *République une et indivisible*, but also of its supposed "democratic" alternative in the Principle of Nationalities and unilateral self-determination. From the analysis of the nation as an open and plural process, Bauer can only denounce as voluntarist, unsatisfactory and incorrect the naturalist and monistic fallacy that preaches that a state should embrace a single nation, as well as its specular investment in the postulate that the only outcome for every self-respecting nation should be the attainment of an independent sovereign state.

The logical corollary of his theory of the nation, for Bauer, is that neither the nation state ("Nationalstaat") constitutes the undisputed rule of the territorial organization of political power, nor can the multinational State (*Nationalitätenstaat*) be considered a mere historical pre-modern residue or an Austrian exception doomed beforehand to failure. In contrast to the different versions, from Herder to Fichte, of the dualism that regards the State as an artificial entity and the nation as a natural entity, our author argues that the national state, in the service of "its" own nation, in no way constitutes a natural formation, since both nations and States are contingent results of equally artificial historical, economic, cultural and political processes. On the other hand, the multi-national State does not constitute in any way an atavistic political structure, destined inexorably to its disintegration in multiple national States, as Bauer counters, the evolutionary historical tendencies that explain the principle of nationalities, without any idealization, with the counter-tendencies that the multi-national State retained in Austria until the Great War. On the other hand, the multi-national State does not constitute in any way an atavistic political structure, destined inexorably to its disintegration in multiple national states. On the contrary, the tendencies of historical evolution underpinning the principle of nationalities may also be contrasted with the tendency towards integration and coexistence within a multi-national state, which characterized the diverse nationalities of Austria-Hungary.[66]

The multi-national State, however, constitutes a complex and conflicting democratic challenge: the possibility of accommodating different nationalities

---

66 Bauer (1907: 153).

on an equal footing, self-government and mutual respect within the same State implies a radical reform of the Imperial structure characterized by inequality and domination among the nations and to reach a difficult pact on an equal footing between nations. Bauer's analysis is prolixic and, given the scientific-social objective of his work, not as detailed and precise as that of Karl Renner. Yet some of the basic conditions that it posits to democratically redesign a multi-national state may be synthesized:

1) If the multi-national State is not conceived as a utopia ideally opposed to the real world, but as an *immanent* conception that takes on impulse and is constructed from the own "internal evolutionary tendencies in Austria",[67] the undeniable empirical fact of multi-nationality increasingly demands the need for a new covenant of peaceful coexistence among the nations that comprise it, a programme of institutional reforms that will overcome the deadlock of national struggles, based on the very different reality of the different nationalities.

2) That the centralist-atomistic liberal view of the Nation State be replaced by an "organic conception", that is, by the sovereignty shared among various nations: *L'ennemi, c'est la souveraineté*, wrote Karl Renner,[68] by the recognition as subjects of law not only of the individual citizens in their relationship with the State, but also of the juridical-political personality of the internal national communities;

3) That these communities be understood as nationalities, in the sense specified above: communities of culture and destiny, plural and contingent rather than as ancient territories, kingdoms and provinces ("Königreiche", "Kronländer", "Länder"), endowed with "historical rights". In *Staat und Nation*, Renner had already stressed that they had become not only authentic "impossible things", because they constituted neither social nor national individualities, but antidemocratic structures of domination which, by integrating several nations with various privileges, were constitutively based on the systematic oppression of national minorities by the majority.

4) That the multi-national State be organized in a *federal* way, as a State of States, through self-government and shared government, although through a federalism that recognizes and accommodates multi-nationality, that is, as a *federal multi-national State*, such as plurinational federalism, replacing the obsolete *kaiserlich und königlich* structure.[69]

---

67   Bauer (1907: 332).
68   See Nagel (2016: 9).
69   Bauer (1907: 377).

5) That the defence of the federalization of the multi-national State be not only based on (1) the denunciation of the secessionist illusion of the fragmentation *ad infinitum* of national States of less territorial scope and the lack of a solution to the problem that all, in turn, pose with their own minorities dominated by the new national majority; but (2), on the assumption that, from the interests of the working classes, it would provide a more favourable political scenario for their demands and a broader economic space in which to advance their social progress, and lead and coordinate their struggles.

From this point of view, for Bauer, the *nationale Autonomie* is the right way for the self-government of nationalities,[70] because, in contrast to the national policy of power of the ruling classes, the working class can oppose their economic, social and political demands, together with the national objective of expanding the cultural community to the masses, towards an authentic and inclusive public community system.

6) Finally, the *federal multi-national State* that Bauer postulates also builds from other additional and hardly insignificant features:

a) Firstly: *democratization*. From the revaluation of democratic socialism posited by Austro-Marxism, the democratization of the state of the old Habsburg monarchy becomes the central axis guiding the reform of the multi-national State as a "democratic multi-national state". Hence the federal formula, which, deeply Republican in origins, requires the democratic quality of both the Union as a whole and the Member States. However, democracy itself must be reformulated in a complex sense in order to cope with multinational accommodation. In the first place, it must assume the dogmatic articulation of the (individual, political and social) rights of citizens, with the collective rights (cultural and political) of the nations *qua* nations within the federation. Secondly, it must guarantee the demand for guarantees of democracy and internal pluralism in each of the nationalities integrated in the federal multi-national State. That is, the federal multi-national State does not dissociate itself from the democratic quality of the federated states (self-government must be carried out through representative mechanisms chosen by universal suffrage, equal and secret, a citizenship endowed with rights and according to a proportional electoral system, etc.). Above all, federal democracy must reconcile the rule of majority decision with respect for national minorities.

---

70 Bauer (1907: 278).

b) Secondly, it reinterprets the unilateral right of self-determination leading to secession, in keeping with the Principle of Nationalities, as the *Principle of internal self-determination* ("innerstaatliches Nationalitätsprinzip").[71] That is, as Karl Renner emphasizes in *Das Selbstbestimmungsrecht der Nationen*,[72] no indisputable *ius secedendi* exists, but the right to self-government, to political autonomy endowed with broad powers and guaranteed constitutionally, does. This, in turn, translates into a vision of horizontal and non-hierarchical, "shared sovereignty" against the classic Westphalian concept and its pretensions of indivisible, unlimited and untransferable sovereignty. Hence the very core of multinational federalism that is built on a double axis: self-government and shared government, unity and national diversity. In this model, there are no absolute communities: all of them are partial and overlapping, and shared sovereignty is exercized through the self-government of one's own powers and shared government in matters of common interest.

This internal self-determination, this autonomy, however, is not limited to the reductive scope of the development by nationalities of their own culture. Contrary to what has often been affirmed, we must emphasize that Bauer's proposal refers not only to a mere *cultural autonomy* of nationalities, but to substantive self-government in fundamental subjects.[73] Political autonomy,[74] which generates an authentic sphere of political power in its own affairs ("eine rechtliche Machtsphere"),[75] which is projected into broad capacities of "self-legislation and self-administration" ("Selbstgesetzgebung und Selbstverwaltung"),[76] and which covers economic, educational, linguistic, official and even military matters in certain respects.

c) Thirdly, because of the undesirable effects (oppression of minorities) of the application of the *pure territorial principle*, Bauer postulates the possibility of introducing the *non-territorial or personality principle*, advanced in the day by Meinecke in *Weltbürgertum und Nationalstaat* (1907) and by Renner in *Staat und Nation* (1898) and *Das Selbstbestimmungsrecht der Nationen* (1918). However, neither Renner nor Bauer consider the Non-Territorial as a complete *alternative* to the territorial principle, but as an element of correction and complementary to the first. Its proposal

---

71 Bauer (1907: 180).
72 Renner (2015: 89).
73 See Czerwinska (2005: 185).
74 Bauer (1907: 277).
75 Bauer (1907: 438).
76 Bauer (1907: 451).

consists in a nuanced articulation of the territorial principle and the personnel. For example, through free individual declaration of nationality and the abandonment of ethnic-racial ascription, territoriality and personality can be combined in plural contexts. In no event is the "pure implementation"[77] of the principle of personality postulated, except for the mechanisms test that, for example, favour the presence of territorial representative bodies together with the possibility of cultural participation (linguistic policies, educational system, administration, etc.), in the sense of reasonable accommodation, by applying the personal principle to the minorities. Thus, among others, dual management mechanisms are proposed in the case of mixed cantons, which allow minorities the right to be cared for in school and in administration in their own language (including linguistic federalism, that is, languages considered as heritage of the whole Union). Unlike, for example, the *millet* of the Ottoman Empire, autonomous national minority communities, instituted by the principle of personality, are organized here: 1) under democratic rules, and 2) based on individual express consent and internal democracy. These and other proposals gave rise to an intense debate, which was soon cut off by the war, on various formulas of *reasonable accommodations* that are highly flexible and varied, personal and territorial, and which was hardly implemented at the end of the Empire. This accommodation, however, did not exclude the eventual assimilation of some minorities. But unlike Kautsky, who conceived assimilation as the obligatory adoption of the language and culture of the majority, Bauer regarded it as a long process and the eventual result of respect for pluralism and diversity, avoiding by all means the national coercion of the majority over the minority.[78]

To conclude, it must be pointed out that this reinterpretation of the right of self-determination as internal self-determination, as autonomy, derives from the pluralistic condition of the federal multi-national State as a superior ethical and political model against the both naive and oppressive principle of nationalities, although the mechanism of secession does not resolve the horizon of political possibilities. This last option remains a *remedial right* before the failure of federal state of nationalities. That is, instead of constituting the eminent and unique strategic political objective of the solution to the problem of nationalities and their demands for self-government, secession remains for Bauer as a final option, negotiated and not unilateral, in the event of the repeated impossibility or irresolvable violent conflict (genocide, ethnic cleansing,

---

[77] Bauer (1907: 312)
[78] Bauer (1980 [1912]: 621).

war, etc.) of multinational federal accommodation. In this sense, it is symptomatic that, even in 1917, Bauer rejects self-determination as a universal political principle, although he does accept it under the critical circumstances of the moment, in the case of the Czech Republic and Poland. The idea of multinational federalism continued to be the rule for him, and the principle of self-determination was the exceptional outcome in response to an irremediable political failure.

Behind the dangerous chimera of an imaginary world of homogeneous and sovereign national states, serving the interests of a single national majority, the reality of national, ethnic and cultural pluralism has not only continued its course in history, but has increased in relevance in the late modern period. In the new context of global society and the multiplication of migrations and refugees, the ideas of multinational federalism and non-territorial autonomy, losers at a given moment, but replete with arguments, concepts and institutional solutions to the ethnic and national problems of collective action, contain valuable contributions for the present. This is precisely the case of Otto Bauer's work. Nearly forgotten from the 1940s, the crisis in the Soviet Union led to a renewed interest in his contributions on territorial and non-territorial autonomy (Latvia, Lithuania, Ukraine) from the 1990s onwards.[79] The English translation of *The Question of Nationalities and Social Democracy* by O'Donnell and edited by Ephraim Nimni[80] decisively contributed to the contemporary reception of Bauer's lucid analysis, and it also highlights the theoretical relevance of the *Non-Territorial Cultural Autonomy* frame. This model demonstrated his potential to inspire public policies and institutional arrangements for implementing accommodation strategies in multi-ethnic and plurinational contexts, as an alternative or a complement to federal solutions.

The accommodation of national minorities through mechanisms of territorial and non-territorial autonomy is regaining prominence in the present world, both in political theory and comparative politics.[81] In this sense, several case-studies have brought to the forefront the "tension between ethnic geography (pattern of ethnic settlement) and political autonomy (degree of self-rule)",[82] as well as the implementation gap between what is stated on recognition in legal texts or the symbolic usage of recognition, on the one hand, and actual autonomy substantive measures concerning issues such as religion,

---

79   See Smith (2013), and Cordell (2017).
80   Bauer (2000).
81   See Nimni et al. (2013); Malloy & Palermo /2015); Mally et al. (2015), and Nimni & Aktoprak (2019).
82   See Coakley (2017: 18).

language and education, on the other.[83] Research projects in the making like Horizon 2020 (2008–2023) *Non-Territorial Autonomy as Minority Protection in Europe*, funded by the European Research Council at the Institute for Modern and Contemporary Research (ÖAW) of Vienna, is good evidence that Bauer's approaches are of inescapable relevance today, 110 years after the time of publication of his flagship contribution.

Bibliography

Agnelli, Arduino (1969), *Questione nazionale e socialismo. Contributo allo studio del pensiero di K. Renner e O. Bauer*, Bologna: Il Mulino.

Bauer, Otto (1907), *Die Nationalitätenfrage und die Sozialdemokratie*, Vienna: Ignaz Brand.

Bauer, Otto (1975–1980), *Werkausgabe*, Vienna: Europaverlag, 9 vols.

Bauer, Otto (2000), *The Question of Nationalities and Social Democracy*, translated by Joseph O'Donnell, Ephraim Nimni, editor Minnesota U. Press: Minneapolis.

Blum, M.E., and W. Smaldone (2015), *Austro-Marxism. The Ideology of Unity. Austro-Marxist theory and Strategy*, Leiden/Boston: Brill.

Bourdet, Yvonne (1968), *Otto Bauer et la Révolution*, Paris: EDI.

Coakley, J. (2017), *Non-Territorial Autonomy in Divided Societies*, London: Routledge.

Cordell, K. (2017), "Non-Territorial Cultural Autonomy", in *50 Shades of Federalism*. http://50shadesoffederalism.com/diversity-management/non-territorial-cultural-autonomy/.

Czerwinska-Schupp, Ewa (2005), *Otto Bauer: Studien zur social-politischen Philosophie*, Frankfurt a. M.: Peter Lang.

Erk, Jan. (2015), "Non-Territorial *Millets* in Ottoman History", in H.T. Malloy & F. Palermo (eds.), *Minority Accommodation through Territorial and Non-Territorial Autonomy*, Oxford: Oxford UP, pp. 119–131.

Fejtö, François (1989), "Les raisons politiques et idéologiques de la destruction de la monarchie", in M. Molnár & A. Reszler. (eds.), *Le Génie de L'Autriche-Hongrie*, Paris: PUF.

García-Pelayo, Manuel (1979), *La teoría de la nación de Otto Bauer*. Madrid: Fundación Pablo Iglesias.

Hanisch, Ernst (2011), *Der grosse Illusionist. Otto Bauer 1881–1938*, Vienna: Böhlau.

Haupt, George, M. Lowy & C. Weil (1974), *Les marxistes et la question nationale 1848–1914*, Paris: Maspero.

---

83 See Osipov (2013).

Kautsky, Karl J. et al. (1978), *La Segunda Internacional y el problema nacional y colonial.* Mexico City: Cuadernos de Pasado y Presente, 2 vols.

Leisse, Olaf (2012), *Der Untergang des östrreichischen Imperiums. Otto Bauer und die Nationalitätenfrage in der Habsburger Monarchie,* Marburg a. Lahn: Tectum.

Luxemburg, Rosa (1979), *La cuestión nacional y la autonomía,* Mexico City: Cuadernos Pasado y Presente.

Máiz, Ramón (2010), "Karl Marx. De la superación del Estado a la dictadura del proletariado", in F. Vallespín (ed.), *Historia de la Teoría Política, 4: Historia, progreso y emancipación,* Madrid: Alianza, 103–170.

Máiz, Ramón (2012), *The Inner Frontier. The Place of Nation in the Political Theory of Democracy and Federalism,* Bern: Peter Lang.

Malloy, Tove H. and F. Palermo, eds. (2015), *Minority Accommodation through Territorial and Non-Territorial Autonomy,* Oxford: Oxford UP.

Malloy, Tove H., A. Osipov & B. Vizi, eds. (2015), *Managing Diversity Through Non-Territorial Autonomy,* Oxford: Oxford UP.

Mann, Michael (2005), *The Dark Side of Democracy: Explaining Ethnic Cleansing,* Cambridge: Cambridge UP.

Mann, Thomas (1983), *Betrachtungen eines Unpolitischen,* Frankfurt a. M.: Fischer [1918].

Meinecke, Friedrich (1963), *Weltbürgertum und Nationalstaat,* Munich: Oldenbourg.

Molnár, Miklós, & André Reszler, eds. (1989), *Le Génie de L'Autriche-Hongrie,* Paris: PUF.

Momsen, Hans (1979), *Arbeitbewegung und nationale Frage,* Göttingen: Vandenhoeck & Ruprecht.

Nagel, Klaus. J., ed. (2016), *Otto Bauer, Karl Renner. Escrits sobre nació i federalisme,* Barcelona: IEA.

Nimni, Ephraim, ed.(2005), *National Cultural Autonomy and its Contemporary Critics,* London: Routledge.

Nimni, Ephraim (2015), "Minorities and the limits of Liberal Democracy. Democracy and Non-Territorial Autonomy", in Malloy and Palermo (eds.), *Minority Accommodation,* pp. 73–98

Nimni, Ephraim, Alexander Osipov and David J. Smith, eds. (2013), *The Challenge of Non-Territorial Autonomy.* Oxford: Peter Lang.

Nimni, E. & Aktoprak, E., (eds.) (2019), *Democratic Representation in Plurinational States: The Kurds in Turkey,* Basingstoke: Palgrave.

Osipov, A. (2013), "Non-Territorial Autonomy during and after Communism" *Journal on Ethnopolitics and Minority Issues in Europe,* Vol 12 N° 1, 7–26.

Renner, Karl (1994), *Schriften* (ed. Anton Pelinka), Vienna: Residenz.

Renner, Karl (2015), *Estado y Nación. El derecho de las naciones a la autodeterminación,* Madrid: Tecnos.

Schmitter, Philippe C. (1994), "Conceptual travels of Transitologists and Consolidologists". *Slavic Review,* 53 (1), p. 176.

Smith, D. (2013), "Non-Territorial Autonomy and Political Community in Contemporary Central and Eastern Europe", *Journal on Ethnopolitics and Minority Issues in Europe*, 12:1, pp. 27–55

CHAPTER 6

New Worlds Tackling on Side-tracks: The National Concepts of T.G. Masaryk and Oszkár Jászi during the First World War (1914–1919)

Bence Bari

War is a thesaurus of horrors – and of opportunities. This observation of Raymond A. Pearson in connection to the Eastern European minority question of the long 19th and early 20th centuries is of special relevance when it comes to the First World War.[1] Due to the latter, the Old World and its inhabitants both underwent revolutionary transformations.

New approaches to the most important questions of contemporary times – nation, class, religion etc. – had already appeared in the *fin de siècle* era. In Eastern Europe, the offset between these and traditional standpoints added to the problems of the nationally diverse Romanov and Habsburg domains. 'New' and 'old' currents clashed within and throughout communities already separated by ethnic differences – and then the Great War arrived with all its impact.

When searching for examples, one could examine the paths of two intellectuals: the Hungarian sociologist Oszkár Jászi (1875–1937) and the Czech philosopher Tomáš Garrigue Masaryk (1850–1937). These reform-minded inhabitants of Austria–Hungary both became influential thinkers and politicians between 1914–1919. The outcome of their activities, however, contrasted each other strongly – like the fate of their respective Hungarian and Czech(oslovak) nations.

As for the current study*, its thesis will be that the intellectuals underwent the same transformation when it came to their ideas; however, the pace and the circumstances of their developments were different. This resulted in varying outcomes for their projects. Consequently, the evolving national ideas of Jászi and Masaryk during the First World War shall be observed and compared. Focus is placed on the concepts used by them: those of 'nation', 'nationality'

---

* I would like to thank Professor Balázs Trencsenyi (CEU) for his comments on an earlier version of this chapter.
1 See Pearson (1983: 190–220).

and 'minority', and how the intellectuals applied their transforming ideas to the multinational settings of the present and the desired future: the Habsburg Empire, historical Hungary and Czechoslovakia. Regarding sources, Masaryk's English and Jászi's Hungarian writings shall be employed, as these were the ones that targeted their main audiences. Nonetheless, it is also important to take into account national and international contexts to both provide background and to show how much the ideas of these intellectuals differed – or did not differ – from those of others. Given the transnational context of the ideological developments in the First World War, it is also important to place the thoughts of Masaryk and Jászi in these contexts and to detect the influences of these on their developing ideas.

1   The Setting: Pre-War Hungarian and Czech Contexts

Although the Revolution and War of Independence of 1848/49 ultimately failed, the on-going struggle with the Habsburg dynasty culminated in a realistic and satisfactory compromise for the Hungarian elite. The *Ausgleich* of 1867 finally made the state of Hungary (Transleithania) an autonomous and influential centre of power within the Monarchy.[2] *It cannot be that all in vain so many hearts have bled* – in keeping with the words of the 'second Hungarian anthem', Mihály Vörösmarty's *Appeal* (1836),[3] the governments of Hungary – led mostly by the so-called 'Liberal Party' (*Szabadelvű Párt*) – defended its hard-won privileges like a tigress throughout the Dualistic Era.

Soon enough, a serious threat materialized in the image of Czech demands to make the Western Slavic nation the third ruling constituent of the empire. The Austrian Emperor and Hungarian King, Francis Joseph I (1848/67–1916), did take this solution into consideration. However, the attempt of a 'Bohemian *Ausgleich*' failed in 1871 due to the resistance of Austrian German parties and, importantly, the Hungarian government.[4] As for the latter, the Transleithanian elite feared losing both its newly acquired position within the dualistic state *and* its control over the multinational domains of historical Hungary that comprised the territories of the Carpathian Basin. This fear had its background in the events of 1848/49, when inter-ethnic fights set the country

---

2   Judson (2006: 262).
3   Mihály Vörösmarty, *Appeal*, translation by Theresa Pulszky and John Edward Taylor. http://www.babelmatrix.org/works/hu/V%C3%B6r%C3%B6smarty_Mih%C3%A1ly/Sz%C3%B3zat/en/3522-Appeal Last Date of Download: 2017. 08. 29.
4   Judson (2006: 295–96).

ablaze. Thus, the successive Hungarian governments rejected all similar claims.[5] Their attitude froze the political conditions of the Habsburg Empire for more than half a century – and amongst others, this made the economically weighty Czech nation a dangerously disappointed loser in that situation.

When it came to arguing for their positions, both the Czech and Hungarian elites used the same conceptual tool of historically based 'state rights' (*Staatsrecht*). As for the former national movement, the mainstream political forces of the late 19th century demanded that the historical 'Lands of the Crown of St. Wenceslaus' – Bohemia, Moravia, Silesia – should gain the same privileges as those of the Hungarian Crown.[6] The reliance of Czech politicians on the sizeable German communities of these provinces as formative parts of the civic nation conceptualized by them is of great importance.[7] However, the emphasis on historical rights and independent existence of the Bohemian lands also stood against the German nationalist claims of dominance within Austria and the Czech provinces.[8] All in all, those were the representatives of a majority subject to the domination of a privileged minority who demanded rights in a way that should have been acceptable to the latter. Naturally, the need to exercize control over all of the historical Bohemian territories also played a part in this decision.

Initially, the leading politicians of Cisleithenia – mostly German Liberals – were only willing to grant individual rights based on citizenship as opposed to demands based on collective or historical rights.[9] However, the December Constitution of the Austrian realms in 1867 assured not only equal chances of development, but also cultural rights to nationalities on a local level. This development was due largely to the influence of the German-Jewish liberal politician Adolf Fischhof (1816–1893) who envisioned the burgeoning of local national cultures under the leadership of the German ethnic element. On the other hand, FISCHHOF also started to support the idea of gradual federalization– which the Hungarian governments could not accept.[10]

This was because while Czechs attempted to gain positions by using arguments based on historical rights, the Hungarian elite built its defence upon this foundation. Being a relative majority within their own multinational country, Hungarians argued that only their community – and that of the Croatians – wielded the attributes of a proper 'nation' (*nemzet*) due to the continuous existence of the Hungarian state throughout history. As opposed to this,

---

5   Juhász (2010: 50).
6   Rees (1992: 1–2).
7   Szpoluk (1981: 103).
8   See Trencsényi et al. (2006: 296–97).
9   Trencsényi et al. (2006: 297).
10 Reifowitz (2001: 441–43).

'ahistorical', stateless ethnicities were called 'nationalities' (*nemzetiségek*) and their demands to acquire political self-government were rejected. This naturally created a tension that led to bloody fights between ethnic groups in 1848/49. Drawing consequences from this outcome, the post-*Ausgleich* elite tried to make an internal compromise between the Hungarian and minority positions. Consequently, the so-called 'Nationalities Law' of 1868 – drafted by Ferenc Deák (1803–1876) and the Minister of Culture and Education, József Eötvös (1813–1871), the Hungarian masterminds behind the Austro–Hungarian Compromise – recognized the existence of minority populations and their cultural rights under the sceptre of the Hungarian 'political nation' (*politikai nemzet*). Since it did not apply any punishments should the government ran counter the law, the theoretically liberal resolves of the Nationalities Law became less and less active over time. On the other hand, the Hungarian elite engaged in a project of assimilative politics ('Magyarization') whilst increasingly and aggressively rejecting the demands of the nationalities in the name of historical nationhood.[11]

As time went by, old tactics proved to be unsatisfactory. The Czechs could not initiate a further transformation of the Habsburg Empire – the Hungarians could not assimilate or sufficiently oppress the non-Magyar nationalities under their rule. Finally, new political forces appeared on both scenes as the dawn of the new century approached.

In Hungary, those were the various approaches to the dualistic system that had defined the differences between parties. Thus, it was no surprise that both the pro-Compromise Liberal Party and its main opponent, the so-called 'Party of Independence' (*Függetlenségi Párt*) – which promoted the extension of Hungarian autonomy within the Habsburg Empire – adhered to traditional liberal principles when it came to other political and social questions. In terms of opposition to them, the end of the 19th century saw the appearance and the rise of the popular Social Democratic mass party in Hungary. However, it could not gain any political capital due to the limited suffrage that defined the electoral system.[12]

In contrast, Austrian governments enfranchised wider and wider strata of the population. In parallel to these developments, middle-class based Czech liberalism lost ground to the emerging mass parties with more radical voices when it came to the questions of political and social life: the Social Democrats, the Agrarians and the National Socialists.[13] Reaching various levels of success, both the Hungarian and the Czech representatives of the 'new wave' realized

---

11   Gyurgyák (2007: 65–78, 82).
12   Judson (2006: 265–68).
13   Trencsényi et al. (2006: 360–61); Orzoff (2009: 35).

the main problems of contemporary times and tried to find alternative ways to solve them – Masaryk and Jászi being the trailblazers amongst these.

2   The New Current(s)

The end of the long 19th century saw the appearance of influential ideas concerning the future of the Monarchy from the political Left. As opposed to the original Marxist standpoint that viewed nationalism as an issue merely deriving attention from class struggle, the leadership of the Austrian Social Democratic Party decided to deal with this problem and re-organized itself along ethnic lines after the Brno Congress of 1899.[14] Famously, the related ideas of Karl Renner and Otto Bauer proposed a federal re-organization of the empire according to the 'nationality principle' (*Nationalitätenprinzip*). The 'Austro-Marxists' asserted that the ethnicities of the Habsburg Empire were in fact full-grown 'nations' – each of their groups tied together through language, history, culture and being entitled with the right to self-determination.[15]

The Czech Social Democrats followed this line of development. In 1897, during their first appearance in the *Reichsrat*, they openly denounced demands based on the historical rights of the Bohemian Crown. The Leftist politicians offered an alternative in their Žofín resolution of 1913, calling for the federalization of the Habsburg Empire along national lines – which, in fact, did not differ from the views of the Austrian Social Democratic framework.[16]

The new and fresh atmosphere, along with the ideas of the Left, influenced many and made them either adopt or come up with new ideas in connection to federalism. As for a rightist example, one can think of Aurel Popovici, the Romanian member of the heir Franz Ferdinand's *Belvedere* circle. The politician published his famous plan for the 'United States of Greater Austria' in 1906, mainly utilizing a racial approach to nationality problems.[17]

As for the Czech context, others also tried to find new ways to solve age-old problems – a notable example being the professor of philosophy at the Charles University in Prague, Tomáš G. Masaryk. Importantly, Masaryk was born in the Southern Moravian borderlands, to a Slovak father and a German mother —he was only assimilated into the Czech nation during his youth.[18] Upon founding

14   Bruegel (1973: 3–4).
15   Tarr (1999: 100–01).
16   Rees (1992: 11).
17   Neumann (2008: 72).
18   Neville (2010: 5–6).

his tiny Czech's People Party – or more famously, the Realist Party – in 1900, the intellectual immediately detached from the concepts of the Bohemian *Staatsrecht* and political nationhood. As Masaryk argued, the political changes of the past epochs – the Habsburg absolutism of the 16th century and the liberal developments of the 19th century – rendered these ideas outdated. Instead of this, he placed emphasis on the natural rights of 'nations' (*národy*), those cultural bodies defined most of all by their languages. One of these rights was self-government, which was needed especially by the cultured and economically developed Czech nation. Based on these statements, the politician demanded the federalization of the Habsburg Empire in a similar style to that of the Social Democrats.[19]

As for Hungary, on the other hand, the local Social Democratic forces were independent of the Cisleithanian movement and did not propose federalization as a solution for ethnic problems. However, the growing tensions between nationalities and the Hungarian nation caused many to examine this problem – Oszkár Jászi being one of those individuals. Like the Masaryk, the Hungarian sociologist did not belong to the traditional elite of the respective nation, as he was from a Jewish background. In contrast to his Bohemian colleague, however, this fact caused difficulties regarding Jászi's political activity due to the problem of Jewish integration into Hungarian society. Regarding the latter, the sociologist's main determination was to conceptualize an ideological tension between his 'New Hungary' – a progressive and democratic concept influenced by Leftist ideas – and the conservative, corrupt and outdated 'Old Hungary' of the traditional elite. Jászi's views were not popular, as his atheist and highly theoretical beliefs fell far from the thinking of the average Hungarian citizen. He did not differ from Masaryk from this aspect either – the Hungarian intellectual proved to be much more influential than his compatriot as Jászi became a reference point within the circles of Hungarian progressives. In this aspect, the sociologist relied on a small group of like-minded people – the so-called 'Galilei Circle' – and also on the influential sociological journal, *Twentieth Century*, which he edited. Finally, Jászi founded his own Radical Party in 1914.[20]

When it came to the nationality question of Hungary, the Hungarian intellectual denounced the rigid attitude of the elite that resisted all non-Hungarian national demands behind the shields of *Staatsrecht*. Jászi stressed the need to grant cultural rights to all ethnic groups so that they could develop their internal lives freely. In addition to this, he also asserted that democratization and

---

19 Szpoluk (1981: 103, 105–06).
20 Gyurgyák (2007: 160–67).

adequate governance would finally solve all related problems in the Habsburg Empire.[21] On the other hand, the sociologist did not agree with the ideas of Austro-Marxism regarding federalization. In contrast, he emphasized the higher needs of political and economic ties as established by imperial and state structures – especially when it came to the Hungarian sphere. The intellectual also profoundly believed that these factors would promote the assimilation of nationalities into the Hungarian nation.[22] Thus, while criticizing the traditional elite for violating the rights of nationalities and maintaining its dominance based on historical state rights, the sociologist still bowed to the latter respecting the structure of the Hungarian Kingdom and also appeared to share opinions on the eventual assimilation of the non-Magyar ethnicities – although with democratic overtones.

Importantly, both Masaryk and Jászi tried to look beyond the provincial circumstances, paying attention to the developments and events of the outside world. Eventually, the latter also came to them in the image of the young Scottish historian, Robert W. Seton-Watson. Interested in the conditions of the distant Habsburg Monarchy, Seton-Watson travelled through the realms of the Eastern empire between 1905–1910. It is of great importance that Seton-Watson was in Hungary during a political crisis that defined the rule of the so-called 'Coalitional Government' —for instance, the Hungarian gendarmerie suppressed a Slovakian national protest with scandalous brutality in the town of Černová in 1907. As he got to know the local conditions along with the members of various national elites, the Scottish intellectual developed a critical point of view on the contemporary political situation that was sympathetic to the cause of nationalities. This was partly because the traveller gained acquaintances mainly within the camp of oppositional figures and new-wave thinkers – Masaryk and Jászi amongst others.[23]

Seton-Watson did not only meet the respective Czech and Hungarian intellectuals, but also remained in correspondence with them. The Scottish historian relied on the co-operation of the these individuals in connection to a project that gradually gained huge importance. He thought that the Western European public should be informed of Eastern conditions and that local national movements should be supported; he therefore initiated the journal of the *European Review*. Unfortunately, the First World War made the publication impossible. On the other hand, while it was once the Scottish intellectual that

---

21 Baka (1980: 697–99).
22 Baka (1990: 171–72, 179–81).
23 Seton-Watson and Seton-Watson (1981: 13–40).

travelled to the Habsburg Empire, in 1914, the latter came to him – in the image of Masaryk, now working for the cause of national independence.[24]

3 For National Independence: Masaryk and Czechoslovak Secessionism (1914–1918)

While the Czech leader consistently argued for the national reform of the Habsburg Empire until 1914, he saw new opportunities emerging with the outbreak of the First World War. From this point on, Masaryk opted for the cause of an independent 'Czechoslovak' state. In fact, the idea that Czechs and Slovaks share the same values of nationhood had appeared already in the mid-19th century. On the other hand, the concept lost its power in time. It took the endeavours of Masaryk and Karel Kálal to revive the idea in the *fin de siècle* era – initially, as an additional tool in the framework of arguing for imperial reforms, and then for the brand-new idea of independence.[25]

However, it was clear that the new cause would not be able to be victorious from within – it needed the support of the outside world. Thus, Masaryk made use of the network of the so-called 'Mafie' based on his circle of Bohemian allies, focusing especially on the cause of foreign propaganda. The Czech leader himself went into exile in December 1914. When he decided to switch sides to the Entente, he called on his local contacts from the period before the war – importantly, Seton-Watson, amongst others.[26]

The Scottish intellectual and the Czech politician had already met in Rotterdam during the October of 1914. Here, the latter was able to convince Seton-Watson that the ancient Habsburg Empire must be destroyed and showed him the plans of a successor state: 'Bohemia'.[27] When Masaryk arrived in London in September 1915, his Scottish patron secured him a position at the newly-founded School of Slavonic and East European Studies – and with it, an excellent opportunity to promote Czechoslovak secessionism. Finally, the Czech politician convinced his friend that the project of the *European Review* must be revived in order to serve the aims of the new times.[28]

This initiative led to the birth of the influential periodical, *The New Europe*, that united the national secessionists from the Habsburg Empire and their

24   Seton-Watson and Seton-Watson (1981: 98–99).
25   Marzik (1990: 191–92).
26   Neville (2010: 7, 21).
27   Neville (2010: 24).
28   Hanak (1962: 102–31, 210).

supporters within Great Britain. Published from October 1916, the journal appeared not only in the British Isles, but also in France, Italy and the United States. The society of the periodical was transnational in its setting, uniting co-workers from Serbia through France to the United States within its ranks. Being far more than a 'mere' originator, Masaryk contributed much to the successes of the *New Europe* by giving further ideas to its editorial board.

Upon his arrival in England, the Czech politician became one of the most energetic champions of the so-called 'principle of nationality'. The journalist C. Ernest Fayle, the leaders of the *Morning Post* and the *Manchester Guardian* already employed the notion to argue for the dissolution of the hostile Habsburg Monarchy into national units in 1914. Naturally, Masaryk and the *New Europe* were eager to follow their examples.[29] The Czech intellectual also convinced the journal's staff to adopt the spatial concept of *Mitteleuropa* (Central Europe). Although it already came into existence at the beginning of the 19th century, the term acquired importance during the First World War, standing for the German designs of imperial expansion as envisioned by the liberal nationalist Friedrich Naumann, the historian Hermann Ocken and the geographer Karl Haushofer, amongst others.[30] On the other hand, it also became a conceptual counter-weapon in the hands of Masaryk and his comrades.[31] In fact, the first leader of the *New Europe* – written by the Czech politician – stated that upon the basis of this foundation of alliances and conquests, Germany aimed for nothing less than 'world domination'.[32] On the other hand, the staff of the periodical also understood 'Central Europe' as a collection of territories to be liberated from the yoke of the hostile Central Powers. In this sense, Masaryk circumscribed the region in his memorandum *The Eleventh Hour* (1916), equating it to 'the East of Germany, Austria–Hungary, the Balkans and the Eastern part of Russia (Poland)' [sic!].[33] Thus, the politician contributed greatly to the transfer of a highly influential geopolitical term from the local to the Anglo-Saxon context.

In addition to this, the Czech intellectual was a useful member of the *New Europe* as an expert of local conditions as well, writing articles on the Habsburg Empire and the concept of Czechoslovakia. The latter shed light on how the politician explained the circumstances of the present, imagined the future

---

29 Hanak (1962: 43).
30 Trencsényi (2017: 166–67).
31 Nolte (1995: 12).
32 T.G. Masaryk, "Pangermanism and the Eastern Question", *The New Europe*, I:1 (16 October 1916).
33 *At the Eleventh Hour*, Seton-Watson Collection (hereafter: SEW), London, UCL School of Slavonic and East European Studies, box 2/3 fold. 3, 29.

and promoted his related ideas in the West – from whose public, however, he also received critiques and impacts.

From this aspect, especially *Pangermanism and the Zone of Small Nations* (14 December 1916) proved to be important with regards to Masaryk's views on the national concept. Following the views of the German philosopher Johann Gottfried Herder, the author made a distinction between the 'organic' national community and the 'artificial' state. This became important in connection the 'Central Zone' of Europe as identified by Masaryk: diverse territories ruled by the multi-ethnic empires of Russia, Austria–Hungary and Germany. The Czech leader argued that, in contrast to nation and state colliding in the West, the Eastern entities were of a 'mixed' or 'special' nature – which was a source of great disturbances and conflicts known as the 'Oriental Question'.[34] In other words, Masaryk took ideas on nationalism that had already been explained to him concerning Great Britain and started to promote these on the pages of the *New Europe*.

Soon enough, a criticism arrived in the image of British historian A.F. Giles' article *What is Nationality?* on 28 January 1917. A Scottish specialist in Ancient history, Giles argued that the Czech intellectual confused the term 'race' (ethnicity) with 'nation'. In contrast, Giles pointed out that the course of history led from the transformation of single races first to mixed nations and then, to statehood.[35] Masaryk failed to answer these points openly in the *New Europe*, although he did present his views on the subject in a letter to Seton-Watson. The Czech politician did accept some points brought up by Giles – for instance, he agreed that the Belgian, Swiss and Scottish communities were the products of the historical combination of ethnicities. On the other hand, Masaryk still viewed nations as entities based on racial foundations. He also suggested that the term 'nationality' would be more adequate to apply to European conditions, based on the languages used by various groups. Finally, he made interesting remarks on Giles' ideas, stating that

> Mr. Giles' objection is typically English [...] [He] confounds this so called [sic!] *"political nation"* with nationality. The state creates in its members the consciousness of common citizenship, but no nationality.[36]

The collision between the Masaryk's and Giles's views of nation – the latter shared by the British associates of the *New Europe* group – were of special

---

34　T.G. Masaryk, "Pangermanism and the Zone of Small Nations", *The New Europe*, I:9 (14 December 1916).
35　A.F. Giles, "What is Nationality?", *The New Europe*, II:14 (18 January 1917).
36　Masaryk, letter to Seton-Watson, 1917, SEW, box 17/16, fold. 6.

importance in connection to the future of Central Europe. The debate signified an important difference between the uses of fundamental terms such as 'nation' when it came to the Central European secessionists and their Western European supporters that set the basis for a transnational discussion over these ideas. In addition to this, it was also true that both the mixed ethnic conditions of the region and the importance of other factors when it came to the conceptualization of the future state system made the existence of national minorities inevitable. The age-old question of Czech–German antagonism also needed a theoretical solution already during the Great War – and Masaryk indeed paid a lot of attention to the problem.

All of these issues appeared for the first time during the Rotterdam meeting of the Czech politician and Seton-Watson in 1914. Importantly, Masaryk brought the *Staatsrecht* concept into the picture again when envisioning the future 'Bohemia':

> His arguments in favour of the **historic** Bohemia-Moravia-Silesia plus the Slovak districts [of Northern Hungary], as opposed to a new Czecho-Slovak **racial** state, rest on the extreme difficulty of drawing a tenable frontier on a basis of ethnography.[37]

This argument received further strengthening in Masaryk's study *The Future Status of Bohemia*, in the *New Europe* volume of 22 February 1917. The Czech leader understood the demands posed by him as a 'fair application of majority'. The politician argued that the insistence on historical borders responded best to the ethnic problems of the Bohemian, Moravian and Silesian landscapes. While he did not reject the idea of future frontier ratifications in favour of Germany, Masaryk made further demands for the Czech-inhabited areas of Lower Austria, Prussian Silesia and the province of Lusatia, populated by the Slavic Sorbs.[38]

One way or another, the future state would undoubtedly be a home to a sizeable German minority – a question addressed by Masaryk from 1914 onwards. When negotiating with Seton-Watson in Rotterdam, the Czech leader proposed that the government of the future state would promote a return to local identity in the form of a renewed Bohemian patriotism as opposed to the threat of German nationalism. Masaryk was positive that the defeat of Germany would accelerate this process. Additionally, the politician promised the

---

[37] Memorandum based on Seton-Watson's 'original notes of conversations at Rotterdam with Masaryk', SEW, box 17/16 fold. 3., 6.

[38] T.G. Masaryk, "The Future Status of Bohemia", *The New Europe*, II:19 (22 February 1917).

establishment of a tolerant national policy that would have secured the cultural rights of minorities.[39] It was especially stressed in *The Future Status of Bohemia* that the Czechs did not seek to oppress Germans – as historically, they only longed for an equal state of affairs. As for the future state, Masaryk proposed the title 'Bohemia' due to its historical and supra-national nature, also referring to the ancient co-existence of various nationalities in these lands.[40] In other words, while 'minority' was conceptualized by Masaryk as a position forced on the defeated, he also looked at Germans and others as possible 'co-nationals' of Czechoslovaks in the common state of the future.

Ironically, this development led to another shift by Masaryk during the First World War – this time, in favour of the political nation repudiated by him earlier. This development reached its peak in the intellectual's own *Nová Evropa* (*The New Europe*), written first in Czech during the Winter of 1917/18. As opposed to his earlier views, Masaryk now made a distinction between 'nation' (*národ*) and 'people' (*lid*). Although he still did not adhere his commitment to the idea of the political nation (*národ politický*), the author asserted that the nation could be explained as a political community. Furthermore, Masaryk now used the terms 'nation' and 'nationality' (*národnost*) distinctively. All of these changes brought the ideas of the author closer to those of his supporters in the *New Europe*. On the other hand, the Czech politician did not talk about the future 'Bohemia' anymore, but the country of the Czechoslovaks (*Československý stát*).[41] This meant that the Masarykian position became more twisted, as it projected a nation-state that would have been a home to various national communities. As for the latter, Masaryk identified the ethnicities of the future Czechoslovakia as 'national minorities' (*národní minority*). Masaryk stated that these groups would receive full national rights – and possibly, extraterritorial cultural autonomy. The author listed Austro-Marxism as an important source of this idea. In a side-note, he also mentioned that territorial designs (*autonomie teritoriální*) were also parts of this concept.[42]

However, in 1917, a new concept appeared on the ideological fronts of the Great War: that of self-determination. It was the Provisional Government of the Russian Empire that first declared its commitment to the principle after the February Revolution.[43] In response to the situation, the Czech politician soon travelled to the seething country to promote the establishment of the

---

39   Memorandum based on Seton-Watson's 'original notes...', p. 4.
40   Masaryk, "The Future Status of Bohemia", p. 171.
41   Masaryk (1920: 74, 178).
42   Masaryk (1920: 93–95, 164).
43   Manela (2007: 37).

famous Czechoslovak Legion. In a Petrograd interview of 21 May 1917, Masaryk supported the statements of the new government and understood their concept as a right of nations to unite and secede from alien rule.[44] In *Nová Evropa*, the politician used self-determination (*právo národů na sebeurčení*) as a fundamental argument for Czechoslovak independence and European reconstruction.[45]

The Czech leader naturally utilized the new concept for the causes of the Czechoslovak movement; on the other hand, the notion played a part in the conceptualization and the propagation of his political community as well. In the absence of Masaryk, it was the publicist Vladimir Nosek who expressed related ideas in the *New Europe* of 14 November 1918. In *The German Minority in Bohemia: A Czech View*, the author pointed out that certain representatives of the Bohemian German population opposed the idea of their separation from the new state. The secession of German Bohemia (*Deutschböhmen*) would also have deprived the remaining territories of precious resources and would have made the successful realization of Czechoslovak self-determination impossible.[46]

By this time, the self-determination discourse of the First World War went through fundamental changes. After the their *coup d'état* of November 1917 the victorious Bolsheviks promoted the idea and utilized it in opposition to the 'imperialistic' designs of the traditional Great Powers. Although the followers of Lenin stood for the understanding of self-determination as a right of nationalities to secede from imperial rules, Masaryk could not take their side due to their anti-bourgeois and radically revolutionary standpoint. On the other hand, the leading politicians of the West eventually decided to counteract Bolshevik propaganda by partially adopting its terminology. Both the British Prime Minister Lloyd George and the American President Woodrow Wilson committed to the idea of self-determination – the latter proving to be more influential. As opposed to the Bolsheviks, Wilson coupled self-determination with his ideas of 'government by consent' and originally interpreted the former as a right of not ethnic, but civic nations.[47] The transforming ideas of Masaryk fitted this agenda. In fact, the Czechoslovak propaganda in the United States had already described the 'Bohemian Question' as

---

44 Zeman (1991: 95).
45 Masaryk (1920: 74–81).
46 "The German Minority in Bohemia: A Czech View", *The New Europe*, IX:109 (14 November 1918).
47 Unterberger (1989: 83–91).

a problem of geography and violated state rights, implying that the solution – the future state of Czechoslovakia – should involve not only the Czech population, but other ethnicities of a larger historical-political entity as well.[48]

The First World War ended officially in November 1918. The Central Powers suffered defeat, and Czechoslovakia – with its National Council recognized by the forces of Entente – proclaimed its independence on 28 October 1918. From that point on, the task of Masaryk and his compatriots was to put their ideas into reality – ideas influenced not only by the experiences of the Czech national past, but the transnational settings of the war as well. On the other hand, the creation of Czechoslovak statehood in late 1918 finally created a dialogue with the Hungary of Oszkár Jászi.

4   For Imperial and National Reform: Jászi's Changing Radicalism (1914–1918)

While Masaryk tried to find support abroad, the Hungarian sociologist stayed in Austria–Hungary after the outbreak of the First World War. In opposition to the opinion of the majority, Jászi condemned the conflict for its destruction and bloodshed. The sociologist also stayed true to the values represented by him before 1914 – for instance, he remained a spokesman of national reconciliation and helped the representatives of nationalities ridden by the Hungarian government. However, Jászi's pacifism did not mean that he would not have seen opportunities coming up from the bloody streams of the war. In fact, the sociologist believed that the conflict would be the source of further development.[49] Retrospectively, it was surprising that he engaged in the support of certain projects – especially when it came to the national question.

One of these was none other than the aforementioned idea of *Mitteleuropa*. While Jászi opposed the militaristic expansion of the Central Powers led by 'Prussia' (Germany), he believed in the necessity of supra-national integration in the region. In his interpretation, the Central European empire of the future was the outcome of the mutual interdependence of local communities which could have created a democratic and pacifist commonwealth together.[50] In

---

48   "What the Papers Say", *The Bohemian Review*, I: I (February 1917); Ch. Pergler, "The Bohemian Question", *The Bohemian Review*, I:4 (May 1917).
49   Litván (2003: 99–101, 113).
50   Baka (1980: 701).

contrast, the sociologist denounced the principle of nationality as one leading into the directions of fragmentation and hostilities driven by chauvinism.[51]

When it came to Jászi's Central European concept, he also believed that the supra-national formation would have eventually solved the nationality question of the region. Already in 1915, he had explained this idea in one of the articles of the *Twentieth Century*. As the sociologist argued, Germans would have constituted more than half of the population – which would have been a firm background for the future state. Complemented with the Hungarian nation, this would have made an economic and cultural commonwealth of 120 million people stable and viable. This – along with the necessities dictated by economic considerations – would have resulted in the democratization, but also in the liberalization and humanization of nationality policies. Interestingly, Jászi projected the imperial expansion of Hungary within Central Europe; as he argued, the geographical position of the former would have predestined the nation to rule the Balkans in alliance with the Germans.[52] The Hungarian sociologist was not alone locally to view the notion in positive terms; in fact, Polish socialists also contemplated the possibility whether their respective nation would benefit from the processes of regional economic integration.[53] This was largely due to the fact that the aforementioned Naumann – who published the most influential work concerning the idea of *Mitteleuropa* – did not aim at abolishing non-German identities; he introduced the imperial concept as one of co-operative hegemony and an alternative to Russian domination for local peoples.[54] Staying true to his socialistic viewpoints, Jászi envisioned a future of transnational and international co-operation for the peoples of Central Europe.

Despite the worrying omens of the First World War, Jászi also maintained the view that the ethnic problems of Hungary did not need solutions as radical as other national questions in the East of Europe. In an early 1918 article of the *Twentieth Century*, titled *The Southern Slavic Crisis* (*A délszláv krízis*), the sociologist supported the idea of Yugoslav unification in the name of self-determination (*önrendelkezés*). On the other hand, he asserted that Hungary – while containing a sizeable Southern Slavic population – did not have any reasons to fear this process. As for the latter, Jászi thought that the combination

---

51   Litván (2003: 101–02).
52   O. Jászi, "A középeurópai gazdasági közeledés és a magyarság jövője" [The Central European Economic Repprochement and the Future of the Hungarian Nation], *Huszadik Század*, 8 (1915), 129–30.
53   Trencsényi (2017: 168).
54   Houžvička (2015: 92–93).

of a 'just' nationality policy and the possibility of co-nationals maintaining contacts through borders would be adequate.[55]

Although being influenced by other ideas of the war, the sociologist showed a strong commitment to these beliefs even during the last moments of the Great War. In October 1918, he published the book *The Future of the Monarchy* (*A Monarchia jövője*). The sociologist pointed out that that as opposed to the West, the diverse domains of Austria–Hungary, Russia and the Balkans only reached a 'pre-national' state, the local structures not providing adequate background for the solution of the 'nationality question' (*nemzetiségi kérdés*). Jászi identified 'nation' as a politically organized, united community in a righteous pursuit of the right of self-determination (*önrendelkezési jog*).[56]

On the other hand, the author did not understand the notion as a right to secession. Importantly, Jászi did not adopt the idea from the Russian revolution – as for references, he looked at Wilson's Fourteen Points as announced by the US president on 8 January 1918. It is not to be forgotten that these talked vaguely about the future of the Habsburg Empire, demanding only the possibility of 'autonomous development' secured for local nationalities – a phrasing that could have gained various meanings through possible interpretations. Jászi opted for a minimalist understanding, asserting that national independence must be achieved in a 'reasonable way'. As for requirements, the sociologist talked about the necessity of possessing adequate material and cultural resources in order to create a proper national state. Additionally, he also asserted that the formation of new structures should have provided a solution for the nationality question – while respecting the economically and culturally viable 'old statehoods'. Finally, the vindication of self-determination must have led towards future co-operation and integration between peoples.[57] Consequently, Jászi argued for the continued existence of the Habsburg Empire in a federalized form as an economic and political necessity in the region.[58]

As for the latter, the sociologist made a distinction between cases where national unity was possible and to be created and those where certain communities could only have existed as 'nationality minorities' (*nemzetiségi kisebbségek*). He applied the former criteria to the future states of the Monarchy: Hungary, Austria, Bohemia (understood as the Lands of the Crown of St.

---

55   O. Jászi, "A délszláv krízis" [The Southern Slavic Crisis], *Huszadik Század*, 7 (1918), 50–52.
56   Jászi (1988: 13–15).
57   Baka (1980: 700–01).
58   Jászi (1988: 75–77).

Wenceslaus), Poland and the Southern Slavic Illyria. As for the latter, Jászi asserted that in some cases, the creation of separate national territories was not possible, either due to the mixed nature of populations or the inadequate states of national developments. As for these, he proposed that the communities of these areas should be called 'nationality minorities' and were to be invested with the right of 'cultural autonomy' (*kulturális autonómia*) as a form of self-government. He admittedly used the ideas of Austro-Marxism as a source when it came to the subject; however, he criticized them for not realizing the difference between the needs of the developed 'nation' and 'nationality'. The sociologist asserted that the German community of Bohemia could acquire its own administrative area within the respective state – thus, Jászi's concept included even the idea of territorial autonomy.[59] In contrast, the sociologist stressed that the Kingdom of Hungary was not in need of reconstruction. The author argued that the country developed organically throughout history by means of geography, administration and law and was under the firm rule of Hungarian 'cultural hegemony' (*kultúrhegemónia*).[60] With this remark, Jászi remained within the boundaries of traditional Hungarian political language concerning the minority question – while in other aspects, he exceeded both his contemporary co-nationals and his earlier self.

However, the generous proposals of the *Future of the Monarchy* could not avoid the effects of the First World War drawing to its end. Many of the national movements that had demanded autonomy earlier aimed for independence in October 1918; it would have been impossible for the secessionists to have stayed within the defeated Habsburg Empire instead of opting for independence. Jászi could not even convince the representatives of Transleithenian nationalities. The pro-Masaryk Slovak politician Anton Štefánek, for instance, accused the Hungarian sociologist of representing the same intention towards 'Magyarization' as those of the government – only masked by a different conceptual language.[61]

Nonetheless, fate gave a chance not only to Masaryk, but also to Jászi to realize his ideals at the end of the First World War. On 28 October 1918 (the same day Czechoslovakia proclaimed its independence), the so-called 'Aster Revolution' broke out in Hungary. As a result, the Austrian Emperor and Hungarian King Charles of Habsburg (1916–1918) appointed the government lead by Count Mihály Károly – the united camp of reform-minded parties, the Radical Party

---

59   Jászi (1988: 16, 38–40, 50, 99, 114–15).
60   Jászi (1988: 24, 69).
61   Litván (2003: 127).

of Jászi being also a part of this coalition. It is no wonder that the second version of *The Future of the Monarchy* now bore the title *The Future of Hungary and the United Danubian States* – a sign that times had changed for the sake of new structures.[62]

5   Great War-era Hungarian and Czech Contexts (1914–1918)

By the end of the First World War, both Jászi and Masaryk gained a chance to prove the worth of their previous commitments. However, both intellectuals were subject to their national contexts when it came to the realization of their ideals. In terms of not only politics but also of concepts, the local political field was dominated by other ideas and political figures up until 1918.

As opposed to the initiatives of Masaryk from 1914 on, the bulk of Czech public opinion counted on the future survival of the Habsburg Monarchy – and still believed in the possibility of reforms in favour of their national goals, the war-time situation providing an adequate background for the realization of these aims. Even though the Young Czech leader KAREL Karel Kramář advocated the view in August 1914 that the Great War was nothing less than an ultimate struggle between 'Slavs' and 'Teutons', no home parties – including his own – stood openly for the cause of independence. Soon enough, even the sprouts of resistance were suppressed by the Austro–Hungarian military that took control of Cisleithenia. Consequently, Kramář was imprisoned along with other national leaders in 1915.[63]

In May 1917, the liberal reforms of the new monarch, Charles of Habsburg, allowed Czechs to openly make their voice heard for the first time during the Great War. On the first session of the re-opened Reichsrat, it was František Staněk who spoke in the name of the Czech Union – the united camp of national parties. The Agrarian politician demanded nothing less than the establishment of an autonomous Czechoslovak province in the Habsburg Empire, referring to self-determination as a leading principle behind these raisings. Retrospectively, the influence of the Masarykian movement was clear when it came to these plans as the secessionists encouraged locals to utilize their ideas for the Czech cause.[64]

---

62   Litván (2003: 125, 135–39).
63   Rees (1992: 10–11, 15–16).
64   Agnew (2004: 164–65, 167–68).

The subsequent speeches of Czech representatives in the Reichsrat mainly followed the lines set on 30 May – in that Austrian Imperial Council that consisted of all the nationalities of Cisleithania. Thus, the national politicians needed to engage in debates with others. Naturally, the greatest opponents of their ideas were the German representatives of the Bohemian provinces who aimed for the separation of their national areas from those of the Czechs. The solution of the Slavic representatives was to propose autonomy (using the German term of *Autonomie*) for the minority community as it was apparent already from the speech of the Young Czech Adolf Stránský on 12 June 1917.[65] On the other hand, the words of Antonín Klofáč on 22 January 1918 were especially interesting in this regard. While pointing out the mixed nature of the Bohemian landscape that prevented the separation of national communities, the Agrarian representative made an explicit reference to the introduction of national-individual autonomy in the Ukrainian People's Republic, claiming that such solutions were characteristic for the Slavic handling of multi-ethnic communities. While proposing a non-territorial solution to the German problem of the Bohemian lands, the Klofáč's was also an example that the Czechs were attentive of their international contexts and did not hesitate to engage in transnational adaptations of ideas for the interest of their multi-ethnic vision of Bohemia.[66]

On the other hand, local parties only made use of all of these concepts to improve their arguments for the reform of the Habsburg Empire and the autonomy of the Bohemian lands. It was not until early 1918 that Czech politicians started to see the creation of an independent Czechoslovak nation-state as an alternative to the imperial framework.[67] As an important step towards this outcome, the so-called 'Epiphany Declaration' of 6 January 1918 demanded independence once more in the name of self-determination. It was a new and telling element of the statement that it did not make any references to the future role of the Habsburg dynasty or their empire in connection to the life of the Czech nation.[68]

---

65   The speech of Adolf Stránský in the *Reichsrat*, 12 June 1917, in: *Stenographische Protokolle des Abgeordnetenhauses des Reichsrates 1861–1918. XII. Legislaturperiode, XXII. Session: 30. 05. 1917 – 12. 11. 1918.* http://alex.onb.ac.at/cgi-content/alex?aid=spa&datum=0022&size=45 &page=1097

66   The speech of Antonín Klofáč in the *Reichsrat*, 22 January 1918, in: *Stenographische Protokolle des Abgeordnetenhauses des Reichsrates 1861–1918. XII. Legislaturperiode, XXII. Session: 30. 05. 1917 – 12. 11. 1918.* http://alex.onb.ac.at/cgi-content/alex?aid=spa&datum=0022 &size=45&page=3772

67   Orzoff (2009: 40, 46–47).

68   Agnew (2004: 170).

Similarly, the thoughts of Jászi only reached the Hungarian mainstream, dominated by conservative approaches to the national question, at a relatively late stage. The intellectual could convince the progressive camp of local political forces to accept his theories by 1917.[69] On the other hand, the latter gathering lacked both the political positions and an authoritative figure equivalent to that of the opposing side: Count István Tisza, the Prime Minister from 1914 to 1917. Focusing on the putative interests of the Hungarian nation, the politician stood for the continuation of war efforts and the preservation of the dualistic structure until late 1918. Consequently, Tisza denounced the principle of national self-determination as a notion posing danger to the existence of Austria–Hungary, clearly belonging to the armoury of hostile forces.[70]

On the other hand, even the political system of Transleithenia, designed to fit the interests of expansive Hungarian nationalism, could not prevent the appearance of transnational debates in relation to the ideas of new times, especially during the worsening war situation of late 1918. In his speech of 19 October 1918 in the Hungarian Parliament, the Slovakian representative Ferdiš Juriga argued for vindication of the right the self-determination for all the 'nations' – and not the 'nationalities' – of Hungary.[71] Even though these ideas already went against the conceptual language of the ethnic Hungarian mainstream, Juriga did not adhere to secessionism – he argued for the federalization of the country. In addition to this, the Slovakian politician used Jászi as a point of reference, claiming that the Hungarian intellectual was the only one to deal scientifically with the national question and the only one capable of its understanding.[72] In view of the impending defeat of Hungary, its political elite and public opinion was also finally ready to accept new concepts by late 1918.[73] Even Tisza made it clear that the 'Wilsonian principles' (the 14 Points and with them, self-determination) must be the founding stones of the future, – although only in case the integrity of historical Hungary was preserved during the process of transformation.[74]

---

69 Litván (2003: 117).
70 Szász (2008: 5–6).
71 The speech of Ferdiš Juriga in the Hungarian Parliament, 19 October 1918, *Képviselőházi napló, 1910. XLI. kötet. 1918. július 24.–November 16*, in: https://library.hungaricana.hu/hu/view/OGYK_KN-1910_41/?pg=359&layout=s.
72 Ibid., https://library.hungaricana.hu/hu/view/OGYK_KN-1910_41/?pg=360&layout=s.
73 Szász (2009: 51).
74 Szász (2008: 7).

6 The Moments of Truth: Czechoslovak and Hungarian Nationality Policies in 1918/19

By the end of the First World War, Masaryk and Jászi had both gained leading positions within their countries, the status of which, however, were sharply different. The leaders of the Entente recognized the Czechoslovak National Council as a representative of a victorious nation allied to them; however, Hungary suffered defeat along with the Habsburg Empire. Consequently, while Masaryk was to create and expand his Czechoslovakia, Jászi faced the task of salvaging what was possible from historical Hungary. For this reason, the Károlyi government appointed the Hungarian sociologist to be the head of the brand-new 'Nationality Ministry' (*Nemzetiségi Minisztérium*) in November 1918. Jászi immediately started to work, trying to subdue the probable effects of defeat by initiating negotiations with the nationalities of Hungary. It transpired soon afterwards that the late war-era propositions of the intellectual fell far from the expectations of these groups – thus, the sociologist came up with a new idea: the creation of an 'Eastern Switzerland'. Hoping that national self-determination could be realized for all parties within Hungary in a negotiated way, Jászi proposed the establishment of territorial autonomies.[75]

This tactic seemed to work in case of a couple of local national movements as Jászi managed to deal with the representatives of Slovaks, Germans and Ruthenians. These results, however, did not last for a long time – as the casting vote belonged to the Entente and its allies: Czechoslovakia, Serbia and Romania, both hungry for territories. Realizing the failure of his tactics, Jászi placed emphasis on the defence of Hungarian ethnic territories from December 1918. The sociologist followed the ideas of Hungarian Social Democrats in this respect. This initiative regrettably failed due to the inadequate defence policy of the Károlyi government – consequently, the forces of states neighbouring historical Hungary substantially occupied wide areas of the country.[76] The end came for Jászi and his allies in the image of the Communist *coup d'état* of 21 March 1919 – after which the intellectual was forced into exile, condemned for the disintegration of his country by the Horthy system of the inter-war period.[77]

If Jászi failed to act successfully as a 'salvager', then Masaryk received the more grateful task of the 'founder' – which did not mean that his position would have been an easier one. It was especially the realization of the Czechoslovak political national concept that proved to be difficult due to the tensions between the

---

75 Szarka (1990: 69–71).
76 Szarka (1990: 71–73).
77 Litván (2003: 164–69).

new government and the representatives of local Germans. The parties of the latter proclaimed the establishment of their autonomous provinces: *Deutschböhmen* ('German Bohemia'), *Böhmerwaldgau* ('Bohemian Woods'), *Sudetenland* and *Süd-Böhmen* ('Southern Bohemia') in the collapsing Habsburg Empire during October and November of 1918. All Bohemian German parties were united in the belief that by relying on the ideas of Wilson, their communities could vindicate their right of self-determination – by which they usually meant their joining of German-Austria or Germany. The Czechoslovak government blocked these initiatives by occupying the respective areas.[78]

Nonetheless, the founders of the new state did not give up on the idea of political nationhood despite these conflicts. It was the Czechoslovak constitution of 1920 that proved the serious nature of Masarykian intentions. The preamble of the latter announced the commitment of the 'Czechoslovak nation' (*národ Československý*) to the ideas of modernity, 'embodied in the motto of self-determination' (*obsažených v hesle sebeurčení*). The entity identified national, racial and religious minorities (*menšin narodnich, nabozenskych a rasových*) and established a system of cultural rights for them. It is of great importance that only one community counted as a 'national minority' according to the constitution: that of the Sub-Carpathian Rusyns with an autonomous, 'self-governing territory' (*samospravné uzemí*).[79] This was due to earlier negotiations between the representatives of the respective national movement and the Czechoslovak leadership. Consequently, the Carpatho-Ruthenians joined Czechoslovakia voluntarily in return for territorial autonomy. This was granted rather easily by the leadership of the latter as, conceptually, the Rusyns were not parts of the Czechoslovak ethnic core of the state.[80] All in all, the Czechoslovak nation became a legal-political construction instead of one limited to an ethnic concept.

7 Two Sides of the Same Coin? Comparison and Conclusions

Nobody living in the *fin de siècle* era could have forecast the changes brought upon the World by the First World War. Neither Jászi nor Masaryk were

---

78   Bruegel (1973: 22–23, 28).
79   *Sbírka zákonů a nařízení státu československého*, Wolters Kluwer, http://ftp.aspi.cz/opispdf/1920/026-1920.pdf (accessed on May 2, 2016) As opposed to Germans, the Rusyn population joined the Czechoslovak state as a result of negotiations between their national leaders and the government of the latter – thus, the outcome was truly a result of their 'self-determination'.
80   Heiman (2009: 37, 68).

exceptions to this rule as shown by the revolutionary transformation of their ideas during the brief period between 1914–1918. The controversies of this development effected their practical policies when it came to the Czechoslovak founding of the state and the Hungarian attempts to preserve the historical borders. Thus, it is important to put their ideas besides each other and to compare them.

Influenced by the ideas of the political Left, both the Hungarian sociologist and the Czech philosopher identified the relationship between ethnicities as a grave problem of the East of Europe, either known as the 'Oriental' or the 'nationality question'. Both saw the solution in the creation of national territories independent of each other, although Masaryk took this step by his own will in 1914. On the other hand, Jászi did this under the pressure of conditions in late 1918. Although he repeatedly reacted to the changes of times, the sociologist treated the territorial integrity of Hungary as a priority through the observed period – this position of defence averted him from reaching the same radical position as his Czech counterpart. From this aspect, the Hungarian representative of the new current mimicked the conservative standpoint of the mainstream national movement.

The positions of Jászi and Masaryk also differed gravely in connection to a supra-national idea of the Great War: that of the German *Mitteleuropa*. While the Hungarian sociologist welcomed the concept rather positively, the Czech leader saw a lethal danger to the cause of the Czech(oslovak) movement in this initiative. This did not mean that Masaryk would have opposed the creation of supra-national entities in the future; however, his priority was to found a nation-state *and* to reconcile this concept with the reality of ethnic diversity. For the Czech politician, the main goal and the desired destination was Czechoslovakia – while for Jászi, the future of multinational Hungary was to be solved within the context of regional problems.

The conceptualizations of 'nation', 'nationality' and 'minority' by the respective intellectuals followed the same approach. Jászi adjusted to the traditions of the Hungarian political language, setting up a hierarchical relationship between the political community of the 'nation' and ethnicity-based 'nationality', also treating the latter as a synonym to 'minority'. In the sociologist's interpretation, 'nation' was a fully developed entity to be entitled with the full right of 'self-determination' – the most radical interpretations of which, however, he did not accept. 'Nationalities' or 'minorities' lacked some of the requirements of national communities; as for them, Jászi stood firmly for the securement of cultural rights for these groups within larger political entities.

On the other hand, Masaryk also used the concepts as they appeared in the framework of Czech nationalism before the war. Thus, those were 'nation' and 'nationality', which acted as synonyms this time, stressing the equality of ethnic communities in the empires of the East. 'Minority', on the other hand, became important in the ideological construction of the nation-state. Firstly, this was to be the position of the defeated; in time, however, Masaryk tried to treat the future communities of Czechoslovakia as co-nationals with full rights within the framework of a political nation. From the philosopher's aspect, 'self-determination' was to be understood in its total meaning: a right to secession. Nonetheless, Masaryk put the same limitations as Jászi on the vindication of this privilege when it came to other ethnicities, treating the territorial integrity of the Bohemian lands as a priority in the name of *Staatsrecht*.

When comparing Masaryk and Jászi from this aspect, one could identify counter-rotating arcs with respect to the transformation of their ideas. The Czech politician completed a round by accepting, negating and accepting the concept of political nationhood again. Importantly, this happened only partly due to the pressure of the outside World (for example, MASARYK's Masaryk's Western relations) as the philosopher also identified the conceptualization of a civic community to be a solution for the ethnic problems of the Bohemian provinces. On the other hand, Jászi only tried to upgrade the idea of the Hungarian political nation as late as 1918. Those were only the contemporary circumstances that made him accept the fact the historical Hungarian Kingdom was about to dissolve and that the future belonged to the system of nation-states.

Consequently, it is also of great importance that both thinkers expressed their ideas and were under the influence of transnational contexts. Masaryk did not only gain a chance to propagate the cause of Czechoslovak secessionism in the *New Europe*; his supporters also pressed him to re-formulate his ideas on 'nation' and the future community of Czechoslovakia. On the other hand, while Jászi was not a part of such a broad international framework, he modified his thoughts by opening up towards other national groups in Hungary – some of which were also attentive towards his ideas in this regard.

When it comes to local contexts, it is of great importance that both intellectuals represented minority positions up until the end of the Great War. Nonetheless, while starting essentially as 'outsiders', both lived to see the acceptance of their ideas by 1918 and consequently, gained leading positions in their newly-founded (or reformed) countries. From this aspect, both their careers were highly successful.

It was their relationship with the outside world that created a real difference between Jászi and Masaryk. The Hungarian sociologist argued and hoped for national and imperial reform from within. In contrast, the Czech politician tried to utilize external forces for his cause and engaged in an extensive foreign propaganda for these aims. Masaryk's work was a persistent and cautious one, counting with the instability of fate. The Czech leader took the survival of the Habsburg Monarchy into consideration until 1916, aiming for the federalization of the empire as a minimum in this case.[81] Fate, however, proved to be graceful for the cause of Czechoslovak independence, that became supported by the Entente by the end of the First World War. Jászi, on the other hand, could only rely on the support of his Hungarian political allies in a huge, hostile and seething World.

> 'I was walking on the same roads, towards the same goals as Masaryk. Our views concerning the World and our understanding of the problems were also similar. And the results? On one side: the foundation of a state and a fully, brightly lived life. On the other? A broken country and a ravaged life.'[82]

These remorseful lines were written by Jászi later and in most aspects, his observations were right as for the comparison between him and the Czech politician. The paths of the emigrant and the founder crossed once more after 1919 as the Hungarian intellectual visited the Czechoslovakian Republic on a few occasions and met Masaryk during the 1920s and 1930s. Being able to voice his opinions only from abroad, Jászi continuously argued for both the need of democratization in Hungary and the necessity of developing closer relations with the neighbouring states. Relying on his own interpretation of Masaryk's words during their exchanges, he also believed that the former would take the rectification of borders in consideration in case of a democratic transformation in Hungary – a hope that lacked a firm background.[83]

As opposed to the Hungarian sociologist, one could correctly see Masaryk as a more active and more daring individual. The dissolution of the Habsburg Monarchy seemed to be impossible in 1914 and was a possibility hardly accepted internationally even by early 1918. The foundation of the Czechoslovakian nation would have been unimaginable without the ideological and propagandistic activities of Masaryk – whose efforts were hardly paralleled in the oeuvre of Jászi.

Bibliography

Agnew, H. (2004), *The Czechs and the Lands of the Bohemian Crown*, Stanford: Hoover Institution Press.

---

81 E.g. Masaryk to Eduard Beneš, 12 September 1916, in Hadler (1995: 355–56).
82 Quoted by Gyurgyák (2007: 163–64).
83 Litván (2003: 247).

Szász, Z. (2008), „Tisza István – a háború jelképe" [István Tisza – the Symbol of the War], *História*, 30:9 (2008), pp. 3–18.

Szász, Z. (2009), "Magyar szemmel Erdély elszakadásáról" [The Secession of Transylviania from a Hungarian Perspective], *História*, 31: pp. 5–6.

Baka, A. (1980), „A nemzetiségi kérdés megközelítésének alakulása Jászi Oszkár koncepciójában" [The Transformation of the Approach to the Nationality Question in the Concepts of Oszkár Jászi], *Jogtudományi Közlöny*, 35: 10, pp. 697–99.

Baka, A. (1990), *Eötvös Józseftól Jászi Oszkárig. A magyar nemzetiségi politikai gondolkodás változásai* [From József Eötvös to Oszkár Jászi. The Changes of Hungarian Thinking on Nationality Policies], Budapest: Közgazdasági és Jogi Könyvkiadó.

Bruegel, J.W. (1973), *Czechoslovakia before Munich. The German Minority Problem and British Appeasement Policy*, Cambridge: Cambridge UP.

Gyurgyák, J. (2007), *Ezzé lett magyar hazátok. A magyar nemzeteszme és nacionalizmus története* [This is what Your Magyar Country has Become. The History of Hungarian National Identity and Nationalism], Budapest: Osiris.

Hadler, F., ed. (1995), *Weg von Österreich! Das Weltkriegsexil von Masaryk und Beneš in Spiegel ihrer Briefe und Aufzeichnungen aus den Jahren 1914–1918. Eine Quellensammlung*, Berlin: Akademie Verlag.

Hanak, H. (1962), *Great Britain and Austria-Hungary during the First World War: A study in the formation of public opinion*, London/New York: Oxford UP.

Heiman, M. (2009), *Czechoslovakia. The State that Failed*, New Haven: Yale UP.

Houžvička, V. (2015), *Czechs and Germans 1848–2004. The Sudeten Question and the Transformation of Central Europe*, Prague: Karolinum Press.

Jászi, O. (1988), *A Monarchia jövője. A dualizmus bukása és a Dunai Egyesült Államok* [The Future of the Monarchy. The Fall of Dualism and the United Danubian States], Budapest: Maecenas.

Judson, P.M. (2006), *The Habsburg Empire. A New History*, Cambridge, MA / London: The Belknap Press of Harvard UP.

Juhász, J. (2010), *Föderalizmus és nemzeti kérdés* [Federalism and the National Question], Budapest: Gondolat.

Litván, G. (2003), *Jászi Oszkár*, Budapest: Osiris.

Manela, E. (2007), *The Wilsonian Moment*, Oxford/ New York: Oxford UP.

Marzik, Th.D. (1990), "The Slovakophile Relationship of T.G. Masaryk and Karel Kálal prior to 1914", in S.B. Winters (ed.), *T.G. Masaryk (1850–1937): Volume 1: Thinker and Politician*, Basingstoke: Palgrave Macmillan, 1990, pp. 191–92.

Masaryk, T.G. (1920), *Nová Evropa. Stanovisko slovanské*, Prague: Nakladem Gustáva Dubského.

Neumann, V. (2008), "Federalism and Nationalism in the Austro-Hungarian Monarchy: Aurel Popovici's Theory", in id., *Essays on Romanian Intellectual History*, Timișoara: Editura Universității de Vest, 65–80.

Neville, P. (2010), *Tomáš Masaryk and Eduard Beneš. Czechoslovakia. The peace conferences of 1919–23 and their aftermath*, London: Haus Publishing.

Nolte, C.E. (1995), "The New Central Europe of Thomas Garrigue Masaryk", in J.S. Micgiel (ed.), *Wilsonian East Central Europe: Current Perspectives*, New York: Pilsudski Institute, pp.

Pearson, R. (1983), *National Minorities in Eastern Europe 1848–1945*, Basingstoke: Macmillan.

Rees, L.H. (1992), *The Czechs during World War I. The Path to Independence*, New York/Boulder, Co: Columbia UP/East European Monographs.

Reifowitz, I. (2001), „Threads Intertwined: German National Egoism and Liberalism in Adolf Fischhof's Vision for Austria", *Nationalities Papers*, 29:3, pp. 441–43.

Szpoluk, R. (1981), *The Political Thought of Thomas G. Masaryk*, Boulder, CO: East European Monographs.

Orzoff, A. (2009), *Battle for the Castle. The Myth of Czechoslovakia in Europe, 1914–1948*, Oxford: Oxford UP.

Seton-Watson, H., & Ch. Seton-Watson (1981), *The Making of a New Europe. R.W. Seton-Watson and the last years of Austria-Hungary*, London: Methuen.

Szarka, L. (1990), "A méltányos nemzeti elhatárolódás lehetősége 1918 végén" [The Possibilites of Reasonable National Separation at the end of 1918], *Regio*, 1:1, 69–71.

Tarr, Z. (1999), "Ethnicity, Nationality, and Nationalism in Early Austrian-Hungarian Social Science", in J. Marcus (ed.), *Surviving the Twentieth Century: Social Philosophy from the Frankfurt School to the Columbia Faculty Seminars*, New Brunswick: Transaction Publishers, pp. 100–01.

Trencsényi, B. (2018), "Central Europe", in D. Mishkova & B. Trencsényi (eds.), *European Regions and Boundaries. A Conceptual History*, Oxford/New York: Berghahn, pp. 166–87.

Trencsényi, B., M. Janowski, M. Baár, M. Falina & M. Kopeček (2006), *A History of Modern Political Thought in East Central Europe. Volume I: Negotiating Modernity in the 'Long Nineteenth Century'*, Oxford, Oxford UP.

Unterberger, B.M. (1989), *The United States, Revolutionary Russia, and the Rise of Czechoslovakia*, Chapel Hill/London: University of North Carolina Press.

Zeman, Z. (1991), *The Masaryks: Making of Czechoslovakia*, London: Tauris & Co.

PART 2

Local Dynamics

CHAPTER 7

Micro-Nationalisms in Western Europe in the Wake of the First World War

Francesca Zantedeschi

> When the President talks of 'self-determination' what unit has he in mind? Does he mean a race, a territorial area, or a community? Without a definite unit which is practical, application of this principle is dangerous to peace and stability... The phrase is simply loaded with dynamite. It will raise hopes which can never be realized [...]. What a calamity that phrase was ever uttered! What misery it will cause!
>
> Robert Lansing, U.S. Secretary of State, at Paris Peace Conference, 1918[1]

∴

1   Introduction*

In January 1918, the US President, Woodrow Wilson, drew up a statement of principles to broker the peace plan that would end World War I. The outlined Fourteen Points called for, amongst others, the abolition of secret diplomacy, the elimination of customs barriers, the reduction of armaments, the protection of the interests of peoples subject to colonial regime, as well as sustaining the "autonomous development" of peoples of the Austro-Hungarian and Ottoman Empires; the establishment of a system of collective security and international law – the League of Nations – in order to maintain world peace and the political independence of both the small and large States. However, these programmatic points were not fully implemented during the Paris Peace Conference, which began in January 1919. From the outset, ideological controversies

---

* This paper is part of a research project funded by the Gerda Henkel Stiftung entitled *From the trenches to regionalist militancy. Regionalism as a form of dissent in the immediate aftermath of World War I* [AZ 50/F/17].
1   Lansing (1921: 97–98).

surrounded the very aims of Wilson's Plan itself. Indeed, its drafting brought to a head the clash between the ideal of a democratic peace and the objective of inflicting a punitive peace on the defeated States, not to mention the conflicting aims of affirming the principle of nationality and the interests of the victorious powers against those of various sub-national ethnic groups; the latter groups often populated entire regions beyond the confines of geographic territorial boundaries, making the application of the principle of self-determination of peoples extremely tenuous and controversial.

Despite the obstacles and practical problems that arose at the time of its implementation, the principle of self-determination brought about new national claims, since many "small nations" now felt empowered to take control of their own political destinie.

In this article, I will address the issue of the immediate repercussions of the principles of nationality and self-determination on micro-nationalisms in Western Europe – paying particular attention to France – in order to analyse the transnational dimension that characterized nationalist phenomena both during and after the War.

Before embarking on this analysis, however, a few introductory remarks about the notion of "micro-nationalisms" are needed. Michael Keating uses the term when writing about the French "submerged nationalities or *micronationalités*", in order to distinguish them "from the overarching and predominant nationality of France and the other 'nation-states' of Europe". As such, in France it accounts for those regionalist movements that did not succeed in integrating cultural, economic and political elements "into a mobilizing ideology based upon the claims of a territorial or ethnic group" and in managing to "relate them to identifiable territories".[2] The term "micro" therefore does not refer to the "size" or "geography" of the territory in question, but rather to the scope of the regionalist movements at issue. Stanley G. Payne, for his part, used the term "regional micronationalism" in relation to Spain, in particular with regard to Catalonia and part of the Basque provinces and their "centrifugal protest against the manifold frustrations attending the process of modernization", which "in part was a reaction against the relative failure of nineteenth-century liberalism in Spain.[3]

In the context of this article, the term "micro-nationalisms" will be used to deal with those national or regional movements whose claims were predominantly cultural as opposed to political, even if at times they did stake claims to minor political ambitions. Unlike major "peripheral" or "sub-state" nationalisms

---

2 Keating (1985).
3 Payne (1991: 482).

(such as, for example, the Catalan, Basque, and Flemish ones), whose political claims were radicalized and whose social base grew considerably after the First World War,[4] these micro-nationalisms never went so far as to claim independence, at any rate not in the 1920s, which is the period under examination. Arguably, they found it difficult to define clear and mobilizing objectives. Secondly, these micro-nationalisms had very limited social and political impact. Hence, the term of "micro-nationalisms" is preferred for the purpose of accounting for the moderateness of their political claims, as well as their limited social and political impact.

A final clarification before getting to the heart of the matter. The primary focus on French micro-nationalisms relates to the fact that in France, in the period under consideration (the aftermath of the Great War), numerous regionalist movements emerged, whose origins lay in the cultural awakening that many historical provinces had known in the previous century. Because of its (successful) model of State building, France had managed to confine the existing cultural and linguistic differences at regional level to a mere folkloric plan, by succeeding in forging a sentiment of national belonging that did not necessarily conflict with the existence of regional specificities. At the beginning of the twentieth century, the national rhetoric that represented France as a "*mosaïque merveilleuse*" was still predominant and was grounded in a conception of nation in which it was the combination of complementary regions that made for an admirable and productive French unity. The years leading up to the First World War were characterized by pervasive cultural regionalism and the growing debate over the administrative decentralization, which was understood as the "necessary redistribution of powers between the State and the local communities".[5] The *Fédération Régionaliste Française* (FRF), established by Jean Charles-Brun in 1901, had the purpose of bringing together the numerous proponents of decentralization, as well as regionalists and federalists irrespective of their political or religious convictions.[6] According to Charles-Brun, regionalism did not constitute a system as such, but rather a method that presupposed knowledge and respect of regional diversities. It represented a "test of conciliation" between tradition and progress, particularism and patriotism; and owing to the knowledge of provincial varieties it presupposed, it sought to balance the various economic forces to increase national

---

4   According to Hechter's definition, "*Peripheral nationalism occurs when a culturally distinctive territory resists incorporation into an expanding state, or attempts to secede and set up its own government (as in Quebec, Scotland and Catalonia). This type of nationalism is often spurred by the very efforts of state-building nationalism* [...]". See Hechter (2000: 17).
5   Boutin & Rouvillois (2003: 7).
6   On Charles-Brun and the FRF, see Wright (2003).

prosperity. The main point of convergence among regionalists was that only a punctual and radical reform of the organization of the State could generate and regenerate the wealth of the French nation. During the First World War, regionalists worked incessantly to disseminate their ideas, also because they believed that only federalism could guarantee world peace. As Charles-Brun explained on the occasion of a lecture delivered to the Ligue d'Action Régionaliste (founded by Jean Hennessy, in 1911) in December 1917, in fact, the idea of a League of Nations "appealed to French regionalists because of both 'tradition' and 'method'", and could prevail only if it was based on federalism.[7] As we shall see in the course of this article, the FRF reached its zenith in the years 1922–1926, also thanks to the influence it exercized on deputies of other parties.[8]

2   The Principle of Self-Determination and Western European Micro-Nationalisms

The principle of self-determination implies the right of a people to choose its own form of government, as well as determine its own political destiny. During the First World War, it was used to "emancipate" the peoples of the Austro-Hungarian and of the Turkish Empires. Accordingly, it was employed to justify the remake of the territorial map of the Central and Eastern Europe, where new boundaries were delineated according to ethnic criteria.

In his narration of the peace negotiations, Robert Lansing explained that the principle of self-determination was set out by Wilson in an address delivered on 11 February 1918, before a joint session of the Senate and House of Representatives, in which he stated that "self-determination is not a mere phrase. It is an imperative principle of action which statesmen will henceforth ignore at their peril". Despite the fact that the original clause containing a formal acceptance of the same was eliminated from the final draft of the Covenant of the League of Nations, it "remained as one of the general bases upon which a just peace should be negotiated", because Wilson never openly disavowed it.[9]

In order to reduce the danger of a resurgence of the national issue in Europe, a system of protection of minorities was therefore established under the

---

7   As Carl Bouchard (2006) has explained, the appeal of the League of Nations' idea for French regionalists lay in the fact that "it represented a unique opportunity to build a federal-type union from the ground up".
8   Núñez Seixas (1998: 185).
9   Lansing (1921: 83–85). In this way, it remained more a political than a legal concept: see Musgrave (1997: 31).

jurisdiction of the League of Nations, which had the task of "watching over the integrity of the frontiers and the egalitarian treatment of minorities within the new States".[10] The final treaty on minorities, which resulted from long and exhausting negotiations was nonetheless imperfect and flawed, since the rights and obligations of national minorities were not only excluded from the peace treaties, being replaced and governed by "specific and separate treaties of minorities" with various States of Eastern Europe (Poland, Yugoslavia, Greece, Czechoslovakia, Hungary, Romania, Bulgaria and the Baltic States), but the rights guaranteed to minorities were rather limited too.[11]

The ambiguities and vagueness of the assumptions of the principle of self-determination engendered numerous problems when it was time to put it into practice: the enormous amalgam of ethnic groups that characterized the territories of the Austro-Hungarian Empire were scattered and divided, as large groups of national minorities were henceforth incorporated into boundaries of new States. Furthermore, it led to the emergence and strengthening of nationalist and regionalist movements not only in Central and Eastern Europe, but also in Western Europe. This was mainly due to the resounding success achieved by the ideology of Wilsonianism, in which the U.S. President "articulated the principle of national self-determination and the closely related concept of collective security". As Wilson stated on 27 May 1916, while advocating the idea of a post-war League of Nations, not only "every people has a right to choose the sovereignty under which they shall live", but also "the small states of the world have a right to enjoy the same integrity that great and powerful nations expect and insist upon. And [...] the world has a right to be free from every disturbance of its peace that has its origins in aggression and disregard of the right of peoples and nations".[12]

The erroneous interpretation of Wilsonian arguments led to the idealization of the figure of Wilson by nationalists of all kinds, who considered him as a "representative of the idealist compromise of the democratic nation embarked on a crusade for the liberation of all oppressed peoples". As Núñez Seixas has observed, all these elements – the propagandistic use of the principle of self-determination, the attempts to legitimize it, and the dissemination of Wilsonian myth – "exercised great influence over the evolution toward nationalism of various groups which had previously concentrated on cultural activities or whose ideological definition was formulated in a regionalist or

---

10   Núñez Seixas (1993: 6).
11   Núñez Seixas (1993: 6–7). See also Azcárate (1969).
12   Ambrosius (2002: 21).

federalist way".[13] As a consequence, the expectations created by the Peace Conference spurred nationalist movements to embark upon a series of propagandist activities and political actions aimed at influencing decisions of negotiators. The desired intent of raising international public awareness about the issue of national minorities, for example, was at the origin of the Union des Nationalités (UN, 1912), promoted by the French journalist Jean Pélissier, and the Lithuanian nationalist leader, Jean Gabrys. Present among twenty nationalities and States, the UN promoted the publication of a monthly bulletin, *Les Annales des Nationalités*, the annual celebration of a Congress of Nationalities (five congresses from 1912 to 1919), and the establishment of the Office Central des Nationalités in Paris (where many nationalities had established the basis of their propaganda operations), with the purpose of promoting "the cause of national and political self-determination of nationalities", and coordinating the international action of nationalist movements. However, even if the UN had a global reach in principle, "*de facto* it concentrated on Central and Eastern Europe, especially on the European parts of the Russian empire",[14] whereas the League of Nations, far from resolving all national issues, created or exacerbated others.[15] In this context, Western European minorities did not succeed in making themselves heard in the international arena.

This was the case of Aosta Valley, where the linguistic rights of the French-speaking population of the region (annexed to the Italian Kingdom in 1861) were principally defended by the clergy and certain ranks of the middle classes up to World War I.[16] In general, in Italy, in the years following the unification, there had been no political claims by allophone minorities, due to the non-existence of nationally significant units, different from the predominant Italian one, on the border of the kingdom. In such a context, the cultural individuality of small ethnic-linguistic communities did not represent a real problem, since their proponents were not particularly interested in claiming the respect for their culture and language from a State with which, after all, they identified.[17]

---

13 Núñez Seixas (1998: 154).
14 Svarauskas (2014).
15 See Núñez Seixas (2001). Furthermore, as Stanisław Sierpowski (1991: 32) has observed, "The League, even though of 'nations', was an organization of autonomous states. Therefore, the organs of the League, particularly, the Council and the Secretariat, considered the minorities' problem mainly from the viewpoint of its members, and not the minorities themselves".
16 Núñez Seixas (1998: 170).
17 On the other hand, the unwillingness of the Italian State to recognize its minorities was due to "the affirmation of the totalizing and discretionary principle of citizenship", which became a basic element in the construction of the unitary state. See Ghisalberti (1994: 25).

Nonetheless, if the numbers of families of foreign extraction in Italy had not been not particularly high prior to World War I,[18] annexations subsequent to the War led to the arrival of more than half a million of new alloglot subjects. Hence, in post-war Italy, the issue of linguistic minorities came to the fore, and the question of minorities became part of mainstream political and cultural debate. Moreover, in Aosta Valley, Alessandro Celi suggests, the incoming of a great mass of "foreigners" (workers and soldiers), together with the social transformations imposed by the War, "provoked in the local population a generalized reaction [...], which constituted the basis of a significant change in the political language and ideological formulations of the Valdostans".[19]

It was in this context that the Ligue Valdôtaine was given renewed impetus. Founded in November 1909 by Anselme Réan with the purpose of defending the official character and the teaching of the French language, the Ligue Valdôtaine was the first movement to take up the debate about the respect for minorities, and the need to grant Aosta Valley a special status.[20] In the immediate post-war years, the Ligue began to advance additional political claims, relying on ethnic reasons to draw attention to the specificity of the region, both in its documents and the local press. This radicalization was partly justified by the fear that the government would grant special status to the German and Slovene minorities —both considered to be "ethnically diverse"— but not to Aosta Valley. Indeed, the Italian government thought that it would be able to resolve the issue of the newly annexed minorities —Germans in South Tyrol, and Slovenes and Croats in Julian Venetia— by allowing them a certain degree of linguistic and administrative autonomy. At the same time, the Aosta Valley elites opposed any attempts by the government to equate them to the newly annexed populations. In an article published in the local weekly *Le Pays d'Aoste* (1913–1926), Monsignor Jean-Joconde Stévenin explained that the comparison of the Aosta Valley question with one of the territories of German and Slovene languages offended the patriotism demonstrated by the region during the conflict.[21]

In 1919, the Ligue Valdôtaine claimed for autonomy in a petition addressed to the Italian premier Vittorio Orlando, who headed the Italian Delegation

---

18 19,091 Albanian, 2,552 Catalan, 19,646 "French", 6,905 Greek, 6,250 Slovenian, 2,199 German families. See Merlo (2012: 249).
19 Celi (2017).
20 As observed by Simona Merlo (2012: 225), it represented the temporary effort of going beyond ideological and political divergences (in particular between Catholics and Liberals) in the name of the common ideal of preserving the linguistic and cultural identity of Aosta Valley.
21 Merlo (2012: 250–55).

to the Peace Conference. The *Pétition pour les revendications ethniques et linguistiques de la Vallée d'Aoste*, attempted to internationalize the Aosta Valley question, and made specific reference to the rights of its people to self-determination. Fomented by the Wilsonian Fourteen Points, and the concessions that the Italian Government made to the German-speaking minority in South Tyrol, these claims did not go beyond linguistic proclamations, making a timid proposal for administrative autonomy, and requesting the opening of a French Consulate in Aosta.

The autumn of 1921 marked a turning point for regionalism, following the Italian Popular Party's request to the government to draft a bill on the establishment of regions within the year. The proposal of decentralization and regionalization made by its leader Luigi Sturzo was not opposed to the unitary conception of the State, but acknowledged regional historical realities as a complement and further development of the existing State identity. These assumptions were at one with those advocated by supporters of an autonomist and regionalist solution for Aosta Valley that was adapted to local specificities, whilst remaining firmly rooted in membership of the *pays*. In 1922, a delegation of the Ligue valdôtaine went to Rome to present a petition in favour of the linguistic and administrative autonomy of Aosta Valley to the new head of state, Benito Mussolini. Despite the fascist regime's promise of conceding to some of its requests, the measures taken by the new regime actually tended to eliminate any trace of the French language in the region.[22] The centralizing and "levelling" policy adopted by the fascist regime, which aimed at forcibly Italianizing the linguistic minorities within its boundaries, was particularly directed towards Germans, Slovenes, and Croats. This was mainly due to the presence of powerful States (Austria, Germany, and Yugoslavia) that could represent potentially strong political references for the separatist claims of these minorities – as actually happened after the War.[23]

---

22 As early as 1923, the hamlet schools, which were the last bulwark of French education, were suppressed. That same year, a legislative decree ordered the removal of all posters in French, even bilingual ones, and in 1926 all the names of the streets of the city of Aosta were changed. From 1925, marriage documents were to be drafted exclusively in Italian. A decree of the same year prohibited any teaching, even if optional, in any language other than Italian in schools. Finally, a Royal Decree of February 1928 imposed the teaching of Italian as the one and only language, and at the same time required the suppression of teaching in any minority languages; http://www.axl.cefan.ulaval.ca/europe/italieaoste.htm.

23 Ghisalberti (1994: 39–40). The internal contrasts with Monsignor Stévenin and Réan's approach to fascism in 1924 eroded the ideological basis of the Ligue and led to two consecutive splits, from which the Groupe valdôtain d'action *régionaliste* and Jeune *Vallée* d'Aoste arose. The *Jeune Vallée d'Aoste* became a clandestine group under fascism, a battlefield

The principle of self-determination exerted some influence on the evolution of the Walloon movement too, which, in the aftermath of war, radicalized and started claiming for the right of self-determination of the Walloon people.[24] The entire history of the Walloon movement has been conditioned by the presence of a strongly assertive Flemish movement.[25] Founded in the mid-nineteenth century, the Walloon movement initially relied on cultural initiatives; it took on a more political identity towards the last two decades of the century, as a reaction to the introduction of the first linguistic laws promoting the Flemish language in the 1870s, with the foundation of a movement to defend Walloon and French-speaking culture and traditions. During its early years, it ardently defended Belgium as a unified state. The situation began to change from 1911 on, when a law aiming at making "Flemish" the University of Ghent contributed to radicalizing the stance taken by the movement. During the Walloon Congress of 1912, organized by the *Ligue Wallonne de Liège*, a committee was set up to analyse the question of splitting from the national government, and an unofficial Walloon Parliament was instituted, the Assemblée wallonne, with a mandate for developing propaganda on Walloons matters. The experience of the Great War pushed the Assemblée wallonne to adopt a nationalist Belgian approach causing resentment among the most recalcitrant and radical *wallingants*.[26]

The Great War was also a turning point for Flemish nationalism, which grew progressively stronger, moving from linguistic and cultural claims towards more political ones,[27] consequently broadening and radicalizing its base. The Walloon movement radicalized too: from the beginning of the 1920s, the Assemblée wallonne opted for systematically rejecting both the administrative separation and the linguistic claims advanced by the Flemish movement, by exploiting the notion of patriotism in order to discredit the adversary. In the context of *union sacrée* characterizing the immediate post-war period, the Assemblée wallonne therefore picked on those *flamingants* who compromised themselves with the German occupiers.[28]

In this period, other concerns of the Assemblée wallonne dealt with the issue of representation: it complained, for example, that no Walloons took part

---

during the Resistance, and a movement that would press claims for the autonomy of Aosta Valley after 1945. The Ligue continued its activity for a few years, but the fascist regime soon put an end to them; its ambitions faded, together with its founder, in 1928.

24   Kesteloot (1993).
25   For an overview on both movements, see Desprez & Vos (2016).
26   Van Ginderachter (2005: 24–25).
27   Shelby (2014).
28   Kesteloot (1993: 26).

in Versailles negotiations. In addition, it was disturbed by the "gradual threat of minorization of Wallonia", that is, the fear of being numerically inferior to Flemish at parliament.[29] As for the administrative organization, the Assemblée wallonne pled for the Belgian unity with unilingual Wallonia and bilingual Flanders.

The *Comité d'action wallonne*, which reunited the more radical activists, resumed its activities soon after the end of the war. Even though it participated in the debates of the Assemblée, certain degree of divergence soon appeared. In 1923, several of its members —who belonged to the Garde wallonne— merged with the Jeune Garde wallonne fédéraliste and the Comités Jeunes Wallons to set up the Garde wallonne autonomiste. The radicalization of the young militants provoked a scission between the Comité d'action wallonne of Liège and the Assemblée wallonne.[30]

Established in Liège, in 1923, the *Ligue d'action wallonne* was a federalist association that sought to bring together all those associations fighting for a greater degree of regional autonomy. Until 1930, it defended unilingualism in Wallonia and bilingualism in Flanders. Amongst its main concerns were the questions of a rapprochement with France, the Walloon representation at the Government, the economic interest of the Walloons, the demographic question, the linguistic rights of the Walloons in official bodies and the statutes of the linguistic border and of Brussels.[31] The autonomy advocated by the Ligue d'action wallonne was based on the Wilsonian principle that people had the right to self-determination, which could take the form of a regional – or European – federalism. In 1930, it founded the Concentration wallonne with the purpose of bringing together the various leanings within the Walloon movement. At its inaugural conference, which was held in Liege, on 27 and 28 September, 1930, the Concentration Wallonne adopted a resolution that emphasized the "French integrity" of Wallonia and acknowledged that the Flemish people were entitled to their own identity. The *Concentration Wallonne* called for regional monolingualism and the establishment of federalism with a system of linguistic freedom for Brussels. As explained by Chantal Kesteloot, the emergence of a Walloon autonomist movement was largely due to the insistence of Flemish claims for cultural autonomy: this made them aware of the

---

29   Kesteloot (2004: 26–27, 37).
30   See: http://www.wallonie-en-ligne.net/Encyclopedie/Congres/Notices/Ligue-Action-wallonne-Liege.htm.
31   Van Ginderachter (2005: 25).

necessity of having their own set of claims by "focusing their struggle on the Walloon space".[32]

3   Transnational Connections: Micro-Nationalisms and Sub-state Nationalisms

The principle of self-determination not only influenced the demands and attitudes of more developed/evolved sub-state national and regional movements, it also had repercussions on micro-nationalisms, albeit not necessarily in a direct way and presumably as a consequence of what Daniele Conversi has defined as the "demonstration effect" of nationalisms on one another. This term refers to the complex play of mutual influences occurring at an ideological, tactical, and strategic level among nationalist movements "across frontiers as stimulated by international events". It is associated to "general influences on nationalist movements exerted by 'external' models".[33] It allowed not only the adoption of similar political practices and national causes, but also legitimized the cause of nationalists, "who generally considered themselves as actors in a world of fighting nations in which each of them has the right to enjoy full freedom and self-government", thus nurturing their feeling of solidarity.[34]

The First World War indeed years were indeed an intense period for the development of imitative practices among nationalist movements. In particular, Irish nationalism was to become the reference model for radical nationalists (such as the Basques and Galicians), especially after the triumph of Sinn Féin at the elections of December 1918. As Núñez Seixas has emphasized, this triumph seemed to demonstrate that "a minority of patriots were able to awaken the national sentiment of an entire people through their own sacrifice, even against the opinion of the majority 'legalist' party: in case of failure, the spiral of repression of the State, in fact, would have pushed the majority of the population to sympathize with the cause of radical nationalism".[35] Plausibly, the

---

32   Kesteloot (1993: 29).
33   Conversi (1993: 246, 249) identifies two kinds of "demonstration effect": instrumental and emphatic. "*Instrumental* models are adopted as examples and inserted into both the ideology and praxis of local nationalism, hence they operate at the elite level, meaning that they can steer some of the political choices of nationalist leaders. *Emphatic* models refer, on the contrary, to a sense of solidarity which can develop among some section of a particular 'oppressed' people and operate both at the elite and the base level thanks to their [universal] mobilizing force".
34   See Núñez Seixas (1992, 2017).
35   Núñez Seixas (1992: 27).

"demonstration effect" concerned not only the most politicized sub-state national movements in Western Europe (such as the Flemish, the Basque and the Catalan movement), but also those micro-nationalisms that were in contact with them. This was the case, for example, of the Catalan and Occitan movements in France, the evolution of which had been strongly affected by the international activities of their more dynamic neighbours south of the Pyrenees: the Catalan nationalists.

In Roussillon, the emergence of a Catalan consciousness was deeply marked and influenced by its relationship with the Catalans on the other side of the Pyrenees. This relationship had started in the nineteenth century, when the Catalan cultural and linguistic revival was set in motion,[36] and increased significantly during the First World War, when left-wing Catalan nationalism openly positioned itself for the allied camp against the Spanish neutrality proclaimed by Alfonso XIII, in the hope of regaining social and electoral weight. The formal announcement of the Allies' war aims, as codified by the Wilsonian Fourteen Points, fully responded to the left-wing Catalanists' programmatic aspirations, which dealt with the right of peoples to organize themselves and participate in the League of Nations.[37] This in fact led to the intensification of the relationship between Catalanist intellectuals from Roussillon and Catalan nationalists.

In April 1915, Catalan nationalists engaged in a zealous international activity aiming to raise awareness of their cause among foreign public opinion, and overtly distance themselves from the neutrality of the Spanish monarchy during the conflict. This propaganda activity revolved around the presence of 12,000 Catalan volunteers in the ranks of the French Foreign Legion, and the mystification of the real motivations that had pushed these "heroes" to risk their lives on the battlefield, in defence of the ideals of freedom and democracy advocated by the Entente.[38] The initiative was promoted by the Unió Catalanista (1891), which gathered many Catalanist centres and organizations, the two Catalan journals *El Poble Català* and *La Nació*, and the left-wing republican weekly *Iberia*, all of them published in Barcelona. In Roussillon, they were ardently supported by the *Revue Catalane*, which echoed their message, and

---

36 Zantedeschi (2003).
37 See Núñez Seixas (2018); Zantedeschi (2006).
38 The figure of 12,000 Catalans out of a total of 15,000 Spanish volunteers would be accepted without reservation by the subsequent Catalan historiography. Actually, it appears that the Spanish volunteers enrolled in the Foreign Legion of the Entente were 2191, of whom only 954 were Catalans; Martínez Fiol (1991: 113–28). See also Esculies & Martínez Fiol (2014).

devoted an increasing amount of space to the Francophile proclamations issuing from across the border.

Throughout the conflict, the international propaganda of Catalan nationalists also centred around the celebration of the Catalan origins of the undisputed hero of the "miracle" of the battle of Marne, General Joseph Joffre, who was originally from Roussillon and celebrated as the most successful incarnation of the Catalan "race". The participation of the president of the Catalan regional council (Mancomunitat) in the celebrations in honour of Joffre, celebrated in Perpignan in February 1919, can be interpreted as one of the last attempts to give international resonance to the autonomist demands of Catalonia, in the hope of resolving the Catalan question legally.[39]

After the war, regionalism gained ground in Roussillon, finding a voice in the journal *La Renaissance Catalane* (July 1918). The new periodical undertook an active campaign in favour of administrative and economic decentralization of France, the abolition of "artificial departments" and their replacement with regions. It was notorious for the allegiance of certain of its editors to the Catalan nationalist cause, paying specific attention to the campaign for Catalan autonomy. Nonetheless, its stance in favour of the Catalan nationalist claims was more a consequence of its firm French patriotism, galvanized by the neutrality of the Spanish crown, rather than the expression of some kind of autonomistic ambition. In fact, Roussillon Catalanists had no political claims, if not an administrative and cultural reform within the French State. All their efforts (for example, the creation in 1921 of the *Colla del Rosselló*, an association that had the purpose of gathering "all individuals willing to develop the intellectual heritage of Roussillon" and restored Floral Games) aimed at promoting local writers and artists, preserving the cult of traditions, and safeguarding the Catalan language. They were proud and respectful of the unity of their *Grande Patrie*, even though they deprecated its excessive centralism, which had declared war on the traditional institutions and had dealt a harsh blow to the intellectual and cultural life of the provinces.

Cultural and political activities of Catalan nationalists also had repercussions on the Occitan movement in the post-war years, when a new generation of Occitan regionalists arose. Relations between Occitans and Catalans also

---

39   For a detailed account of the event, see: *Joffre*, Barcelona: La Novel·la Nova, 1919. Another attempt to exploit Joffre's Catalan origins for autonomous purposes took place in May 1920, in Barcelona, on the occasion of the Jocs Florals, the presidency of which was assigned to Joffre. However, on that occasion, French and Spanish diplomats acted jointly to curb any attempt at exploitation by the Catalans, especially bearing in mind that, in August 1919, Spain had made its official entry into the League of Nations. See Zantedeschi (2003: 197–201).

dated back to the mid-nineteenth century, when, during the early stages phases of their respective linguistic and literary revivals, they began to dream of a federation that would unite all peoples of the "Latin race", beyond their belonging to different states. In the Occitan territories, the cultural and linguistic revival, which had been championed by *Félibrige* since 1854 was to remain quite extraneous to political claims.[40] But, as elsewhere in Europe, the post-war Occitan generation also had to come to terms with the new geo-political organization of the continent, which had been deeply reshaped by the peace treaties and the principle of nationality that had dictated their course of action.[41] This generation criticized traditional Félibrige's lack of initiative in promoting Occitan, its academicism, and lack of courage in furthering the teaching of the language at school, as well as its failure to endorse social and political causes.

The creation of the Comité d'Action des Revendications Nationales du Midi (1922), by Mistral Neveu, was the prelude to the foundation of the Ligue de la Patrie Méridionale-Fédération des Pays d'Oc (1923).[42] This committee was made up of several smaller committees responsible for drawing up a federalist programme. Within it, the Ligue pour la Langue d'Oc à l'école was perhaps the only committee that existed in practice. With a federalist mission, the Ligue de la Patrie Méridionale worked on the restoration of the Occitan language by promoting the creation of an Institut d'Études Occitanes, sustaining the publication of manuals, and contributing to the establishment of an Occitan library. Ultimately, it was doomed to failure. Its main proponents, Camille Soula and Ismaël Girard, published the periodical *oc* (1923), which fought hard to give impetus to the Occitan culture and build a modern Occitan movement by breaking away from the Félibrige's traditionalism and provincialism.

In this period, many Occitan ventures were influenced by Catalanism, following the renewal of the Catalan-Occitan friendship soon after the end of the War.[43] It was owing to the support of Catalans, for example, that the *Societat d'Estudis Occitans* (SEO) was established in Toulouse, in 1930. Actually, the

---

40 The *Félibrige* was a literary association of Provençal poets, which was founded by Frédéric Mistral and other young writers, in 1854, in order to save Provençal language from obliteration.

41 Abrate (2001: 155–60).

42 Lespoux (2009).

43 Moreover, the "Catalan cause" became very popular among French public opinion following the discovery, in November 1926, that a Catalan organization was preparing an armed incursion into Catalonia from France to free it from Primo de Rivera's dictatorship. The organization was led by Francesc Macià, who had gone into exile in France after Primo de Rivera's coup d'état. Macià was judged in Paris and sentenced to two months' imprisonment.

fledgling association could be considered as a kind of branch of the Institut d'Estudis Catalans. The connection between Occitanism and Catalanism flourished during the 1930s: the SEO was greatly inspired by Barcelona, Louis Alibert's *Gramatica Occitana* was published in 1935 in Barcelona, and the Occitanist movement was partially funded by the Catalanist movement.[44]

In those years, the main Occitan activists organized and acted outside Félibrige.[45] One of the major proponents of Occitanism, Charles Camproux, founded several youth organizations and journals, including *Occitania* (1934), which was the expression of a modern Occitan movement, committed to federalism.[46] In 1935, Camproux and the editorial staff of *Occitania* founded the Parti Occitaniste. Leaning towards the left of the French political arena, Occitanists were opposed to Félibrige, whom they claimed did not fight for the unification of the Occitan territories (which they called Occitania), but merely sought to promote the Provençal language and culture. Despite their activism and commitment to economic, political, and cultural revitalization of the South, however, and as Andrew Smith has observed, these small movements remained isolated and "the ability of these young regionalists to appeal politically was limited".[47]

The story of the Catalan-Occitan relationship illustrates how the "effect demonstration" went well beyond the simple imitation or iteration of political claims and ideological and tactical strategies, and influenced the establishment of cultural and linguistic institutions in the interwar period. It also shows how linguistic and cultural affinities continued to function during and after the War, representing an ideal of civilization capable of transcending states' borders. However, both in the Occitan case as with others, the French internal situation proved to be equally influential as (if not more influential than) the international context in both fostering and containing the regionalist movements that were developing in France at that time.

In fact, after war had galvanized national fervour and unity and fomented French patriotism, the return of peace and the geopolitical reorganization of Europe based on the principle of national sovereignty rekindled the debate about the need to reorganize the French territory on a federal basis among the young regionalists. The re-annexation of Alsace and Lorraine which, under the German Empire, had enjoyed a certain degree of autonomy, renewed the debate on the excessive centralism of the French State, and reawakened the

---

44 Amit (2014: 52–72).
45 Lafont (1974: 165).
46 Abrate (2001: 259).
47 Smith (2016: 131).

issue of minorities in France. In 1926, Eugène Ricklin founded the *Heimatbund* (Homeland Union), which published a manifesto that condemned French policies of cultural assimilation in the region, and called for autonomy within the boundaries of France.[48] In the following years, a certain number of autonomist newspapers were founded in Alsace, such as the *Volksstimme* and *Die Wahrheit* (which even called for the independence of Alsace and Lorraine), as well as autonomist parties – the *Elsässische Fortschrittpartei* (Alsatian Progressive Party, 1927) and the *Elsass-Lothringischer Heimatbund* (Parti Autonomiste d'Alsace-Lorraine, 1927).[49] In November 1927, the French government began repressing autonomist initiatives and banned the autonomist newspapers, since it considered them a threat to "the integrity of the Republic". Moreover, in 1928, proceedings were instituted (the Colmar Trial) to quash the Alsatian-Lorrain autonomists.

4 Transnational Connections: Pan-Nationalisms

The Alsatian autonomist campaign was passionately followed by *Breiz Atao*, which published the manifesto of the *Heimatbund* in June 1926. *Breiz Atao* was a bilingual French/Breton periodical published from 1919 on by the Groupe régionaliste breton (GRB), a newly founded party, set up by Job de Roincé, Henri Prado, and Morvan Marchal, in September 1918.

The Great War represented an important break also for the history of the Breton movement, which entered its "second phase".[50] The first Breton regionalist party, the *Union régionaliste bretonne* (URB), founded in 1898, was a largely conservative, clerical and monarchical party. Even if it embraced the French cause during the war by adhering to the *union sacrée* in defence of France, after the War, in the light of the small nations being granted the right to self-determination, it presented a petition to the Peace Conference. The petition,

---

48 As noted by McGillicuddy (2011: 175–76), "the manifesto was a reflection of the extent of dissatisfaction in some circles in Alsace but was certainly not representative of all those who supported the principle of autonomism. Its significance lies principally in the fact it encapsulated all the elements necessary to develop a national Alsatian political programme".

49 McGillicuddy (2011: 177).

50 The first phase of regionalist movement in Brittany, which lasted up to 1914/18, represented "a reaction by the existing territorial elites against the threat to their position posed by the modern, democratic and secular republic and its inroads into Brittany" (Keating 1988: 109). On the Breton movement during and after the First World War, see also Chartier (2010).

written by Régis de L'Estourbillon, one of the founding members of the URB, and endorsed by several hundred signatures, essentially claimed the right to speak and teach Breton freely and to have Breton traditions and beliefs respected. Quite predictably, the petition was ignored.[51]

Interestingly, in Brittany, the idea of liberating peoples was not only stimulated and propagated by the success achieved by the principle of self-determination. Here, the pan-national rhetoric of Celticism also had a considerable influence, affecting the evolution of Breton nationalism in the immediate aftermath of the war. In particular, the events of the Easter Rising (1916) and the War of Independence "inspired a resurrection in Breton, Scottish, and Welsh nationalist activity".[52] According to the members of Breiz Atao, fraternity with the Welsh, Scottish and Irish people would regenerate both the Breton national sentiment and race.[53] It was the first political party to officially espouse Pan-Celticism, and, in 1923, it sent a delegation to Wales to discuss its policy.[54] That same year, Olier Mordrel published an article in the periodical *Breiz Atao* – which, by now, had as its sub-title "monthly magazine of Breton nationalism and inter-Celtic relations" – in which he explained the benefits that Pan-Celticism would have on Breton cause: "Pan-Celticism will redeem Brittany. [...] Pan-Celticism will make us come out from our petrified environment, and will merge us within an intense current of life that will awake a sleeping genius, sensitivity and character, which were corrupted by a too long serfdom".[55]

Between 1923 and 1925, *Breiz Atao* published a supplement with articles in Welsh and English, *Panceltia*, that soon launched the idea of founding a nationalist party of Gauls. The supplement was directed by William Ambrose Bebb, a Welsh historian, writer and politician, and informed about the political

---

51 Keating (1988: 110) explains that "Some evidence of support, at least verbal, for the Briton idea is provided by the growing number of deputies who included reference to Brittany in their election manifesto [...] but this seems to reflect the use of Breton symbolism by the old elites rather than a challenge to the system".

52 The *Unvaniez Yaouankiz Breiz* (Union of Breton Youth, 1919), which formed around the periodical *Breiz Atao*, consisted of young ethnonationalists inspired by the Irish Easter Rising and the events that followed it. In 1919, a pamphlet titled *Irlande à jamais!* was published and distributed throughout Brittany. See Stover (2012). However, despite the inter-Celtic connections established by Breton militants, "assistance from Germanic regionalists within France exercised an equally profound influence upon the development of Breton nationalist ideology, and ultimately impacted upon its very conceptions of Celticism": see Leach (2010: 630).

53 Carney (2015: 70 and ff.).

54 Berresford Ellis (2002: 100).

55 Quoted in Carney (2015: 71).

and cultural news of Wales, Scotland and Ireland.[56] However, also because of the "general ignorance of Brittany prevailing in Celtic nationalist movements",[57] this Breton Pan-Celticism was very soon forsaken in favour of a European federalism.

Indeed, federalism was dictated by the international context of that time.[58] Morvan Marchal, who would be the main instigator of the movement up until 1931, was a committed federalist, and exposed the theoretical foundations of a national movement in *Breiz Atao*. For him, the future laid in federalism. As he wrote in 1925: "We have no doubt: Breton nationalism is federalist". In 1926 the periodical changed its sub-title from *"revue mensuelle du nationalisme breton et des relations interceltiques"* ("monthly magazine of Breton nationalism and inter-Celtic relations") into *"revue mensuelle du nationalisme breton et du fédéralisme international"* ("monthly magazine of Breton nationalism and the international federalism").

On the other hand, Breton movement found support "in the eastern peripheries of the French state".[59] Indeed, the political-electoral success of autonomist Alsatians from 1925 onwards gave the Breton nationalist group the impetus to found a new party, the Parti Autonomiste Breton (PAB), the constituent congress for which took place in Rosporden, on 9 September 1927. As clearly stated in the statute of the PAB (adopted by the congress of the party in Châteaulin, in August 1928), the party was not separatist, nor anti-French. It opposed French centralism and its "mystic dogma of the one and indivisible Nation". It therefore laid claim to administrative and political autonomy to be represented by a Breton parliament, which would resolve certain questions relating to public education, administration, justice, social legislation, tax, and so on. The PAB advocacy was essentially federalist: "the reorganization of the world will be accompanied by secessions and regroupings, and [...] will take place, not between large States, whose historic role will be finished, but between the nationalities they are made up of, which will come together according to their ethnic, linguistic and cultural affinities".[60]

That same month of September 1927, on 12, some representatives of the Alsatian, Corsican and Breton movements met in Quimper to create the *Comité central des Minorités nationales de France* [CCMNF], whose main promoter was

---

56   Carney (2015: 72). However, it failed to penetrate even the Welsh language circle: see Leach (2010: 633=.
57   Leach, "A sense of Nordism", p. 633.
58   J.-Y. Guiomar, "Régionalisme, fédéralisme et minorités nationales en France entre 1919 et 1939", *Le mouvement social*, 70 (1970), pp. 89–108.
59   Leach (2010: 633).
60   *Déclaration et Statuts du Parti Autonomiste Breton*, Rennes: PAB, 1929, p. 17.

the Breton, Maurice Duhamel. In addition to grouping the autonomist parties of Brittany, Alsace and Corse, the committee maintained contacts with the Flemish, Catalans and the Basques. It would publish the *Bulletin des minorities nationales* (1936) and then subsequently the monthly periodical *Peuples et Frontières* (1937–1939). The bye-laws of the Comité claimed "the right of people to self-determination and international federalism":

> Modern states based on force, whose antagonisms can only lead to ever more terrible wars, have been made obsolete by the world's growing economic interdependence. [The CCMNF] advocates replacing them with a Federation of Peoples, where each nationality will be able to determine its own political status and pursue its own cultural development, according to its traditions and trends, and whose economic unity will be ensured by the abolition of customs and the practice of free trade.[61]

It was the first time that various minorities met to study a common solution to their problems and try to lay down the foundations of a transformation of France into a federal country. Yet, due to the 1929 crisis and the resurgence of international political tensions, federalism made little headway. The splitting up of the *Parti Autonomiste Breton* in 1931 led to the abandonment of the federalist claims in favour of separatism.[62]

Representatives of the Breton movement established connections also with Flemish regionalists, in particular with its main proponent, Abbé Jean-Marie Gantois. After the War, French Flanders —which was crossed by the Yser Front— adopted a pragmatic approach, and pressurized the French government to seek compensation for war damage from Germany, to be able to proceed to the reconstruction of the region.[63] As elsewhere in France, the war had galvanized national fervour and unity and fomented French patriotism. In such a situation, the main concerns of the members of the Comité flamand de France were reconstruction, maintenance of the scientific level and

---

61 Quoted in Gras & Gras (1982: 99).
62 Guiomar (1970: 100).
63 The First World War had a profoundly unsettling effect on French Flanders, which was crossed by the Yser Front (or West Flemish Front, a section of the Western Front during World War I held by Belgian troops from October 1914 until 1918). Moreover, the region had been already affected by the religious conflicts of the beginning of the century that had led to the split of the archdiocese of Cambrai and the subsequent establishment of the archdiocese of Lille in 1913, a few months before the commencement of hostilities. See Baycroft (2005).

independence from Belgium.[64] At the same time, the consolidation of the FRF in the region gave rise to different regionalist periodicals, such as *The Beffroi de Flandre* (founded by G. van den Bussche, Dunkerque, 1919), and *The Mercure de Flandre* (founded by Valentin Bresle, Lille, 1923).

In the 1920s, the regionalist idea gained credence as a way of resurrecting the ancient province in opposition to the *department*: this would allow the preservation of the Catholic faith and local idiom and traditions, as well as the reconstitution of an "authentic France" through the establishment of a federation with other French provinces. Several new *flamingant* organizations were founded, and renewed efforts to promote Flemish culture and language were made.[65] In 1924, the *Union des Cercles Flamands de France* was founded under the presidency of Jean-Marie Gantois. It brought together a few clerical circles, published a Flemish periodical, *Vlaemsche Stemme in Vrankryk* (until 1926), and launched a campaign to advocate preaching and teaching in Dutch at primary schools. In July 1926, the Union changed its name into Vlaamsch Verbond van Frankrijk (Union Flamande de France, VVF), breaking with its strictly clerical orientation and opening Flemish regionalism to lay people. It attracted canon Camille Looten (Professor at the University of Lille and president of the Comité flamand de France since 1899) and Nicolas Bourgeois (leader of FRF), and joined the regionalist movement by associating itself with the FRF.

Gantois was of the idea that the VVF must necessarily be interested in the efforts of other similar movements present on French soil, such as those in Breton, Alsace, and Provence. If his contacts with Provence were not very intense, the same cannot be said for those with Alsace (where Gantois had done military service as an assistant at the garrison library) and, above all, with Brittany. Here, Gantois had come into contact not only with the Bleun Brug, a cultural and regionalist movement of Catholic inspiration directed by Jean-Marie Perrot, but also with Mordrel and Debauvais of *Breiz Atao*. However,, the largest influence on Gantois was the Belgian Flemish movement. Gantois struck up a deep friendship with Vital Celen, a Belgian professor and linguist, who promoted the Flemish culture of French Flanders in Belgium and would help VVF publications financially. From 1925, Gantois became the representative of French Flanders at the *Algemeen Nederlands Verbond* (1895), whose headquarters were in The Hague, and which had the purpose of "propagating and strengthening awareness of the cultural and ethnic unity of the Dutch

---

64 The *Comité flamand de France* was founded in 1853 by Edmond de Coussemaker in order to study and disseminate Flemish culture and Catholic religion. See De Coussemaker-Van Robais (2012), as well as Baycroft (2004).

65 Baycroft (2004: 159).

people living in three States". By the end of the years 1920s, the activists of the VVF launched two new periodicals: *Torrewacther* (1929; from January 1938, supplement of *Le Lion de Flandre*), and *Le Lion de Flandre* (1929, directed by Gantois). These focused on the dissemination of Dutch culture and language, and established contacts with Breton, Alsatian, Occitan, and Belgian Flemish nationalists. The idea of French Flanders cultivated by Gantois in the 1920s had now given way to the idea of the "French Netherlands" (which also included Artois and part of Picardy). Under the influence of the "Greater Netherlands" idea of the Flemish nationalists, Gantois began an ideological evolution that led him to abandon the linguistic criterion to embrace racist and anti-Semitic arguments.[66]

5 Conclusion: The "Drama" of Western European Micro-Nationalisms

In Europe, where the majority of States were multinational, the idea of self-determination proved to be capable of satisfying the most coveted independentist aspirations of all the stateless national peoples. It gained further legitimacy among the liberal public opinion of Western Europe watching over the aspirations of the micro-nationalities of Central and Eastern Europe, and considered them as "a democratic revolt against tyranny".[67] However, the acceptance of the inalienable right of a people to self-determination by the powers of the Triple Entente was by no means unanimous, given both their reluctance to intervene in the internal affairs of a sovereign State, and the discontent of national minorities in three of them. Accordingly, if the right to self-determination of the peoples was used to justify the remake of the territorial map of the Central and Eastern Europe, in the territories of the Allies there had never been any such intention.

Following the enthusiasm aroused by the principles of nationality and the right to self-determination of the peoples, micro-nationalisms in Western Europe also witnessed a new burst of regional enthusiasm and fervour. However, these movements seemed to have three things in common. First of all, while the principle of self-determination invigorated regional movements, the war effort had bolstered State patriotism in all the countries involved. In such a context, the principle of self-determination contributed to reawakening or fomenting of the people's national (or regional) consciousness, giving legitimacy to cultural and linguistic claims that occasionally resulted in minor political

---

66 See Defoort (1977).
67 Macartney (1994).

demands. Nonetheless, in the immediate aftermath of the war, neither regionalism nor federalism, which had taken foothold among these micronationalisms, were in principle opposed to the unitary conception of the State.

Secondly, echoing Chantal Kasteloot's remarks about the Walloon case, and extending them to the other cases presented in this paper, the lack of political formations close to these movements shows that they were integrated into the political system of the state to which they belonged, and therefore militants continued to rely on traditional parties.[68] In other words, the debates centring on regional issues were subordinate to national political debate.

Finally, these movements were characterized by political and social – but also cultural – marginality. In Brittany too, which was the most politically active of the cases considered here, nationalist movements had limited social penetration. As a matter of fact, as Michael Keating has emphasized, the second phase of the Breton regionalist movement, which corresponds to the period between the two wars, was "ineffectual, spawning a variety of groups perpetually in conflict over separatism versus regionalism, clericalism versus anticlericalism, left versus right and Breton-speakers versus Francophones".[69]

These movements were therefore minority —if not marginal— within their respective regions. They actively took part in the political life of the State that they belonged to, and they relied on traditional national parties. The low level of political and social resonance they enjoyed within their own linguistic and cultural communities was but the other side of the same coin.

Bibliography

Abrate, L. (2001), *1900/1968 Occitanie des idées et des hommes*, Toulouse: IEO.

Ambrosius, L.E. (2002), *Wilsonianism. Woodrow Wilson and His Legacy in American Foreign Relations*, New York: Palgrave Macmillan.

Amit, A. (2014), *Regional Language Policies in France during World War II*, Basingstoke: Palgrave Macmillan.

Azcárate, P. de (1969), *La Société des Nations et la Protection des Minorités*, Geneva: Centre Européen de la Dotation Carnegie.

Baycroft, T. (2004), *Culture, Identity and Nationalism. French Flanders in the Nineteenth and Twentieth Centuries*, London: Royal Historical Society/Rochester, N.Y.: Boydell Press.

---

68   Kesteloot (1993: 25).
69   "Finally, the strongest element in the Breton movement veered to the extreme right and adopted an explicitly Fascist policy" (Keating 1988: 110).

Baycroft, T. (2005), "The Versailles Settlement and Identity in French Flanders", *Diplomacy & Statecraft*, 16:3, pp. 589–602.

Berresford Ellis, P. (2002), *Celtic Dawn: the Dream of Celtic Unity*, Y Lolfa: Constable (2nd).

Bouchard, C. (2006), "From French Federalism to World Federalism: Jean Hennessy's Société Proudhon", *Proceedings of The Western Society for French History*, 34, pp. 233–246.

Boutin, C., & F. Rouvillois, eds. (2003), *Décentraliser en France*, Paris: François-Xavier de Guibert.

Carney, S. (2015), *Breiz Atao! Mordrel, Delaporte, Lainé, Fouéré: une mystique nationale (1901–1948)*, Rennes: Presses Universitaires de Rennes.

Celi, A. (2017), "La Grande Guerra e le origini dell'autonomismo valdostano", in G. Zanibelli (ed.), *La Grande Guerra in Provincia Comunità locali e fronte interno: fonti e studi su società e conflitto*, Siena: Nuova Immagine Editrice, 2017, pp. 325–337.

Chartier, E. (2010), "La première guerre mondiale, un élément fondateur pour l'*Emsav*", in G. Denis (ed.), *Mémoire et trauma de la Grande Guerre. Bretagne, Catalogne, Corse, Euskadi, Occitanie*, Rennes: Publication du CRBC Rennes-2/Université Européenne de Bretagne.

Conversi, D. (1993), "Domino Effect or Internal Developments? The Influences of International Events and Political Ideologies on Catalan and Basque Nationalism", *Western European Politics*, 16:3, pp. 245–270.

De Coussemaker-Van Robais, S. (2012), "Le Comité Flamand de France (1853–1940), société savante ou mouvement régionaliste?", *Histoire, économie & société*, 4, pp. 59–73.

Defoort, E. (1977), "Jean-Marie Gantois dans le mouvement flamand en France (1919–1939)", in C. Gras & G. Livet (eds.), *Régions et régionalisme en France du XVIIIème siècle à nos jours*, Paris: PUF, pp. 327–336.

Desprez, K. & L. Vos (2016), *Nationalism in Belgium: Shifting Identities, 1780–1995*, London: Palgrave Macmillan (2nd ed.).

Esculies, J., & D. Martínez Fiol (2014), *12.000! Els catalans a la Primera Guerra Mundial*, Barcelona: Ara Llibres.

Guiomar, J.-Y. (1970), "Régionalisme, fédéralisme et minorités nationales en France entre 1919 et 1939", *Le mouvement social*, 70, pp. 89–108.

Ghisalberti, C. (1994), "Stato nazionale e minoranze. L'esperienza italiana", in U. Corsini & D. Zaffi (eds.), *Le minoranze tra le due guerre*, Bologna: Il Mulino, pp. 23–40.

Gras, S., & C. Gras (1982), *La révolte des régions d'Europe occidentale de 1916 à nos jours*, Paris: PUF.

Hechter, M. (2000), *Containing Nationalism*, Oxford/ New York: Oxford UP.

Keating, M. (1985), "The Rise and Decline of Micronationalism in Mainland France", *Political Studies*, XXXIII, pp. 1–18.

Keating, M. (1988), *State and Regional Nationalism*, New York/London: Harvester Wheatsheaf.

Kesteloot, Ch. (1993), "Mouvement wallon et identité nationale", CRISP, 1392 (7), p. 24.

Kesteloot, Ch. (2004), *Au nom de la Wallonie et de Bruxelles français. Les origines du FDF*, Bruxelles: Éditions Complexe.

Lafont, R. (1974), *La révendication occitane*, Paris: Flammarion.

Lansing, R. (1921), *The Peace Negotiations. A Personal Narrative*, Boston/New York: Houghton Mifflin Co.

Leach, D. (2010), "'A sense of Nordism': the impact of Germanic assistance upon the militant interwar Breton nationalist movement", *European Review of History/Revue européenne d'histoire*, 17:4, pp. 629–646.

Lespoux, Y. (2009), "Aux origines de la revendication occitaniste en faveur de l'enseignement de la langue d'oc: les propositions du Nouveau Languedoc et d'Occitania", *Lengas*, 65, pp. 29–48.

Macartney, C.A. (1994), "Stati e minoranze nazionali", in S. Woolf (ed.), *Il nazionalismo in Europa*, Milan: Unicopli, pp. 95–114.

Martinez i Fiol, D. (1991), *Els "voluntaris catalans" a la Gran Guerra (1914–1918)*, Barcelona: La Magrana.

McGillicuddy, A. (2011), *René Schickele and Alsace: Cultural Identity Between the Borders*, Bern et al.: Peter Lang.

Merlo, S. (2012), *Fra trono e altare. La formazione delle élites valdostane (1861–1922)*, Soveria Mannelli: Rubbettino.

Musgrave, T.D. (1997) *Self-Determination and National Minorities*, Oxford: Oxford UP.

Núñez Seixas, X.M. (1992), "El mito del nacionalismo irlandés y su influencia en los nacionalismos gallego, vasco y catalán (1880–1936)", *Spagna Contemporanea*, 2, pp. 25–57.

Núñez Seixas, X.M. (1993), "Il nazionalismo catalano e la diplomazia spagnola di fronte al sistema di protezione delle minoranze nazionali della Società delle Nazioni (1919–1930)", *Storia delle relazioni internazionali*, 6:2, pp. 3–65

Núñez Seixas, X.M. (1998), *Movimientos nacionalistas en la Europa del siglo XX*, Madrid: Síntesis.

Núñez Seixas, X.M. (2001), *Entre Ginebra y Berlín. La cuestión de las minorías nacionales y la política internacional en Europa, 1914–1939*, Madrid: Akal.

Núñez Seixas, X.M. (2017), "Ecos de Pascua, mitos rebeldes: El nacionalismo vasco e Irlanda, (1890–1939)", *Historia Contemporánea*, 55, pp. 447–82.

Núñez Seixas, X.M. (2018), "Catalonia and the 'War of Nations': Catalan Nationalism and the First World War", *Journal of Modern European History*, 16:3, pp. 379–398.

Payne, S.J. (1991), "Nationalism, Regionalism and Micronationalism in Spain", *Journal of Contemporary History*, 26:3–4, pp. 479–491.

Shelby, K.D. (2014), *Flemish Nationalism and the Great War: The Politics of Memory, Visual Culture and Commemoration*, Basingstoke: Palgrave Macmillan.

Sierpowski, S. (1991), "Minorities in the System of the League of Nations", in: P. Smith (ed.), *Ethnic Groups in International Relations*, New York/Aldershot: NYU Press/Aldershot, 1991, pp. 13–37.

Smith, A.W.M. (2016), *Terror and terroir: The winegrowers of the Languedoc and modern France*, Manchester: Manchester UP.

Stover, J.D. (2012), "Modern Celtic Nationalism in the Period of the Great War: Establishing Transnational Connections", *Proceedings of the Harvard Celtic Colloquium*, 32, pp. 286–301.

A. Svarauskas, "Union des Nationalités", in: 1914–1918-online. International Encyclopedia of the First World War, ed. by U. Daniel et al., issued by Freie Universität Berlin, Berlin 2014-10-08. doi: 10.15463/ie1418.10262.

Van Ginderachter, M. (2005), *Le chant du coq: nation et nationalisme en Wallonie depuis 1880*, Gent: Academia Press.

Wright, J. (2003), *The Regionalist Movement in France, 1890–1914: Jean Charles-Brun and French Political Thought*, Oxford: Clarendon.

Zantedeschi, F. (2003), "Il malinteso roussillonese-catalano. Un approccio comparativo per lo studio del catalanismo in Roussillon (1880–1920)", M.A. Thesis, Università Ca' Foscari, Venice.

Zantedeschi, F. (2006), "La Catalogna e l'autodeterminazione per l'autonomia negli anni della Grande Guerra", *Memoria e Ricerca*, 21, pp. 113–132.

CHAPTER 8

The Language Brotherhoods: European Echoes in the Development of Galician Nationalism (1916–1923)

Ramón Villares

> "A lawyer, no", said Edith, O'Brian's sister, who until then had remained silent. "No, my dear friend. You [Adrián Soutelo] shall be a poet, a fighter. You would make a fine Fenian!"
>
> R. Otero Pedrayo, *Os camiños da vida* [The Roads of Life], 1928.

∴

Scholarship agrees that the Language Brotherhoods (LB), founded in A Coruña in May 1916, represent the starting point of modern political nationalism in contemporary Galicia. Explicitly linked to the defence of the Galician language in the cultural sphere and seeking an "integral" autonomy in the political sphere, their ideological and political evolution shifted from regionalist positions towards nationalism, a definition that the LB adopted at their first political assembly, held in Lugo in November 1918. The LB were the beginning of a new political movement in Galicia that was progressively equated with similar and preceding initiatives undertaken in Catalonia and the Basque Country, which were a response to the challenges brought about by the 1898 crisis, the great debate on the regeneration of Spain and, naturally as of August 1914, the repercussions of World War I. The LB participated in this historical context, even though they emerged relatively late, and the fact that they coincide in time with one of the most outstanding events of that period, the Easter Rising in 1916, can only be considered circumstantial. The founding of the LB can therefore be understood more as an internal epochal phenomenon than an event connected directly with the emergence of European organizations of nationalities or national minorities before and after 1914 (e.g. the *Union des Nationalités*, 1912). In addition, the LB must be understood as a generational break, to the extent that new social, mesocratic and urban levels try to settle scores with their ancestors and gain access to public life. This settlement is perfectly summarized in Antón Villar Ponte's metaphor of "living words" (e.g. nationalism) as an antidote to "dead words" (e.g. "healthy and conformist" regionalism), which seem like distant echoes of *fin-de-siècle* Darwinism applied, in this case, to the transition from regionalism to cultural and political nationalism that the LB led when they were first established.

The objective of this chapter is to analyse the appearance of and first steps taken by the LB between 1916 and 1923, as the Galician expression of a process that can be explained in endogenous terms, as well as one forming part of a much broader trend that was Iberian and European in dimension, and in which there are some decisive references for understanding the emergence of Galician nationalism. The Galician context in which the LB appear is marked by several milestones. Firstly, the structural changes that occurred in fishing and farming, that is, in the modernization of agriculture and the emergence of an authentic industrial revolution in maritime activities, the expansion of fishing, the creation of a manufacturing sector led by the canning industry and the carryover effects that these activities had on shipbuilding and other annexed industries.[1] Secondly, the strong social mobilization represented by the agrarianism of Basilio Álvarez' *Acción Gallega* (Galician Action) movement, and a programme of technical reform for agriculture presented at the Monforte Agrarian Assemblies (1908–11), which attempted to respond to long-standing demands of the Galician peasantry concerning the elimination of the old methods of transferring land (*foros*, or chartered tenancies) and, above all, to promote a broad process of possessive individualism through massive access by farmers to full ownership of the land and the incorporation of small agricultural operations in the market.[2] Thirdly, the existence of a strong migratory current, destined essentially for the American republics, which radically transformed Galician rural society, both due to the exodus produced and its return effects, through visible remittances of capital and invisible remittances of a cultural and symbolic nature, that decisively changed Galician society in the first third of the twentieth century.[3]

In this framework, they also had a decisive influence on some external facts or echoes that make it possible to understand both the appearance of the LB and the previous process through which a Galician cultural and political elite experienced a prise de conscience, leading to the founding of this movement. The reformist ("regenerationist") reflections on the limits of the Spanish political system and the need for its reform encouraged new political alternatives, initially defined as regionalist, since the crisis of 1898. In fact, Catalan

---

1 Carmona & Nadal (2005).
2 See Villares (1982), and Cabo Villaverde (1998).
3 See Núñez Seixas (1998), and Vázquez (2015).

regionalism appeared as such from 1901 and some of its strategies, such as the alliance with various political forces (from Republicans to Carlists), caused the first cracks to appear in the Restoration system after the 1905 and 1907 elections.[4] This example of "new politics" outside *turnismo*, or peaceful alternating bipartite political power sharing, was a stimulus for the LB and their first organizational steps, when they attempted to establish specific alliances with the Catalan nationalism represented by its leader, Francesc Cambó. On the other hand, the Great War that broke out in August 1914 had a decisive influence on European national policies, as shown by the example of Ireland, and also by the reinforcement or emergence of national movements in many small European countries, which would have its most notable expression in the enthusiastic acceptance of US president Woodrow Wilson's Fourteen Points to "reconcile and link the idea of democracy with the principle of nationalities".[5] In addition, the war had profound effects on the ideological positions of the great traditional parties, which through the *Union Sacrée* quickly turned towards nationalism, "a universal European phenomenon in 1914".[6]

The evolution of World War I and the preparation of peace treaties after 1918 opened many expectations about a new historical era in which new nations would replace the old empires. In addition, the nationality policies of the Soviet revolution since October 1917 reinforced the idea that social revolution and national identity seemed compatible, an idea apparently respected in the denomination of the USSR as a union of Soviet republics. Everything seemed to announce, from Ireland to *Mitteleuropa* or from the theoretical positions of Wilson to Lenin, that a new horizon for the national question was emerging in the immediate post-war period, which was more problematic than expected. As Florentino López-Cuevillas, a member of the *Nós* (Ourselves) group, stated, "when the conflict seemed to reach an end, a threat emerged in distant Russia: the ghost of social revolution".[7] The euphoria of the late 1918s encouraged the leaders of the LB, which reinforced their nationalist definition as a strategy not only to face the state crisis in the Spain of King Alfonso XIII, but also to avoid the social consequences of the Bolshevik revolution. In addition, this context favoured external alliances or, at least, mirrors in which self-examination could take place: Ireland and Portugal, preferably. These two mirrors allow a comparative analysis of the great challenges of the LB: an organizational model and tension between strategic priorities (cultural nationalism or political

---

4 Riquer (2001: 185 and ff.).
5 See Núñez Seixas (2001: 62).
6 See O'Brien (1999: 10).
7 *Nós*, 1, January 1920.

nationalism), and also confront the results of the first Language Brotherhoods with the diagnosis of one of their main theorists and leaders[8] regarding those hindrances which, in the opinion of the Ourense writer, were experienced by two political parties, the agrarian and the nationalist, that were the subject of Risco's dreaming at that time.

1 A Regionalist Manifesto

The LB appeared in May 1916, as a specifically cultural movement, defining itself as regionalist in the political sphere. The organization and mobilizing capacity of Galician regionalism had been quite remarkable in the last decade of the nineteenth century, under the leadership of Manuel Murguía and Alfredo Brañas, who managed to place Galicia in the context of the so-called regional Spain, *España regional*, the name of a magazine published in Barcelona that defined the political debate of peninsular regionalism until the crisis of 1898. In the case of Galicia, organizations such as the *Asociación Regionalista Gallega* (Galician Regionalist Association, Santiago) or the *Liga Gallega* (Galician League, A Coruña), as well as the promotion of powerful symbols or *lieux de memoire*, such as the Pantheon of the Illustrious Galicians, the Carral Martyrs monument or the creation of the Galician Language Academy, are examples of this regionalist work that also received powerful help from Galician community associations in the Americas.[9] However, the invocation of regionalism by the early LB was not a guarantee of organizational continuity, because unlike in the Basque Country, and in particular in Catalonia, Galician regionalism was not able to transform into political nationalism as a result of the deep political impact that the colonial defeat of 1898 had on Spain, despite the fact that attempts were made, such as *Solidaridad Gallega* [Galician Solidarity] (1907), that were clearly influenced by the experience of the broad coalition *Solidaritat Catalana* [Catalan Solidarity], but which experienced much more frustrated political results.[10] The emergence of the LB was, therefore, somewhat different from what had occurred in the range of peninsular regionalisms, both because of the seriousness of the situation and the lack of political organizations in Galicia capable of leading mobilization processes that were regionalist in nature, and against the political system of Spain's Restoration, "oligarchical and despotic", in the words of Joaquín Costa.

---

8   See Risco (1930).
9   See Máiz (1984), and Villares (2017).
10 Cabo Villaverde (2006).

The LB were founded in a truly unique time and context. They are born in a "neutral" Spain in the European conflict, with ideological and political influences from Joaquín Costa's Reform movement ("Regenerationism") and social Catholicism, but also from the internal experience of *Solidaridad Gallega* and the Monforte Agrarian Assemblies. From the former, they inherited the name of their mouthpiece, *A Nosa Terra* [Our Homeland] founded by the members of *Solidaridad Gallega* in A Coruña in 1907. From the latter, a programme of technical reform for the Galician rural sector and the experience of several leaders, amongst which must be highlighted the figure of Rodrigo Sanz, a figure well connected with the Catalan regionalist leader Cambó. To this regionalist and "solidary", agrarian and vaguely republican tradition, the impulse from a nucleus of Galician residents in Madrid and, of course, the societal strength of Galician emigration in the Americas, should be added. The person who opted for this variety of influences was the journalist Antón Villar Ponte, with the publication of his booklet, *Nacionalismo gallego. Nuestra afirmación regional* [Galician Nationalism. Our regional affirmation]. It was published in April 1916 and was the cornerstone of the first meeting of a LB branch in A Coruña. This initiative was well received, both in Galicia and in the Galician diaspora in America.[11]

The manifesto of Villar Ponte was the result of a climate of opinion that had been evident for two years, both in Galicia and Madrid, regarding the two problems that would be focused on by the LB's ideology: the defence of the Galician language and the study of Galicia's economic problems. Two years previously, the promoter of the LB had published an article, "Galician should not die",[12] in which he maintained that one's native language was synonymous with "thinking for oneself" and a way of fighting the "separatism" of the central State, which marginalized the peripheral regions. The political context was also marked by debates on political regionalism with the creation of the first Catalan self-government institution or *Mancomunitat de Catalunya* (1913), a parliamentary debate on the co-officiality of the Catalan language (1915) or, for the specific case of Galicia, the creation of a university chair in Galician literature (1913) at the University of Madrid and not the Minerva of Santiago de Compostela. In addition to these cultural affirmations, the appearance in Madrid of the journal *Estudios Gallegos*, edited by Aurelio Ribalta, which was the "fuse for the resurgence of Galicianism in Galicia",[13] was decisive. A publication whose outlook was regenerationist and which had "solidarity" influences, its

---

11 Beramendi & Núñez Seixas (1995).
12 *La Voz de Galicia*, 9 May 1914.
13 Beramendi (2007: 429).

list of contributors was extensive, and included among others Lois Porteiro or Rodrigo Sanz, the author of a series of articles that summarized the work undertaken by the Monforte agricultural assemblies. In fact, this group of Galician people settled in Madrid defended a thorough reform of Galician agriculture, the improvement of communications and the abandonment of tariff protectionism, which was a substantial part of the future LB programme and, therefore, of Galician nationalism during the Spanish Second Republic (1931–36).

In addition to the Galician and Madrid context, the emergence of the LB was connected with movements from outside of Galicia which ended up, more or less accidentally, stimulating the Galician process. An obvious example was the Irish Republican Brotherhood, which achieved significant social and cultural mobilization in the "pre-revolutionary" era, particularly through its infiltration of the Gaelic League.[14] A rather later observation by Risco, in the first issues of the *Nós* magazine that dealt with the Irish question, confirmed this parallelism, when he noted that "The Gaelic League was formed in Ireland long before [1893], with the same purpose as that of our Language Brotherhood".[15] The LB brethren idea had a certain relationship with the notion of "Franciscan" fraternity,[16] which distanced the LB movement from the political party concept. Membership of the LB had something of a social apostolate about it, which was linked to a Catholic conception of the world, because the Brethren (*irmandiños*) allowed the solidarity of its members to be strengthened through ties that were stronger than ideas. The later definition of the LB by the Ourense group, *Nós*, whose intellectual roots were to a great extent orientalist and neosophical, would clearly insist on these ideological and organizational traits in which a certain secrecy and occultism would be common practices.[17]

2 From Regionalism to Nationalism

The Language Brotherhood founded in A Coruña was immediately replicated in other cities and towns in Galicia, surpassing twenty nuclei, from Compostela to Monforte, Vilalba, Betanzos, Ferrol, Viveiro, A Estrada and Pontevedra. The largest territorial implantation of the LB coincided to some extent with the nuclei of the preceding *Solidaridad Gallega*, which was stronger in the

---

14 See Foster (2014: 90), and Paseta (1999: 149).
15 *Nós*, 8 (1921).
16 Agra-Mariño (2017).
17 Ventura (2010: 110).

northern provinces than southern Galicia. The constitution of these local LB groups was the result of successive press campaigns, and also of tours or visits to each locality on the part of the Brethren from A Coruña who, in the manner of a religious mission, transmitted the good news to local mesocratic groups. In fact, the LB fully represent the common practice of the nationalist groups at that time in Spain: to be more a movement than a party, create a loose militancy for its members, defend a collegial direction of the movement, which as a whole implied maintaining decentralized action and a predominance of indirect affiliation, whether with figures on a personal basis or cultural bodies which, at the local level, were the best mouthpieces for the LB's "idearium". As Vicente Risco often asserted, the value of an individual "brother" was more valuable (whether it was the poet Ramón Cabanillas or the "brilliant artist" Alfonso R. Castelao) than a whole local grouping, because the triumph of Galicianism would depend more "on a remarkable novel written in Galician" than "all material progress".[18]

During the first two years of the LB movement's existence, the rapid and successive creation of local circles was accompanied by two tensions that were solved partially in the first LB Assembly, held in Lugo in November 1918. The first tension involved the model of organization of the Brotherhood branches and the need to forge a shared strategy and a common programme. The degree of affiliation of the LB groups was low and, above all, very uneven. The LB in A Coruña had hundreds of members, while other local circles did not exceed half a dozen. A pessimistic Vicente Risco confessed at the end of 1918 that in the city of Ourense, the Language Brethren had no more than three members, which was "something of a cause for curiosity, when not for laughter", whilst on his visit to Santiago de Compostela two months later, he commented "I did not find anyone who would take me to the Brethren or introduce me" to militants he already knew.[19] Apart from these negative impressions, the truth is that the LB had from the beginning the will to be a movement and not a political party, given the lack of faith that parties had in political life at that time. One of the strongest leaders in the early period of the LB, Lois Porteiro Garea, stated in the summer of 1916 that "we are not a party", because this new movement had no intention of "corrupting us by going after votes and engaging in the ungodly comedy of the deputies".[20] The search for votes, however, was undertaken in the parliamentary elections of February 1918, with four candidates presented in the districts of Pontedeume, Noia, A Estrada and Celanova. They failed to get

---

18   *A Nosa Terra*, 10 July 1918.
19   Ventura (2010: 13, 25).
20   Seixas Seoane (2016: 36).

elected, despite the support and strategic guidance provided for them by the Catalanist Francesc Cambó, to organize the election campaign.[21]

The LB's electoral failure accelerated the need to provide a better organizational structure and, at the same time, set an ideological and political agenda. The organizational boost was the work of the LB's main director in A Coruña, Lois Peña Novo, who drafted a regulation that changed the objectives of the movement (including the political autonomy of Galicia) and opened the way for a coordinated action of the LB. This initiative would be reflected in the Brotherhoods' first political assembly, held in Lugo on 17–18 November, 1918, which brought together 60 people representing 16 local groups and that changed the political profile of the LB.[22] The changes introduced at the Lugo assembly were of an organizational and political nature. At the organic level, the Lugo meeting was the first in a series of assemblies that were held on an annual basis (Santiago, Vigo, Monforte) until February 1922, when a split in the movement took place and an attempt, commanded by Risco, to create a more centralized structure through the *Irmandade Nazonalista Galega* [Galician Nationalist Brotherhood]. The second consequence was of an ideological and political nature, by the public and solemn declaration that "we declare ourselves, now and forever, Galician nationalists". It was the end of a two-year period of uncertainties, in which the LB's ideological direction oscillated between political regionalism, social Catholicism and the conservative politics of the Spanish reformist leader Antonio Maura. For the more moderate sector of the LB, the decision taken at the Lugo assembly was received with many reservations, in such a way that the regionalism in the "solidarity" tradition, which dreamed of finding allies in some sectors of the dynastic parties, ended with the electoral failure of 1918 and with the full incorporation of the "brethren" movement of the Ourense group, in particular Losada Diéguez and Vicente Risco, who defined the theoretical and even organizational line of the Language Brotherhoods from 1918 until the Primo de Rivera dictatorship in September 1923.

The lax militancy that characterized the LB meant that the number of members of the various local groups was not high. At the Monforte assembly (1922), according to Risco's own estimates, there should have been around 600 members present, since it was estimated that the A Coruña grouping, which had three hundred, represented half of all the movement. In terms of comparison, LB membership was genuinely low, since the Gaelic League, in 1908, had about

---

21 Beramendi (2007: 452–55).
22 Beramendi (2007: 464 and ff.).

47,000 members,[23] even though the total population of Ireland in 1911 barely duplicated that of Galicia for the same dates. The LB's sociological profile, with the known details of its 433 members in the 1918–1924 period, reveals that the most relevant sectors were the liberal professions, such as lawyers and surgeons (25.6%), property owners and entrepreneurs / traders (23.1%), as well as the intellectual professions (teachers, writers and journalists), with 22.6%. These three sectors comprised more than seventy percent, which explains the low membership numbers of adherents from the lower classes, but also from the Church, Army or Civil Administration. As a whole, the LB's sociological base had a "clear predominance of liberal and intellectual professionals", from where almost all its leaders or "guiding figures" hailed.[24] In similar organizations such as the Gaelic League, according to T. McMahon's analysis, the social profile of its leaders, by 1912, would be even more mesocratic: 47.2% of liberal professionals and 44.6% of civil servants, trade workers and craftsmen (Allegue 2017). These Galician and Irish sociological traits confirm the general periodization of the "Nation-Building Processes" of non-dominant ethnic groups, in whose "phase B", when political claims are voiced, the role of "erudite scholars" who define the territory, build their history and codify their language continues to be essential.[25]

The LB's elite had generally a university background (Law, Medicine, Humanities, Teaching), with attendance at non-Galician educational institutions (Madrid, Deusto), as happened frequently in the Irish case, where many leaders of the revolutionary generation studied in England or France. However, unlike the Irish example, where the role played by the Catholic schools of the Christians Brothers and by higher education bodies such as University College Dublin (1908),"a microcosm of political sentiment in Ireland" where "many dozens" of that generation were educated,[26] was crucial; neither secondary nor university studies in Galicia experienced a process of assuming a commitment to Galician culture and language, given the distance of the Catholic Church from the regionalist movement and, later on, from the Brotherhoods. This deficit in the preparation of the LB elites was partially compensated by an informal education acquired in journalism and through emigration to Cuba and Argentina. In short, an education of the "self-taught, with training acquired in activism related to agriculture and associations, and the adventures of emigration".[27]

---

23   Allegue (2017).
24   Beramendi (2007: 698 and ff.).
25   Hroch (2015: 34 and ff.).
26   See Pasetta (1999:53 and ff.), and Foster (2015: 31 and ff.).
27   Villar Ponte (1977: 27).

The social profile of the LB membership and leadership was not, therefore, very different from other nationalist movements of that time, with the middle classes, who were the expression of a rising social mobility and high cultural awareness, clearly predominant. "The republic of poets" was the title of one of the articles on Ireland published in the Madrid liberal newspaper *El Sol* by Ricardo Baeza, who noted that in the top ranks in the political struggle of *Sinn Féin* were poets, dramatists, writers and historians such as Griffith, Russell, Childers, FitzGerald or Green, not to mention fellow travellers like the distinguished poet, W.B. Yeats.[28] The Galician writer and nationalist leader, Ramón Otero Pedrayo, must have been thinking about something similar when he came up with the profile of "Fenian poet and fighter" —and not a lawyer— for the protagonist of "The Student", a part of his 1928 novel *Os camiños da vida* [The Roads of Life] which narrates a sporadic trip to Ireland from Paris.

The LB programme had characteristics that were clearly sourced from the foundational texts and previous tradition of the solidarists and land reformers. But it also underwent a remarkable transformation after the first political assembly held in November 1918, where the transition from regionalism to political nationalism was formally approved. During the first two years of its existence, the LB concentrated their efforts on two main objectives, contained in the editorial text of the first issue of *A Nosa Terra* November 1916). The first objective was the "affectionate" defence of Galician, according to their own definition as friends and members of the "language brotherhoods". By placing the question of the language at the forefront, the LB were breaking with the entire Galician cultural tradition inherited from the *Rexurdimento* (or Galician literary and cultural renaissance of the late nineteenth century), in which the use of Galician was reserved for poetic expression, while in prose, in family and epistolary relations or in political meetings, its use was sporadic. This challenge aspired to overcome the legacy of speaking the popular language entailing a negative social effect, which had already been criticized by *Rexurdimento* poets like Rosalía de Castro. The LB strategy attempted to reverse the process and this was, without a doubt, its main contribution to contemporary Galician culture, given the importance that had been conferred upon the cultural (but not so much to the linguistic) field since regionalism. In an analysis of the contents of *A Nosa Terra* magazine, the hegemony of culture is constant, with rates between 30 and 35% in the thematic distribution of articles published from 1908 to 1930.[29]

---

28   Baeza (2010: 113 and ff.).
29   Beramendi (2007: 353, 649).

The LB's political program underwent changes or adaptations over time, within a stable structure summarized in the "nationalist decalogue" written by Vicente Risco, from the agreements of the Lugo political assembly and then published with various formats and titles in *A Nosa Terra*.[30] Taking this decalogue as a starting point, in addition to other contemporary doctrinal texts, we can group the LB's programmatic contents into three categories. The first consists in the re-galicianization of Galicia, understood in a similar way to what was attempted by the Irish nationalists, although the intensity of the process was modulated. In the Galician case, the central proposal was the recovery of Galician as an expression of a "palingenetic, redemptive" endeavour, as Ramón Villar Ponte would state years later. This recovery of the language (or "speech") should be accompanied by a programme of reconstruction of Galician culture as a whole, thought and expressed basically in Galician and across the most diverse registers: literary practise, social communication, theatre, choral music and, of course, in the institutional and political arena.

The final objective, also analogous to the Irish process, was to "de-castilianize" Galicia and, therefore, to "galicianize" Galicia. Just as there was an attempt to build an "Irish Ireland" through an energetic "de-Anglicization", in which "being Irish meant not being English",[31] the overarching LB project was to achieve a Galician monolingualism that, actually, was only practised among the militants and sympathizers of the Brotherhoods. In fact, in the aforementioned Decalogue, the linguistic issue is only present in one of the ten mandates (the third one), in which they advocate a "co-official status of the Galician and Castilian languages", an idea that will remain prevalent until the Galicianist Party in the 1930s. However, the LB's cultural programme went beyond the linguistic issue itself. LB members, whether the most liberal-democrat in the group from A Coruña, or the most traditionalist-Catholic in the Ourense group, *Nós*, conferred great importance upon the construction of a symbolic repertoire of a Galician nationhood. To this end, initiatives such as the declaring of 25 July, the feast of St. James's, as the Galician National Holiday, the mythification of the historical and legendary figure of the "marshall" Pardo de Cela, captured and executed in 1483 by Castilian troops, or the resignification of monuments such as the one dedicated by the regionalists to the "martyrs of Carral", liberal soldiers who had risen up against the monarchy of Isabel II in 1846 and converted, by twentieth-century Galician nationalism, into defenders

---

30   Ventura (2010: 105).
31   Pasetta (1999: 120).

of Galician freedoms as had been the *comuneros* in Castile, who revolted against Emperor Charles V in the sixteenth century.[32]

A second programmatic block was constituted by the objective of achieving a state of political autonomy for Galicia, sometimes described as "integral", within the framework of the debates that were taking place in Spain in the first decades of the twentieth century. This was the first point of the Decalogue which, in addition, was reinforced with other demands such as "municipal autonomy" and "equal civil and political rights" for men and women. The political programme of the LB had two pillars on which to sustain itself: to turn Galicia into a political subject by means of achieving a system of integral autonomy and, secondly, to overcome the limitations of the oligarchical liberalism of the Restoration regime, by combatting political clientelism ("anti-boss rule", *anti-caciquismo*) and a determination to regenerate political life or participation, which the Spanish philosopher Ortega y Gasset called at that time the "new politics". However, the political results obtained by the LB during this initial phase, from 1916 to 1923, were relatively poor. Participation in political life was reduced to a symbolic presence in the municipal sphere, as attempts to enter the Madrid parliament were blocked in the February 1918 elections. Galician nationalism did not compete electorally again until the constituent elections of the Second Republic (June 1931), although in this case, better results were attained (four deputies from a total of 47 elected in Galicia). The purposes of political regeneration of the system, especially in the fight against clientelism that were upheld by an important part of the LB (that which came from the "solidarity" and federal tradition) were postponed in the face of the strenuous resistance of the Galician political structure, in which between 1876 and 1923 only one deputy, out of 945 elected, would not belong to the two dynastic parties.[33]

The third block of the LB programme was undoubtedly the one that was more developed, because it came from the "solidarity" tendency, from the debates of the Monforte agricultural assemblies and the *Estudios Gallegos* journal group. It referred to the defence of free trade against the protectionism that was characteristic of economic policy that began in Spain after 1891.[34] More than a programme to resolve the chartered tenancy system and progress towards land ownership by the peasantry (which was the banner of the land-reform movement), the LB enthusiastically supported free trade ideology, which, at a certain historical moment, would cause a strong disagreement with

---

32 Villares (2017).
33 Villares (2005: 211).
34 Serrano (1987).

Cambó when he was minister of several governments of Spain. The free trade of the LB, which was defended by various agricultural experts and reformers, was especially insistent in obtaining the "free import of corn", as a necessary measure for the food consumption of the rural population and also as animal feed that would allow the Galician agricultural sector to be competitive in its strategy of exporting empty cattle to the main meat consumer markets in Spain. The free-trade arguments of Galician nationalism were well synthesized in the agreements of the second Monforte agrarian assembly of (1910): "In Galicia, wheat and corn are needed [...]; men and livestock need much more corn than we produce".[35] This demand for tariff-free trade had no political and institutional recourse, both due to the protectionist firmness of Spanish economic policy and the contradictions that this entailed for customs freedom for a farming economy that was being inserted into the Spanish domestic market, which sold thousands of tonnes of meat produced in Galicia.[36] However, it was a demand that fitted perfectly into nationalist ideology and only some contemporary experts, such as Cruz Gallástegui, reviewed or denounced what they considered a clear contradiction, since it was Spanish and not Galician agriculture that was the most deficient in corn production: "The Spanish make us speak and Galicia speaks and demands corn only for other regions to benefit".[37]

Compared to contemporary Catalan and Basque models, the Galician Brotherhoods were founded late, and they were also late in adopting the structure of a political party, not doing so until 1931 when the *Partido Galeguista* (Galicianist Party) was founded. But the LB's work was essential for shaping modern Galician nationalism, because it was able to create a new political project, which broke not only with the old regionalism, but also with the old politics of Spanish liberalism. Their forces were limited and the capacity to craft a cross-class and mass political project was not possible until the times of the Second Republic. But the foundational phase of the LB, from 1916 to 1923, was important for two reasons. Firstly, because they developed the ideological and doctrinal foundations of Galicia as a nation, in which the defence of the Galician language was essential. The LB tried to create a national consciousness based on cultural identity. The second important contribution was to consider the case of Galicia within the Iberian and even European context, thus seeking external alliances and complicities that made Galician national reality visible.

---

35   *Estudios* Gallegos, 2 (1915).
36   Villares (1982).
37   Gallástegui (1930).

3 Internationalizing Galician Nationalism

The Language Brotherhoods were founded, as expressed in texts and articles by several of their leaders, with an "internationalist vision", in the sense of seeking alliances with political and cultural movements that could be considered analogous or close to those of Galicia. This connection with the outside world was basically conceived as working in three directions: the relations within the Spanish State with Basques and, above all, Catalans as a continuity of the period of "regional Spain"; secondly, building with Portugal a cultural "reference point for reintegration" that, incidentally, served as an intermediary to enter into some, and notably French, European cultural circles; and, thirdly, connecting with the most emblematic example of national struggle at that time, which was Ireland. Despite the fact that the LB leaders were fully aware that they needed to garner support and develop external relations that reinforced their internal action, in particular to better define their political strategy, the results achieved were scarce, both within the Iberian Peninsula and in possible relationships with Ireland or the joining of European platforms such as the *Union des Nationalités* or the League of Nations associations, such as the Catalan *Amics d'Europa* or the magazine *Messidor*.[38]

The delay with which the LB appeared clearly prevented the Galician national issue from being part of Wilsonian euphoria of 1918. An essential point was the absence of a specific strategy in relation to the Great War, which was hardly found except for fleeting mentions in nationalist newspapers. An enormous contrast with what happened in the case of Catalonia, where Catalanists presented the several hundreds of Catalan volunteers enlisted in the French Army as fighters for Catalonia's freedom alongside the Czech or the Polish Legions and organized an enthusiastic welcome for Marshal Joseph Joffre, who had familiar connections in the Catalan-speaking Roussillon. In addition, the war divided the field of nationalism, between the most Germanophile positions of Enric Prat de la Riba and the pro-allied Antoni Rovira I Virgili. The latter author was the one who clearly defended the opportunity to link the principle of nationalities to the struggle for freedom and progress represented by the allied powers, which forced "all nationalism to have an international policy", that is, a diplomacy of its own.[39] The same thing happened in Ireland, whose volunteers (particularly Ulster) participated in the battlefields against Germany but also, on the part of the Fenians, sought support from the central empires that weakened the strength of the British empire. The war was,

---

38 Núñez Seixas (2010: 63–75).
39 Núñez Seixas (2010: 34–43).

therefore, an opportunity to internationally project the Irish question, as O'Brien recalls concerning two relatives who died almost simultaneously, one in the Battle of Somme (Thomas Kettle) and another (Francis Skeffingtom) during the Easter Rising.[40]

The discussion of this problem was not raised openly by the LB, even after the assembly held in Lugo, which opened a door of "pan-Galicianism" to Portugal that would be extended to other partners in subsequent assemblies. As "indispensable issues to deal with", Risco proposed in January 1921 several points that should be discussed at the third meeting of the LB, to be held in Vigo the following month: "Attitude towards of Ireland", "Relations with Portugal" and "Relations with the Basque Country and Catalonia".[41] This thematic list allows these relations to be examined in order to calibrate the degree of internationalization of Galician nationalism until 1923.

The first external relations that the LB sought to establish, in the fully regionalist stage, were with moderate Catalanism led at that time by Cambó. These relations were conceived in the framework of a domestic political strategy of combatting the Restoration system, a task to which the Catalan leader was especially committed from the drafting of the *Espanya Gran* project (1916) and the profound political crisis of 1917. But these relations with Cambó went in a short period from euphoria to disappointment. Certainly, there was a strong current of sympathy towards Catalonia in Galicia, which was evident since the times of *fin-de-siècle* regionalism and *Solidaridad Gallega*, which made the Catalan example a political reference and a model to follow: "We have to imitate Catalonia", it was stated in the journal *Revista Gallega* in 1907.[42] This Catalan connection was present from the founding of the LB, when they were still debating between regionalist and nationalist positions. In 1917, the LB established contact with Cambó's party (*Lliga Regionalista*), which led to Galician leaders visiting Barcelona in November of 1917, and a reciprocal visit by Cambó to Galicia. The climax of this relationship was the February 1918 elections, in which Cambó dreamed of being "President of the government with an obedient Parliament", but that dream of breaking the political structure of the Restoration ended in complete failure, after no more than 25 deputies were obtained, none of which were from Galicia.[43]

From that moment on, Galician nationalism ceased to have any dialogue with the *Lliga* and Cambó; these were not replaced immediately by other peers

---

40   O'Brien (1999: 14 and ff.).
41   Ventura (2010: 80).
42   Beramendi (2007: 403).
43   Riquer (2013: 93 and ff.).

such as the more radical party *Acció Catalana*, founded in 1922. In September 1923, the "Triple Alliance" was organized in an ephemeral fashion, preceding the Galeuzca pact of 1933.[44] The 1918 electoral failure left a panorama of scorched earth. Cambó's presence in various monarchist governments (1918 and 1921) accelerated opposition to the laws of tariff protection that the Catalan minister had promoted, which resulted in a campaign to discredit Cambó, about whom a negative (and even anti-Semitic) image was formed amongst Galician nationalists, and which also appeared in Catalan radical nationalism as of 1919.[45] As is evident in the agenda of the LB assembly in 1921, hardly any trace was left of the relations with the Basque Country, at least until the Triple Alliance of 1923, despite the influence that a "bascophile" like Losada Diéguez exercized in the Brotherhoods.

More relevant were the relations woven by the Galician nationalists with Portugal, which were substantiated on two different levels. The foreground, most clearly political, consisted of the conversion of Portugal into a positive referent of reintegration, founded on the cultural and linguistic brotherhood and also on the opportunity posed by the Portuguese Republican regime for a future Iberian federal republic. Villar Ponte defended both "pan-Galicianism" as an "integral Iberianism", that translated into one of the most well-known agreements of the Lugo assembly: "Galicia has to consider Portugal, because it is axiomatic, like the bulwark of its spiritual independence".[46] This appeal to Portugal, allowing it to serve as a counterpoint to the negative reference that was Castile, was one of the strongest currents of contemporary Galician nationalism, reaching in the work of A.R. Castelao, *Sempre en Galiza* (Forever in Galicia) (Buenos Aires 1944), its most absolute expression, where Portugal is regarded as an expression of what Galicia might have been. In this pro-Portuguese position that was republican and federal in tendency, the group from A Coruña was highly active through the journalism and essays of Antón Villar Ponte or Xoán V. Viqueira, who also upheld an approximation, even orthographical, of Galician to Portuguese language. Even an intellectual somewhat at a remove from the LB, like Eloy Luis-André, defended the use of Galician as a universal language because "a language employed by thirty million people cannot die".[47] News and references to Portuguese culture and politics were very frequent in the pages of *A Nosa Terra*, and some Portuguese leaders, such as the minister Leonardo Coimbra, visited Galicia at the invitation of the

---

44   Estévez (1991).
45   Ucelay-Da Cal (2006: 87).
46   Villar Ponte (1971: 211).
47   *A Nosa Terra*, 25 January 1917.

A Coruña Brotherhood. However, this approach to Portugal had few echoes in the neighbouring country, where it was not possible to create any movement of an irredentist nature that claimed a Galician-Portuguese political union, except in poems such as "A Galiza. A modo de velho cantar" ["To Galicia. In the manner of an old ballad"], by the poet Afonso Lopes Vieira: "Leave Castile and come to us", which was echoed in the LB mouthpiece.[48] Murguía had alluded to Portuguese "indecision" in his time and, in 1920, a Castelao vignette took up the same idea when a grandfather could not tell his grandson whether those who lived beyond the River Miño were more foreign than those from Madrid. Almost non-existent irredentism in Portugal and more cultural than political reintegrationism in Galicia were two sides of a coin that would have hardly any circulation.

Cultural reintegration is the background of the relationship with Portugal, prioritized by the *Nós* Group in particular, and specifically by Vicente Risco, who confessed in 1921 that "I have full powers from the Language Brotherhoods Assembly to reach an understanding with our friends from Portugal".[49] This relationship was based on the forging of a cultural alliance with Portuguese authors and magazines that allowed a presence of Galician literary culture not only in Portugal but also through its intermediation in French publications. The main Portuguese interlocutor was the poet Teixeira de Pascoaes, editor of *A Aguia* magazine and leader of the intellectual group, *A Renacença Portuguesa* (1911), whom Risco greeted as "brother and friend" in their correspondence. Thanks to this relationship, a regular collaboration of Galician authors was established in Portuguese magazines and vice versa, with Pascoaes himself contributing with a poetic text published in the first issue of *Nós* magazine. But the most important was the connection with the French literary critic Philéas Lebesgue, a regular contributor to the *Mercure de France* magazine, where he regularly provided news of Galician culture in the *Lettres portugaises* section.[50] Although these relations were mediated by Portugal, the truth is that the works of Galician authors were disseminated through this French magazine, which explains why Risco himself regarded Lebesgue as "the defender of our literature in erudite France".[51]

The most important external reference for Galician nationalism, in which a purportedly long-standing Celtic brotherhood was also present, was Ireland, the mirror that captivated the eyes of most Western European nationalities, as

---

48   *A Nosa Terra*, 10 September 1917.
49   Cameirâo (2010: 465).
50   Figueroa (1996).
51   *Nós*, 30 October 1920.

Poland had done in the nineteenth century. The presence of the Irish question in Galicia had had some importance in the *fin-de-siécle* Galician regionalism, when an author, such as the notary, Diego Pazos or the regionalist leader, Alfredo Brañas, followed closely the Irish agricultural struggles that led to the Land Act of 1881, which transformed the structure of land ownership in favour of the Catholic settlers, and which penalized the "Protestant" Thomas Parnell as a political leader.[52] The highly praised poetic text of Alfredo Brañas appealing to the Irish example as a model for Galician peasant farmers (*"Ergue labrego, érguete e anda/ como en Irlanda, como en Irlanda"* ["Rise up, peasant, rise up and take a stand / As in Ireland, as in Ireland"], is part of an Irish connection that did not continue until the odyssey of the Language Brotherhoods was well under way. It can be stated that the Irish mirror, despite the apogee of the paradigm of Celticism in the formation of the idea of Galicia by Manuel Murguía, disappeared completely from view until 1920, four years after the Easter Rising took place. The news about Ireland in *A Nosa Terra* during the years 1916 to 1923, were "a chronicle of absences, passion and silence"[53] and, it could also be added, unexpected twists due to internal conflicts rather than ideological coherence with the fractions of Irish nationalism. An ignorance or stagnation of political processes which, on the other hand, is not recorded in somewhat analogous contexts, such as Catalonia, where the Irish question had "an incalculable impact"[54] or in the Basque Country, where "the Irish influence was intense and enduring".[55] The Irish echoes also reached Brittany, where some of the *brétonnant* leaders spent sleepless nights during Easter 1916, waiting for news from Ireland, or made paintings on a wall in Rennes.[56] In the Galician case, Villar Ponte or his friends did not do anything like that in any of the Galician cities.

However, the interest of the LB's nationalism in the political evolution of Ireland was strong as of 1920, in the context of the political hegemony of Sinn Féin, the conflicts around the 1921 Treaty and subsequent Civil War. There were three aspects of Irish politics that particularly captivated Galician nationalists, because they in some way related to the internal divisions that the LB were experiencing and which were made explicit in the split at the Monforte Assembly of 1922: the debate on political or cultural nationalism, which was reflected in the controversy between Peña Novo and Risco; the conflict between

---

52 O'Brien (1994: 52).
53 Madriñán (2017).
54 Ucelay-Da Cal (1984: 218).
55 Núñez Seixas (2017: 450).
56 See Carney (2016: 77 and ff.), and Le Cloarec (2016: 60).

those who were "pro-treaty" and "anti-treaty"; and thirdly, the effects of political violence and the "sacrificial mystique" that had begun with those who died in Easter 1916, followed the death of the mayor of Cork, MacSwinney and culminated in the Irish civil war and its devastating effects on so many families. Without going into the periphery followed by the Irish revolutionary generation, it is important to examine the reception and the echoes of that process in Galicia.

These Irish echoes came quite late, despite the Celtic brotherhood that united the two peoples. Neither the conflicts caused by the Great War itself, or the change produced in 1916 with the Easter Rising and the subsequent elimination of the "constitutional nationalism" defended by the Irish Parliamentary Party, which led to the overwhelming victory of the Republicans of Sinn Féin in the first elections of the post-war period (73 Fenian deputies over 6 "redmondist" deputies), had any special impact on Galicia. It was probably not through ignorance, because in the Galician daily press itself (*La Voz de Galicia, El Noroeste*) and in Madrid (*El Sol*) or Barcelona (*La Vanguardia*), news and authored articles appeared on the Irish question. Reference should be made to the pervasive series of articles by Ricardo Baeza, published in *El Sol* during the 1920–1921 period, in which a reference is made to the sons of Breogán, the discoverer of Éirinn: "the Galicians are morally obligated to be interested in the future of Ireland, and I fear that despite the masses held for the late mayor of Cork, not enough has been done up until now".[57]

It was from 1920 that the LB, once defined as nationalists, began to pay attention to Irish politics, radicalized after the Versailles Treaty and led by the Sinn Feiners, who rejected parliamentary policy and campaigned for independence. During 1920–1923, Galician nationalist mouthpieces (*A Nosa Terra* and *Nós*) included extensive news on Irish issues, whether concerning literature and history, or about an episode that had enormous repercussion for European public life: the hunger strike and subsequent death in jail of the mayor of Cork, Terence MacSwinney, in October 1920, between "surprising" support from the Catholic Church (there were theological doubts about whether it was really a suicide) and reservations about his attitude on the part of people close to him, such as Michael Collins, who did not entirely agree with that personal sacrifice of "dying for Ireland".[58] However, one year later, the cultural magazine *Nós* dedicated an entire issue to the memory of the Irish martyr, with biographical details on MacSwinney and a version in Galician, produced by Antón Villar Ponte, of the work of W.B. Yeats, *Cathleen ni Houlihan*, the literary expression,

---

57 Baeza (2010: 104).
58 See Baeza (2010: 131 and ff.), and Foster (2015: 273 and ff.).

in the words of its translator, of "the struggles of a fraternal country of ours to become independent from foreign imperialism".[59] The choice of *Nós* magazine was a homage in every way, after years of indecision, regarding which path to follow in the approach of the Irish revolution and as a way of promoting the Galician cause abroad. A hundred copies of this issue of the magazine was sent to the Irish delegate in Madrid in order "to be sent to Ireland" and they also undertook to sell portraits of the mayor of Cork to raise money for the "Irish White Cross".

This position of *Nós*, which partly moved away from that of *A Nosa Terra*, clearly connected with the internal debates of the LB who, in February 1922, would hold a decisive political assembly that led to a split in the movement. The split could be understood, mutatis mutandis, as a Galician version of the break between the supporters of the Treaty, with whom the Coruña branch of the Brotherhoods sympathized, and the Republicans led by Éamon de Valera, with whom the *Nós* group felt greater affinity. The attention dedicated by the magazine to the Irish question was also the result of intense communication, even on the diplomatic level, with the Irish representative in Madrid, for whom a young Fermín Penzol acted as an effective intermediary.[60] Vicente Risco took special care to maintain relations with the Irish delegation in Madrid in order to avoid the intrusion of the defenders of the "disgusting treaty", informing about the political situation in Galicia and reiterating support for the position of De Valera. The echoes of Ireland could be heard in Galician internal code without something analogous happening in the opposite direction, given the obsession of the Irish delegation in Spain with establishing a diplomatic relationship with the Spanish government.

The efforts made by the LB, especially by Vicente Risco to put the issue of Galician nationalism on the international agenda was meritorious but very limited. This does not lessen the value of Risco's opinion, in 1921, that "We, without outside support, can never do anything".[61] The outer connection worked better through personal contacts, such as those maintained with Teixeira de Pascoes or Philéas Lebesgue, and less at institutional levels, except for the sporadic relationship with the Catalanists. Their organizational weakness did not allow them to reach large European forums where the nationality question and the problem of national minorities, were debated.[62] There was no material means to achieve this (no figures like Cambó or the Basque Ramón de

---

59 See *Nós*, 8 (December 1921); Insua (2005: 196–97).
60 Cabrera (2016).
61 Ventura (2010: 94).
62 Núñez Seixas (2001).

la Sota), nor were the social roots of nationalism in Galicia comparable to the cases of the Basque Country and Catalonia and, of course, those of Ireland. This outward projection of Galician nationalism would only achieve a certain dimension in the times of the Second Republic and, then, in exile, with actors from the first Brotherhoods, such as Castelao and other, younger figures such as Plácido Castro, who, nevertheless, could never become the Galician counterpart of Cambó's lieutenant charged with the internationalization of the Catalan question in the 1920s, Joan Estelrich.

4   An Assessment: Challenges and Hindrances

A final assessment on three key aspects can serve as a recapitulation of this article and also as a comparative reflection. Firstly, it is necessary to evaluate to what extent there is continuity or rupture in the "Galician generation of 1916", with respect to its predecessors. Secondly, the reasons for the hegemony of cultural nationalism over political nationalism which distances the Galician case from the nearby examples of the Basque Country or Catalonia and, above all, from Ireland. Finally, it is necessary to respond to the question posed by Risco in 1930, on the non-confluence of the two political parties that he regarded as strictly Galician: the nationalist ("fledgling") and the agrarian ("ill-fated"). In that blind spot, the diagnosis of Galicia's political problem, performed during the annus mirabilis of 1930, was summarized by the person who was the main intellectual and organic leader of Galician cultural nationalism.

A break or continuity? The main leadership of the first Brotherhoods comprised a small group of people that we could identify as the generation of 1916, in accordance with the later testimony of Ramón Villar Ponte (1977). Its main members would be young people, born in the 1880s (Porteiro Garea, Viqueira, the brothers Villar Ponte, Castelao, Risco, Losada Diéguez, Otero Pedrayo) and the 1890s (Peña Novo, Víctor Casas). It was a generation that could be equated, by its social profile, to those who led other decisive changes, such as the 1901 Generation (*generació de 1901*) in Catalonia, defined as such by the journalist Agustí Calvet *Gaziel* and comprising more experienced members than those of the LB; to the Spanish generation of 1914, defined by the leadership of Ortega y Gasset or, in the Irish case, to the generation of 1916, which was the protagonist of the greatest change of that time in Western Europe, responsible for what "all changed, changed utterly", in the powerful lines by W.B. Yeats. What characterizes all these generations was to have shared intense experiences, such as a war (1898, 1914) and their proposal to react against their predecessors, a reaction was very inconsistent in its intensity. In the case of the Great War, the influence on the generation of the Brotherhoods was almost irrelevant; however, they were fully aware that they should be different from their predecessors, although with nuances. For Antón Villar Ponte, generational colleagues such as Porteiro or Viqueira could be defined as the "continuation" of the "precursors", those that Murguía defined as the leaders of the Galician *Rexurdimento*, which, however, was not referred to in the founding manifesto of the LB.[63] On the other hand, several members of the generation who produced a narrative of their intellectual formation, such as Otero Pedrayo or Risco, did not strictly recognize the earlier teaching by those Galician authors, although they did not lack teachers, who they found in the European cultural current that flowed from Romanticism to the conservative revolution at the end of the nineteenth century.[64] In short, the self-perception of the LB leadership is closer to being a break than a continuity. In addition to Risco's opinion, Antón Villar Ponte did not fail to emphasize his initiative of May 1916 as "the greatest and highest [event] that occurred in our Homeland", because "thanks to us [the promoters of the first LB], our children will have a country".[65] The peculiarity of the Galician case is undoubtedly the organizational and mobilizing weakness of *fin-de-siècle* regionalism that approached the 1898 crisis in a situation of theoretical and programmatic "atony".[66] On the contrary, the Catalan generation of 1901 defined itself as an alternative to a conservative regionalism that was implicated in the political dynamics of the Restoration system until the crisis of 1898, from whose consequences it swiftly distanced itself.[67] The Irish revolutionary generation was the result of an intense "radicalisation, polarisation and collision" developed from 1890 until the explosion of 1916, in which intense political and even parliamentary action was combined with a cultural reconstruction in the Irish context.[68]

A nationalism with "two souls", cultural and political? Certainly, in the LB's strategic choices, the existence of these "two souls", so frequent in contemporary nationalist parties, could be seen from 1918. Initially, there was a tendency towards political action and intervention in the electoral processes, which was mainly upheld by a part of the A Coruña Brotherhood, which connected with the Catalan experience of the *Lliga* and, in another way, with the Irish experience of the parliamentary struggle in favour of Home Rule. It was those that

63 Villar Ponte (1916, 1971: 61 and ff.).
64 Villares (2018: 205 and ff.).
65 *A Nosa Terra*, 5 March 1931.
66 Beramendi (2017: 347 and ff.).
67 Riquer (2001: 185 and ff.).
68 Foster (2015: XV).

Risco would contemptuously call the Galician "redmondists". This commitment to politics lost at the Monforte assembly, as was highlighted in the subsequent debate on a "fundamental disparity": whether nationalism was a "problem of culture" (Risco) or a "problem of liberties" (Peña Novo). The standpoint of Risco and many other members of the LB, from Villar Ponte to Castelao, was that it was a priority to "create a people" and to forge "a strong national awareness that makes us completely and authentically Galician", clearly rejecting the practise of politics under the liberal oligarchical system of the Restoration. Expressed with somewhat bombastic words by Antón Villar Ponte, it would be a divergence between supporters of the "victory of the ideal" and those who preferred the "ideal of victory", an idea that the LB's leader had already expressed months before,[69] when he referred to the "two classes of Galicianists": those of an "apostolic temperament" and those of a "political temperament". In this debate, the echoes of disputes that occurred in Catalonia, the Basque Country and Ireland, were clearly perceived at a time of "generalized nationalist splits".[70] However, the essential difference of the Galician Brotherhoods was in the almost total abandonment of the political struggle in favour of cultural nationalism.

Nationalism and agrarianism? This choice refers to the problem expressed later on by Vicente Risco, on the paths that could be followed in the future (he made the criticism that they had obviously not been followed in the past) by the two parties which, in his perspective, could be called strictly Galician: the agrarian and the nationalist: "If the agrarian is an ill-fated Galician party, the nationalist is a fledgling Galician party. The political force that defends the interests of the region must be formed one day from the integration of both, if the Galician farmers manage to wake up and realize their true interests".[71] This article will not examine Risco's wishes and a possible counterfactual history. It is relevant, however, to analyse why this integration did not take place in the founding years of the Brethren and what blockages produced that lack of understanding between a powerful land-reform movement and the nascent nationalist movement. Moreover, in this case, the Irish mirror can help to understand the Galician subject, where some mutual similarities can be found: a fight over the land between the Catholic farmers and the great Protestant landowners, with an intense peasant ownership which was accompanied by a strong rural exodus. However, it is clear that the rhythms and achievements of both processes were very different.

---

69   *A Nosa Terra*, 15 July 1921.
70   Ucelay-Da Cal (2006: 110).
71   Risco (1930: 212).

In the case of Ireland, the Land War favoured not only an intense social mobilization, but the penetration of nationalism in the rural world as a result of a replacement of the English liberal party by the Irish parliamentary party, after the elections of 1885. It was the beginning of a political struggle for Home Rule that reached the eve of the Great War, when a second shift opened the way to the hegemony of the Fenians and, therefore, to the struggle for independence from the British Empire. The analogies of the Galician case with this panorama are merely formal. In Galicia, since the crisis at the end of the nineteenth century, there was an "agrarian malaise" that led to the appearance of the first agrarian organizations (57), "livestock associations" and "farmers' societies" founded until 1900, but there is no connection between land-reform movement and parliamentary political action, despite the attempts of figures such as Manuel Portela Valladares (elected in 1905 as a liberal deputy in an "agrarian" district) or the abbot Basilio Álvarez, promoter of the most important agrarian organizations since 1907: Galician Action (1912), and the Regional Confederation of Galician Farmers (1922). The reformist rhetoric of the agrarian leaders, expressed in the Agrarian Assemblies of Monforte, kept agrarianism not only distant from Galician regionalism but also from Spanish liberalism. The most mature and intense stage of Galician agrarianism was 1918–1923, when a dense associative network was consolidated, comprising nearly a thousand organizations (unions, societies and leagues), which accounted for 15% of all of Spain. The land-reform movement was able to engage on an intense mobilization, promoting strategies such as the default of rents on *foros* and the fight to suppress them.[72] In spite of this temporary coincidence, there were few points of contact between agrarianism and nationalism, and therefore no permeability between both movements. However, what is most surprising is to verify that the LB's agricultural program was so dependent on issues such as free trade and the "free import of corn", that it forgot to address the central issue, which was the reform of land ownership and the integration of smallholding farming in the market, aspects in which agrarian organizations were especially efficient.[73]

Therefore, the paths followed by Galician nationalists and agrarian reformers, as Vicente Risco pointed out in 1930, did not meet. But what the former "Supreme Councillor" of the Galician Nationalist Brotherhood was not aware of was the strong limitation that this divergence entailed for nascent nationalism, at least in key aspects. Nationalism lost the mobilizing capacity of the rural population that agrarianism possessed, as well as the leadership exercised

---

72 See Cabo Villaverde (1998), and Domínguez Castro (2005).
73 Cabo Villaverde (2017).

in the local environment by return migrants, whom nationalists despised for being presumptuous "Argentinians" (*chés*) or "philistines". It was also deprived of the co-operation of the Church which, on the contrary, leaned heavily in the direction of agrarianism, where it controlled hundreds of Catholic unions embedded in the Galician Catholic-Agrarian Federations and in the National Catholic Agrarian Confederation.[74] Finally, a very obvious absence in the field of nationalism: the "sacrificial mysticism" and capacity to suffer, which was so relevant in the Irish case and that only in an episodic way was displayed in the field of Galician agrarianism, but never in that of nationalism. In fact, the social conflicts in which agrarianism was involved ended on several occasions with deaths: five peasants in Nebra (1916), three in Guillarei (1922) and others in different Galician villages (Sofán, Antas de Ulla and Chantada) which, in general, were the result not so much of a "primitive protest" but of proactive collective action. These events did not produce "heroes' widows" as in Dublin, but they did encourage agrarian militancy and its confluence with republicanism in the municipal elections of 1931, which opened the door to the Second Republic. Faced with the explicit recourse to violence, from the Easter Rising to war with Britain, the incentives provided by Galician nationalism were weak, both to expand membership of the movement (clearly inferior to the mobilization of agrarianism), and to identify a personal sacrifice with the "victory of the ideal". If "to dye for Ireland", as proposed by the "heroes of Easter" and so many others, was an explicit take on that ideal, nothing analogous can be found in the Language Brotherhoods movement. In Galicia, the few examples of political violence at that time are in the field of land-reform agitation.

As a general conclusion, it should be stated that for the LB, the seven years that passed between 1916 and 1923 were of great historic intensity, both inside and outside of Galicia. The experience of the LB went through very different phases: a regionalism that remained indecisive until February 1918, when it failed in its first electoral experience; a clearly nationalistic definition from November of 1918 and a determination to create a political party that was still "fledgling" in 1930; and a hegemony of cultural nationalism towards politics, certainly from the same year of 1918, when the Ourense group joined, but which became more apparent after the split in 1922. The most striking feature of the LB's trajectory was that, in the space of several years, they carried out a more ideological than organizational process of decantation, without reaching a degree of social mobilization comparable to the contemporary Galician agrarian movement. With this backdrop, the three indicators chosen as a final balance show that the distances between Galician nationalism and that of

---

74   Martínez (1995).

Catalonia, the Basque Country and, of course, Ireland, are enormous. But it is also clear that the path taken by the LB was qualitatively decisive: they reacted against their predecessors and were aware of being part of a new generation: that of 1916. They opted to create a national conscience that would allow the "victory of the ideal" to be established within the framework of Risco's pessimistic diagnosis, which considered Galicia as a "suicidal people", in a private letter of 1921.[75] They also disregarded engaging in politics, by conviction or by impossibility, which ruptured any option of turning the cause of Galician nationalism into a political problem within and beyond Galicia. Having followed paths parallel to Galician agrarianism was undoubtedly the main limitation of this phase of the Language Brotherhoods. If Easter 1916 was sung by Yeats as the occasion when a "terrible beauty is born", the leading Galician poet of a similar stature, Ramon Cabanillas, deployed his finest poetic skills to sing of agrarianism and nationalism. But whereas in his 1917 poem, *En pé!* [Stand up!], Galician brothers were invited to take action "around the blue and white flag, around the Galician flag", in his poem dedicated to the "Sobredo martyrs", or the hymn composed for Basilio Álvarez's Galician Action (1915), the invocation to violence is much more direct. Agrarianism beat nationalism in poetry too:

Irmáns! Irmáns gallegos!	Brothers! Oh Galician brothers!
Dende Ortegal ó Miño	From Ortegal to the Miño river,
a folla do fouciño	let's make shimmer
fagamos rebrillar! [...]	the billhook's blade! [...]
Antes de ser escravos,	Before we're enslaved,
irmáns, irmáns gallegos!	Brothers! Oh Galician brothers!
que corra a sangre a regos	Let the blood run as rivers
dende a montana ó mar	from the mountains to the ocean waves

Bibliography

Agra, M.X. & M. Mariño (2017), "A Fraternidade nas Irmandades da Fala 1916–1922", in J. Beramendi *et al* (eds.), *Repensar Galicia. As Irmandades da Fala*. Santiago de Compostela: Xunta de Galicia /Museo do Pobo Galego, pp. 87–104.

---

75 Ventura (2010: 109).

Allegue, A. (2017), "As Irmandades da Fala e a Liga Gaélica. Puntos en común e diverxencias de dúas iniciativas a prol da lingua minorizada", in Beramendi *et al.* (eds). *Repensar Galicia*, pp. 359–374.

Baeza, R. (2010), *La isla de los santos. Itinerario en Irlanda*, Tarragona: Igitur [1930].

Beramendi, J. (2007), *De provincia a nación. Historia do galeguismo político, 1840–1930*, Vigo: Edicións Xerais.

Beramendi, J.G., and X.M. Núñez Seixas (1995), "The Historical Background of Galician Nationalism (1840–1950)", *Canadian Review of Studies in Nationalism*, XXII: 1–2, pp. 33–51.

Cabo Villaverde, M. (1998), *O Agrarismo*, Vigo: A Nosa Terra.

Cabo Villaverde, M. (2006), "Solidaridad Gallega y el desafío al sistema de la Restauración, 1907–1911", *Ayer*, 64, pp. 235–59.

Cabo Villaverde, M. (2017), "As Irmandades da Fala perante o agrarismo: expectativas e realidades", in Beramendi *et al.* (eds), *Repensar Galicia*, pp. 359–374.

Cabrera, M.ª D. (2016), "Saúde e Patria! Cartas de Victor Casas a Fermín Penzol", *Grial*, 212, pp. 55–65.

Cameirâo, L. (2010), *Epistolário espanhol de Teixeira de Pascoaes (Cartas de intelectuais espanhois a Teixeira de Pascoaes)*, Lisbon: Assírio&Alvim.

Carmona, X. & J. Nadal (2005), *El empeño industrial de Galicia. 250 años de historia, 1750–2000*, A Coruña: Fundación Pedro Barrié de la Maza.

Carney, S. (2015), *BreizAtao! Mordrel, Delaporte, Lainé, Fouéré: une mystique nationale (1901–1948)*, Rennes: Presses Universitaires de Rennes.

Domínguez Castro, L. (2005), "Agrarismo y sociedad campesina en Galicia", in J. de Juana & X. Prada (eds.), *Historia contemporánea de Galicia*, Barcelona: Ariel, pp. 461–91.

Estévez, X. (1991), *De la Triple Alianza al Pacto de San Sebastián (1923–1930), Antecedentes del Galeuzca*, San Sebastián: Mundaiz.

Figueroa, A. (1996), *Lecturas alleas. Sobre as relacións con outras literaturas*, Santiago de Compostela: Sotelo Blanco.

Foster, R.F. (2015), *Vivid Faces. The revolutionary Generation in Ireland 1890–1923*, London: Penguin Random House.

Gallastegui Unamuno, C. (1930), *Esbozo de programa agrario para Galicia. Conferencia pronunciada en Vigo el 3 de diciembre de 1930*, Pontevedra: Imp. Celestino Peón.

Hroch, M. (2015), *European Nations. Explaining their Fomation*, London: Verso [Göttingen 2005].

Insua, E.X. (2005), *Sobre "O Mariscal", de Cabanillas e Villar Ponte*, A Coruña: Universidade da Coruña.

Le Cloarec, B. (2016), "*Breiz Atao* e il rinnovamento del nazionalismo bretone nel primo dopoguerra", *Nazioni&Regioni*, 8, pp. 51–65.

Madriñán, X.R. (2010), *A nacionalización do pasado irlandés, 1845–1937*, Santiago de Compostela: Centro Ramón Piñeiro.

Madriñán, X.R. (2017), "Irlanda en *A Nosa Terra*: Unha crónica de ausencias, paixón e silencio", in Beramendi *et al.* (eds). *Repensar Galicia*, pp. 359–374.

Máiz, R. (1984), *O rexionalismo galego. Organización e ideoloxía, 1886–1907*, Sada: Ediciós do Castro.

Martínez, A. (1995), *Cooperativismo y transformaciones agrarias en Galicia, 1886–1943*, Madrid: Ministerio de Agricultura, Pesca y Alimentación.

Núñez Seixas, X.M. (1998), *Emigrantes, caciques e indianos. O influxo sociopolítico da emigración transoceánica en Galicia, 1900–1930*, Vigo: Edicións Xerais.

Núñez Seixas, X.M. (2001), *Entre Ginebra y Berlín. La cuestión de las minorías nacionales y la política internacional en Europa, 1914–1939*, Madrid: Akal.

Núñez Seixas, X.M. (2010), *Internacionalitzant el nacionalisme. El catalanisme polític i la qüestió de les minories nacionals a Europa (1914–1936)*, Valencia: Afers/PUV.

Núñez Seixas, X.M. (2017), "Ecos de Pascua, mitos rebeldes: el nacionalismo vasco e Irlanda (1890–1939)", *Historia Contemporánea*, 55, pp. 447–82.

O'Brien, C.C. (1994), *Ancestral Voices. Religion and Nationalism in Ireland*, Chicago: Chicago UP.

O'Brien, C.C. (1999), *Memoir. My life and themes*, London: Profile Books.

Paseta, S. (1999), *Before the Revolution. Nationalism, Social Change and Ireland's Catholic Élite, 1879–1922*, Cork: Cork UP.

Riquer i Permanyer, B. (2001), *Escolta Espanya. La cuestión catalana en la época liberal*, Marcial Pons Historia, Madrid.

Riquer i Permanyer, B. (2013), *Alfonso XIII y Cambó. La monarquía y el nacionalismo político*, Barcelona: RBA.

Risco, V. (1930), *El problema político de Galicia*, Madrid: Compañía Ibero-Americana de Publicaciones.

Seixas Seoane, M.A. (2016), *Luís Porteiro Garea e As Irmandades da Fala*, Santiago de Compostela: Concello de Santiago.

Serrano Sanz, J.M. (1987), *El viraje proteccionista de la Restauración. La política comercial española, 1875–1895*, Madrid: Siglo XXI.

Ucelay-Da Cal, E. (1984), "El Mirall de Catalunya: models internacionals en el desenvolupament del nacionalisme i del separatisme català, 1875–1923", *Historia Social*, 28–29, pp. 213–19.

Ucelay-Da Cal, E. (2006), "Entre el ejemplo italiano y el irlandés: la escisión generalizada de los nacionalismos hispanos, 1919–1922", *Ayer*, 63, pp. 75–118.

Vázquez, A. (2015), *Emigrantes galegos, transportes e remesas 1830–1930*, A Coruña: Fundación Barrié de la Maza/Consello da Cultura Galega.

Ventura, J. (2010), *Epistolario de Vicente Risco a Antón Losada Diéguez*, Ourense: Deputación Provincial.

Villar Ponte, A. (1916), *Nacionalismo gallego. Nuestra "afirmación" regional. Apuntes para un libro*, A Coruña: Tipografía Obrera.

Villar Ponte, A. (1971), *Pensamento e Sementeira, Leiciós de patriotismo galego*, Buenos Aires: Ediciones Galicia.

Villar Ponte, R. (1977), *A xeración do 16*, A Coruña: Real Academia Galega [1951].

Villares, R. (1982), *La propiedad de la tierra en Galicia, 1500–1936*, Madrid: Siglo XXI.

Villares, R. (2005), "Restauración y Dictadura en Galicia (1874–1930)", in J. de Juana & X. Prada (coords.), *Historia contemporánea de Galicia*, Barcelona: Ariel, pp. 203–27.

Villares, R. (2017), *Identidades e afectos patrios*, Vigo: Galaxia.

Villares, R. (2018), *Fuga e retorno de Adrián Solovio. Sobre a educación sentimental dun intelectual galeguista*, Vigo, Galaxia [1st ed., 2007].

CHAPTER 9

The Galician Language Brotherhoods and Minority Languages in Europe during the First World War

Johannes Kabatek

1   Introduction*

The following reflections on the Galician Language Brotherhoods (LB, *Irmandades da Fala*), an intellectual movement in favour of the emancipation of the substate regional language spoken in Northwest Iberia and founded in 1916, aim at contextualizing this movement on two axes. The first one is the contemporary context of linguistic thought and debates on language diversity at the beginning of the 20th century; the second one is the socio-diachronic evolution of Galician. One hundred years later, Galician has become the co-official language of a politically autonomous region. Alongside Spanish, it is the language of official usage, of education, mass media and of a broad range of written discourse traditions up to scientific prose. It is a "normalized" language in the sense that since the 1980s there is an official written standard and in the sense that it may be used for all social purposes, even if the overall prestige of Spanish is very strong and makes Galician frequently assume the role of a secondary language in a diglossic situation.

The historical evolution that led to the current situation has often been considered under a rather idiosyncratic perspective, sometimes accompanied by certain anachronistic or teleological viewpoints, where Galician is described as a kind of historical victim that finally achieved its merited status after hundreds of years of oppression. This might be explained by the intention of investigators to justify language emancipation, but it should also be contextualized by broader comparative views.

Galicia is one of the numerous European territories where a local vernacular emerged out of Latin after the decline of the Roman Empire, and like other vernaculars expanded due to political reasons in medieval times. "Galaico-Portuguese" became a written language of both Galicia and Portugal, but

---

*   I would like to express my deepest gratitude to Xosé M. Núñez Seixas for his valuable comments on a previous version of this chapter

Galician became separated early from its southern Portuguese expansion territory with its new centre in Lisbon and remained under the political influence of León and Castile. When, from the fifteenth century onwards, other European vernaculars (including the closely related neighbouring Portuguese) underwent standardization processes, Galician, like many other European languages, did not participate and became dialectalized under the dominant Castilian/Spanish. Galician remained a spoken vernacular and the local, monolingual majority was linguistically disconnected from the Spanish speaking power, a fact that is criticized during the Enlightenment by some intellectuals who postulated, as in other European regions, the access of popular classes to the prestige language and culture. The 19th century brought, as all over Europe, a so-called "Renaissance" to the local language, expressed mainly by popular poetry, some prose texts and several metalinguistic reflections on the lexicon, grammar and the origin of the language. By the end of the century, as in other regions, the language is linked by local intellectuals to the identity of the people and to regional political and economic interests. Even if geographically distant from many other European regions and even if unique in its particularities, the Galician evolution can therefore be seen in the context of other European regionalist movements. This paper primarily focuses on one key moment in this evolution at the beginning of the 20th century, a moment when the tendencies of the previous century are bundled into a concrete social and linguistic program without which the following evolvement would hardly be imaginable. The remainder of the text is structured as follows: I will first contextualize the general linguistic programme of the brotherhoods and show how it contradicts overall assumptions of contemporary linguistic thought. Section 3 is dedicated to two general principles, *discursive transversality*, on the one hand, and the antagonism between *universalism* and *particularism*, on the other hand. Section 4 turns back to the particular Galician case showing how transversality with Catalan is crucial in order to understand the particular Galician case. Section 5 opens the context to further European cases in the same period.

2 The *Irmandades da fala* and the Belief in Change

The foundation of the Galician Language Brotherhoods in 1916 coincided with the year of publication, in Lausanne and Paris, of Ferdinand de Saussure's *Cours de linguistique générale*, a book that is generally considered to be the foundational document of modern linguistics. In Saussure's view, linguistics should be —following the tradition of the nineteenth-century "Neogrammarians" (and Saussure himself was originally a Neogrammarian)— an exact science.

However, its main object (at least according to his famous *Cours de linguistique générale*[1]) should be —in opposition to the Neogrammarians— the study of *langue* as a synchronic, abstract mental system. Even if Saussure discusses in depth the relationship between the object *langue* and speech production, *parole*, both himself and his structuralist followers have focused on language as a separate and autonomous entity, a projection we can contemplate without taking into account the "real" activity of speakers and hearers. This view became dominant in modern linguistics, and behind it there is Émile Durkheim's sociological theory about the *fait social*,[2] which Saussure used to refer to in his lectures, together with contemporary psychological thought. The *fait social* —and language is one of Durkheim's examples— as separated from the individual. The individual is unable to change the social fact and must reproduce what is collectively fixed:

> "The particular language is the social side of language; it is located outside the individual who can neither create or modify it alone; it only exists as a kind of contract between the members of the community."[3]

In opposition to Saussure's thought, the Galician *Irmandades da fala* shared a completely different view on language. They proposed consciously to use the Galician language, and they did so because they believed that by using the language, they would contribute to the change of its status:

> "Since speech is that characteristic that most distinguishes peoples, and what more than anything else shapes their character, and therefore, in this case, in order to create a common Galicianist spirit, the Brotherhood shall propagate the use of our language by all available ways."[4]

Linguistics only focused in the second half of the century on interaction, on language and society and on language planning, demonstrating amongst other things how languages can be revitalized or how language contact can be modelled. The movement of the Brotherhoods anticipated implicitly some of the principles of modern language planning as it was characterized by the belief that a language situation might be changed consciously by individuals if there

---

1 Saussure's most famous book was actually published by his disciples after his death, and the priority given to synchronic studies seems partly more due to the intervention of the editors than to the author's original intention. As for criticism, see, amongst others, Bouquet (2012).
2 See Durkheim (1895).
3 Saussure (1916: 31). My translation.
4 *Regramento das Irmandades da Cruña*, A Coruña: n. ed., 1918.

were a common will to do so. It is here of course more the relationship of the languages in general (Galician as opposed to Spanish) than the particular forms within a language that should be changed, but there was a conviction that the propagation of the language made sense and that it would contribute to alter the current situation.

In fact, the most important step taken by the Brotherhoods in order to emancipate the Galician language was to use it also in written and spoken formal contexts. Many of the intellectuals who participated in the 19th century Renaissance using Galician for poetry spoke Spanish rather than Galician as a family and private language. Even the foundation of the Galician Academy in 1905, an institution shaped in imitation of similar language academies, took place in Spanish:

> "This Academy has been founded in order to recollect Galicia's real lexicon, in order to release knowledge of its grammar, and to affirm its existence. Because languages are the peoples' purest and most powerful instruments, characterizing their nationality. [...] A people that forgets its language is a dead people [...]. Those persons who speak a language which is not of their own do not belong to themselves."[5]

Until the second decade of the twentieth century, Spanish continued to be the formal communication language even among defenders of Galician. This gap between Spanish as a formal language and Galician as popular language was filled by the Language Brotherhoods for the first time in the modern history of Galicia. They used the language because they wanted it to become more important: in the preceding history of Galician, its speakers simply spoke the language because it used to be their normal way of expressing themselves. Now, some speakers intervened consciously against the traditional diglossia that characterized Galician sociolinguistic history.[6] They did this not only in a meta-linguistic way, treating the language as an external object, but also incorporating it into their own linguistic behaviour. In a way, they were both linguists (as they thought consciously about language planning) and speakers at the same time. This was completely new in Galician history, and this is what made and makes the Language Brotherhoods so important for contemporary commemoration at a time when conscious, institutionalized language planning is firmly established in Galicia and when the roots of the present situation are highlighted in history.

---

5   *Boletín de la Real Academia Gallega*, 6–7 (20.11.1906), my translation; see also Ínsua (2014).
6   For this concept and the history of Romance diglossias, see Kabatek (2016).

3   Discursive Transversality, Universalism and Particularism

The innovation of the Galician Language Brotherhoods was not only built on local grounds. It was connected to other European social movements and received inputs from outside. This section introduces some general concepts of variational linguistics which will be the background for the description of this cross-cultural influence.

Linguistics is not uniform in defining the dimensions of linguistic variation. However, in the Romance tradition, a threefold distinction between *diatopic* (dialectal), *diastratic* (sociolectal) and *diaphasic* (situational) varieties is generally accepted. A "language variety" is thus a form of language determined by space, social group and situation. All varieties are functionally "languages", but few undergo standardization and become "historical languages" in Coseriu's (1980) sense. A more recent view orders all varieties under one universal and central dimension along the continuum between "immediacy" and "distance".[7] These are universal poles linked to communicative practices and these are characterized by a series of conditions of interaction. In written cultures, "distance" is associated with written language but does not causally depend on it, whereas "immediacy" is associated with spoken language.[8] These notions are important for our purpose, since we are basically dealing with the *status* of language and varieties and with so-called *Ausbau*, the elevation of a former language of "immediacy" to domains of "distance".[9]

Taking up again the example of modern Galician, we can see that the language had for centuries been restricted to uses of "immediacy", and that the so-called *Rexurdimento*, the Galician literary Renaissance of the nineteenth century, had established some written traditions of "distance". However, before the emergence of the Language Brotherhoods, there was almost no spoken formal tradition, and in a very short period, Galician activists managed to generate a considerable amount of formal spoken texts, as the first Brotherhood's founder Antón Villar Ponte stated in 1918. That year, "more elaborated Galician has been spoken than previously for a whole century".[10]

Modern linguistics stresses the distinction between "normative" and "descriptive" approaches, giving clear preference to the latter. The task of the linguist is to offer adequate description and explanation of linguistic phenomena,

---

[7]   Koch & Oesterreicher (2011).
[8]   Kabatek (forthcoming).
[9]   See Kloss (1967).
[10] Villar Ponte (1918), quoted by Ínsua (2016:17).

not to change or modify the object.[11] However, in the tradition of linguistics, the dominant tradition is probably rather a normative one, if we think of traditional definitions of grammar as the art of writing and speaking correctly or of language apologies in the sixteenth century postulating the change of status of vernaculars. Language is categorized, and people speak about language not only in order to describe it, leaving the object untouched, but in order to shape the object in a certain manner. This means that speakers are conscious of a bilateral relationship between the object language and metalinguistic discourse; it also means that they can propose changes in the object.

As we know from discussions on language planning, proposals to change language or language prestige do not have a direct impact on the object, as Einar Haugen stated: "The planner proposes, and the community disposes".[12] Direct, immediate language planning is impossible in the case of natural, non-artificial languages, where we must consider a triangle between planning, language activity and language.[13]

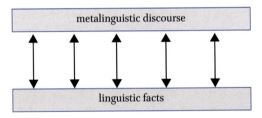

FIGURE 9.1 Mutual relationship between linguistic facts and metalinguistic discourse

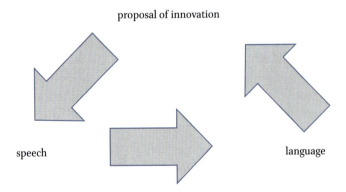

FIGURE 9.2 The triangle of language planning

---

11   It goes without saying that also sheer description may alter the object (in sociolinguistics due to what is called the observer's paradox, and even in natural science, if we think of Heisenberg's uncertainty).
12   Haugen (1966: 24).
13   Kabatek (1996: 43),

Language is not an artefact. It presupposes collective knowledge, and the introduction of innovations can only be proposed to individuals, not directly imposed. A complex process of adoptions within the speech community is needed to make innovations become generalized. This also means that perhaps the most efficient way of language planning is not by proposing innovations in a laboratory, but by performing examples. If we look again at the Language Brotherhoods, this is exactly what they did. They did not only propose metalinguistically to overrun the sociolinguistic situation, but they also behaved in an innovative and proactive way, acting as models for a different conception of the division of language domains in Galician society.[14]

In general, on the premise that metalinguistic discourse can propose changes in languages, and according to the particular situation, there is a potential for changes, a range of possible goals (with its limits) which might be achieved. Metalinguistic reflection thus becomes a political issue in Bismarck's sense of politics as "the art of the possible".

Metalinguistic discourses which propose changes in the current linguistic setting might be generated *in situ*, or they might be adopted from elsewhere, from other places and examples, as part of a process of cultural transfer. A closer look at the history of linguistic thought makes it possible to identify a number of innovative foci where ideas and models were crafted, from where they spread to other places. This is what we can call *discursive transversality*, when a metalinguistic reflection generated in and deriving from a particular situation is adopted by others, and applied to a different situation.

Discursive transversality does not only allow for the adoption of analyses of language situations elsewhere; it also allows for the adoption of proposals to change those sociolinguistic situations. Moreover, discursive transversality presupposes *communication*: only if there are ways of communication or

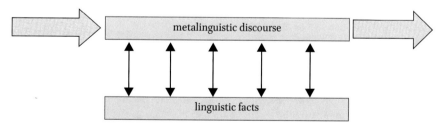

FIGURE 9.3 Discursive transversality

---

14   For some general information on the history of the Galician language, see Monteagudo (1999). For a more detailed view on the history of the Language Brotherhoods, see Beramendi (2007), Cochón (2016) and Ínsua (2016), as well as Ramón Villares' chapter in this volume.

individual (sometimes also institutional) contacts, is a real adoption of discourses and its application to a new situation possible. This also means that, when analysing historical changes in language situations, the trace of those individuals who are responsible for the introduction of innovative discourses must be found.[15]

A further relevant aspect of discursive transversality is that the situation in which the discourse originally emerged and the situation into which it is imported must be comparable (otherwise an importation would make no sense) and will at the same time be somehow different. An imported discourse may encounter a fertile ground in a transposed situation; however, it may also be confronted with different realities or with stronger rejection than in the original area. Moreover, it will obviously change during the process of transposition, and it may eventually be adapted to the new situation, as Lenin adapted the Marxist discourse to the agrarian society for which it had not been originally conceived.

When describing human language, it is useful to distinguish between three different levels: the universal, the historical and the individual level.[16] Language is what makes human beings be human, and since Aristotle it is commonly accepted that the human being is a *zoon politikón* due to the *logos*. Humans recognize human language and intuitively distinguish it from other noises; they know that they are virtually able to acquire any of the existing languages, and they feel that there is a series of common characteristics amongst different languages of the world. But it is not possible to refer to "language" as such; languages in plural are historically grown entities, and human beings are part of a shared history, according to the language(s) they speak. We do not in fact even speak "a language" as a whole: we produce individual utterances situated in time and space.

In the history of linguistic thought, language frequently used to be reduced to the universal level, but the antagonism between the universal and the historical level has also led to an opposition in discourse on language. Speaking is always a social act: only when the speaker and the listener both speak a shared language will there be understanding, although they also know that both speak

---

15   See Leersen (2006). In Kabatek (2005) I have shown, with the example of the "Bolognese Renaissance" in the twelfth century, how a new discourse generated in Bologna spread throughout Europe enhancing the creation of vernacular texts in different places. We could even invert the view and claim that when elaborate vernacular texts suddenly appeared in a certain region, a link to the Bologna-connection was supposed to be involved.

16   See Coseriu (1985).

slightly different from the interlocutor and that they have something purely individual. What on a personal, interactional level is the antagonism between identity and alterity (in a Hegelian sense), on a social level is reflected in the antagonism between universalism and particularism. Universalism is often accompanied by the dream of a universal language and the overcoming of the Babelian confusion: a merge between the historical and the universal level. On the other hand, particularism stresses differences, sometimes reducing the universal to the historical level.

The opposition between universalism and particularism can be traced back to the ancient world,[17] but the discourse on linguistic universalism and particularism in the twentieth century has two dominant anchors in more recent times, mainly in the eighteenth and the nineteenth century: the universalist thought of French philosophers of the enlightenment, culminating with the main linguistic paradigm of the French Revolution by the end of the eighteenth century, and its particularist counterpart, which stresses the difference of each particular language and the shape of nations by linguistic diversity, a position defined and defended by German idealist philosophy from Herder to Wilhelm von Humboldt.[18]

A utopian objective of the French Revolution was the propagation of French as the universal language, an idea which was rooted in the writings of Étienne B. de Condillac, Antoine de Rivarol and others, and which was carried out with specific language policies during the second phase of the Revolution. *Anéantir les patois*, 'wipe out the dialects', Abbé Grégoire's formula, was only one aspect of a complete programme of uniformization and universalization.[19] The aim of the Jacobine language policy was to purify the French language, damning the vocabulary of the Ancien Regime to oblivion. Not only diatopic varieties and different languages were considered to be enemies of the Revolution; also, language variation according to social stratification, as well as the diversity of styles, was to be destroyed for the sake of the aim of linguistic *égalité* without any differences. The uniformization of metric systems, space, time and all other aspects of human cultural organization did not leave language aside. The opposite model was that proposed by German romanticism, with its focus on the equal dignity of all languages and interest in diversity and plurality in nature and culture.[20]

---

17 Bossong (1990).
18 Coseriu (2015).
19 See Schlieben-Lange (1996).
20 (Forster 2010).

The French Revolution also attempted to establish a link between linguistic universalism and political bias. It associated linguistic universalism with a progressive, left-wing ideology, whereas particularism was linked to reaction and monarchy. This correlation remains a constant factor in linguistic ideologies until present, although not exclusively: in contrast with this general tendency, some sub-state regionalist and nationalist movements, as well as some ethnic minority parties, have also tried to merge particularism with left-wing ideology.[21] This shows that different discursive elements can be separated and newly combined: the Humboldt brothers, for example, were sympathetic for some of the main tenets upheld by the French Revolution, and they also had friends involved in the movement of the *Idéologie*. Wilhelm von Humboldt travelled to Paris after the storming of the Bastille and corresponded with Destutt de Tracy.[22] However, both Wilhelm and Alexander merged the idea of equality and brotherhood with their interest for diversity.

One of the central issues concerning the antagonism between universalism and particularism at the beginning of the twentieth century would be the way in which both could be combined with different political ideologies, and how universalist or particularist movements were able to merge their aims with the struggle for social equality. Historians have diverged on the question as to whether the evolution of particularism from literary romanticism into political agitation and a mass movement was a continuous process with different phases (Hroch 2015), or whether the most decisive steps should rather be considered as largely independent from their romantic roots.[23] Be it as it were, the local evolution of ideas and movements in a region such as Galicia, independently from its geographic distance to centres of reference, cannot be understood coherently without its connection to imported discourses.

4   The Catalan Connection

The Galician language movement that led to the establishment of Galician as a spoken formal language, and which settled the basis for what from the 1970s onwards has been labelled "linguistic normalization", is an interesting case

---

21   See e.g. Augusteijn & Storm (2012), as well as Núñez Seixas & Storm (2018).
22   Gipper & Schmitter (1979).
23   For the Catalan case, see Marfany (2008: 273 and ff.).

which allows for an illustration of some of the general ideas presented in the previous sections.

The connection to France and French eighteenth century thought was present in the ideas of the Galician Enlightenment, when Spanish intellectuals discussed the necessity of improving the educational system.[24] At the beginning of the nineteenth century, after a long period of scarce or absent literary activity in Galician, sporadic written texts were published, which acted as landmarks of the beginning of a new regionalist tendency. An interesting example was *Proezas de Galicia*, penned by José Fernández Neira and printed in 1810 in A Coruña, a polemic anti-French dialogue which took place in the context of the Peninsular War, and served for the purpose of fostering Spanish patriotic mobilization among the Galician peasantry, which could be better addressed in its own language. Alongside some other contemporary writings,[25] this was one of the texts that opened the way for the Galician literary recovery, the so-called *Rexurdimento* ('Re-flowering', or cultural renaissance) in the second half of the nineteenth century.

Certainly, it would be difficult to imagine the movement of the Language Brotherhoods in the absence of this background. However, there were two innovative elements of the Galician linguistic discourse in the early twentieth century: the aforementioned aim of elevating Galician to formal spoken domains, and the link between regionalism and popular classes. This latter phenomenon was already present in nineteenth-century Galician-language poetry, particularly in the female poet Rosalía de Castro's work. But there was no clear social project during the nineteenth century, and the main protagonists of the Galician *Rexurdimento* mostly had no systematic political programme that merged linguistic with social emancipation (Hermida 1992; Beramendi 2007).

Those individuals who set up the Language Brotherhoods movement, particularly Antón Villar Ponte (1881–1936) and Aurelio Ribalta (1864–1940), deserve further comments. Villar Ponte was the Galician journalist and intellectual who can be considered to be its main founder. He denounced the enduring Galician backwardness and the overwhelming influence of political clientelism in regional politics, and he repeatedly stressed that Catalonia, and the Catalan movement, was the model to be followed. In fact, Catalonia had already served as model for the creation of Galician Solidarity (*Solidaridad Gallega*), a political grouping founded in 1907 as a mirror of Catalan Solidarity.

---

24   See Monteagudo (1999: 259).
25   Mariño Paz (1992).

This consisted of a coalition of Republicans, Catalanists and Traditionalists, which managed to win the majority of the Catalan seats at the Spanish elections in 1907. Although the sociolinguistic situation in Catalonia was quite different from Galicia, in several aspects it was also comparable: the frequently cited "Catalan Bourgeoisie", which was supposed to be the backbone of the regionalist movement, was largely assimilated and Spanish-speaking at the beginning of the twentieth century. Moreover, no clear link was consolidated between social emancipation and the recovery of the vernacular among the working classes, which were overwhelmingly Catalan-speaking.[26] The Spanish language, thanks to its wider geographic range, seemed to offer for large sectors of Catalan society greater advantages than Catalan. However, although the *Solidaritat Catalana* aimed at becoming an all-Spanish political movement directed against the political regime of the Restoration monarchy, it also marked a turning point, as the Catalan language became much more present than before in public life. However, in Villar Ponte's adoption of Catalanist discourse and strategies, he regarded the regional language, Galician as a crucial element for strengthening the Galician nation against "absurd centralism".[27] The other head of the movement, Aurelio Ribalta, published an essay on "militant Catalanism" in Madrid in 1901, the year when the Catalan Regionalist League (*Lliga Regionalista*) was founded. He had intensive contacts with Catalan intellectuals and the Catalan regionalist movement at the beginning of the century. For him, there existed a clear link between the use of the regional language and a political regionalist program, and he started a debate on an adequate orthography for Galician and is author of an unpublished Galician grammar. His dream was the creation of a free Galicia which would serve as a bridge between neighbouring Portugal and Castile.

In fact, the discursive transversality from Catalonia to Galicia, and the frequent cultural and political transfers between Barcelona and the Galician towns was a constant factor in Galician language emancipation processes throughout the twentieth century. Thus, during the years of the Second Spanish Republic (1931–36), the Galician Statute of Autonomy from 1936 was partly based on the Catalan model from 1932, establishing Spanish and Galician as official languages (with Spanish as the only language for external relationships). Similarly, after General Franco's death, Catalan nationalist politicians, in alliance with Basque and Galician nationalists, put forward the co-officialization of the regional languages in the new Spanish Constitution of 1978. The current model of three levels of language legislation (constitution – statute of

---

26   See Nagel (1991), Marfany (2001) and Anguera (1997).
27   Villar Ponte (1916: 5).

autonomy – law for linguistic normalization) was adopted from Catalonia, and the contemporary Catalan discourse on independence has also been partly imitated by Galician nationalists. Catalans have widely used international platforms such as UNESCO for the propagation of their ideas, and the European Charter for Regional or Minority languages was strongly influenced by Catalan representatives. This is how the Catalan discourse on language has spread to and influenced other regions, to the point that some laws on linguistic diversity in the Americas also reflect some Catalan inspiration. Certainly, the Catalan influence on the discourse on language rights should not be exaggerated, but it was one of the leading foci of non-state language nationalism already at the dawn of the twentieth century. On the other hand, Catalan sociolinguistics strongly adopted elements from Québec in the 1970s and based several of the central sociolinguistic and socio-political terms on Canadian models.

5 European Languages around the First World War

As in Galicia, universalism and particularism were the two main forces that characterized the antagonism of European linguistic landscapes before and after the First World War. It is not my aim here to trace a comprehensive panorama of the whole continent, so I will limit my remarks to a few general aspects that show how the Galician movement should be seen in general European context.[28] What characterizes this context is a profound reordering of social, political, cultural and linguistic spaces, especially in those parts affected directly by the war, but also beyond those territories.

If we look at the overall evolution from the bird's-eye view, the most outstanding tendency before and after the war is the one towards linguistic levelling and homogeneity, together with the emergence of new political units —successor states that acted as *nationalizing states*[29]— which implemented their respective official languages. Before the Great War, there were 22 independent states in Europe; in its aftermath, their number rose to 30, half of them republics and most of them democratic.[30] Polish was re-established as an official language in the new Republic of Poland, and languages as Czech or the different Baltic languages also became national languages of their emerging national states. A striking example was that of the lands of the former

---

28 For a general view, see Walter and Declercq (2016).
29 Brubaker (1996).
30 See Grzega (2012: 70).

Habsburg monarchy.[31] In the nineteenth century and throughout the beginning of the twentieth century, there had been in this area two basic models of linguistic organization. The first one corresponded to a French-inspired monolingual and homogeneous unified nation (in the eastern part of the empire, the Cisleithanian or Hungarian zone since the Compromise (*Ausgleich*) of 1867, where monolingual laws of Magyarization were already enacted from the end of the eighteenth century onwards. The second one was characterized by a respect of diversity, and on all levels of social organizations several languages were co-present, and was common in the Transleithanian area under Vienna's rule.[32] As occurred at the time of the end of the Ancien regime, this diversity was implicitly associated with the defence of premodern social order, the monarchy and tradition.

After 1918, emerging territories like the new Republic of Austria or Czechoslovakia defined themselves as monolingual states in practice. In the case of Czechoslovakia, the nation-state was built upon an apparently unified construct, the so-called Czechoslovakian language, which de facto meant the hegemony of Czech within a multilingual state, where local languages such as German, Hungarian or Russian just preserved certain minority rights.[33] Minority rights were also protected by the League of Nations from 1920 onwards and violations were constantly reported to the headquarters in Geneva. Tomás G. Masaryk, president of the republic from 1918 to 1935 and one of the main leaders of the Czech national movement, was strongly influenced by Herder, as well as by the idea of a language reflecting the spirit of the nation. Therefore, he considered the Czechs and the Slovaks to be one single nation (*národ*) possessing a common language (*jazyk*). This was in fact a fiction, but it was defended officially from 1918 until the 1930s, with attempts to avoid linguistic differences and with language planning commissions which tried to unify the terminology in both languages.

In France, Italy and Germany, intense contacts among soldiers from different regions at the trenches during the war were considered to have had an important impact, on the one hand, on the awareness of the existing linguistic diversity; on the other hand, this intensive social intercourse also heavily influenced the process of building up national linguistic coherence.[34] Dialect levelling as the dominant linguistic tendency of the twentieth century seems to have been accelerated in these countries in wartime and beyond, completing

---

31 See Goebl (1999) and Scheer (2016).
32 See Goebl (1999).
33 See Csernicskó & Fedinec (2015).
34 See Walker and Declercq (2016)

the nation-building process started decades before.[35] This was also a consequence of increasing population movements, the spread of new mass communication media (telephone, radio) and the increase of language contact across the continent. Whereas Italy and Germany were relatively recent national states, France had long been a political unit, where unifying tendencies in written communication traced back to the sixteenth century. However, contrary to the aforementioned ideology of the French Revolution, linguistic unity was not yet achieved at the beginning of the twentieth century. However, the generalization of primary schooling and compulsory education from 1870 onwards strongly contributed to linguistic unification and continuation of dialect loss.[36] Some minority groups in the French periphery, from Brittany to Corsica, were influenced by the diffusion of the principle of nationality and took up the defence of minority languages now definitely challenged by the diffusion of the state language.[37] The interwar period, saw the creation of parties within different regionalist movements such as the Sardinian Action Party (*Partito Sardo d'Azione*, 1921), in Sardinia, the Corsican Action Party (*Partitu Corsu d'Azzione*, 1922), in Corsica, and, some years later, the *Strollad Emrenerien Vreiz* (Breton Autonomist Party, 1927) in Brittany. These had in part similar programmes and interchanged their main ideas.

Political independence did not always lead to real linguistic emancipation. In the case of the Ireland, the Constitution Act of the Irish Free State, established in 1922, declared official in Art. 4 the Irish language as a "National Language" alongside with English, which, however, was not considered to be a second "National Language". Irish became a language of teaching and of official usage but it remained marginal in comparison with dominant English. Mezo has compared the Irish case with the Basque Country, where it took much longer to officialize the vernacular language and where the overall social support for the local language was lower than in Ireland. Paradoxically, the result of the slower and less direct language policy in the Basque country gave more fruitful results, which shows how manifold the factors for success or failure in attempts to steer linguistic evolutions politically are.[38]

Another interesting case was that of Switzerland, a country surrounded by belligerent countries which managed to maintain a neutral status during the conflict. In Switzerland, the war contributed to the maintenance of a different nation model not based on linguistic unity, but, in a way, on a "negative"

---

35 See De Mauro (2002); Auer et al. (2005).
36 See Weber (1976) and (Thiesse 1999).
37 See the chapter by Zantedeschi and Núñez Seixas in this volume.
38 See Mezo (2009).

identity enhanced by its encirclement by fortified borders during the conflict. This also helped to maintain in the German-speaking part of the country a pluri-dialectal landscape which is completely opposed to the general European tendency towards levelling and homogeneous standard orientation. Swiss German dialects are the normal means of oral communication, and speakers from different regions keep speaking their dialects when coming together in linguistic interaction, presupposing passive pluridialectal competence. Standard German (*Hochdeutsch*) in turn is a functional language for written usage, as well as for certain public issues; but it is barely used as a spoken language in the private sphere. Proposals of creating a Swiss German standard have been absolutely marginal, since Swiss-ness is expressed by dialect use and non-linguistic, political and ideological identity features.[39]

Further cases could be added. What is common to the discourse in many places is that there is a dynamic situation with social movements and establishments of new orders. These new orders affect languages and varieties and they use languages and varieties as arguments for their goals. And they seem convinced, against the idea of the unconsciousness of language change expressed by contemporary linguists, that language situations can be changed and that languages can be planned. The Prague linguistic circle is an interesting example of how a single group of linguists deals with this apparent contradiction: the Prague phonologists are the most immediate successors of Ferdinand de Saussure's doctrine, and at the same time, other members of the group are dedicated to the standardization and the elaboration of the Czechoslovakian literary language. In Galicia, the language practice and the social programme of the Galician Language Brotherhoods also coincides with metalinguistic activities or with spelling proposals such as Aurelio Ribalta's phonetic orthography for Galician presented in 1910 in his *Libro de Konsagrazión*: the common idea is that languages can be planned internally, with reference to the corpus, and externally, with reference to their status.[40]

6 Conclusions

The Galician Language Brotherhoods or *Irmandades da Fala* were undoubtedly a very particular movement, but they are part of a common European language history. In that history, languages emerged, died, emancipated, degenerated, and they did so due to the activity of their speakers, as well as to

---

39   See Zimmer (2003, 2005), as well as Werlen (1993) and Christen (1998, 2010).
40   See Ribalta (1910).

ideological discourses which were created, adopted and reproduced. Global historical events, such as the impact of the First World War, had a destructive impact and left behind millions of victims on the battlefields, and starving families throughout the countryside and the rear. But the turmoil of war also allowed for political disruptions, for the death of the old order identified with the long nineteenth century, and for the emergence of new orders and for emancipations of the repressed, as Antón Villar Ponte also affirmed:

> "Perhaps this great evil of the monstrous war in whose vortex, more or less, we all dance, shall conclude by bringing us enormous good. It does not matter that it is at the cost of so many unbearable pains and so many tears and suffering. Every great ideal is always reached after having left in its wake a new Appian Way lined with crosses."[41]

I do not share Villar Ponte's view that terrible moments were necessary in order to build up a new order, as in Jorge Luis Borges' *Deutsches Requiem* (included in his book *El Aleph*, 1949) or in Yeats' "a terrible beauty is born", referring to the Irish Rising, 1916. The monstrous war was not to be the last one of the century, and Villar Ponte's dream of social equality, as well as of a Galician society where the Galician language was spoken on all levels, would still take much time before it became true, and we are still unaware as to whether the Brotherhoods simply arrived too late.

Galicia used to be an almost monolingual territory until well into the twentieth century. Only small groups of elites used to speak Spanish in their daily interaction and the vast majority used exclusively Galician. However, the rather marginal tendencies to reverse this situation from the nineteenth century onwards were confronted with strong Castilianizing tendencies during the twentieth century. Even if there was an almost successful attempt to officialize Galician during the Second Republic, which failed due to the fact that the Galician state of Autonomy, approved by referendum three weeks before the outbreak of the Spanish Civil War, was never implemented, the two Spanish dictatorships (1923–30 and 1939–75) which dominated the century (mainly the Francoist regime and its unifying language policies), strongly contributed to the spread of massive Castilianization. Post-war economic modernization was almost exclusively associated with Spanish, while the Galician language increasingly became the language spoken by the peasantry and older generations. Intrafamiliar diglossia, where more or less bilingual adults try to bring up their children in the dominant language, while speaking Galician only with

---

41   (Villar Ponte (1917), quoted by Ínsua (2016: 47).

other adults, became a more and more common phenomenon. Democratization after the death of Franco also allowed for a Galician revival, and the 1978 Constitution served as a legal frame for political emancipation and "linguistic normalization". Galician became the co-official language of the 'Autonomous Community' of Galicia, the language of the regional parliament, of public instruction and of mass-media. However, the process of linguistic assimilation has continued to advance, and all the political measures implemented have not been able to inhibit the tendency of an ongoing language shift towards Spanish.[42] One century later, Antón Villar Ponte and the founders of the Language Brotherhoods would certainly acknowledge that some of their claims were fulfilled, yet they would also dislike some of the ongoing linguistic processes in present-day Galicia.

Bibliography

Anguera, Pere (1997), *El català al segle XIX*, Barcelona: Empúries.

Augusteijn, Joost, & Eric Storm, eds. (2012), *Region and State in Nineteenth-Century Europe. Nation-Building, Regional Identities and Separatism*, Basingstoke: Palgrave.

Auer, Peter; Frans Hinskens & Paul Kerswill, eds. (2005). *Dialect Change. Convergence and Divergence in European Languages*, Cambridge: Cambridge University Press.

Beramendi, Justo G. (2007), *Galicia, de provincia a nación. Historia do galeguismo político, 1840–2000*, Vigo: Edicións Xerais.

Bossong, Georg (1990). *Sprachwissenschaft und Sprachphilosophie in der Romania: Von den Anfängen bis August Wilhelm Schlegel*. Tübingen: Narr.

Bouquet, Simon (2012), "Principes d'une linguistique de l'interprétation: une épistémologie néosaussurienne", *Langages*, 185, pp. 21–33.

Brubaker, Rogers (1996), *Nationalism Reframed: Nationhood and the National Question in the New Europe*, Cambridge: Cambridge UP.

Cochón, Luís, ed. (2016), *Arredor das Irmandades da Fala. Pensamento, política e poética en Galicia (1914–1931)*, Vigo: Edicións Xerais.

Consello da Cultura Galega (2005), *A sociedade galega e o idioma: evolución sociolingüística de Galicia (1992–2003)*, Santiago de Compostela: Consello da Cultura Galega (available at: http://consellodacultura.gal/mediateca/extras/CCG_2005_A-sociedade-galega-e-o-idioma-evolucion-sociolinguistica-de-Galicia-1992-2003 .pdf).

Coseriu, Eugenio (1980). "Historische Sprache' und 'Dialekt", in J. Göschel, P. Ivić, & K. Kehr, (eds.), *Dialekt und Dialektologie*. Wiesbaden: Steiner, pp. 106–16.

---

42   See Consello da Cultura Galega (2005).

Coseriu, Eugenio (1985), "Linguistic Competence: What is it Really?", The Presidential Address of the Modern Humanities Research Association, *The Modern Language Review*, 80:4, pp. XXV–XXXV.

Coseriu, Eugenio (2015), *Geschichte der Sprachphilosophie: Band 2: Von Herder bis Humboldt*, ed. by Jörn Albrecht, Tübingen: Narr.

Christen, Helen (1998), "Convergence and Divergence in the Swiss German Dialects", *Folia Linguistica* 32 (1–2), pp. 53–67.

Christen, Helen (2010), "Vertikale und horizontale Variation: Beobachtungen zum Schweizerdeutschen", in P. Gilles et al. (eds.), *Variatio delectat. Empirische Evidenzen und theoretische Passungen sprachlicher Variation: für Klaus J. Mattheier zum 65. Geburtstag*, Frankfurt a. M. et al: Peter Lang, pp. 145–159.

Csernicskó, István, & Fedinec, Csilla (2015), "Language and Language Policy in Transcarpathia between the Two World Wars", *Minority Studies: Demography, Minority Education, Ethnopolitics* 18, pp. 93–113.

De Mauro, Tullio (2002), *Storia linguistica dell'Italia unita*, Bari: Laterza.

Forster, Michael Neil (2010), *After Herder. Philosophy of Language in the German Tradition*, Oxford: Oxford UP.

Durkheim, Émile (1982), *The Rules of Sociological Method and Selected Texts on Sociology and its Method*, ed. by S. Lukes, New York: Free Press [1895].

Gipper, Helmut, & Schmitter, Peter (1979), *Sprachwissenschaft und Sprachphilosophie im Zeitalter der Romantik*, Tübingen: Narr.

Goebl, Hans (1999), "Die Sprachensituation in der Donaumonarchie", in I. Ohnheiser, M. Kienpointner and H. Kalb (eds.), *Sprachen in Europa. Sprachsituation und Sprachpolitik in europäischen Ländern*, Innsbruck: Institut für Sprachwissenschaft, pp. 33–58.

Grzega, Joachim (2012), *Europas Sprachen und Kulturen im Wandel der Zeit: eine Entdeckungsreise*, Tübingen: Stauffenburg.

Haugen, Einar (1966), *Language Conflict and Language Planning. The Case of Modern Norwegian*. Cambridge/Mass: Harvard UP.

Hermida, Carme (1992), *Os precursores da normalización: defensa e reivindicación da lingua galega no Rexurdimento (1840–1891)*, Vigo: Edicións Xerais.

Hroch, Miroslav (2015), *European nations: explaining their formation*, London: Verso.

Ínsua, Emilio X. (2014), *Antón Vilar Ponte e a Academia Galega. Contributos para a historia crítica dunha institución centenaria*, Vigo: Edicións do Cumio.

Ínsua, Emilio X. (2016), *A nosa terra é nosa. A xeira das Irmandades da Fala (1916–1931)*, A Coruña: Baía.

Kabatek, Johannes (1996), *Die Sprecher als Linguisten. Interferenz- und Sprachwandelphänomene dargestellt am Galicischen der Gegenwart*, Tübingen: Niemeyer.

Kabatek, Johannes (2005). *Die Bolognesische Renaissance und der Ausbau romanischer Sprachen. Juristische Diskurstraditionen und Sprachentwicklung in Südfrankreich und Spanien im 12. und 13. Jahrhundert*. Tübingen: Niemeyer.

Kabatek, Johannes (2016), "Diglossia", in A. Ledgeway & M. Maiden (eds.), *The Oxford Guide to the Romance Languages*, Oxford: Oxford UP, pp. 624–633.

Kabatek, Johannes (forthcoming), "Spoken and written language", in: *MRL Galician*.

Kloss, Heinz (1967), "Abstand Languages' and 'Ausbau Languages", *Anthropological Linguistics*, 9, 7:29–41.

Koch, Peter, & Oesterreicher, Wulf (2011), *Gesprochene Sprache in der Romania: Französisch, Italienisch, Spanisch*, Berlin: De Gruyter.

Leerssen, Joep (2006), *National Thought in Europe: a cultural history*, Amsterdam: Amsterdam UP.

Marfany, Joan-Lluís (2001), *La llengua maltractada: el castellà i el català a Catalunya del segle XVI al segle XIX*, Barcelona: Empúries.

Marfany, Joan-Lluís (2008), *Llengua, nació i diglòssia*, Barcelona: L'Avenç.

Mariño Paz, Ramón (1992), „Estudio fonético, ortográfico e morfolóxico de textos do prerrexurdimento galego (1805–1837)", Ph. D. Dissertation, Universidade de Santiago de Compostela.

Mezo-Aranzibia, Josu (2008), *El palo y la zanahoria: política lingüística y educación en Irlanda (1922–1939) y el País Vasco (1980–1998)*, Madrid: Centro de Estudios Políticos y Constitucionales.

Monteagudo, Henrique (1999), *Historia social da lingua galega. Idioma, sociedade e cultura a través do tempo*, Vigo: Galaxia.

Nagel, Klaus-Jürgen (1991), *Arbeiterschaft und nationale Frage in Katalonien zwischen 1898 und 1923*, Saarbrücken/Fort Lauderdale: Breitenbach.

Núñez Seixas, Xosé M., & Storm, Eric, eds. (2018), *Regionalism and Modern Europe. Identity Construction and Movements from 1890 to the Present Day*, London: Bloomsbury.

Ribalta, Aurelio (1901), *Catalanismo militante*, Madrid: Imprenta de Romero.

Ribalta, Aurelio (1910), *Libro de Konsagrazión. Feixe de poesías gallegas*, Madrid: Impr. Sucesores de Hernando.

Saussure, Ferdinand de (1916/1984), *Cours de Linguistique Générale*, ed. by T. de Mauro (1ª ed. 1972, based on the original edition by Bally, Sechehaye and Riedlinger from 1916), Lausanne - Paris: Payot.

Scheer, Tamara (2016), "Habsburg Languages at War: 'The linguistic confusion at the tower of Babel couldn't have been much worse'", in Walker & Declercq (eds.), *Languages*, pp. 62–78.

Schlieben-Lange, Brigitte (1996), *Idéologie, révolution et uniformité de la langue*, Sprimont: Mardaga.

Thiesse, Anne-Marie (1999), *La création des identités nationales: Europe XVIIIe-XXe siècle*, Paris: Seuil.

Walker, Julian, & Declercq, Christophe (eds.) (2016), *Languages and the First World War: Communicating in a Transnational War*, London: Palgrave Macmillan.

Villar Ponte, Antón (1916), *Nacionalismo gallego. Nuestra afirmación regional*, A Coruña: Tipografía obrera.

Weber, Eugen (1976), *Peasants into Frenchmen: the modernization of rural France, 1870–1914*, Stanford: Stanford UP.

Werlen, I. (1993), *Schweizer Soziolinguistik*, Neuchâtel: Institut de Linguistique.

Zimmer, Oliver (2003), *A contested nation: history, memory and nationalism in Switzerland, 1761–1891*, Cambridge: Cambridge UP.

Zimmer, Oliver (2005), "Nation, nationalism and power in Switzerland, c. 1760–1900", in L. Scales (ed.), *Power and the nation in European history*, Cambridge: Cambridge UP, pp. 333–353.

PART 3

The Legacy of the First World War and the Nationality question

∴

CHAPTER 10

The Impact of the First World War on the (Re-)Shaping of National Histories on Europe

Stefan Berger

1   Introduction

The First World War marks the culmination of nineteenth-century historiographical nationalism, and after 1918, it continued to engage the minds of many historians in the interwar period, which saw a major transnational debate on the question of war guilt and the justification of the peace treaties of 1919. This chapter will begin by tracing those debates as a prime example of the continued purchase of historiographical nationalism on diverse European historiographies in the interwar period. The end of the First World War also saw the end of empires in Eastern Europe and the emergence of a whole range of new nation states. The second section of this chapter analyses how those nation states swiftly established historical institutions which not only played an important role in professionalizing historical writing, but also in providing those new nation states with historical legitimacy. After the old Europe had disappeared at the end of the First World War, the liberal national historiographies of the long nineteenth century found themselves under attack from the political left and right. The third section of this chapter will discuss the various ideological commitments of national history writing in this period. Finally, the chapter will pay special attention to borders and borderlands and their impact on historiographical nationalism in the interwar period. After all, the map of Europe had changed considerably at the end of the First World War.

2   The War Guilt Debate

After the First World War, all states published substantial document collections that had the explicit purpose of justifying their actions. Whilst they were keen to disseminate this official scholarship nationally and internationally to academic and popular audiences, they also tightly controlled the archives by using censorship, where necessary, in order to prevent views other than those that were officially sanctioned to emerge from the documents. Germany was the first to produce a major government-funded source collection on the origins of the conflict which set out to prove one thing and one thing only: that Germany was not, as article 231 of the Versailles Treaty stated, the sole guilty party in the outbreak of war in August 1914. *Die grosse Politik der europäischen Kabinette, 1871 – 1914 (The High Politics of European Governments, 1871 – 1914)* was published in 40 volumes between 1922 and 1927 – under the general editorship of Friedrich Thimme (1868 – 1938), who willingly sacrificed his own scholarly benchmarks when they clashed with political expediency.[1]

The planning of the collection started as early as 1919, and a foreign office memorandum of 1921 could not have been clearer on the political functionalization of history for the interests of the nation: 'The great document publication is not being prepared so that its volumes (...) might only gather dust in archives or be studied by isolated historians with effects which will be apparent only after years'.[2] The historians working on it were not given access to the archives of the war office, the navy office and the General Staff, as the foreign office clearly felt that unpalatable facts might surface here. Before embarking on its own collection, the foreign office had put considerable efforts into repressing the separate edition of documents prepared by the socialists Karl Kautsky (1854–1938) and Kurt Eisner (1867–1919) in 1919. The latter had been no less instrumental in their history politics, but they were keen to demonstrate that the elites of the old Imperial Germany had been guilty in provoking war in 1914 and their argument was that the new democratic republic should not be held responsible for the reckless policies of the empire that had been swept away in the German revolution of 1918.

Versailles seemed to prove that the allies were unwilling to make that distinction, and hence the foreign office in the Weimar Republic did everything to dispel the idea of German war guilt – with the help of a little army of historians and archivists. It established a War Guilt Section in the Foreign Ministry which worked tirelessly to prove 'scientifically' that Germany was not responsible for the outbreak of war in 1914. It published its own journal entitled *Die Kriegsschuldfrage*; it financed a research centre for the study of the causes of the war; it set up the coordination of all those associations which worked on the question of German war guilt and it assisted the Parliamentary Committee of Enquiry into the war guilt question.[3] German historians insisted that the pre-war alliance system had led to an encirclement of Germany which in turn produced a defensive war directed in the main against autocratic Tsarism in Russia.

---

1 Epstein (1973: 174).
2 Cited in Wilson (1996: 11).
3 Herwig (1996: 88–90).

Germany's opponents in the First World War were slow to react to the challenge of the German historical offensive after 1919, but when they did react, they were also not reluctant to draft history into the service of the nation. As Austen Chamberlain wrote to George Peabody Gooch (1873–1968) on 30 July 1926: 'My first duty is to preserve peace now and in the future. I cannot sacrifice that even to historical accuracy'.[4] In 1924, the British foreign office finally gave its approval to a document collection that it perceived as a reply to German scholarship, and asked the internationally renowned and respected G.P. Gooch to head this undertaking. A modest three volumes were to appear until 1927 and the foreign office invested nowhere near as many resources into the undertaking as their Berlin counterparts. As in Germany, particular sets of sources remained out of bounds for historians, e.g. the files of the India Office and the Committee for Imperial Defence.

In France, the Commission de Publication des Documents Relatifs aux Origines de la Guerre de 1914–1918 was established in 1928 to combat what was perceived as very effective German propaganda. In the Soviet Union, it was not a case of justifying the actions of the pre-revolutionary Tsarist government. Rather, the 'red' historians of the Soviet Union were keen to indict the whole pre-war capitalist system for throwing Europe into the cauldron of war.[5] If national historians worked for national governments in the national interest, the whole historians' controversy surrounding the question of war guilt also had a strong transnational dimension to it. For example, British and American historians and politicians worked closely together throughout the 1930s, in order to ensure that their respective document collections contained nothing that would put the other nation in a relatively bad light. Demands for censorship of manuscripts were complied with as a matter of routine. The two international pariah states of the interwar period, Germany and the Soviet Union, co-operated over the publication of documents relating to the pre-history of the First World War. All nations in the interwar period were searching for reciprocal agreements that would allow foreign scholars access to national archives other than their own. The German foreign office often directly supported those foreign scholars whom it perceived to be in sympathy with German demands for a revision of the Versailles Peace Treaty. The history politics of the victorious allies were arguably less successful because they came later, were much more limited and not as dissemination-oriented as the German efforts.

---

4 Cited in Fair (1992: 199).
5 Cited in Spring (1996: 72).

Germany had lost the military war but it was winning the history war in the interwar period.[6]

3 Emerging New States and Historiographical Nationalism

Historiographical nationalism was not just visible in the history politics pursued by nation states with the active help of historians-cum-politicians. It surfaced strongly in the many new-found nation states in East-Central and Eastern Europe after the collapse of empires at the end of the First World War. Like the new-found nation states of the nineteenth century, they were investing heavily in the historical sciences and their professionalization and institutionalization. Soon after Finland gained independence in 1917, the University of Turku was re-founded (in 1920) in order to rival the Swedish-speaking and allegedly unpatriotic university in Helsinki (which had moved from Turku in 1828). The nationalist Finnish intelligentsia organized a nationwide fundraising campaign to endow the university, which was indeed to become one of the bulwarks of Finnish nationalist history, represented by Jalmari Jaakkola (1885–1964), in the interwar period.[7] Jaakkola developed his fantastic theories of a great past of Finnish peasant society, stretching into the medieval period as a nationalist statement directed against those who had dominated Finland before independence, i.e. the Russians and the Swedes. Jaakkola also became active as a war-time propagandist after 1941, calling on fellow Finns to defend the homeland and its proud past against the foreign invaders. The Fennoman nationalist historical narrative, developed during the nineteenth century, became institutionalized at Finnish universities in the interwar period and became the dominant academic historical narrative. Its teleological and homogenizing perspective on Finnish history moved other perspectives to the side-lines. Thus, for example, class perspectives were hardly present in the universities and instead developed in association with the Finnish labour movement outside of the universities. Ethnic, cultural and religious diversity was also hardly ever discussed and became another story silenced by the strength of the nationalist Fennoman narratives.[8]

After national independence in 1919, Latvian national historians concentrated very much on establishing a Latvian national master narrative and

---

6 Generally, regarding the interwar source editions on the First World War, see Zala (2001: 47 ff.).
7 Haapala & Kaarninen (2010: 75).
8 Aronsson, Fulsås, Haapala & Jensen (2008).

refuting in particular the claims of Baltic German historiography over their territory. They focussed on agrarian history, in order to show that the claims of Baltic Germans to the land were spurious and that redistribution of land to Latvian small-holders was historically justified. In 1936, the Latvia History Institute was founded at Riga which had the explicit task, written into its foundational document, of studying 'the past in the light of nationalism and truth'.[9] In the Baltic states, archaeological and ethnographic evidence became especially important in justifying new state borders and policies of cultural homogenization of what were intensely multi-cultural societies in Imperial Russia. In Lithuania, for example, nationalist historians, often taking their cue from Germany, used an explosive mixture of biology, eugenics and Social Darwinism to trace the Lithuanian nation as far back in history as possible.

The Irish Free State, established in 1922, also saw the emergence of a strongly nationalist professional historiography in the interwar period. Intriguingly, it was modelled on what should have been its arch-enemy, Britain. The Irish Manuscripts Commission was founded as a government-funded agency and it took its cue very much from the British Historical Manuscripts Commission. It was given the task of surveying, editing and publishing documents of national interest located in British and continental European archives. The key historians, who were to professionalize Irish historiography from the 1930s onwards and who laid the groundwork for the Irish national master narrative, were all British-trained. As the Irish Free State lacked well-trained nationalist historians of Ireland, it sent some of its best postgraduates on scholarships to Britain, especially University College London, where they benefited from the Institute of Historical Research (IHR), which had been established at the University of London in 1921. Robert Dudley Edwards (1909–1988) and Theodore William Moody (1907–1984) were arguably the most notable Irish historians to emerge from such training. In 1936, they founded the Irish Historical Society and the Ulster Society for Irish Historical Studies. Two years later, these societies began publishing *Irish Historical Studies,* edited by Edwards and Moody. Entrenched in the bastions of Irish historiography in University College Dublin and Trinity College Dublin respectively, both scholars came to stand for a new professional style of history writing based on scientific principles. Yet they managed, like many historians before and after them, to combine their adherence to scientificity with strong doses of nationalism which was also visible in the way they trained the next generation of scholars, archivists, administrators

---

9 Šnē (2010: 82).

and schoolteachers in Ireland-putting equal weight on issues of scientificity and nationalism.[10]

In the new composite state of Czechoslovakia, the professionalization and institutionalization of history writing was also given a major boost by the formation of the new state which promptly sought to give itself historical legitimation. Reference to ancient Slavs, Great Moravians, Hussites, the Slavonic congress, the 1848 revolution and the Czechoslovak legions in the First World War all served the purpose of underpinning nation building after 1918. However, such a Czechoslovak national narrative was deeply contested, with Slovak historians, in particular, keeping their distance. Daniel Rapant (1897–1988), for example, vehemently denied the existence of a common Czechoslovak history during the interwar period. He admitted some commonalities, but stressed that overall, the differences were far more important. In particular, he denied the notion that the current Czechoslovak state was the direct heir to the state created by the Bohemian crown during the middle ages, as such a construction would make Slovakia a mere appendix of an essentially Czech state. Given such differences, it is little surprising that the institutionalization of history writing took place along separate Czech and Slovak lines. The new Czechoslovak master narrative combined emphasis on ancient Slav traditions with an endorsement of Hussitism and its Slovak version, the Bratriks. It celebrated the Great Moravian empire of the Middle Ages and the coming together of Czechs and Slovaks in the First World War. Yet anyone examining this Czechoslovak master narrative will find that it was developed and espoused almost exclusively by Czech historians. Their Slovak counterparts did not seriously question the political unity of the Czechoslovak state in the interwar period, but, whether Catholic or Protestant, they wrote a history that proudly asserted the separate cultural, linguistic and ethnic identity of Slovakia as an independent nation.[11]

In interwar Turkey, the vast majority of the younger Turkish historians had joined the Türk Yurdu (Turkish foyers) just before the First World War, and over the course of the next two decades they were at the forefront of formulating a Turkish historical master narrative in the service of Kemal Atatürk's political regime. After 1931 the official Türk Tarih Kurumu (Turkish History Society) provided the framework for a number of quasi-official historical projects. Some of its leading historians, such as Yusuf Akçura (1876–1935) or Reşid Saffet Atabinen (1884–1965) subsequently became members of parliament, underlining the proximity of historical studies and politics in the Republic of Turkey. Atatürk

---

10 Brady (2011); O'Dowd (2010: 172); Ellis (1991).
11 Hudek (2010: 152); Heiss, von Klimó, Kolář & Kováč (2008); Kolář (2010: 149–50).

personally encouraged the history society to develop the Türk Tarih Tezi (Turkish History Thesis), which argued that Turkish was the original language of mankind and glorified Turkishness as the cradle of humanity. It declared Turks as Aryans and identified contemporary Turks with ancient Hittites, thereby moving the foundation story of Turkey backwards by several centuries.[12]

The determination of newly founded nation states to promote nationalism, including the scientific study of national history, in the interwar period only found its limits in their financial prowess, or rather, the lack of it. Economic crises and instability meant that major investments were often not forthcoming. In some cases, initiatives from within civil society stepped into the breach. In the newly independent Poland, for example, existing scientific societies and historical journals experienced a struggle for survival in the interwar period, as source editions had to be abandoned and journal editors constantly struggled with lack of funds. Nevertheless, a number of new universities were founded, e.g. the Universities in Poznań, Vilnius, and the Catholic University of Lublin. At the University of Warsaw, L'viv and Kraków, new history departments were established. The pre-war Towarzystwo Historyczne (Historical Society) became the Towarzystwo Miłośników Historii (Polish Historical Association) and subsequently the Polskie Towarzystwo Historyczne (Polish Historical Society) in 1924, which held national history conferences in 1925, 1930 and 1935, and published its own journal, the *Kwartalnik Historyczny (Historical Quarterly)*.

4 Ideological Commitments and Challenges

British national historiography was undoubtedly the strongest bulwark of liberal history writing in the interwar period. The nation state was not in question and a homogeneous and strong liberal national master narrative had already been established in the course of the nineteenth century. When George V opened the British parliament in 1935, his speech had been written by the historian George Trevelyan (1876–1962): 'It is to me a source of pride and thankfulness that the perfect harmony of our parliamentary system with our constitutional monarchy has survived the shocks that have in recent years destroyed other empires and other liberties (…). The complex forms and balanced spirit of our Constitution were not the discovery of a single era, still less of a single party or of a single person. They are the slow accretion of centuries, the outcome of patience, tradition and experience constantly finding outlets (…) for the impulse toward liberty, justice and social improvement inherent in our

---

12   Kieser (2005).

people down the ages'.[13] These sentences were a patriotic assertion of the Whig view of historiography that had associated constitutional liberties and democratic traditions with Englishness throughout the long nineteenth century.

Herbert Butterfield (1900–1979) became famous for demolishing the theoretical underpinnings of Whiggism in the interwar period, but in practice, he could not free his own writing from a continued belief in a national history that followed a civilizational path towards greater liberty.[14] In addition, Lewis Namier (1888–1960), for all his effective and iconoclastic anti-Whiggism, was nevertheless the life-long admirer of British political institutions which he held in the highest regard. As Linda Colley (*1949) has written: 'For him [Namier], Britain was the epitome of constitutional wisdom and organic development, whereas Germany, Britain's counterpoise, was characterized by violence, chaos and ineptitude'.[15] The ongoing celebration of the English constitution and English constitutionalism in British political history in the interwar period was striking. It was picked up by social and cultural historians who stressed that the peculiarities of English constitutionalism also explained the development of social harmony and cultural refinement, thus linking other areas of history to the exact same master paradigm of the forward march of civilization and progress characterizing English (and by extension) British history. Economic history rose to prominence in interwar Britain and was similarly infused with strong doses of nationalism. It celebrated the proud achievements of the Industrial Revolution as a British, actually mainly English, affair, rooted in an alleged English progressivism and achievement- and growth-orientation. They were not shy to offer their patriotic services to the education of a future business elite in their country, as they firmly believed that their research had practical implications for the contemporary management of businesses.[16]

Britain was by no means the only country upholding liberal national historiographical master narratives in the interwar period. Historians associated with the *Annales* in the interwar period upheld the commitment of French historians to the values of the French revolution. In so far as they wrote national history, they tended to do so within a cosmopolitan and non-ethnic orientation. In other well-established republican states, such as Switzerland, the defence of liberal traditions also came to the fore in the interwar period. The nationalist appropriations of the medieval past of the Old Confederacy reached its highpoint in and around the Second World War, when homeland defence

---

13   Cited in Hernon Jr. (1976: 86).
14   Bentley (2000, 2011).
15   Colley (1989: 14 ff.). On Namier's iconoclastic anti-Whiggism, see also Colley (1989: 46 ff.).
16   Coleman (1987).

against Nazi Germany became a key issue. It was depicted in terms of the defence of the ancient neutrality and freedoms of the Swiss. But already in the 1920s, Swiss history politics had combined notions of the Alps as protector of the sources of major European rivers with ideas of Switzerland as home for the new League of Nations, a new international organization for conflict resolution, first suggested by the American President Woodrow Wilson in 1918 and eventually established in post-war Geneva, that would bring peace, liberty and democracy to the world. It was Switzerland's historical mission to facilitate the harmonious co-existence of European peoples. Freedom, justice, and federalism became the hallmarks of Switzerland.[17]

In Norway, two of the most famous historians, Halvdan Koht (1873–1965) and Edvard Bull Sr. (1881–1932), took office as Social Democratic foreign ministers in the interwar period, thereby continuing the strong politicization of Norwegian nineteenth-century historiography. The close alliance between liberal democracy and historiography in the nineteenth century was to give way to an equally strong alliance between Social Democracy and historiography in the twentieth century.[18] The strong development of social history at Norwegian universities put a strong emphasis on questions of social inequality and on discrimination in term of class and, later, gender. It thus legitimated the Social Democratic project of better chances for workers in Norwegian society and for a greater share of the nation's wealth. History here became a weapon for a political project aiming at making Norway a more socially responsible and just society.

Czechoslovakia provided one of the few cases of a successful liberal national historiography. The dominating influence of Tomáš Garrigue Masaryk's (1850–1937) led to an identification of Czech national history with the progress of humanity. The Reformation played a key role in the constitution of the Czech nation, which he saw as a precursor of the nineteenth century Czech national movement that found its culmination in the foundation of the Czechoslovak state after the First World War. National history, for Masaryk and his followers, was an important resource for justifying the new-found nation state. However, unlike many of the other new-found nation states of East-Central and Eastern Europe, the Czechoslovak national master narrative was one that co-existed harmoniously with notions of liberal democracy. Masaryk was, after all, a champion of the European Enlightenment, an admirer of both French republicanism and Anglo-Saxon constitutionalism and liberalism. He provided a liberal-democratic framework for the national state which was not without

---

17 For further details, see Marchal (2006).
18 Björk (2011).

its prominent critics, including Jaroslav Goll (1846–1929) (the so-called Goll school), and Josef Pekař (1870–1937).[19]

Some historians were devoted to upholding liberal and social democratic principles in the midst of strong illiberal turns of historiographical traditions. If we take the example of Italy, after the fascists took power in 1923, a strong liberal national historical master narrative was increasingly replaced by an official fascist one. After 1932, the regime ensured that all historical journals had chief editors who were in broad sympathy with fascism.[20] As in National Socialist Germany, few out and out apologists for fascism could be found among Italy's professional historians. The historian of the fascist movement, Gentile, perhaps comes closest to the role played by Frank in Germany. Gentile's *Risorgimento e Fascismo* (*Risorgimento and Fascism*), published in 1931, celebrated fascism as fulfilment of the national ideals that had enthused Italians during the Risorgimento. Liberty, Gentile argued, was not the liberty of the individual, but the liberty of the fascist state. If few went as far as Gentile in identifying the making of the Italian nation with fascism, many, including Gioacchino Volpe (1876–1971), were happy enough to cooperate with the regime, endorsing it when necessary and benefitting from it in terms of resources and advancement. Volpe's national history, *L'Italia in cammino* (*Italy on the Move*, 1927), was also identifying fascism with the project of completing national unity that had started with the Risorgimento.[21]

Yet some historians chose resistance. One of the strongest critics of fascist Italy, Croce, continued to live in the country throughout fascism and even managed to publish his national history, *Storia d'Italia dal 1871 al 1915* (*History of Italy from 1871 to 1915*, 1928). Here, he upheld the nineteenth-century view of liberty against its enemies from the right and the left. Celebrating the achievements of liberalism, he depicted the victory of fascism as a complete break with the legacy of the Risorgimento. Another prominent example of an attempt to uphold the liberal tradition in Italian historiography and develop it further is Carlo Rosselli (1899–1937), the founder of *Giustizia e Libertà* (Justice and Liberty), a centre-left antifascist organization composed of intellectuals, some of which went on to found the short-lived *Partito d'Azione* (Action Party) in 1943. Together with his brother Nello Rosselli (1900–1937), who worked under Gioacchino Volpe at the School of Modern and Contemporary History in Rome, they not only took a political stance against fascism, but also sought to explain the success of fascism in relation to Italy's somehow deficient national

---

19   Kořalka (1992: 1027); Řepa (2011); Neudorfl (1993).
20   Tortarolo (1999); Fogu (2003: 24).
21   Clark (1999).

history. The Risorgimento, they argued, had been unfinished, and claims of the fascist regime to be the heir of the Risorgimento had to be contested historically. An alternative, republican and socialist Risorgimento had to be upheld against the rival claims of the fascist state. The Rossellis were influential in defining the antifascist struggle as a 'second Risorgimento', a trope that became popular in Resistance circles during the Second World War. It sought to create the unity of the Italian nation on the basis of social justice and emancipation.[22]

In continental Europe, liberal national historiographies were under threat. In Weimar Germany, the majority of mainstream national historians remained impeccably opposed to republicanism and parliamentary democracy. Georg von Below (1858–1927), readily dismissed the historical writings of 'democrats lacking scholarly profundity', and was instead committed to the 'cloud-cuckoo-land of cosmopolitanism'.[23] The most important methodological innovation in interwar German historiography was the inclination towards *Volksgeschichte*, which had distinctly illiberal political connotations. Walter Goetz (1867–1958) was one of the few who called on fellow historians to leave behind the monarchist, Prussian nationalist perspective which, he argued, blinded German historians and made them unable to accept the political settlement of the post-First World War period.[24] The weak liberal tradition of German national historiography was either silenced or exiled with the coming to power of National Socialism. The most committed of National Socialist historians, such as Walter Frank (1905–1945), at the *Reichsinstitut für Geschichte des neuen Deutschland* (National Institute for the History of the New Germany), sought to infuse German national history with the racial paradigms championed by the regime.[25] More mainstream historiography retained its distance from such racialization of historical writing, but conservative étatist historians supported aspects of the regime's policy and were enamoured by the regime's foreign policy successes. Many were willing to promote the regime and its aims in diverse contexts.[26]

A comparison of Germany with Hungary is instructive. As in Weimar Germany, the peace treaties at the end of the First World War produced a national outcry. Like in Germany, the collapse of an empire resulted in a liberal and, immediately afterwards, communist revolution, which was ultimately defeated.

---

22 See Morgan (2008).
23 Von Below (1924: 42, 29).
24 Goetz (1957: 419). The essay on German contemporary historiography was first published in 1924.
25 Heiber (1966).
26 Schönwälder (1996: 211). See also Gilbert (1947: 51).

A much more authoritarian political regime emerged in interwar Hungary, which broke with the liberal history cult surrounding the 1848 revolution that had been established before 1918.[27] Whereas in Germany, the events of 1848 never really fitted into the dominant storylines of national unification that came to be focussed on Bismarck and the 'wars of unification' between 1864 and 1871, in Hungary, historians had successfully integrated 1848 into the official national history, albeit a sanitized version of 1848 that excluded its more radical political aspects. It helped that Hungarian historians could portray 1848 as a moment of national defence against a hostile foreign power, i.e. Russia, whereas German historians found it much more difficult to do so. In the interwar period, the Hungarian state generously financed historical studies that had the aim of demonstrating how historically unjustified the Treaty of Trianon was. The comparative history of Hungary with its newly sovereign neighbouring states became popular, precisely because such comparison showed these states' lack of historical legitimacy. Hungarian comparative history was thus born out of the spirit of historiographical nationalism in the service of the revision of the much-hated Treaty of Trianon, which had reduced Hungary to under a third of its pre-war territory (it lost 72 per cent of its territory to neighbouring states).[28]

In many of the new nation states of East-Central Europe, historians, who participated in projects to establish liberal democratic national master narratives, battled against the odds. Many intellectuals, including historians, were attracted to the construction of national essences, which in turn contributed to the radicalization of nationalism. In Hungary, Bulgaria and Romania, the discourse on national characterology paved the way for historical interpretations that undermined liberal democratic thought and instead endorsed more radical ideologies.[29] In Poland, the national(ist) perspective became vital for justifying the rebirth of the Polish nation at the end of the First World War. Hence, some of the key debates in interwar Poland took place between those historians, who justified a Jagellonian view on national history, taking the imperial history of the Polish-Lithuanian Commonwealth as a benchmark for national history, whilst others warned against imperial overstretch and instead

---

27   Von Klimó (2003: 55 ff.).
28   Thomas Szerecz has completed a PhD dissertation at Central European University in Budapest on the subject of comparative history writing in Hungary (defence 2017). I am grateful to him for alerting me to this intriguing connection between comparative history and methodological nationalism in Hungary.
29   Trencsényi (2011).

preferred to consolidate Poland around the national-democratic state that had been created in 1919.

In Spain, a strong nineteenth-century liberal historiographical tradition was replaced with a fascist and Catholic master narrative with the onset of the Franco dictatorship. It found expression in the routine idealization of medieval Christendom, the stress on the moral purity of Spanish Catholic nationality, and the strong role of Opus Dei in history departments and historical education more generally. The nation became synonymous with the church and the monarchy. One of the foundational texts of the new Catholic master narrative was Julián Juderías' (1877–1918) *La Leyenda Negra* (*The Black Legend*), first published in 1914. It countered the liberal idea that Catholicism was a dark (black) influence in Spanish national history throughout the ages, and lamented the absence of a Catholic master narrative that was capable of defending 'the Catholic conception of life' underlying the Spanish national character and its idealism. The liberals, he argued, had invented the black legend of Spanish national history in order to put the nation down. What was needed, instead, was the celebration of Spain's moral superiority that found expression, above all, in Miguel de Cervantes' successful novel *Don Quijote*. Pedro Sáinz Rodríguez (1897–1986), in his lectures at the University of Madrid in 1924/25, argued that Spanish decadence was rooted in the abandonment of the Catholic ideals that had produced the Golden Age of Spain. National Catholic historical writing celebrated 'mother Spain', and produced a cult of ancestry that was to inspire uncritical love for the 'genius' of the Spanish 'race'. In its imperial inflection, national Catholicism came to celebrate *Hispanidad* as the principle affirming the spiritual community of all Hispanic nations, embracing the Latin American republics.[30] Ciriaco Pérez-Bustamante (1896–1975) was a good example of those historians who became apologists for Francoism among the Spanish academics.[31]

The liberal national historiographies emerging from the long nineteenth century were not only challenged by the political right in interwar Europe. In 1917, the victory of the Bolsheviks in the Soviet Union for the first time allowed a Marxist-Leninist historiography to emerge as state historiography. Bolshevik historiography stood in a tradition of Marxist historiography, best represented in Russia by Georgij Plechanov (1857–1918). Plechanov's *Istorija russkoj obščestvennoj mysli* (*History of Russian Social Thought*), published in 1909,

---

30 Boyd (1997), Chapter 6.
31 See Pasamar (1991); for a summary in English see also Pasamar (2010), Chapter 3, which is especially good on the exiled liberal historians Américo Castro and Sánchez Albornoz. See also Antolín-Hofrichter (2018) and Álvarez-Junco (2017).

prioritized class over nation in line with Marxist thinking and stressed Russian backwardness vis-à-vis the West.[32] Many Bolsheviks shared the belief in Russia's backwardness. Trockij, in his *1905* and his *Istorija russkoj revoljucii* (*History of the Russian Revolution*), upheld notions of Russian peculiarity which he traced back to its oriental character and strong *étatisme*. Lenin and Stalin, by contrast, already argued before 1917 that Russia's historical development was in line with that of the West and therefore could take the lead in the world-wide destruction of capitalism.

Michail Pokrovskij, who became the undisputed leader of Soviet Marxist historiography in the 1920s, was nicknamed 'Supreme Commander of the Army of Red Historians'.[33] He gave early Soviet historiography an internationalist orientation, abhorred Russian nationalism and was adamant that it was important for Marxist historians to look beyond the narrow confines of national history. As People's Commissar for Education, he prohibited any history teaching that promoted nationalism. In his own writings, he placed heavy emphasis on social and economic developments in history, which, he argued, were essential to document the class struggle in history. Despite all this, he still could not escape national history. His *Russkaja Istorija v samom sžatom očerke* (*Brief History of Russia*) was approved by no less a figure than Lenin and it served as bible for the first generation of Marxist-Leninist historians in the Soviet Union. As a national history, it was indeed trying to establish a new national master narrative, which portrayed the history of Tsarist Russia as 'dark other', where not only the working classes but also the non-Russian nationalities were repressed. He contrasted the Russian past sharply with the bright Communist future of the Soviet Union under Bolshevism.

Whilst Pokrovskij had insisted on the importance of solid empirical evidence and spoken out against the falsification of historical facts in pursuit of political aims, Stalin, in his attack on evidence-based historiography, could build on Leninist notions that the party line was to guide the historians more than historical evidence, as true objectivity could only be achieved through identifying with the Communist Party's explication of the laws which governed historical processes (*partijnost'*). The Communist Party, representing all 'progressive' traditions in history, held the key to historical interpretation, and all deviations from its line were necessarily 'reactionary'. With the implementation of the personality cult around Stalin, the fountain of all historical wisdom was not even the Party anymore, but its 'great leader'.

---

32 Baron (1963).
33 Enteen (1978).

Stalin's turn away from internationalism and towards the theory of 'socialism in one country' had important implications for Soviet historiography, as he now charged historians with producing patriotic narratives which were to legitimate Bolshevik rule in the Soviet Union.[34] Historians were to prioritize the history of Russia over the history of all other Soviet republics, as it was Russian history which was perceived as anchor-point of Soviet state building. Russian ethnic particularism was to characterize much of Soviet historical writing from the 1930s to the 1950s.[35] Stalin perceived history as major ally in his drive to construct unity and purpose around the notion of Soviet patriotism. The enemies of the working classes thus became enemies of the Soviet people, or the Russian people and its sister peoples. Historians now harked back to many of the traditional heroical myths underpinning nationalist histories of Russia already in Tsarist times. One of Russia's greatest writers, Alexandr Puškin (1799–1837), was transformed into a Stalinist icon.[36] Ivan the Terrible (1530–1584) and Peter the Great (1672–1725) became national heroes once again, and the making of a strong national Russian state was commented on approvingly, even if it was an oppressive class state.[37]

In Andrej Vasil'evič Šestakov's (1877–1941) *Short Course in the History of the USSR*, published in 1937 to replace Pokrovskij's earlier work, the Russian past was linked positively to the Soviet present. In Pokrovskij, the Russian past had been the necessary precondition for the Soviet present, but it had not figured positively, quite the contrary. In Šestakov's text, on the other hand, the reader is expressly invited to identify with the heroes of Russian history. Thus, the book begins: 'The USSR is the land of socialism. There is only one socialist country on the globe-it is our motherland'. And it closes: 'We love our motherland and we must know her wonderful history well. Whoever knows history will better understand current life, will fight the enemies of our country better, and will consolidate socialism'.[38] Soviet patriotism and love for the socialist motherland became guiding lights of Soviet national historiography thereafter.[39]

The ICHS, which continued to organize the world historical congresses in the interwar period, struggled to maintain the liberal tradition against the advances of authoritarian right-wing, fascist and Communist attempts to dislodge it. The history of the ICHS in the interwar period was, to a considerable extent, the history of the nationalist re-assertion of history through and in the

---

34   Powell (1951).
35   Martin (2001).
36   Litvin (2001); Petrone (2000).
37   Perrie (2001); Black (1962); Benjamin Schenk (2004).
38   Cited in Mazour (1958: 204).
39   Brandenberger (2002).

transnational arena. The ICHS, at its 1928 Oslo congress, affirmed the national principles in its modes of representation which meant that it accepted delegations from the Communist Soviet Union, fascist Italy, and, later on, from National Socialist Germany and Francoist Spain as national delegations, whilst it refused officially to acknowledge the exile historiographies from all these countries. It was a victory for the communist and fascist dictatorships within the ICHS that they now alone represented their respective national historiographies in front of the world community of historians. Moreover, they were not shy in pushing their particular ideological history politics onto the world historical congresses. For example, German historians were able to peddle the agenda of a racist *Volksgeschichte* in the service of a comprehensive revision of the Versailles Peace Treaty quite successfully in the 1930s.[40]

Transnational histories were sometimes written out of the desire to overcome historiographic nationalism. Toynbee, for example, changed his views on nationalism as result of the First World War. Before 1914 he applauded the liberal national liberation movements in various parts of Eastern Europe and at the peace conference in 1919, he still was an advocate of the principle of national self-determination. However, thereafter he increasingly came to abhor the ugly and destructive side of nationalism, which he saw as responsible for endless acts of violent and brutal barbarism. His *Study of History*, started in the 1920s, was motivated by the desire to write against the impending disasters that nationalism was about to produce but even Toynbee could probably not have imagined the intensity with which hypernationalism was to wreak havoc on a global scale during the Second World War.[41]

5   The Historiographies of Changing Borders and Borderlands in Interwar Europe

In the heated nationalist atmosphere of the interwar period, the cases of Yugoslav national history or German *Volksgeschichte* demonstrate the utmost importance that historians attached to borders and borderlands. Especially where those borders were contested, and there happened to be an astonishing number of contested borders in the interwar period, one invariably finds vociferous historiographical debates over such borders often involving whole national historiographies. Take, for example, the battles between Polish and German historians after 1919 about the new eastern borders of Germany. On the German

---

40   Harvey (2003), Chap. 6.
41   McNeill (1978: 448 ff.).

side, outrage over the Versailles Treaty spurned on historians to seek the revision of the new borders with historical arguments. On the Polish side, historians feverishly propagated the historical right of Poland to the territories it had gained under the Versailles Treaty. Thus, for example, historians were extremely active on both sides to provide arguments in the political battles surrounding the plebiscites in Eastern Prussia and Upper Silesia in 1920/21 that decided the national belonging of those regions in the interwar period. German *Ostforschung* battled it out with Polish *Westforschung* in an intricate historians' war that lasted for the entire interwar period only to be resumed under the circumstances of the post-Second World War territorial order.[42]

Similar history wars can be found in many parts of interwar Europe: Czech and German national histories clashed in Bohemia and Moravia; Italian and Austro-German narratives competed over South Tyrol and Trentino; Slovene and Austro-German accounts provided distinct stories of Lower Styria, Carinthia, and Carniola —to give just a few prominent examples of the importance of borders to interwar national histories.[43] In the new nation state of Lithuania, historians were busy nationalizing multicultural areas such as Vilnius and its surroundings by reference to an allegedly primeval Lithuania. The neighbouring disciplines of archaeology and ethnography justified claims that a population that was subjectively nationally indifferent was nevertheless objectively Lithuanian.[44] The influence of Social Darwinism and biological determinism only increased the strength of those claims to nationalize particular territories in Eastern and East-Central Europe, where nation states had emerged from the ruins of empires after 1918.

The peace settlements at the end of the First World War produced what became known as Greater Romania in the interwar period. The provinces of Bessarabia, Bukovina and Transylvania now became part of Romania. They included universities in Cluj and Cernăuţi that had to be Romanianized. Thus, an *Institutului de istorie naţională* (Institute for National History) was set up at Cluj, in addition to Romanian state-sponsored research institutes, regional branches of state archives and museums, all of which had the task of integrating the new regions into the enlarged Romanian state.[45]

The defeat of the Austro-Hungarian state in the First World War, and the dissolution of the Habsburg empire brought a whole range of border conflicts

---

42 Piskorski, Hackmann & Jaworski (2002); Hackmann (2011).
43 For a good survey of those overlapping histories and their impact on national historical master narratives see the contributions in Frank & Hadler (2011).
44 Wendland (2008: 428).
45 Murgescu (2010: 99).

and changes which had consequences for national history writing. Austria was one of the strangest cases: a new-found state without a national history and a national movement. Had many Austrian Germans subscribed to transnational Habsburgism before 1914, the vast majority now turned to German nationalism and would have happily merged with the German Reich, had the Allies allowed such a move. As it was, the Allies pushed through the foundation of an independent Austrian state, which was faced with the task of state-building (not to mention nation-building) – a process to which few of its elites actually subscribed or actively wanted. Under the circumstances, it was not surprising that Austrian historians developed contacts with their German counterparts and many, led by Heinrich von Srbik (1878–1951), who held the chair of general history at the University of Vienna between 1920 and 1945, developed a pan-German version of history that legitimated the eventual merging of Austria with Germany in 1938. Very few historians, e.g. Ernst Karl Winter (1895–1959), attempted to construct an independent Austrian national identity.[46]

6   Conclusion

The First World War reshaped national historical master narratives in Europe in a major way. The debates surrounding the war guilt question of the First World War had major repercussions on interwar politics – with the German government-sponsored campaign successfully spreading the message of the injustice of the Versailles Peace Treaty. The new nation states founded on the territories of those European empires that had imploded at the end of the First World War were usually keen to deploy history to underline the legitimacy of their new-found statehood. Contested borderlands became sites of intense struggle between different national histories in the 1920s and 1930s, ensuring that borders were often given high priority in national histories.

In the politically charged atmosphere of the interwar period, it does not come as a surprise that the discipline hardly developed in a politics-free space. Liberalism and parliamentarism were under threat in a number of European nation states in the 1920s and 1930s, and as has been documented above, for some countries at least a weakening of liberal national master narratives contributed to their demise into more authoritarian forms of government. Historiography was to some extent a barometer of political change, reflecting and at the same time helping to pave the way for such change. At the extreme ends of

46   Suppanz (1998).

the political spectrum was, on the one hand, the rise of fascist regimes to power and, on the other, the victory of Communism in the Soviet Union. Fascism and communism significantly reshaped historical professions in Europe. Overall, historiographical nationalism was extremely strong in the interwar period. Even where liberal national historiographies could prevail, they often did so against the backdrop of a strong liberal nationalism.

Bibliography

Alvarez-Junco, J. (2017), "History and National Myth", in J. Moreno-Luzón & X.M. Núñez Seixas (eds.), *Metaphors of Spain: representations of Spanish national identity in the twentieth century*, New York/Oxford: Berghahn, pp. 9–32.

Antolín-Hofrichter, A. (2018), *Fremde Moderne: Wissenschaftspolitik, Geschichtswissenschaft und nationale Narrative unter dem Franco-Regime, 1939–1964*, Munich: Oldenbourg.

Aronsson, P., N. Fulsås, P. Haapala, & B.E. Jensen (2008), "Nordic National Histories", in S. Berger & Ch. Lorenz (eds), *The Contested Nation: Ethnicity, Religion, Class and Gender in National Histories*, Basingstoke: Palgrave Macmillan, pp. 256–282.

Baron, S.H. (1963), *Plekhanov. The Father of Russian Marxism*, Stanford: Stanford UP.

Bentley, M. (2000) "Butterfield at the Millenium", *Storia della Storiografia*, 38 (2000), pp. 17–32.

Bentley, M. (2011), *The Life and Thought of Herbert Butterfield* (Cambridge: Cambridge UP).

Björk, R. (2011), "The Overlapping Histories of Sweden and Norway – the Union from 1814–1905", in T. Frank & F. Hadler (eds), *Disputed Territories and Shared Pasts: Overlapping National Histories in Modern Europe*, Basingstoke: Palgrave Macmillan, pp. 17–34.

Black, C.E. (1962), "The Reforms of Peter the Geat", in id. (ed.), *Rewriting Russian History. Soviet Interpretations of Russia's Past*, New York: Praeger, 2nd ed., pp. 235–248.

Boyd, C.P. (1997), *Historia Patria. Politics, History, and National Identity in Spain, 1875–1975*, Princeton, NJ: Princeton UP.

Brady, C. (2011), "Arrested Development: Competing Histories and the Formation of the Irish Historical Profession, 1801–1938", in Frank & Hadler (eds), *Disputed Territories*, pp. 275–302.

Brandenberger, D.L. (2002), *National Bolshevism: Stalinist Mass Culture and the Formation of Modern Russian National Identity 1931–1956*, Cambridge, MA: Harvard UP.

Clark, M. (1999), "Gioacchino Volpe and Fascist Historiography in Italy", in S. Berger, M. Donovan & K. Passmore (eds), *Writing National Histories. Western Europe since 1800*, London: Routledge, pp. 189–201.

Coleman, D.C. (1987), *History and the Economic Past. An Account of the Rise and Decline of Economic History in Britain*, Oxford: Oxford UP.

Colley, L. (1989), *Lewis Namier*, London: Palgrave Macmillan.

Ellis, S.G. (1991), "Historiographical debate: representations of the past in Ireland: whose past and whose present?", *Irish Historical Studies*, 27, pp. 289–308.

Enteen, G.M. (1978), *The Soviet Scholar-Bureaucrat. M.N. Pokrovskii and the Society of Marxist Historians*, University Park: Pennsylvania State UP.

Epstein, F.T. (1973), *Germany and the East*, Bloomington: Indiana UP.

Fair, J.D. (1992), *Harold Temperley: a Scholar and Romantic in the Public Realm*, Toronto: University of Toronto Press.

Fogu, C. (2003), *The Historic Imaginary. Politics of History in Fascist Italy*, Toronto: University of Toronto Press.

Gilbert, F. (1947), "German Historiography during the Second World War: A bibliographical Survey", *American Historical Review* 53:1, pp. 50–58.

Goetz, W. (1957), *Historiker in meiner Zeit. Gesammelte Aufsätze*, Cologne: Böhlau.

Haapala, P., & M. Kaarninen, "Finland" (2010), in I. Porciani and L. Raphael (eds), *Atlas of European Historiography: The Making of a Profession, 1800–2005*, Basingstoke: Palgrave Macmillan, pp. 74–76.

Hackmann, J. (2011), „German East or Polish West? Historiographical Discourses on the German-Polish Overlap between Confrontation and Reconciliation, 1772–2000", in Frank and Hadler (eds), *Disputed Territories*, pp. 92–124.

Harvey, J.L. (2003), "The Common Adventure of Mankind. Academic Internationalism and Western Historical Practice from Versailles to Potsdam", Ph.D. thesis. Pennsylvania State University.

Heiber, H. (1966), *Walter Frank und sein Reichsinstitut für Geschichte des neuen Deutschland*, Stuttgart: Deutsche Verlags-Anstalt.

Heiss, G., Á. v. Klimó, P. Kolář & D. Kováč (2008), "Habsburg's Difficult Legacy: Comparing and Relating Austrian, Czech, Magyar and Slovak National Historical Master Narratives", in Berger and Lorenz (eds), *The Contested Nation*, pp. 367–404.

Hernon Jr., J.M. (1976), "The Last Whig Historian and Consensus History: George MacAulay Trevelyan, 1876–1962 ", *American Historical Review*, 81:1, pp. 66–97.

Herwig, H. (1996), "Clio Deceived: Patriotic Self-Censorship in Germany after the Great War", in Wilson (ed.), *Forging*, pp. 87–127.

Hudek, M. (2010), "Slovakia", in Porciani and Raphael (eds), *Atlas*, pp. 152–53.

Kieser, H.-L. (2005) „Die Herausbildung des nationalistischen Geschichtsdiskurses in der Türkei (spätes 19. – Mitte 20. Jahrhundert)", in M. Kroska & H.-Ch. Maner (eds.), *Beruf und Berufung. Geschichtswissenschaft und Nationsbildung in Ostmittel- und Südosteuropa im 19. und 20. Jahrhundert*, Münster: Aschendorff, pp. 59–98.

Kolář, P. (2010), "Czech Republic", in Porciani and Raphael (eds), *Atlas*, pp. 148–150.

Kořalka, J. (1992), "Czechoslovakia", *American Historical Review*, 97:4 (1992), pp. 1026–1040.

Litvin, A.L. (2001), *Writing History in Twentieth-Century Russia*, Houndmills: Palgrave Macmillan.

Marchal, G.P. (2006), *Schweizer Gebrauchsgeschichte. Geschichtsbilder, Mythenbildung und nationale Identität*, Basel: Schwabe.

Martin, T. (2001), *The Affirmative Action Empire: Ethnicity and the Soviet State 1923–1938*, Ithaca: Cornell UP.

Mazour, A.G. (1958), *Modern Russian Historiography*, Princeton, NJ; Princeton UP, 2nd ed.

McNeill, W.H. (1978), *Arnold J. Toynbee: A Life*, Oxford: Oxford UP.

Morgan, Ph. (1999), "Reclaiming Italy? Antifascist Historians and History in 'Justice and Liberty'", in Berger, Donovan & Passmore (eds), *Writing National Histories*, pp. 150–160.

Murgescu, B. (2010), "Romania", in Porciani and Raphael (eds), *Atlas*, p. 98–100.

Neudorfl, M.A. (1993), "Czech History, Modern Nation Building and Tomás G. Masaryk (1850–1937)", *Canadian Review of Studies in Nationalism*, 20, pp. 13–20.

O'Dowd, M. (2010), "Ireland", in Porciani and Raphael (eds), *Atlas*, pp. 172–174.

Pasamar, G. (1991), *Historiografía e ideología en la postguerra española. La ruptura de la tradición liberal*, Zaragoza: IFEC.

Pasamar, G. (2010), *Apologia and Criticism: Historians and the History of Spain, 1500–2000* (Bern: Peter Lang).

Perrie, M. (2001), *The Cult of Ivan the Terrible in Stalin's Russia*, New York: Palgrave Macmillan.

Petrone, K. (2000), *'Life has become more joyous, comrades': Celebrations in the Time of Stalin*, Bloomington: Indiana UP.

Piskorski, J., J. Hackmann & R. Jaworski, eds (2002), *Deutsche Ostforschung und polnische Westforschung im Spannungsfeld von Wissenschaft und Politik. Disziplinen im Vergleich*, Osnabrück/Poznan: Fibre Verlag/PTPN.

Powell, A. (1951), "The Nationalist Trend in Soviet Historiography", *Soviet Studies*, 2:4 (1951), pp. 361–379.

Řepa, M. (2011), "The Czechs, Germans and Sudetenland: Historiographical Disputes in the 'Heart of Europe'", in Frank and Hadler (eds), *Disputed Territories*, pp. 303–328.

Schenk, B. (2004), *Alexandr Nevskij: Heiliger–Fürst–Nationalheld. Eine Erinnerungsfigur im russischen kulturellen Gedächtnis (1263–2000)*, Cologne: Böhlau.

Schönwälder, K. (1996), "'Taking Their Place in the Front Line'. German Historians during Nazism and War', *TelAviver Jahrbuch für Deutsche Geschichte*, 25, pp. 205–219.

Šnē, A. (2010), "Latvia", in Porciani and Raphael (eds), *Atlas*, pp. 82–83.

Spring, D. (1996), "The Unfinished Collection: Russian Documents on the Origins of the First World War", in Wilson (ed.), *Forging*, pp. 63–86.

Suppanz, W. (1998), *Österreichische Geschichtsbilder. Historische Legitimation in Ständestaat und Zweiter Republik,* Cologne: Böhlau.

Tortarolo, E. (1999), „Die *Rivista Storica Italiana* 1884–1929", in M. Middell (ed.), *Historische Zeitschriften im internationalen Vergleich,* Leipzig: Leipziger Universitätsverlag, pp. 83–92.

Trencsényi, B. (2011), *The Politics of 'National Character'. A Study in Interwar East European Thought,* London: Routledge.

Von Below, G. (1924), *Die deutsche Geschichtsschreibung von den Befreiungskriegen bis zu unseren Tage,* (Munich: Oldenbourg), 2nd revised edition.

Von Klimó, A. (2003), *Nation, Konfession, Geschichte. Zur nationalen Geschichtskultur Ungarns im europäischen Kontext (1860–1948),* Munich: Oldenbourg.

Wendland, A.V. (2008), "The Russian Empire and its Western Borderlands: National Historiographies and their 'Others' in Russia, the Baltics and the Ukraine", in Berger and Lorenz (eds), *Contested Nation,* pp. 405–441.

Wilson, K., ed. (1996), *Forging the Collective Memory: Government and International Historians through Two World Wars,* New York/Oxford: Berghahn.

Zala, S. (2001), *Geschichte unter der Schere politischer Zensur. Amtliche Aktensammlungen im internationalen Vergleich,* Munich: De Gruyter.

CHAPTER 11

From Nationalities to Minorities? The Transnational Debate on the Minority Protection System of the League of Nations, and Its Predecessors

Stefan Dyroff

1   Introduction*

The "Minority Question" in Central and Eastern Europe is an established object of research in the humanities, law and social science. Mostly, the Minority Protection System (MPS) of the League of Nations is seen as a milestone of universal Human Rights regimes.[1] While the legal forerunners and successors of the MPS are often mentioned in the literature,[2] its discursive interpretation and the legal, political and academic discourse about its improvement are rarely taken into account. As the system was never really reformed and abandoned in 1945, one can bring forward that the whole discourse about the MPS produced "hot air" only and deserves no attention. But I would argue that analyses of these discourses reveal a lot about the way the problems that were to be tackled by the MPS were comprised by political elites. Hereby, transnational organizations and a handful of transnational activists played a key role. They were the authors and the driving forces of platforms for transnational discussions that attracted the attention of the media, diplomats, scholars etc. and

---

*   The following paper draws on my current research project on 'The Minority Protection System of the League of Nations, 1920–1934', especially an already finished chapter of about 100 pages on 'Opinions and Expectations'. The part on the period before 1920 draws on secondary literature as well as occasionally additional research and is therefore less comprehensive. I also rely partly on a paper on 'The Minority Protection System of the League of Nations and the Legacy of the Habsburg Empire', which I discussed at an international workshop on "After Empire. The League of Nations and the former Habsburg Lands" in December 2015. As some notions cannot be translated one-to-one, I mention some original quotations in German or French in the annotations.

1   Lauren (2003: 114).
2   See Jackson Preece (1997) and Fink (2000).

thereby multiplied the impact of their political thoughts.[3] Although members of nationalist movements tried to make their thoughts part of these discussions, they rarely succeeded. Apparently, they were more interested in political support than in the evolution of political thought on a given problem. Therefore, voices of liberal and conservative thinkers will prevail.

In this article, it will not be possible to present the activities of all such organizations. The focus will be on continuities and changes of pre- and postwar discussions with special attention to the key terms and headlines used to conceptualize and identify the underlying 'problem'. So far, conceptual history (*Begriffsgeschichte*) did not bother most historians of the 'minority question' in the interwar-period. For instance, Sabine Bamberger-Stemmann regarded the terms "minority, nationality, national group or national minority" as equivalent.[4]

I would like to challenge this perspective and convince you that the contemporary use of the terms was neither interchangeable nor accidental. Behind the different terminologies one can find different contextualizations of the underlying 'problem'. Truly, it is not easy to do conceptual history when the meaning of the words "minority" and "nationality" are not entirely synonymous in the languages that were relevant for the transnational discourse: English, French and German. In addition, not all participants of the discourse knew about the semantic differences between their mother tongue and the languages of their contributions. Another problem is that in German alternative terms such as "Volksstamm" and "Volksgruppe" were used as well. While the first term originated in the Austrian constitution of 1867, the second one was linked with racial (völkisch) nationalism and became more popular in the 1920s and especially the 1930s. Despite such methodological difficulties, I hope that this approach will shed new light on the different concepts of how to solve the so-called minority or nationality problems in Eastern, Central and Western Europe beyond established frameworks like revisionism, kin and host state, ethnic bargaining etc. which are all situated in the realm of power politics.[5]

---

3 See Dyroff (2013). I use the term "transnational" to indicate that these organizations and activists aimed to create alternatives to a state and government centered system of international relations.
4 Bamberger-Stemmann (2000: 10).
5 Jenne (2007).

2 Nationality Question and National Minorities before 1918

As a starting point of the analysis, an article on the conceptual history of the term "national minority" is very helpful.[6] Therein, Kai Struve argues that the origins of the term can be found in the 1848 Frankfurt Parliament and its debates on 'nationality question' within the territories of Prussia and Austria. However, he observes that the term 'minority' was rarely used by the parliamentarians who spoke mostly of nationalities, e.g. during the famous Poland debate.[7] He could only find the concept 'national minority' in the debates of the Austrian Reichsrat 1848/49. Nevertheless, Struve claims that 'nationality' was used more often than 'national minority' before because Austria was not regarded as a 'national state' but a 'multinational state' (Nationalitätenstaat). In consequence, after the downfall of Austria-Hungary in 1918, the 'nationality problem' of the multinational state became the 'minority problem' of the national state. According to Struve, the term 'national minority' replaced 'nationality' in the inter-war years. This genealogy of the minority problem suggests that we need to have a closer look at continuities and discontinuities between the 'minority problem' after 1918 and the 'nationality problem' until 1918'.

2.1 Nationality Questions and the Inter-Parliamentary Union (1889–1918)

I start this approach with a closer look at the Inter-Parliamentary Union (IPU) that was founded in 1889. Unfortunately, the latest book on the IPU before World War One appeared in 1988 so that the latest research trends in International History were not applied to this organization yet. Nevertheless, Uhlig's monograph is a good starting point for cursory research in the IPU archives. However, his claim that minority protection was part of the IPU's program before 1914 cannot be verified by a rereading of his primary sources.[8] For example, when the Romanians raised the topic in 1893 it was always as "question des nationalités". Thereby, Vasile Urechia was most prominent in trying to bring the situation of Romanians in Transylvania on the agenda.[9] Although the IPU failed to comply with this request, the Romanians stirred up some trouble

---

6 Struve (2004).
7 For the Poland debate see Geiss (2013: 42).
8 See Uhlig (1988, 477, 548).
9 See especially the correspondence from 1893 in boxes 18 and 19 and the Proces-verbaux des séances de la Conference Interparlementaire Bern 1892. In Bern, it was Aurel Popovici that tried unsuccessfully to bring the topic on the agenda. There is a clear connection with the transylvania Memorandum from 1892 in which Romanians asked Emperor Franz Joseph for equal rights with the Hungarians. According to Uhli (1988: 179), the Romanians wished to

behind the scenes, especially in advance of the 1896 conference in Budapest. Thereby, they prepared the ground for later attempts to discuss nationality questions as a potential danger to peace. The next effort came from the Poles within the Austrian delegation in Vienna in 1903. Gustaw Rozskowski and Karol Lewakowski raised the topic in their speeches. Roszkowski named the existence of populations of the same nationality on both sides of a state border as a danger to peace.[10] Likewise, Lewakowski named the fate of nations that found themselves as a minority in their state, as a possible cause of war. Therefore, he advocated rights concerning language, culture and religion for members of national minorities.[11] This was the first time, the notion "minorité nationale" came up in the discussion.

To sum up, delegates from non-dominant nationalities within the Austro-Hungarian Empire, especially the Romanians and the Poles, tried to raise "nationality questions" in different contexts since the early 1890s. Thereby, to a certain degree, they managed to bring their domestic problems to an international audience. However, they failed to bring the "nationality questions" as a whole on the agenda. In the discussions and the correspondence, most partcipants did not use the notion of minorities but nationalities and mentioned concepts such as autonomy and federation. Concepts for minority protection in order to settle disputes were never debated or even clearly voiced. Although the IPU made it possible for delegates of non-dominant nationalities to participate in the discussions, they could never bring their topic of rights of nationalities itself on the agenda.

2.2 Nationality Questions and the Union des Nationalités (1912–1918)

The idea to found the Union of Nationalities (UN)[12] emerged in a different context than the IPU that wanted to serve as a testing ground for new ideas and initiatives leading to peace and international co-operation. It emerged at the margins of the Universal Race Congress in London in July 1911 at which the participants discussed race relations and how to improve them. At that time, as can be seen in the 1908 publication of 'Racial Problems in Hungary' by Robert William Seton-Watson, the problems of races and nationalities were not

---

bring the question of „national minorities" on the agenda of the conference that was scheduled for 1893. This is however, a misreading of the sources.

10   *Compte rendu de la XIe conférence tenue à Vienne, Palais du Reichsrat, du 7 au 9 septembre 1903*, Vienna: n. ed., 1903, 62.

11   *Ibidem*, 122 and 114.

12   See Watson (1995); Soutou (1995); Núñez Seixas (2001: 111–39); Demm (2002); Demm & Nikolajew (2013). Svarauskas (n. d.) is a poor contribution that does not represent the state of the art.

clearly distinguished linguistically. At the London conference, Juozas Gabrys, a Lithuanian nationalist in French exile, met Jean Pélissier. The latter was famous as a special correspondent travelling through Austria-Hungary and the Balkans, thereby dealing intensively with the nationality problems in the region. Both decided to organize a First Universal Congress of Nationalities in Paris in 1912. After the congress, they established a Central Office for Nationalities in the French capital. The organization became known under the name Union des Nationalités and published the journal *Annales des Nationalités*, which consisted mostly of special issues on particular nationalities. The UN united representatives of nationality groups from East Central and Western Europe as well as some Muslim nationality groups from North Africa and the Caucasus. A conference in February 1914 was attended by diverse groups that looked for transnational platforms to promote their causes, among others by Irish and Egyptian nationalists as well as the Anti-Slavery Society and the Friends of Liberty in Russia.

The outbreak of World War One pushed the Union in its final direction, it became a "first international of nationalities" that united non-dominant national movements.[13] It served as a platform for ethnic groups that wanted autonomy within an empire, national independence or already had a national state and wanted to enlarge it on ethnic grounds. In 1915, representatives of the Serbs, Bulgarians, Czechs, Latvians, Lithuanians, Rumanians and Armenians attended the next conference; written reports from the Irish, Ukrainians and Basques were presented. In 1916 delegates represented the Albanians, Algerians, Basques, Belgians, Catalans, Circassians, Daghestans, Egyptians, Estonians, Fins, Georgians, Irish, Jews, Kumyks, Luxemburgians, Lithuanians, Poles, Ruthenes, Romanians, Tartars, Chatagais, Tunisians and Ukrainians.[14]

The activism of French and Belgian intellectuals like Charles Seignobos, Henri La Fontaine and Paul Otlet helped to secure prestige and attention for the UNs activities.[15] However, due to the growing significance of 'national questions' and 'nationality politics' as a potential resource in warfare and peace-making,[16] the founding fathers of the UN lost control over the organization. The French participation was hampered by Pélissier's work for the French Secret Service in Greece, Switzerland and Ukraine as well as the relocation of the UNs headquarters to Lausanne. In addition, Gabrys started to take money

---

13 See Esculies & Petronis (2016: 343, 351).
14 Office de l'Union des Nationalités (ed.), *IIIe Conférence des Nationalités, Lausanne 27 juin 1916*, Lausanne: Union des Nationalités, 1916.
15 For LaFontaine and Otlet see Laqua (2013: 26–30).
16 See Chernev (n. d.).

from the German Foreign Office and cooperated with Friedrich von der Ropp, a German from Lithuania who was the founding father and secretary general of the "League of Foreign Nationalities of Russia".[17] To a certain extent, von der Ropp organized and steered the 1916 conference of the UN. Thereby, the UN lost its original syndicat character as well as its democratic, socialist and modernist tendencies.[18] With the breakthrough of the nationality principle in international relations in 1917/18,[19] the UN lost its usefulness for most participants and the organization went into oblivion before it dissolved itself in 1919. Notably, most of the nationality groups had reached their aims and were therefore no longer interested to uphold the organization.

From our point of interest, the question if nationality or minority were the preferred terms in its publications and discussions, we can note that nationality prevailed while the notion of minority rights was rarely used. Independence, autonomy, self-government or federal principles appear much more often. This clearly shows that minority rights were not the preferred option of the representatives of nationalities as well as the French and Belgian intellectuals that participated in the UN. However, Théodore Ruyssen, the later secretary general of the International federation of League of Nations Societies (IFLNS), already envisioned mutual guarantees for fair treatment of all minorities by the contracting powers at the coming Peace Conference.[20] Nevertheless, Gabrys himself claimed "Nationality Rights" and did not mention minority rights but autonomy as a subitem.[21]

From 1917 on, the Central Organization for a Durable Peace (CODP)[22] took the lead in transnational discussions of the Central and Eastern European nationality problems, mainly because the activities of other organizations such as the IPU were paralyzed by the Great War and the UN was regarded as pro-German since 1916. Nevertheless, the UN provided a starting point for the internationalization of certain nationality questions and the formation of a transnational network of representatives of non-dominant nationalities. It

---

17 It is very difficult to find a good equivalent for "Fremdvölker". Instead of "nationalities" one could also refer to "peoples" or "nations". See Zetterberg (1978).
18 Esculies & Petronis (2016: 351).
19 Fisch (2015).
20 Quote from a letter from Ruyssen to Gabrys as reprinted in: Office de l'Union des Nationalités (ed.), *IIIe Conférence des Nationalités, Lausanne 27 juin 1916*, Lausanne: Union des Nationalités, 1916, pp. 211–212.
21 The „Droits des Nationalités" are printed in Pélissier (1918: 219–221). Gabrys thought in a more elaborated version can be found in Gabrys (1917).
22 Surprisingly, there is no new research on the CODP. The standard volume therefore still is Doty (1945). The only work that used archival sources is Zechlin (1962).

served as a platform for the exchange of knowledge on technologies of lobbying on an international scale as well as for the exchange of knowledge on concrete legal models that promised to guarantee more rights for nationality groups within a given state.

In 1915, the CODP had published a minimum program for a durable peace that advocated a guarantee of civil equality, religious liberty and free language usage for all nationalities within a state. From 1916–1918, the CODP released four volumes with 'scientific studies' to underpin their minimum program to guarantee a durable peace. In the first volume, the Englishman Charles Roden Buxton, the Lithuanian Jouzas Gabrys, the Hungarian Oskar Jaszi and the Swiss Albert Forel contributed their thoughts on the nationalities problem. None of them made a substantial contribution with concrete proposals how to solve the current nationalities problems peacefully. Most of them rather described the situation and remained in a national respectively personal perspective. Roden-Buxton praised Home Rule and the British handling of the Boer question. Gabrys presented the work of the UN, Jászi exhibited his own ideas how to reform the Hungarian nationalities policy[23] and the Swiss Albert Forel claimed proportional representation for minority representatives in government. The American Levermore followed this path in the second volume and advocated democratic government as the only workable solution of the nationalities' problem. Roden-Buxton as well as Levermore made it clear that the current discussion is on rights for nationalities in Central and Eastern Europe only and thereby excluded groups such as the Egyptians and the Irish that had participated in the UN.

In the third volume that appeared in 1917, the Swede Karl Hildebrand[24] and the Austrian Rudolf Laun, published their views on the problem of nationality. Both referred to claims, repressions and freedom of national minorities as

---

23 Jászi was a socialist opponent of the conservative elites that ruled Hungary. In 1912, he had published a book on „The Formation of National States and the nationality issue. A Selection". However, as a planned German translation was not realized, Jaszi's thoughts did not become part of a transnational discourse before 1914. In 1918, his book on the breakdown of dualism and the future of the Danube States received much more consideration. Therein, he advocated autonomy. From 1918 to 1919, Jaszi served as a government minister. See Jászi (1912). On his thought, see Litván (2006). More detailed are Haslinger (1993) and Fischer (1978). Although Jászi participated in the OCPD his thoughts, like those of other East Central European political thinkers, did not become points of reference in transnational discussions. Nevertheless, the theoretical debate on the question of nationalities in the region itself was particularly rich. See Balász Trencsényi et al. (2016: 495–512).

24 Hildebrand was a journalist and had visited the German-French front from both sides in 1914/1915. His published impressions show that he was rather pro-German than neutral. See Hildebrand (1915).

well as autonomy. Laun wrote of a "special protection requirement of national minorities".[25] In a different line of argumentation he referred to the contributions in the previous volumes of the CODP to show that national egoism is always present in discussions on the nationality problem and that members of a ruling nation within a state will always have problems to fully understand the position of a minority. He then points to Austria as the "cradle of national minority protection and hopefully likewise the cradle of the prospective nationality rights of the world".[26] On the other hand, Laun rejected the idea that the Austrian nationality rights should become part of post-war international law and thereby be applied in other states as unrealistic in the current political situation. For the same reason, he advised against the establishment of an international supervisory commission and an international court for nationality rights.[27] Moreover, he argued, that all guarantees of nationality and minority rights are worthless if they are not implemented in practice. Therefore, he regarded the inclusion of members of all nationalities in the legislative, the executive and the judicative organs of the state at the central as well as the regional level as the best guarantee that nationality rights will be respected.

Although Laun was everything but impartial and whitewashed Austria's nationalities policy, one cannot deny that he tabled the best contribution so far. Thereby, he profited from his engagement in the juridical debate about *Länderautonomie* that took place in Vienna in 1917.[28] He delivered some constructive comments and advanced the transnational discussion significantly. To a great degree, Laun's perspective on the nationalities question became the official standpoint of the CODP at the first gathering in 1917. One reason was that due to travel restrictions for citizens of the Entente states, only citizens of Germany, Austria-Hungary, Switzerland and the Scandinavian states could attend the meeting in the Norwegian capital Kristiania (today Oslo). Furthermore, Laun managed to convince the more idealistic Scandinavians that their more radical ideas would never be accepted by the Great Powers.[29]

---

25 Rudolf Laun, "Zur Nationalitätenfrage", in *Recueil de Rapports sur les différents points du programme-minimum, troisième partie*, The Hague: n. ed., 1917, pp. 21–44, especially p. 22. The German original is "besonderes Schutzbedürfnis der nationalen Minoritäten".

26 *Ibidem*, esp. 29. Laun uses the term "Nationalitätenrecht".

27 Zechlin, 'Die Zentralorganisation für einen dauernden Frieden',..469f.

28 The opinion of 14 renowned legal scholars that were written before the discussion and a commented summary are published in the *Österreichische Zeitschrift für öffentliches Recht in 1916/17*.

29 Although there seems to be no research on this aspect, it is tempting to assume that Scandinavians viewed the nationality question from a Nordic point of view. For instance, in

As a result, the CODP published two draft proposals for international treaties that touched upon the nationality problem. The Swede Theodor Ädelsward composed the draft treaty on the transfer of territories that included minority rights and the Norvegian Halvdan Koht the draft treaty on the rights of national minorities.[30] Ädelsward and Koht focused on religious and language rights and mentioned national registers as desirable tool to implement minority rights. In Ädelsward's bibliography, the writings of the UN are mentioned at first place. In Koht's comments on his draft, a pamphlet by Gabrys is mentioned among the seven reports that the CODP published on the topic. Furthermore, he recommended Gabrys' recent book on "The Nationality Problem and Durable Peace" as further reading. This suggests that Gabrys and the UN had a decisive impact on the work of the CODP.

Koht's support for the idea to protect national minorities by international conventions is another important point in his draft. As a tool to implement such treaties, he suggested supervisory commissions and a nationality tribunal. Likewise, he proposed to give the right to appeal to the tribunal to the supervisory commission and the national minorities themselves. Finally, Koht names two aims of minority protection: first, to protect national minorities and their historical development; second, to forestall internal discord that could weaken and dismember a state. Remarkably, the first article of his draft treaty, followed article 19 of the Austrian constitution from 1867. In a comment on the two drafts that included some details about the proceedings in Kristiania, Laun made a remarkable comment that is especially important for an analysis of the linguistic shift from nationalities to minorities. He advocated that Austria should no longer accept the role as the accused in transnational discussions of nationality questions. In contrary, it should become the accuser of other states by demanding the protection of national minorities".[31] According to this, Austria should have started to attack the nationalities policy of

---

1905, the Union between Norway and Sweden had been dissolved peacefully after a plebiscite in Norway. In addition, the struggle for the preservation of the autonomy of Finland within the Russian Empire and the contemporary debates on increased autonomy or independence after the February Revolution in Russia could have played a role. The same was surely true for the "language strife" between Swedes and Fins in Finland which could have been the prism of the Swedish perception of the language strife between Germans and Czechs in Bohemia and Moravia.

30   Halvdan Koht, *Avant-projet d'un traité général relatif aux droits des minorités nationales*, The Hague: n. ed., 1917; Theodor Adelswärd, *Avant-projet d'un traité général relatif aux transferts de territoires*, Stockholm: Oskar Eklund, 1917.
31   See Laun (1917). Among others, the article aimed to influence the September session of the Austrian parliament.

other states but use the term minorities' policy in order to avoid any associations with Austria-Hungary.

The fourth volume of the CODP that was published in 1918 contained two more discussions of Austria's nationality policy, both from German-speaking Jews: One appraisal by Eugen Ehrlich from Bukovina and a critical praise by Franz Oppenheimer from Berlin. While Ehrlich followed the line of Laun and tried to reject the current criticism of Austria's nationality policy by giving concrete numbers for press confiscations, political trials etc.,[32] Oppenheimer brought in some new arguments. He linked the nationality problem to questions of class and rural-urban migration movements, concluding that a definite settlement of a nationality problem on a territorial base is impossible. On the other hand, the German-Italian sociologist Robert Michels rejected the whole idea of international minority protection. For him, all promises of fair treatment for heterogeneous populations were an illusion.[33] But this was the position of an outsider that could not influence the progress of the discussion.

After the downfall of the Habsburg monarchy and the founding of the Austrian Republic at the end of October 1918, Laun immediately joined the Foreign Office where he was responsible for nationality questions in the former territory of Austria-Hungary. In March 1919, he attended the last CODP conference in Berne. In May 1919, he became a member of the Austrian delegation to the Paris Peace Conference. He stayed in Paris until August 1919 but his designs and proposals for the handling of nationality questions in national and international law are not taken into account by the peacemakers.

To sum up. Austrian respectively Habsburg political thought dominated the transnational discourse about possible international regulations of the nationality question and the configuration of minority rights at the sunset of World War One. Thereby, ideas that were shaped to reform Austria's nationality policy and that had not yet proved itself in practice, were presented as a model for national and international regulations. Therefore, the term "nationalities" dominated the discourse although "minorities" and "minority rights" grew in significance.

---

32 The main arguments of Ehrlich can also be found in a pamphlet that was distributed in Englisch, French and German in 1918. I was only able to contact the French version: E. Ehrlich, *Quelques aspects de la Question Nationale Autrichienne*, Geneva: Atar, 1918.

33 Robert Michels, "Notes sur les moyens de constater la nationalité", in *Recueil de Rapports sur les différents points du programme-minimum, quatrième partie* (The Hague: n. ed., 1918), pp. 64–73, especially p. 73.

3 Transnational Discussions of the Minority Question after 1918

3.1 The Postwar Legay of the CODP: Laun and Adelswärd as Participants and Creative Minds of the Transnational Minority Discourse

Although the CODP failed to influence the outcome of the Paris Peace Treaties significantly, its intellectual potential and heritage survived in several transnational associations that were active in the postwar years. This is especially true for associations with a pacifist or humanitarian background. For our case of nationality and minority rights, two key figures are the Swede Theodor Adelswärd and the Austrian respectively German Rudolf Laun.

Adelswärd became the IPU's unofficial spokesman on minority rights and guided the work of its committee on ethnic and colonial affairs and an additional sub-committee on minority rights in the early 1920s. His appointment was a personal decision by the IPUs Norwegian Secretary General Christian Lange who also advised him what publications he should contact to inform himself.[34] In 1921, in his opening speech of the Stockholm gathering of the IPU, Adelswärd mentioned that their 'old word', the rights of nationalities respectively the rights of minorities is no more only a word but became a generally accepted principle. Likewise, in the index, nationality rights and minority rights are both mentioned with the same reference to just one page. Only a year later, in 1922, the keyword nationality rights is no longer present while "minority rights" has several entries in the printed version of the proceedings of the IPU conference. Nevertheless, the word "national minority" had not yet gained sovereignty over the discourse. The debates were about disputes between dominant nationalities and minority nationalities.[35] In his speech that opened the debate on the protection of national minorities, Adelswärd made long references to the work of the CODP in which he participated, in order to underline that unofficial movements[36] such as the IPU were not newcomers to this topic. The other speakers did not contribute to a general discussion of the problem but mostly named concrete examples of the violation of minority rights or praised their own state's minorities' policy as exemplary. Only in 1923 and thanks to a report of the Swiss Paul Usteri did the IPU start to discuss new

---

34 Lange to Adelswärd, 29.02.1922, in: IPU Archives in Geneva, Box 36, Correspondence 1922 I. There is another letter from 21.03.1922, in which Lange uses exclusively the notion „minorités" and advises Adelswärd to read recent German books and document collections about „nationale Minderheiten".

35 See e.g. the speech of Adelswärd in Union Interparlementaire (ed.), *Compte rendu de la xxe conférence tenue à Vienne du 28 au 30 Août 1922* (Geneva: Union Interparlementaire, 1922), pp. 89–113, especially p.111. In French "nationalités minoritaires".

36 The notion „unofficial movement" is borrowed from Macartney (1934: 212).

ideas, among others paritative committees. Those should consist of members of all ethnic groups in the region or the state and help to settle disputes between members of minority groups and the state. Another resolution from 1923 demanded the establishment of a permanent minorities committee by the League of Nations.

These resolutions can be regarded as representative for two different strands of the discourse. While the first aimed to look for ways to solve conflicts between majority and minority groups within a given state, the second preferred to strengthen the respective organs of the League of Nations in order to better supervise the implementation of the minority treaties into practice. At the end, both approaches failed because most resolutions of the IPU were not followed by attempts to put them into practice by the national groups. As Ädelsward pointed it out in a public speech on the activities of the IPU in Geneva in 1926, a spirit of reconciliation and goodwill would have been necessary to reconcile the different nationalities in most concerned states.[37]

Adelswärd had managed to transfer his CODP expertise to the IPU and was one of the initiators of the discussion on minority problems after 1918. Thereby, he was supported by Christian Lange, the IPUs Secretary General who had been involved in the CODP as well.[38] As the IPU's president from 1922 to 1928, Adelswärd made authoritative statements on minority problems in public. However, the IPU decided to have as Swiss as the chairman of its new founded minorities committee. Although this deprived Adelswärd of further influence on the work of this committee, this was of minor significance. The IPUs work on minorities was less productive than the CODP because it was hampered by the greater number of the participants and their less visionary conduct of the work. Most delegates from East Central European states defended the national interest of their states (respectively their nationality groups) so that constructive work became extremely difficult. Representatives from Western European states like Ireland and Spain did not participate in the discussions or the committee work. In addition, no references to the situation in these states were made. The minorities problems that were discussed by the IPU were either linked to the MPS of the League or recent border changes. Only in 1932 did the Catalan Joan Estelrich start to participate in the work of IPU-Committee but was only nominated as one of the minority representatives in the sub-commission in 1937.

---

37   See Th. Adelswärd, "Discours d'ouverture", *Supplément au Bulletin interparlementaire*, 5 (1926), pp. 3–7 (here: p. 7).

38   See Tønnesson (2013).

Laun who became German by accepting a chair at the University of Hamburg in October 1919 was the legal authority and consultant for nearly all German-speaking scholars and activists that worked on minority rights in the early 1920s. Already in autumn 1920, the German Schutzbund and the German Association for the League of Nations founded a committee for minority rights. The first referent at its first meeting in October 1920 was Rudolf Laun.[39] Later on, the participants voted Laun's resolution "On the Protection of National Minorities". It was also printed as 'Laun's assumptions' in a periodical of the German Association for the League of Nations and thereby known to a wider audience.[40] The same year, Laun published a draft treaty on the international protection of national minorities, thereby expressing his conviction that the already existing minority treaties are not the final stage in the protection of national minorities by International Law.[41] Laun also chaired the committee for minority rights within the German Society for International Law. His encyclopaedia entries on nationality and minority rights certainly influenced the thinking of contemporary law scholars and law students. For instance, in 1921 Laun published "The Nationality Question including Minority Rights" in the German "Dictionary of International Law and Diplomacy" and the entry on "People and Nation, self-determination, national minorities" in the Handbook of German Constitutional Law in 1930.[42]

As these examples show, Laun was regarded as an authority in nationality and minority questions in International Law in Germany and Austria but was no longer an inspiration in the transnational discourse. One reason was that Adelswärd and other Scandinavians that had accepted Laun's expertise in the CODP became marginal figures in the discussions on the MPS and minority questions. Another reason was that Laun did not attend any international meetings and left it to others to defend the legacy of Austria's nationality policy.

---

39   *Rundschreiben Nr. 1 Ausschuss für Minderheitenrecht*, 15.09.1920, in Political Archives of the German Foreign Office in Berlin (PAAA), R 60364, Ausschuss für Minderheitenrecht 1920–21.
40   "Die Entschließungen der Tagung für Minderheitenrecht. Die rechtlichen Forderungen (sog. Laun'sche Thesen)", *Neue Brücken*, 10/11 (October/November 1920), p. 3.
41   Laun (1920).
42   Laun (1925, 1930). The treatment of nationality and minority rights in his 1933 work (Laun 1933), is also remarkable but it has to be assumed that this massive volume did not have a broad readership. Nevertheless, for the transnational context it is remarkable that this scholarly piece won the first prize in an open contest of the Catalanist *Institució Patxot* in Barcelona in 1930.

3.2 Further Protagonists: The IFLNS

As shown above, Adelswärd and Laun very soon began to lose their influence and new figures dominated the transnational minorities' discussions. For instance, Adelswärd was sidelined from the very beginning in the minority commission of the IFLNS which was dominated by the French Théodore Ruyssen, the Englishman Sir Willoughby Dickinson and the Swiss Ernest Bovet. Thereby, the corporate thinking of nationality and minority rights lost ground to particular discussions on how to improve the MPS. As minority protection treaties had only been signed by states in Central and Eastern Europe, the nationalities in Western Europe drifted out of the focus. A clear example for this can be found in the reports of the IFLNS. This association talked about minorities only and passed the task to draft a Magna Charta for minorities to a juridical committee. A sub-committee debated on possibilities how to improve the procedure.

Autonomy came on the agenda of the IFLNS only in connection with the situation in Eastern Galicia before its final assignment to Poland in 1923. Notably, everybody understood that this was a Polish-Ukrainian problem and nobody even mentioned that there could be any other Galician nationality question in Europe. The term Galicia was never linked with Spain. In addition, only at the Warsaw meeting in 1925 did a first Spanish delegate (Tomás Elorrieta) attend a meeting of the minorities' commission. Notably, this was at the request of the executive of the IFLNS that had especially invited a Spanish delegation after a Catalan delegation asked to discuss the question of the Catalan Minority.[43] In 1927, Joan Estelrich, the most important representative of the Catalan movement abroad, took part at the discussions for the first time. As a consequence, the Catalan question was put on the agenda for the next session again.[44] Although the discussion was cancelled anew, Estelrich participated in the next three meetings before he stopped to attend the meetings. According to the official bulletin, there was even no Spanish delegate at the gathering in Madrid in May 1929.[45] From 1930 to 1932, Alfonso Albéniz, the Spanish representative at the League of Nations, attended the meetings as a Spanish delegate.

---

43   Núñez Seixas (2010: 131). However, the Catalan request was withdrawn from the agenda in the last minute: *Bulletin de L'Union Internationale des Associations pour la Société des Nations*, 3 (October 1925), p. 41. The question came up as a consequence of a Catalan minority petition to the League in 1924. For the handling of the petition by the League see Núñez Seixas (2010: 121–29), as well as a description in Cussó (2013).

44   *Bulletin de L'Union Internationale des Associations pour la Société des Nations*, 5 (November/December 1927), p. 66.

45   Núñez Seixas (2010: 185) sustains (relying upon Esterlich's private papers) that Estelrich attended the meetings.

Remarkably, Estelrich noted that the IFLNS looked for solutions to the problems of minorities and nationalities,[46] thereby giving a lively example that in practice the nationality and the minority problems still overlapped, at least for political representatives of an autonomy movement. Nevertheless, he did not describe the Catalonians as a national minority but a nationality.[47] It was Sir Willoughby Dickinson who during a discussion in the House of Lords in June 1931 spoke of the Catalan and the Basque minority in Spain that "claimed to be separately governed from the rest of Spain".[48]

3.3 The CEN

In the Congress of European Nationalities (CEN) that united representatives of non-dominant nationalities from (nearly) all over Europe delegates from Spain played a more prominent role. From 1926, a representative of the Catalans was a member of the board. In addition, Joan Estelrich was chosen to deliver six speeches from 1928 to 1931. Nevertheless, in contrast to the UN-activities from 1912 to 1914, Catalan political thought did not play any significant role in the transnational discussions on minority and nationality problems. This is a clear sign that problems of nationalities in Western Europe played a secondary role in this discourse, among others because it was considered as politically unwise to put nationality questions in France and the United Kingdom on the agenda.

Nevertheless, for our main point of interest, the question if minority problems were the successor of nationality problems, the CEN's discussions provide valuable source material with a lot of interesting citations. The invitation to the first conference in 1925 announced the first European Conference on Nationalities (erste europäische Nationalitätentagung) and it seems that no discussion on the choice of this name had taken place. However, the term minorities was used much more often than nationalities by the speakers. Some of them even called their gathering Congress of European Minorities (*Congrès des Minorités Nationales*) or minority gathering (*Minderheitsversammlung*). Interestingly, only Jews and Germans from the former Russian Empire and the Hungarian part of the Habsburg Empire used the term "nationalities". Probably, these groups had identified themselves as nationalities before 1914 and therefore did not adopt the new terminology at once. The Catalan Fancesc Maspons i Anglasell who participated in 1926, also fits in this pattern of explanation. But the sources strongly suggest another interpretation. Werner Hasselblatt in 1926 presented Estonia's law on cultural autonomy as transformation

---

46 Quote after Núñez Seixas (2010: 166).
47 J. Estelrich, "Die Katalonier", *Süddeutsche Monatshefte* 26 (1928/29), pp. 725–26.
48 HL Deb 10 June 1931 vol 81 cc52-76.

of minority rights in national law, adding the words "nationality rights".[49] This implies that the term Minority Rights was used in conjunction with International Law and Nationality Rights in conjunction with Domestic Law.

However, as not all participants were lawyers, we cannot generalize this finding. In addition, the journalist Ewald Ammende, the secretary general of the CEN, used both notions in the opposite way in 1929 when he referred to "the Nationality Problem and particular Minority Questions".[50] This implies that minority questions were seen as part of the nationality problems while not all nationality problems were regarded as minority problems. A statement from the Slovene president Josip Wilfan in 1932 confirms this. He rejected that the European Nationality Problem is a problem of national minorities in some concrete states only.[51] But before one over-interprets such citations, one should take into account that the same Wilfan stated in 1927 that the notions "minorities", "national minorities" and "nationalities" are used haphazardly in the discussions.[52]

Nevertheless, after a close reading of the sources, one cannot say that the notions "nationality" and "minority" were used haphazardly in the CEN. One should rather remark that the usage was not consistent. Persons that had been members of the ruling nation until 1918 and whose home region had been ceded to another state at the Paris Peace Conference, tended not to use the term "nationality" but referred to "minorities" only. On the other hand, delegates from Spain rarely used the term "minorities" and if they did do, this was in conjunction with the MPS of the League.

To sum up, the transnational discussions within the IFLNS and the CEN have clearly shown that the terms "minorities" and "nationalities" were sometimes used haphazardly but more often with a special purpose. For instance, minorities was not regarded as the right term to describe the situation in Spain. Minorities implied a reference to Central and Eastern Europe or to population groups that were protected by an international treaty or obligation. However, nationalities was not used exclusively to refer to population groups that were not protected by an international treaty or obligation and that did not live in to

---

49   The German original is „Wandlung des sogenannten Minderheitenrechts in ein nationales Eigenrecht, ein Nationalitätenrecht." See *Sitzungsbericht des Kongresses der organisierten nationalen Gruppen in den Staaten Europas*, Vienna: Braumüller, 1926, p. 48.

50   *Sitzungsbericht...* , Vienna: Braumüller, 1929, pp. 1–8. In German: „das Nationalitätenproblem und die einzelnen Minderheitenfragen".

51   *Sitzungsbericht...*, Vienna: Braumüller, 1932, p. 4. In German: „Von vielen Seiten wird das europäische Nationalitätenproblem bloß als das Problem der nationalen Minderheiten aufgefaßt."

52   *Sitzungsbericht...*, Vienna: Braumüller, 1927, p. 103.

Central and Eastern Europe. When the term "nationalities" was used in conjunction with Central and Eastern Europe this mostly implied the placing of the problem in a domestic context and the support for ideas like autonomy and self-government. In contrast, the use of the term minorities suggested that the underlying problem should be solved internationally.

4 Conclusion and Outlook

In 1929, in a lecture for the European Branch of the Carnegie Endowment for International Peace in Paris, the French sociologist Celestin Bouglé underlined that it is important to distinguish national minorities from nationalities.[53] According to him, nationalities want to live as a nation, while a national minority cannot found a state. In consequence, he compared a nationality to a soul without a body. Likewise, the Austrian lawyer and IFLNS activist Josef Kunz underlined that a nationality can belong to the majority in a state and must not necessarily be a minority, giving the Flemings in Belgium as well as the Croats and Slovenes in Yugoslavia as an example.[54] Although these definitions were not accepted by most activists that participated in the transnational discussion on the minorities question in the inter-war period, they remind us that we should care more about the conceptions that were present in this discourse.

Even though concrete definitions were rarely given by the speakers, most of them did not equate nationalities and minorities. The term minority was used much more often after 1918 because there were international minority treaties and obligations while nationality was not a legal term in this context. Leading representatives of nationalities that were not protected by International Law tried to participate in the transnational minority discourse but did not adopt the dominant conception of minority rights. Nevertheless, the term "minorities" had gained sovereignty over the discourse at the end of the 1920s when the debate over a possible reform of MPS reached its peak in the run-up to the 1929 League Assembly in Madrid. Thereby, alternative solutions to "nationality problems" such as autonomy, federalization or domestic paritative commissions took a back seat until they were rediscovered in the early 1930s when it had become obvious that minority protection treaties would not help to secure

---

[53] Celestin Bouglé, 'Le principe des Nationalités et les Minorités Nationales', in: *Publications de la Conciliation internationale. Bulletin trimestriel*, 1929/2, 87–114, 101. In French: "Qu'est maintenant la minorité nationale? Il importe de la distinguer nettement de la nationalité".

[54] Kunz (1932).

peace. It is therefore no coincidence that Jouzas Gabrys and Jean Pélissier revived their activities in 1931 and published a new journal on nationalities and national minorities, the 'Revue des Nationalités et des Minorités Nationales'. The same year Hermann Raschhofer published his book on 'The Main Problems of the Rights of Nationalities'.[55] Also in 1931, Ewald Ammende, the secretary general of the CEN, deepened his interest in the situation of nationalities in Spain after travelling to the country and rediscovered the European significance of the autonomy solutions that were advocated by the Catalans and the Basques. Ammende also mentioned the Galicians, in his words "primoridial Portuguese" that lived above of Portugal.[56] Likewise, the Ukrainian Parliamentarian Club congratulated the president of the "Catalan Republic" for the attainment of self-determination.[57] In 1933, Gilbert Murray, the public face of the British League of Nations Union and a respected transnational expert in minority questions underlined that "autonomy is the only remedy, and even autonomy could scarcely become real in a world like the present, exasperated by political and economic nationalism".[58]

This suggests that the semantic pendulum swang back from minorities in the direction of nationalities and that both terms had become irreversibly associated. In 1945, the American Jewish scholar Oscar Janowsky published a book on *Nationalities and National Minorities* and advocated "national federalism" as "the solution proposed for the unyielding problems of nationalities and minorities" in East Central Europe.[59]

The conclusions of my conceptual approach to nationality and minority problems that centred on transnational associations and debates point in a similar direction. It was not revisionism or border changes that were discussed as possible solutions to minorities' questions in the 1920s and early 1930s but minority rights, autonomy and federalization. The seizure of power by Adolf Hitler in Germany and the turn to authoritarian regimes in Europe stopped the renaissance of autonomy in the 1930s. Revisionism and border changes became respectable as a political demand and were equally considered by transnational activists. Already in 1933, the above mentioned Gilbert Murray spoke of cases "in which the common feeling of the world will agree that the demand

---

55   Raschhofer (1931).
56   Ewald Ammende, 'Spanien als Faktor der Europäischen Nationalitäten-Politik. Barcelona – Madrid – Bilbao. Reisebericht Oktober 1931, PAAA, R 60529. In the German original „Urportugiesen".
57   „Ukraïn'skii Kliub do Katal'ontsiv" *Dilo*, 90 (26 April 1931). This shows that the Ukrainians also followed the situation in Spain.
58   Murray (1933:130).
59   Janowsky (1945).

for territorial revision is just".[60] But this already touches upon other aspects of the transnational debate on minorities and nationalities in the inter-war period that cannot be dealt with in this paper.

Coming back to the starting point, I hope that I was able to convince you that by comprising nationality questions as predecessor and alter ego of the minorities' problem, we get a different perspective on the MPS than by placing it alongside international treaties that provided special rights for minority or nationality groups before 1918 and after 1945. Internationally guaranteed minority rights were not the only way to solve nationality and minority problems.

Bibliography

Bamberger-Stemmann, S. (2000), *Der Europäische Nationalitätenkongreß 1925 bis 1938. Nationale Minderheiten zwischen Lobbyistentum und Großinteressen*, Marburg a. Lahn: Herder Institut.

Chernev, B. (2017), "Shifts and Tensions in Ethnic/National Groups", in: *1914–1918-online. International Encyclopedia of the First World War*, ed. by Ute Daniel et al., DOI: 10.15463/ie1418.10210.

Cussó, R. (2013), "La défaite de la SDN face aux nationalismes des majorités. La Section des minorités et l'irrecevabilité des pétitions «hors traité»", *Études Internationales*, 44:1, pp. 65–88.

Demm, E. "Die 'Union des Nationalités' Paris/Lausanne und die europäische Öffentlichkeit 1911–1919", in J. Requate and M. Schulze Wessel (eds), *Europäische Öffentlichkeit. Transnationale Kommunikation seit dem 18. Jahrhundert*, Frankfurt a. M./New York: Campus, 2002, pp. 92–120.

Demm, E., & Ch. Nikolajew, eds. (2013), *Auf Wache für die Nation. Erinnerungen. Der Weltkriegsagent Jouzas Gabrys berichtet (1911–1918)*, Frankfurt a. M.: Peter Lang.

Doty, M.Z. (1945), *The Central Organisation for a durable Peace (1915–1919). Its History, Works and Ideas*, Ambilly: Imprimerie Franco-Suisse.

Dyroff, S. (2013), "Avant-garde or supplement? Advisory bodies of transnational associations as alternatives to the League's Minority Protection System, 1919–1939", *Diplomacy & Statecraft*, 24:2, pp. 192–208.

Esculies, J., & V. Petronis (2016), 'Self-proclaimed diplomats: Catalan-Lithuanian cooperation during WWI', *Nationalities Papers*, 44:2, 340–356.

Fink, C. (2000), "Minority Rights as an International Question", *Contemporary European History*, 9:3, pp. 385–400.

---

60   Murray (1933: 129).

Fisch, J. (2015), *The right of self-determination of peoples: the domestication of an illusion,* New York.

Fischer, H. (1978), *Oszkár Jaszi und Mihály Károlyi: ein Beitrag zur Nationalitätenpolitik der bürgerlich-demokratischen Opposition in Ungarn von 1900 bis 1918 und ihre Verwirklichung in der bürgerlich-demokratischen Regierung von 1918 bis 1919,* Munich: R. Trofenik.

Gabrys, J. (1917), *Le problème des nationalités et la paix durable,* Lausanne: Librairie Centrale des Nationalités.

Geiss, I. (2013), *The Question of German Unification 1806–1996,* London: Routledge, 2nd ed.

Haslinger, P. (1993), *Arad, November 1918. Oszkár Jászi und die Rumänen in Ungarn 1900 bis 1918,* Vienna: Böhlau.

Hildebrand, K. (1915), *Ein starkes Volk. Eindrücke aus Deutschland und von der deutschen Westfront (Dezember 1914 und Januar 1915),* Berlin: Mittler.

Jackson Preece, J. (1997), "Minority rights in Europe: from Westphalia to Helsinki", *Review of International Studies,* 23, pp. 75–92.

Janowsky, O.I. (1945), *Nationalities and National Minorities (With Special Reference to East-Central Europe),* New York: Macmillan.

Jászi, O. (1912), *A nemzeti államok kialakulása és a nemzetiségi kérdés: válogatás,* Budapest: Grill Károly Könyvkiadóvállalata.

Jenne, E.K. (2007), *Ethnic bargaining: the paradox of minority empowerment,* Ithaca/London: Cornell UP.

Kunz, J. (1932), "Review of Hermann Raschhofer, Hauptprobleme des Nationalitätenrechts", *Zeitschrift für Öffentliches Recht,* XII, pp. 116–18.

Laqua, D. (2013), *The Age of Internationalism and Belgium, 1880–1930. Peace, progress and prestige* Manchester: Manchester UP.

Laun, R. (1917), "Das Nationalitätenrecht als internationales Problem", *Österreichische Zeitschrift für öffentliches Recht,* 3, pp. 397–418.

Laun, R. (1920), *Entwurf eines internationalen Vertrags über den Schutz nationaler Minderheiten,* Berlin: Karl Hermann Verlag.

Laun, R. (1925), "Nationalitätenfrage einschließlich des Minderheitenrechts", in K. Strupp (ed.), *Wörterbuch des Völkerrechts und der Diplomatie. Zweiter Band: Maas-Utschiali,* Berlin: Walter de Gruyter, pp. 82–108.

Laun, R. (1930), "Volk und Nation; Selbstbestimmung; nationale Minderheiten", in G. Anschütz & R. Thoma (eds), *Handbuch des deutschen Staatsrechts,* Vol. 1, Tübingen: Mohr Siebeck, 244–257.

Laun, R. (1933), *Der Wandel der Ideen Staat und Volk als Äusserung des Weltgewissens,* Barcelona: Institució Patxot.

Lauren, P.G. (2003), *The Evolution of International Human Rights. Visions Seen,* Philadelphia: University of Pennsylvania Press, 2nd. ed.

Litván, G. (2006), *A twentieth-century prophet: Oscar Jászi, 1875–1957*, Budapest: CEU Press.

Murray, G. (1933), "Revision of the Peace Treaties", in Leonard Woolf (ed.), *The Intelligent Man's Way to Prevent War*, London: Gollancz, pp. 67–153.

Pélissier, J. (1918), *Les principaux artisans de la Renaissance nationale lituanienne: hommes et choses de Lithuanie*, Lausanne: Bureau d'information de Lituanie.

Macartney, C.A. (1934), *National States and National Minorities*, London: Oxford UP.

Núñez Seixas, X.M. (2001), *Entre Ginebra y Berlín. La cuestión de las minorías nacionales y la política internacional en Europa, 1914–1939*, Madrid: Akal.

Núñez Seixas, X.M. (2010), *Internacionalizant el nacionalisme. El catalanisme polític i la qüestió de les minories nacionals a Europa (1914–1936)*, Valencia: PUV/Afers.

Raschhofer, H. (1931), *Hauptprobleme des Nationalitätenrechts,* Stuttgart: Verlag Ferdinand Enke.

Soutou, G.-H. (1995), "Jean Pélissier et l'Office central des Nationalités, 1911–1918: un agent du gouvernement français auprès des nationalités", in id. (ed.), *Recherches sur la France et le problème des nationalités pendant la Première Guerre Mondiale (Pologne, Ukraine, Lithuanie)* Paris: Presses Univ. Paris-Sorbonne, pp. 11–38.

Struve, K. (2004), "Nationale Minderheit–Begriffsgeschichtliches zu Gleichheit und Differenz", *Leipziger Beiträge zur jüdischen Geschichte und Kultur*, 2, pp. 233–258.

Svarauskas, A. (n. d.), 'Union des Nationalités', in: *1914–1918-online. International Encyclopedia of the First World War*, ed. by Ute Daniel et al, issued by Freie Universität Berlin, Berlin 2014-10-08. DOI: http://dx.doi.org/10.15463/ie1418.10262.

Tønnesson, Øyvind (2013), *With Christian L. Lange as a prism: a study of transnational peace politics, 1899–1919*, Oslo: University of Oslo.

Trencsényi, B., et al. (2016), *A History of Modern Political Thought in East Central Europe. Volume i: Negotiating Modernity in the 'Long Nineteenth Century'*, Oxford: Oxford UP.

Uhlig, R. (1988), *Die Interparlamentarische Union 1889–1914. Friedenssicherungsbemühungen im Zeitalter des Imperialismus*, Stuttgart: Franz Steiner.

Watson, D.R. (1995), "Jean Pélissier and the Office Central des Nationalités, 1912–1919", *The English Historical Review* 110:439, pp. 1191–1206.

Zechlin, E. (1963), "Die 'Zentralorganisation für einen dauernden Frieden' und die Mittelmächte. Ein Beitrag zur politischen Tätigkeit Rudolf Launs im ersten Weltkrieg", *Jahrbuch für internationales Recht*, XI (1962), pp. 448–496.

Zetterberg, S. (1978), *Die Liga der Fremdvölker Russlands 1916–1918. Ein Beitrag zu Deutschlands antirussischem Propagandakrieg unter den Fremdvölkern Russlands im ersten Weltkrieg*, Helsinki: Suomen Historikallinen Seura.

CHAPTER 12

Agrarian Movements, the National Question, and Democracy in Europe, 1880–1945

Lourenzo Fernández Prieto and Miguel Cabo

1   Introduction*

In order to speak of nations and the agrarian question in Europe, or even the world in 1916, four central questions must be kept in mind: the issue of land and property rights, from the point of view of workers/farmers; the mobilization and organization of farmers in the conflictive contexts as well as the expression of a civil society in the rural world that interacted with the State (politics) and the market; nationalism: stateless nations in conflict with old empires and with nation-states constructed in the previous century; and lastly, the farmer-based overseas migrations and their returns in terms of capacity and all sorts of new ideas.

The overarching theme we shall attempt to encompass —the international context in which the Galician Language Brotherhoods emerged— calls for an approach which is plural, conceptual, discursive, ideological, political, cultural as well as material-social. This is necessary in order to appreciate the productive and reproductive interests of the nation's (theoretical) subjects: farmers which constituted —in cases such as Galicia— the majority of society. 100 years ago, on 12 October 1916, the deaths at Cans occurred (in Nebra, Porto do Son, A Coruña). The Civil Guard shot down four women and a man and wounded many more when protesters attempted to hinder a neighbour's forcible eviction. It was the time of struggles (community-based and associative) for land and against the old *foro* or chartered tenancy system that regulated the rent paid to landowners by farmers working the land.[1] Those deaths in the Galicia of 1916, the year the Irmandades were founded, were over land, not Patriotism. They died for the land of home and of everyone, within the

---

*   HISTAGRA Research Group. This work is a part of the project *Los vectores del cambio estructural de las agriculturas atlánticas ibéricas: moto-mecanización y especialización lechera*, HAR2016-77441-P

1   More than a century has passed since these deaths, now firmly rooted in memory (http://nebra.blogaliza.org/tag/martires-de-cans/). Regarding this case and its context, see Villares (1982) and Cabo (1998).

framework of a collective and grassroots action. We shall examine, therefore, the complexity of this dynamic from below, from the point of view of farmer's interests, and from above, from the logic and perspective of the elites, the architects of the discourse itself. Focus is placed on Galicia in 1916, but the lens is multi-scale, encompassing Europe and America —more transcontinental than transnational, in order to ponder the relationship between the Language Brotherhoods, minority nationalism and the agrarian question. This begins with the fact that farmer majorities are voters who intervene in the political system in a decisive manner, in European territories where small plot farming is dominant but there are still unresolved conflicts regarding land (Galicia, Ireland, Catalonia, etc.).

Rurality generally plays a key role in nationalist discourse, even though academic publications, paradoxically, do not always stress this connection with the emphasis it deserves.[2] The interaction between agrarian and nationalist movements in interwar Europe must, in our view, begin with a detailed analysis of the ruralist component present in its discourse, which offers an essential meeting point. Rurality and peasantry also play a key role in contemporary processes of politicization and democratization and all political forces (socialist, liberal, social catholic, etc.) had to incorporate this peasant reality into their analyses, which even in spite of predictions by economic or Marxist theory, demonstrated themselves to be surprisingly stubborn survivors. Following this discourse analysis, a second section will chart the functioning of the rural world in nationalist ideosystems. In closing, we will offer reflections on national questions from the point of view of agrarian movements and parties during the interwar period.

2   The Characterization of Ruralism

The exaltation of the virtues of rural reality boasts an ample history extending back to the classic age and offers a strand of continuity not only in Europe but also in the United States via the Jeffersonian tradition.[3] Nevertheless, during the 19th century interesting nuances will be added, paralleling the accelerated transformations in all areas (urbanization, industrialization, mass society,

---

[2] Thus, recent and ambitious syntheses succeed neither in successfully addressing rural paradigms nor the peasants' realities. See Breuilly (2013); Delanty and Kumar (2006); Herb and Kaplan (2008); Morales Moya, Fusi and de Blas Guerrero (2013). Quite a different matter are monographs and case studies, several of which will be mentioned later.
[3] Caro Barjoja (1963); Stock (1996).

etc.). The ruralist component will therefore be more aggressive the quicker these advances in each country ensue, with the German case probably being the most extreme.[4]

Despite sharing many common characteristics, it is necessary to differentiate the European ruralist discourse insofar as its United States counterpart is concerned (reaching its height with the late 19th century populism which ends when it is absorbed into the Democratic Party): in the United States, the *farmer* was praised as an individual (*farmer* and not *peasant,* which has different implications in the English language). This individual aspired to respect competitive capitalism's established norms against the monopolistic tendencies of large corporations and the railroad companies. In Europe, broadly speaking, the ruralist discourse placed the rural *community* at centre stage (and not the individual to such a large extent), exalting a way of life and certain values within it, and behind this, economic activity.

The high point of ruralism would be what is known as the turn-of-the-century agrarian crisis (from approximately 1875 to 1895), with the massive arrival in Europe —due to advances in means of transport— of products from America, Australia and New Zealand at extremely competitive prices. The sudden alarm sparked decisive debates regarding tariff policy, the viability of family farming, the necessity of state intervention as opposed to liberal dogma or possible adaptations of productive systems (such as the livestock farming in order to take advantage of the cheap fodder costs), as well as the *agrarian question* at the heart of the Socialist-oriented Second International.

Faced with the threatening sensation spreading throughout European rural societies, the elites and political representatives crafted a discourse which would praise and uphold its virtues, refining the traditional clichés: harmony and organicism as opposed to the atomization and individualism of the urban world, communion with Nature as opposed to artificiality, family and tradition pitted against moral disorder, patriotism and frugality as opposed to egoism and hedonism: a catalogue of virtues contrasted by vices seen as belonging to workers and cities. The property-owning farmer—or at least someone who was well established on their land—became the paradigm of this idyllic vision.[5] Ruralism enabled intellectual elitism to synthesize a disdain for the masses with an idealization of the peasantry, which were numerous but were

---

4 Bergmann (1970).
5 Though conceived from a contemporary perspective, see for an understanding of all aspects that fall outside of this idealizing perspective (women, alternative sexuality, the poor, ethnic minorities, etc.) Cloke & Little (1997).

not a *mass* due to the fact that they were not atomized.[6] Advancing sciences such as hygiene, demographics and criminology came to the aid of these prejudices, legitimizing them, and giving them advantages when these same elites are faced with the need of gaining social and electoral support in order to intervene in the democratic politics of universal (male) suffrage.

Although this was enacted mainly from above, this discourse possessed the clear potential to be shared by the majority of the rural population as well, since it played on shared fears: the dependence of financial capitalism and its intermediaries, the primacy of industrial lobbies in the Administration's priorities, the loss of identity and the organizational advantages of the workers. In fact, the broad associative movement that moved across Europe in different forms beginning in the last quarter of the 19th century, cultivated the same discursive frames and translated them into a popular message. Every social movement calls for the elaboration of frameworks of collective action — definitions and explanations of reality which justify and legitimate them in the eyes of its collective parts while at the same time reinforcing its internal solidarity.[7] For the several rural-based associative manifestations in particular, these frameworks utilized arguments along the lines of those already mentioned (agriculture as a basic economic activity superior to any other, the importance of food security in the case of war, etc.) and some images and rhetorical resources which were surprisingly similar—defying linguistic and cultural barriers (comparisons with animals in reference to antagonists, calloused hands as a sign of identity, etc.).

The term *ruralism* must be closely analysed due to its ambiguity and potential confusion with its purely literary uses. Barrington Moore offers an excellent starting point when he points out five elements in its composition:[8]

1) The necessity of a profound moral regeneration masking the absence of a realist analysis of existing social conditions.
2) Organicism, in that rural society was considered to be a harmonious whole, although internally hierarchical, in contrast to the atomized and disintegrated urban civilization.
3) Irrationalism, in terms of the rejection of excessively elaborated intellectual constructions and of a vitalist and *natural* approach to reality.
4) Mistrust towards the foreign and cosmopolitan.

---

6   Carey (1992).
7   Tarrow (1994).
8   Moore (1977).

5) In the artistic sphere a preference for local and costumbrist references reflecting the popular spirit, and which facilitated the viewer or reader's immediate connection.

Taking these aspects as a starting point, the ruralist discourse should possess a generally conservative potential, due to the weight on it of defensive or reactive elements. Arno Mayer qualifies this among the strategies of the traditional elites for lengthening their influence and thus the 'persistence of the Old Regime'.[9] To a certain extent, this solves the paradox Zeev Sternhell detected in the sequence of thinkers rallying against the Enlightenment and its offshoots: the direct rejection of mass culture compatible with the cult of a supposed popular spirit.[10]

Nevertheless, other important nuances are at work. Firstly, the commitment to a rural reality and the social role of the peasantry can be focused towards movements or agrarian parties of a progressive sort, as was the case in Denmark with the liberal *Venstre*,[11] or the agricultural support for the Galician Language Brotherhoods.

Secondly, the apparently nostalgic ruralist discourse did not really endeavour to recuperate a lost past but rather to legitimize completely new goals. Examples of these were equality in the access and active participation of the peasantry in political life and in the market, such as the Galician agrarian reform movement, as well as many others.[12] It can thus be understood that even for organizations of a clearly moderate ideological tenor expressions such as 'conservative modernization' are used.[13]

The result is that at the beginning of the 20th century the ruralist myth –or identity or collective cultural reference- ends up acquiring a surprising transversality and is present in the most diverse ideological variables. Thus, in the United Kingdom, the pioneer of industrialization and urbanization, both liberals and Labour Party members were able to vie for Tories' hegemony in the rural districts. This was done not only through propaganda and programmatic proposals but also by creating an interpretation of the past and the ideal British identity (William Morris, John Ruskin, John and Barbara Hammond). At the same time, the historical period before the enclosures is revised (*Merry England*) as an extension of the organic communities that guaranteed the

---

9   Mayer (1981: 253).
10 Sternhell (2006: 21).
11 Østergård (1992).
12 Lourenzo Fernández Prieto, *Labregos con ciencia. Estado, sociedade e innovación tecnolóxica na agricultura galega, 1850–1939* (Vigo: Xerais, 1992); Cabo, *O agrarismo*.
13 See e. g. for Austria Ernst Bruckmüller, *Landwirtschaftliche Organisationen und gesellschaftliche Modernisierung* (Salzburg, Verlag Wolfgang Neubauer, 1977).

expression of Anglo-Saxon qualities before the triumph of the landlords. Rooting themselves in pre-existing communal elements, they combined them with newer ones in a new future ideal on behalf of the British workers' movement. These authors attribute old roots to novelties in order to set it into a tradition which had not yet disappeared, but was only dormant.[14] This happy time would end after the Middle Ages due to the excessive ambition of landowning nobles. Both liberals (the agrarian reforms of Gladstone and Lloyd-George) and Labour justified their reforms with the revamped recovery of the preindustrial past.[15]

Another important example is that of France, where republicanism sets its sights on gaining the support of the peasantry in order to consolidate the Third Republic by fomenting a compact associative network and filling out the pre-existing ruralism with the myth of the *paysan-soldat* as a defender par excellence of the homeland in the trenches.[16] Even the SFIO would adopt these theories. Even more, when the communist separation occurred, French communists took up the defence of family farming (with co-operativism as the mechanism that would facilitate the move towards collectivism in the long term). The USSR would constitute a primary exception to this tendency by identifying the Russian countryside with backwardness and superstition, inexorably dismantling its structures through Stalinist collectivization: the same structures that the Slavophile tradition and the populists held up as the pinnacle of the Russian spirit in the face of Western materialism and rationalism.[17]

The transversality of ruralism is also evident in anarchism, a critique of all the social and economic transformations of capitalist modernity,[18] and on the far opposite end of the ideological spectrum, the exaltation of the peasantry and of the rural reality formed part of the fascist 'common minimum'.[19] The ruralist discourse therefore manages to become generalized in such a way in the interwar period that it begins to lose its value as a differentiating mechanism,

---

14 Alun Hawkins, *Reshaping Rural England: a Social History, 1850–1925* (New York: Harper & Collins, 1991).

15 Krishan Kumar, *The Making of English National Identity*, Cambridge: Cambridge UP, 2003, p. 209; Clare V. Griffiths, *Labour and the Countryside. The Politics of Rural Britain 1918–1939* (Oxford, Oxford UP, 2007); Paul Readman, *Land and Nation in England* (Woodbridge, The Brydell Press, 2008); Matthew Cragoe and Paul Readman (eds.), *The Land Question in Britain, 1750–1950* (Basingstoke, Palgrave Macmillan, 2010).

16 Lynch (2006).

17 The classic study by Carr (1979) bridged a very acute description of this process of forced collectivization and destruction of the kulaks. A recent reappraisal in Smith (2014).

18 Casanova (1988); Paniagua (1982).

19 Fernández Prieto, Pan-Montojo & Cabo (2014).

unless a deep, detailed analysis is undertaken to explore the role it played in each ideosystem and its interaction with the remaining components.

Aside from its political manifestations, ruralism also showed fertile development in the literary and artistic sphere, although here we will not focus upon this facet. Nevertheless, it is worth noting how writers from many countries like George Sand, Frédéric Mistral, Berthold Auerbach, Ippolito Nievo, Liviu Rebreanu or René Bazin were key to the creation of a ruralist discourse and to its social dissemination. We will only make reference here to a fact that appears striking: this literature hardly brings into its plots positive and self-generated changes, such as co-operativism or technical changes. It only incorporates the results of transformations produced in the urban environment and which end up having an effect (usually considered to be menacing) on rural societies. In this way, the peasant-based formation of associations that spreads throughout the continent is hardly reflected at all in ruralist literature, as we have confirmed in the Galician case or how it is exemplified in an anecdote about Émile Guillaumin, a successful writer (and farmer) who actively fosters the creation of an agrarian union but does not mention it in any of his novels.[20]

3 Nationalism in the Face of the Rural World

All nationalisms, as a national project, must construct and disseminate a narrative that explains a human collective's past and the present, justifies the existence of the bonds which links its members (in turn differentiating it from other groups), reinforces its reciprocal solidarity and directs its political praxis. Without exception, ruralism was a part of this discourse which reinforces the 'imagined community' recreated by nationalisms[21] —that common past to which the original characters of the nation can be traced and that leaves its mark on its members even when the link of many of them with the land has become weak. Interestingly, the rural imprint provides the national identity for a good part of the emotional component it requires for its internalization.[22]

---

20   Cabo (2002); Ponton (1977).
21   Anderson (1983).
22   Nairn (1997: 106); Edensor (2002: 39). A state of late creation and marked heterogeneity, in 1830 Belgium attempted to create a new national imaginary based on the peasantry, giving protagonism to uprisings against successive occupying powers (Austria and the Netherlands) in the new patriotic narrative, as analysed by Van Molle (2013).

Prolific as they are in the creation of myths, a large part of those stemming from nationalism respond to what Levinger and Lytle call a 'triadic structure'.[23] These authors apply it namely to the vision of history, but the same diagram in three phases can be identified for the evolution of the rural world. As a starting point, an idyllic situation is described, a golden age; secondly, a decadent present, a product of threats (processes derived from the advance of industry and cities) which deteriorated and altered the nature of primordial splendour; lastly, the promise of revitalization through the recovery of this lost past.[24]

These constructions remove two dimensions from the rural world that specialized historiography has placed emphasis upon in recent decades. The first of these is change. They are located in an atemporal limbo with no clear beginning and in which the only evolution would be those negatives that lurk behind external factors related to modernity; other than this they are configured in almost geological terms. On the other hand, recent agrarian historiography has indicated the evolutionary capacity of rural societies. This is patent in early Modern History for example, with the spread of foreign crops such as corn or the potato which required a drastic shift in both agricultural practices and calendar. In the same vein, recent studies on the paradigmatic agricultural revolution at the turn of the 18th century show how scientific innovations and gentlemen farmers came down from their pedestals in order to place emphasis on what has been referred to as *hidden improvements*, based on the daily routines and accumulated knowledge of anonymous farmers (more complex crop rotations, the replacement of the sickle with the scythe, of oxen with horses, seed selection and livestock improvement via empirical observation, etc.). Many of the essential traits that scholars at the service of the national ideal (as well as ethnographers and folklorists in general) pinpoint in rural society as perennial elements preserved since time immemorial are, in reality, under the magnifying glass of present day historians, relatively recent. They can be grouped under the category of *invented traditions* as described by Hobsbawm and Ranger.[25]

The second characteristic often left unaddressed by the nationalist story are the conflictive elements present. The rural world is usually portrayed as a harmonious space, in which hierarchies are uncontested and elements of

---

23   Levinger & Lyttle (2001).
24   A present-day demonstration of this can be found in surveys by Michael Skey. The English, citizens of the country most precocious in terms of urban and industrial development, still base their national identity on elements coming from an idealized rural life removed from post-war transformations (immigration, motorization, new family models, etc.). See Skey (2011: 43).
25   Hobsbawm & Ranger (1984).

opposition and dissensus (land ownership, collection of rent, communal use of resources, to name a few) are diffused by shared values and interests, such as a common drive towards increased production, the network of reciprocal duties, the strength of local communities, etc. However, rural history spanning over recent decades has carefully studied the various ways in which this conflictive nature is expressed, including endemic ones between communities described by Charles Tilly as 'forms of horizontal violence'[26] or the 'everyday forms of peasant resistance' ('weapons of the weak') described by James C. Scott. These are developed in apparent calm over periods of time not yet ripe for open defiance (occupying lands, foregoing payment of rent, etc.) by hegemonic groups or institutions.[27]

Beyond the level of discourse, it is extremely meaningful that nationalisms constantly face difficulties when it comes to managing agrarian conflicts, in particular in terms of land ownership. Either its existence is denied or the problematic is simplified in order to blame exogenous factors, such as the supposedly oppressive State, industrialization or ethnic groups outside of the national community. A clear example can be found in the Irish case, when in the 19th century sixties and early seventies, Fenians hesitated to take part in the complex web of interests and struggles around the use of land ownership on the island (cattle breeders vs. farmers, tenant farmers vs. day labourers, the role of local money-lending shopkeepers, etc.). The predominant idea here was that confronting such questions would have the consequence of dividing the national community before the British Administration and therefore it was more convenient to postpone its resolution until after independence was achieved. Lastly, at the end of the seventies, the Land War united claims for land and the national cause, though at the price of taking a reductionist stand with regard to the agrarian situation. According to this, everything was subordinated to the opposition between the tenant farmer and the landlords who had benefitted from the historical plundering following the island's conquest. Three trenches overlapped: the social (landowners vs. tenants), the religious (Anglicans vs. Catholics) and ethnic (Anglo-Saxons vs. Celts), at the expense of leaving out infinite nuances and interests that did not fit into this interpretation.[28] Once independence was achieved was when hidden conflicts could no longer be postponed; problems could not be blamed either on the dependency

---

26 Tilly (1978). An approach to the Galician case can be found in Cabo & Vázquez Varela (2015).
27 Scott (1986).
28 Historiography on this topic is inexhaustible, but the last attempt to systematically connect agrarian and national issues is Bull (1996). For the specific period of the *Land War* the most recent analysis can be found in Kane (2011).

of the United Kingdom. Disatisfaction with the decisions taken by the Dublin governments led to the emergence of specifically agrarian parties.[29]

Another example is provided by the Galician national movement, which always handled the regional question of the 'foros' awkwardly.[30] Other facets of the Galician land question offered a vantage point in which Galicia's position was compromised because of the lack of legal recognition of its peculiarities (such as commons) or due to being marginalized by a centralist Spanish state more attentive to the interests of the grain producing regions and large landowners. It is along these lines that protectionism is denounced, claiming that tariffs impeded Galicia from following a path similar to the Danish one (fodder importation, specialization in dairy products, and a cooperative export oriented agricultural industry). Rather, the *foro* problem didn't fit within this sort of dichotomy since both rent payers and recipients were local. To this can be added the gentry imprint on a good part of the nationalist ideologues, the result being that Galician nationalists lagged behind the movement against the foro. Only shortly before the dictatorship of Primo de Rivera (1923–1930) did they confront the issue, and when they finally did they adopted a middle-ground posture in which rentiers' interests were safeguarded, while at the same time paying tribute to the historic role of the *foro*.

Speaking broadly, it is undeniable that nationalisms held rurality and the peasantry to be of special importance, maintaining (particularly in periods of oppression or decadence) essential traits: the language, popular literature, the manner in which the territory was occupied, folklore, etc. Keeping in mind the division between civic and ethnic nationalisms espoused by Hans Kohn in the forties (taking into account later criticism and that these merely embody ideal types for the purpose of analysis), the latter are, by their own logic, those that go further towards an exaltation of the peasantry and of rurality.[31] Nevertheless, civic or voluntary nationalisms, once they are institutionalized, end up adopting similar stances. Thus, in the paradigmatic French case, an initial distrust of the revolutionaries regarding the rustic milieu (suspected to be reactionary and papists) shifts and evolves into an alliance between the Third Republic (the radical party in particular) and the *paysans* who are favoured by

---

[29] Dooley (2004); Varley (2010).

[30] The *foro* or chartered tenancy was a long-term contract of medieval origin with a division of domains, hereditary in practice, while the tenant, or *foreiro*, would continue to pay rent annually.

[31] Tom Nairn goes to the extreme when he affirms that "Ethnic nationalism is in essence a peasantry transmuted, at least in ideal terms, into a nation", and that the ruralist heritage in countries of the European Union compromises the projects of civic nationalism at its core. See Nairn (1997: 90, 107).

public policy and considered to be the main supporters of the regime, not to mention the nation itself.

It is revelatory to observe the peasantry from the perspective of nationalism as a *national class*, as upholding ethnicity, in the reaction occurring when another force usurps this nationalism in terms of mobilizing the peasantry. Nationalists considered themselves to be the privileged guides of the rural folk, the ones to lead them from a *latent* nationalism to a *conscious* one. This is the case in Galicia, where nationalists, considering their weakness at the time of the *Irmandades da Fala* (founded in 1916), promoted an autonomous organization independent of any state federation (whether the catholic CNCA, the socialist UGT, or any other) for the agrarian movement which had been growing since the last decade of the 19th century. They waited for the moment when the confluence would occur —natural and inevitable to their minds, barring interferences— between the aspirations of the agrarian societies and those of the Irmandades, later the Galicianist Party (*Partido Galeguista*, 1931–36). They thought it would be the way to have a massive electoral base at their disposition, a goal which began to take shape during the Second Republic only to be ended by the Coup d'etat.[32] A reaction harbouring a certain resemblance to that of Irish nationalists who ferociously attacked the co-operativism promoted by Horace Plunkett for its not taking into account ideological and confessional divisions. In their eyes, it was simply a manoeuvre from London to 'kill it [Home Rule] with kindness'.[33] In the same vein, in a Croatia under Hapsburg domination, the primary nationalist party (HSK) was hostile to the emergence of the Stjepan Radić's Croatian Peasant Party, despite it being a defender of Croatian identity and working towards its recognition within a federal structure.[34]

The effective success of the nationalist movements in mobilizing rural workers required, however, aspects that went beyond the simple recognition of their cultural contribution. Nationalist leaders and intellectuals had to convince them that their demands (access to land ownership, the safeguarding of farming against industry and on commercial circuits, mediation with the State and the Market, support for technological innovation, etc.) would be resolved in a more satisfactory manner within their own State or as a result of political autonomy, depending on the case. This was not a straightforward task for nationalist parties for a variety of reasons, the most frequent of these being the

---

32 Beramendi (2007: 717); Cabo (1998).
33 Aalen, (1993).
34 Such fears would certainly prove to be founded given that in time Radić's party became hegemonic among Croatians, successfully combining the double nature of being a peasant party while also a defender of its ethnic minority (first within the Austro-Hungarian Empire, and then from 1918 within a centralist Yugoslavia). See Biondich (2000: 105).

lack of leaders from the rural ranks or the aspiration to become catch-all parties representing all social groups, amongst which the rural sector would be one of many members. The successful cases of sub-state nationalist movements that achieved strong rural support, such as the paradigm of Ireland, included popular demands within their programmes, an effective collaboration with agrarian associations and their (productive and reproductive) interests, and a management of all these factors in administrative spheres that they could gradually control at a local level.

4 The National Dimension in the Diverse Forms of Associationism

Beginning in the last two decades of the 20th century, triggered by the turn-of-the-century agrarian crisis, an acceleration can be observed in the mass politicization process in addition to associationism and an organization of interests in all areas, both in cities and the countryside. The importance of states in solving the crisis (tariffs, fomenting technical change, opening up ways towards land ownership, etc.) became apparent, and therefore the inevitability as well that each social group or economic interest was able to represent themselves before the state in a coherent and well-organized way. The structure of available opportunities began to broaden —with obvious nuances and rhythms belonging to each country— due to the extension of the right to suffrage, the right to associate, the weight of the agrarian question in political and cultural debates and the advances of literacy. Return migration, both international as well as internal within the state itself, also facilitated the broadening of social capital and both material and intangible resources in the villages —an element to bear in mind, particularly intense in cases such as the Irish or Galician.

The majority of farmers participated in the political system and in the output markets (emigrant workforce, cattle, agrarian products) and inputs (technological, emigration consignments: monetary, but also social and cultural). Their interests were quite defined in relation to ownership (in order to assure the full control of the land), and to the market (where they want to compete on equal terms). In this context, the relationship with politics and also with the processes of technological innovation must also be understood.[35] Societies with a strong peasantry at this time, such as Galicia, are based around farmer's homes and in communities enjoying large degrees of autonomy, a prize won, as in many other European territories, due to a combination of resistance and resilience. This happened over time, from the exit from the Lower Medieval

---

35   See for the Galician case Fernández Prieto (1992).

crisis, through the fin-de-siècle crisis, and filtering through that important Rubicon that was the crisis of the Ancien Regime. It is an autonomy which is not only economic but also cultural, although often the romantic elites would erroneously identify it with poverty, unaware that they are were confronted with the powerful weapons of the weak.[36]

In this context, 'agrarian defence', as expressed by Pierre Barral,[37] assumed different forms between the crisis at the turn of the century and the Second World War on the European continent, broken up into four categories. We will present each and then pull the national dimension into its analysis, a procedure we find appropriate for synthetically treating such a broad question. It must be kept in mind that they are neither successive periods nor exclusive modalities, since they can be combined together (for example, a pressure group or an agrarian party can arm themselves with cooperative networks or a federation of cooperatives can present their own candidates in electoral processes).

a) Pressure groups

Pressure groups appear when a harmony is lacking between the necessities of a certain economic and/or social sector and state politics. An example of this is the influential German *Bund der Landwirte* (*Agrarian League*, BdL) which appears in 1893 when the chancellor Caprivi enacts a series of commercial agreements that imply a reorientation of tariff policy towards free-trade. As explained in the now classic study by Hans-Jürgen Puhle,[38] this organization knew how to introduce into the conservative praxis modern elements of mass mobilization at the service of large Eastern landowners, attracting a great number of small to medium-sized farms while never losing of control in a restricted management monopolized by the *Junker* class. A difference from what occurred in the past is that a greater part of these groups possessed stable organization and never interrupted their activity even after their goals were accomplished. Complete and rapid achievement of their desired ends could nevertheless cause these groups to die of success, as was the case with the *Lega di difesa agraria*, formed in Turin in 1885 by large Padano tenants seeking an implementation of tariffs on grain importation. They obtain this in 1887 owing to the support of nearly two hundred legislators, while the BdL could not allow itself to relax in a State which was much more industrialized and exposed

---

36   Scott (1984).
37   Barral (1968), but also in another classic study, by Urwin (1980). The expression has been criticized because it can be taken to imply the unity of interests linked to agriculture, a view we do not share.
38   Puhle (1967). More recently, see also Aldenhoff-Hübinger (2002).

to an alteration of the balance of power benefitting export industry pressure groups.[39]

The usual tactic of pressure groups was to gain parliamentary support through the election of candidates who agreed to support their agenda, independently of the party they belonged to. However, Social Democrats were obviously excluded from this, and success was better with conservative parties (clearly the case as regards Germany), the automatic option by one of them always being avoided. For this tactic to be feasible, it was necessary to gain control of the most substantial portion of rural votes, which at that level could only come from small and mid-sized farmers. Thus, a discourse was crafted which combined agricultural interests and an exaltation of their social and economic role, but which also portioned out cooperative services as well as other types of benefits, such as legal and technical consultation as an incentive. Furthermore, this discourse would serve to fulfil one of the basic requisites of any pressure group, namely, presenting its interests as advantageous for society in general.

Within pressure groups, differentiate subgroups would be those made up of associations of professional producers of certain products, generally with a clear commercial interest (wine, beets, etc.) and with a purely economic and professional discourse with little ruralist rhetoric. This would be the case for France with the *Syndicat général des sériciculteurs de France* (1887), the *Syndicat des viticulteurs de France* (1888), the *Confédération générale des vignerons du Midi* (1907), the *Confédération générale des planteurs de betteraves* (1921) or the *Association générale des producteurs du blé* (1924).

What role does nationalism play as far as pressure groups are concerned? The main aspect resides at the level of their support base's cohesion. This was the central axis on which the discourse of the German BdL rested —a conservative, romantic tone while incorporating biologically racist overtones and marked anti-socialism and anti-Semitism.[40] Given that they had to negotiate with the State, these pressure groups adopted the national identity promoted from that same source and helped to reinforce it through their mediation with the rural masses.

b) Currents within existing political parties.

Here reference is made to wings within established parties, such as the agrarian component in German and Belgian Catholic parties, the former based on the *Christliche Bauernvereine* and the latter in the Flemish *Boerenbond*, which tried to direct the behaviour of the party in the desired direction,

---

39   Malatesta (1989).
40   Puhle (1967: 83–92).

competing with other segments, representatives of industrial businesses or worker unions.[41] The risk was remaining a minority in the face of other types of interests (for example the workers unions that struggled for cheap prices for basic nourishment). In the German case, Catholic-based unions worked to integrate (the same as Zentrum as a whole) important peasant sectors of Western and Southern Germany in the Second Reich following *Kulturkampf*, while the case of *Boerenbond* was more complex. Mobilizing Dutch-speaking peasants, it inevitably suffered tensions in the interwar period as Flemish nationalism grew in opposition to the Belgian state. This lasts until 1932 when, pressured by the ecclesiastic hierarchy, it is forced to release a public declaration of condemnation. In such cases the pattern resembles regional demands subordinated to the nation state and therefore the ethnic question is centred more around cultural, rather than political, aspects.

c) Unions and cooperatives

These were the most common forms of defence, making up a motley ensemble solidified at the end of the 19th century with idiosyncrasies according to each State or each region —consisting of eminently local phenomena— but which does not of course exclude the creation of federative structures to a greater degree. In fact, several scholars point out the communitarian imprint which marks them, channelling the strength of pre-existing solidarities at the local parish-wide level. Even though unions and cooperatives are interested in different ends and often under distinct legal ordinances, they can be grouped together in the same category for analytical purposes. This is because they share a similar foundation, that of the smallholders (leaving aside the unions made up solely of agricultural workers) and it is difficult to trace a clear dividing line in practice (which is why *syndicats-boutiques* became a very popular name for the French unions due to their emphasis in consumer cooperatives). The larger part of the affiliates would come from the peasantry, which by no means excludes the participation of elements pertaining to non-peasant groups of the rural society or mixed figures (part-time farmers or other elements derived from strategies of families involving multiple activities).

Although generalization proves difficult, in may be said that these agrarian associations were the result of the combination of stimuli from the local communities and external elements (workers' movements, social Catholicism, etc.). The main expression was the cooperative or small-scale agrarian association, which coalesced around practical necessities (economies of scale in the cooperative business, an increased representational capacity vis-à-vis the State, electoral aspirations, etc.). In those countries where national identity

---

41   See Hübner (2014) and Van Molle (1990).

represented by the State was uncontested, agrarian associationism (as well as other types of worker or cultural associations, falling outside our focus) played a nationalizing role. This is even the case of associations inspired in ideologies hostile to the very concept of nation and formed around an anti-system and internationalist discourse, as has been demonstrated for the red agrarian *leghe* in Central and Northern Italy, which indirectly (and involuntarily) would have contributed towards confronting the rural masses with the idea of nation by pushing their integration into the market and political system, connecting local demands with larger scale problematics and finally by systematically fostering feelings of solidarity with co-religionists of other regions of the country.[42] Moreover, this is the case where the national project pushed by the Administration knew how to give an active protagonism to an ample associative popular movement, as was the case in Denmark following their defeat in the Second Schleswig War.[43]

In multi-ethnic European states, associationism tended to be organized according to ethnic lines (or national lines insofar as they were granted political meaning). Exceptions occurred mainly on a local scale, where if only one organization existed, it was able to accept minority members (supposing that they didn't fulfill the requirements to be able to form their own one). Thus the development of co-operativism from the beginning in Central and Eastern Europe was determined by ethnic cleavages,[44] a process that was by no means unique to rural society.[45] Although the majority of agrarian associations did not posit the dissemination of a particular national identity as their conscious priority, much of their activity functioned in this sense as a secondary effect. Often, the taking up of a position in this regard was implicit at the territorial level of the larger federations and the criteria for the admission of partners, the language in which the statutes were written and the symbology (name, seal, etc.). In this manner, and slightly abusing the term popularized by Michael Billig, it is possible to speak of 'banal nationalization'.[46]

Here, two mutually reinforcing factors come into play:

—Firstly, for the elites that pushed associationism, this must work to reinforce the material position of its members in the face of other ethnic groups. For example, the fomentation of co-operativism was often accompanied by antisemitic messages as the epitome of the intermediaries. Furthermore, it had to

---

42 Zangheri (2000).
43 Østergård (1992).
44 See Lorenz (2006).
45 For a masterful local study, see King (2005).
46 Billig (1995).

serve to recreate an alternative society that would find full expression when it gained political recognition of the national specificity. Thus, each association, each cooperative, turned into miniature glimpses of the yearned for future national State: prosperous, capable of training its own elites (co-operativism served as a springboard for many political careers) and capable of maintaining the values that accounted for the group's identity. National identity was created in the lap of these organizations in those cases where state resources were not available (or were scarcely available through local institutions, for example) in the nationalizing resources generally thought of as nationalizing instruments (schools, military service, etc.).[47] Lastly, they would serve to disseminate an alternative identity among the masses and in this way give a decisive push to the elite's demands, the 'C step' in the classic terminology forged by Miroslav Hroch.

—Secondly, associationism in general, and co-operativism in particular, called for strong doses of 'social capital', translatable in mutual solidarity and the common capacity for action. Let us think for example of the case of the Raiffeisen credit cooperatives that included its members' unlimited solidarity clause, addressing possible fraud or irresponsibility by other members of the group. The coexistence of members of different cultures and languages could serve to stabilize this crucial mutual trust. We can establish an interesting parallel with the Dutch case, where despite ethnic homogeneity, the potent organizational structures were governed by excluding mechanisms which had been created from ideological/confessional variables (the *zuilen* or Catholic, Protestant and liberal columns).[48]

d) Agrarian parties

Agrarian parties were at their zenith in the interwar period due, on one hand, in Central and Eastern Europe to redistributive Agrarian Reforms, and on the other in Scandinavia, (in this case with more solid roots) due to a fertile previous co-operativist network and early peasant access to the electoral arena.[49] Agrarian parties of countries where identity was not a major issue, such as the case of Nordic countries, adopted a nationalist discourse with ruralist trappings but lacking decisive weight in their everyday activities, far less at any rate than economic, educational and other concerns. It could also be a

---

[47] In accordance with the classic nationalization model for the masses taken from the French case by Weber (1976). Associationism is one of the means of nation-building which is independent from the state, and to which Weber did not pay sufficient attention.

[48] The most recent and complete panorama is by Rommes (2014).

[49] The only available comprehensive analysis of this grouping continues to be Gollwitzer (1977).

demand-based regionalist discourse against the political centre (akin to the Bavarian *Bayerischer Bauernbund* with its anti-Prussian discourse) but without passing the limit of the demand for its own statehood.

In multi-ethnic contexts, on the contrary, the agrarian parties tended to represent a concrete minority, in the sense that in the Yugoslavia created though the dismantled Hapsburg Empire, the peasant parties were Croatian, Serbian and Slovenian. In Czechoslovakia, there was a Czechoslovakian agrarian party continuously present in the governmental coalitions and those corresponding to the German, Magyar and Ruthenian minorities. Thus, the ethnic component was quite strong, and, through the identification of the 'peasantry' with 'nation', they were able to proclaim themselves to be defenders par excellence of the latter. This was the case in Radić's Croatian Peasant Party, first demanding autonomy within the Austro-Hungarian Empire and then after 1918 defending Croatian specificity against Serbian centralism.

In all of this, the nationality issue rarely played the most important part in their ideology, except in cases of marked ethnic opposition between large land owners and the peasantry.[50] In general terms, in agrarian parties the issue of 'class' took preference over national concerns.[51] Proof of this is that even in contexts of strong interethnic tension, so common in the successor states after World War I, the agrarian parties understood how to form alliances beyond national barriers, such as in Czechoslovakia when the Agrarian Party (Republican) managed to communicate effectively with the agrarian party of the German minority (the *Bund der Landwirte*, which was independent on the Second Empire pressure group mentioned above), and even incorporate it into the government presided over by the agrarian Antonin Svehla in 1926.[52] Similarly, the Serbian Agrarian Party was the only Serbian party in interwar Yugoslavia that supported federalism and regularly allied itself with its Croatian counterparts in parliament.[53] It should also be added that the nationalist component of central and Eastern European agrarian parties was devoid of the aggression present in other groupings. Two eloquent arguments suffice to demonstrate this. The first is their trajectory both within opposition and where they held power, with a foreign policy agenda that eschewed war as an instrument of such and encourage peaceful relationships with countries that

---

50 As occurring in Estonia, according to Koll (2006).
51 For an illustration of this thesis for Ruthenians and Poles in Eastern Galicia during the Hapsburg Empire, see Struve (2005: 295).
52 Sobieraj (2002: 85).
53 Biondich (2000).

had been enemies during the First World War.⁵⁴ Secondly, agrarian parties put forward proposals for a regional confederation within the parameters of na international and collaborative structure at a European level. Both pacificism and Europeanism were aspects of the identity of the *International Agrarian Bureau* (1921–1938) based in Prague, which grouped together the larger part of European agrarian parties in the Interwar Years.

e) Finally, a category can be distinguished that is not included in any of those listed previously because they are not exactly pressure groups, agrarian parties, factions of existing parties, associations or trade unions. Following the crisis at the end of the 19th century and during the first decades of the 19th century, the creation at that point and not before of mixed spaces of communication and relationships between elites and the peasantry can be identified. There is a confluence, on the one hand, of actors highly connected to a type of political action that can be defined as "populist" in historical and contextual terms, whether in the United States, in the Russia of the *narodniki* or in the Galicia of *Acción Gallega* and the *Irmandades*. These spaces of communication between elites and peasantry also constructed networks of knowledge, information and action.⁵⁵ In the Galician case, the most visible spaces are the Asambleas Agrarias (Agrarian Assemblies), imitated later by the Irmandades themselves under the name of Asambleas Nazonalistas (Nationalist Assemblies).⁵⁶ These spaces, which were relatively abundant in Europe before 1945, blended at least three types of actors: those of a new politics that was an alternative to liberalism (at times populist, at other times, classist), the agents of the new scientific and professional technocracy, agrarian specialists who grew in number and influence due to the development of new systems of state and sector innovation by rural workers themselves who had the ability to represent their interests in the political and social sphere of liberalism. These were often return migrants, affluent sectors or peasantry with aspirations to social mobility or who were representatives of their community in mediation with the State or Market.⁵⁷

---

54 This was the case of the Stamboliski government in Bulgaria, which approached Yugoslavia in spite of having ceded to this latter country some territories as a result of the Treaty of Neuilly-sur-Seine in 1919. This conciliatory policy was highly disliked by the Macedonian nationalist and terrorist organization IMRO, which contributed to its later defeat in 1923.

55 Cf. the *Nets of knowledge* defined in the session of the same name at the EURHO Bern conference (2013) by Yves Segers and L. Van Molle. www.ruralhistrory2013.org.

56 Both processes have, and not by chance, a historiographical treatment inversely proportional to their importance and genuine influence.

57 See Cabo (1998), as well as Soutelo (1999). On the emergence of state-sponsored systems of innovation, see Fernández Prieto (2007).

5 Conclusions

Ruralism, embodying a vast tradition since Classic Antiquity, exhibited an extraordinary ideological protagonism and reformulated its manifestations paradoxically in the historic moment in which rurality and agriculture began to lose steam in the West. A surprising fact is the transversality it encompasses, given that it is present in a broad range of ideological discourses. A polyvalent element, ruralism played a key role in the self-portraying of nations, even though in this process ideologues would alter the historical reality of the rural societies, adapting it to their needs. Conversely, in different organizational variants of agrarian interests detectable in Europe between the turn of the 19th century and World War II (pressure groups, agrarian wings within parties, associationism/cooperativism and agrarian parties), the national variable plays an important part but with extremely varied effects depending on each country. The ruralist discourse offered a shared meeting point between agrarian associationism and nationalisms (with or without the State, depending on the case) with great potential for mutual collaboration even while pursuing objectives held only partially in common.

The forms of organization we have presented throughout this work allowed for the creation of communication routes between elites and the peasantry which gave rise to networks of knowledge, information and action. In the Galician case, these more visible spaces are the Agrarian Assemblies, beginning in 1909 in Monforte, and which designed an ambitious reform program for Galicia in all areas—a vision which ended up being the predominant one until the Spanish Civil War. These spaces, quite abundant in Europe prior to 1945, combined a new politics (populist at times, class oriented at others) with the new technocracy of the agrarian technicians that spawned a number of new systems of state innovation and with the peasants themselves, now capable of representing their own interests in liberalism's political and social sphere.[58]

Though briefly, it is worth taking on the question of whether the multiple forms of agrarian associationism on the European continent from the end of the 19th century and interwar period constituted a democratizing factor. It seems evident that it promoted the politicizing of the rural population, but both terms are not necessarily synonyms.

---

[58] As regards Galicia, see Cabo (1998). For Spain, Fernández Prieto (2007); on the collaboration of technicians and cooperative movements on the other side of Europe, see Bruisch (2014).

We can take as an example the thesis regarded as neo-toquevillian in Political Science, inspired by the author of *Democracy in America*. The authors grouped beneath under this label link the vitality of associationism in its diverse forms to democratic stability in a given society.[59] It is tempting to establish a nexus between associative habits and democratic culture and tolerance but it still presents some dark areas. For example, in a merely quantitative analysis so dear to political scientists, they in fact underplay the *quality* of these associations. It is paradoxical that a statistical focus ultimately weighs the Ku Klux Klan or (for the case argued here) the *Comités de dèfense paysanne* of Henri Dorgères on the balancing scale of the elements which contributed to the consolidation of democracy.[60] The fact that Wilhelmian and Weimar Germany were among the European countries with the highest associative density and still this did not impede the slide into authoritarianism also raises doubts. With the necessary exceptions, we hold that European agrarian associationism constituted a primary element in the shift from a politics of notables to one of masses. The perspective is complimented by the debate as to whether the various types of agrarian associations constituted *schools of democracy,* and the response in general terms must be positive. Despite the undeniable manifestations of personality cults, the presence at times of practices of communitarian transition practices such as collective voting in electoral processes or the influence of dignitaries, each agrarian cooperative or society offered a space for socialization in politics, of public discussion and dissemination of the concept of *accountability* of public office. This extended to the creation of cadres and social capital in civil society and for acquiring practical and necessary skills for such budget accounting (for markets), keeping minutes of meetings and of formalizing agreements. In each assembly of members and in each meeting ordinary people (in many cases women as well) regularly had the opportunity to take part, on a small scale, in the democratic process regarding issues that most directly affected them. Normally, these individuals would not possess voice in public matters in any area at all. The sum of an infinite number of modest actions at the heart of voluntary associations marked a substantial contribution towards consolidating a democratic *habitus* in European society as a whole.

---

59   Among others it is necessary to note Hoffman (2003); Bermeo and Nord (2000); Putnam (1993, 2000).
60   Paxton (1996).

Bibliography

Aalen, F.H.A. (1993), "Constructive Unionism and the Shaping of Rural Ireland, c.1880–1921", *Rural History*, 14:2, pp. 137–64.

Aldenhoff-Hübinger, R. (2002), *Agrarpolitik und Protektionismus: Deutschland und Frankreich im Vergleich 1871–1914*, Göttingen: Vandenhoeck & Ruprecht.

Anderson, B. (1983), *Imagined Communities: Reflections on the Origin and Spread of Nationalism*, London: Verso.

Barral, P. (1968), *Les agrariens français de Méline á Pisani*, Paris: Armand Colin.

Beramendi, J.G. (2007), *De provincia a nación. Historia do galeguismo político, 1840–2000*, Vigo: Edicións Xerais.

Bergmann, K. (1970), *Agrarromantik und Großstadtfeindschaft*, Meisenheim am Glan: Anton Hain.

Bermeo, N., & Ph. Nord, eds. (2000), *Civil Society before Democracy*, Lanham: Rowman & Littlefield.

Billig, M. (1995), *Banal Nationalism*, London: Sage.

Biondich, M. (2000), *Stjepan Radic, the Croat Peasant Party, and the Politics of Mass Mobilization, 1904–1928*, Toronto: University of Toronto Press.

Bruisch, K. (2014), *Als das Dorf noch Zukunft war: Agrarismus und Expertise zwischen Zarenreich und Sowjetunion*, Vienna: Böhlau.

Breuilly, J., ed. (2013), *The Oxford Handbook of the History of Nationalism*, Oxford: Oxford UP.

Bruckmüller, E. (1977), *Landwirtschaftliche Organisationen und gesellschaftliche Modernisierung*, Salzburg: Verlag Wolfgang Neubauer.

Bull, Ph. (1996), *Land, politics and nationalism: A study of the Irish land question*, Dublin: Gill & Macmillan.

Cabo, M. (1998), *O agrarismo*, Vigo: A Nosa Terra.

Cabo, M. (2002), "Da revolución á cooperativa: visións literarias do agrarismo galego", in M. Romaní & M. Novoa (eds.), *Homenaxe a José García Oro*, Santiago de Compostela: USC, pp. 65–84

Cabo, M. & X.M. Vázquez Varela (2015), "Las otras guerras de nuestros antepasados: la violencia comunitaria en la Galicia rural contemporánea", *Hispania*, 251, pp. 781–804.

Carey, J. (1992), *The Intellectuals and the Masses*, London: Faber & Faber.

Caro Baroja, J. (1963), "The City and the Country: Reflections on some ancient Commonplaces", In J. Pitt-Rivers (ed.), *Mediterranean Countrymen: Essays on the Social Anthropology of the Mediterranean*, Westport: Greenwood, pp. 27–40.

Carr, E.H. (1979), *The Russian Revolution: From Lenin to Stalin (1917–1929)*, London: Macmillan.

Casanova, J. (1988), *El sueño igualitario: campesinado y colectivizaciones en la España republicana, 1936.1939*, Zaragoza, Institución Fernando el Católico.

Cloke, P. & J. Little, eds. (1997), *Contested countryside cultures. Otherness, marginalisation and rurality*, London: Routledge.

Cragoe, M., & P. Readman, eds. (2010), *The Land Question in Britain, 1750–1950*, Basingstoke: Palgrave Macmillan.

Delanty, G. & K. Kumar, eds. (2006), *The SAGE Handbook of Nations and Nationalism* London: Sage.

Dooley, T. (2004), *"The Land for the People". The Land Question in Independent Ireland*, Dublin: UCD Press.

Edensor, T. (2002), *National Identity, Popular Culture and Everyday Life*, Oxford: Berg.

Fernández Prieto, L. (1992), *Labregos con ciencia. Estado, sociedade e innovación tecnolóxica na agricultura galega, 1850–1939*, Vigo: Edicións Xerais.

Fernández Prieto, L. (2007), *El apagón tecnológico del franquismo: Estado e innovación en la agricultura española del siglo XX*, Valencia, Tirant Lo Blanch.

Fernández Prieto, L., J. Pan-Montojo & M. Cabo, eds. (2014), *Agriculture in the Age of Fascism. Authoritarian Technocracy and Rural Modernization, 1922–1945*, Turnhout, Brepols.

Gollwitzer H., ed. (1977), *Europäische Bauernparteien im 20. Jahrhundert* (Stuttgart: Gustav Fischer Verlag).

Griffiths, C.V. (2007), *Labour and the Countryside. The Politics of Rural Britain 1918–1939*, Oxford, Oxford UP.

Hawkins, A. (1991), *Reshaping Rural England: a Social History, 1850–1925*, New York: Harper & Collins.

Herb, G.H., & D.H. Kaplan, eds. (2008), *Nations and Nationalism: A Global Historical Overview*, Santa Barbara: ABC Clio, 4 vols.

Hobsbawm, E.J., & T. Ranger, eds. (1984), *The Invention of Tradition*, Cambridge: Cambridge UP.

Hoffman, S.-L. (2003), *Geselligkeit und Demokratie. Vereine und Zivile Gesellschaft im transnationalen Vergleich 1750–1914*, Göttingen: Vandenhoeck & Ruprecht.

Hübner, Ch. (2014), *Die Rechtskatholiken, die Zentrumspartei und die katholische Kirche in Deutschland bis zum Reichskonkordat von 1933*, Berlin: LIT

Kane, A. (2011), *Constructing Irish National Identity. Discourse and Ritual during the Land War, 1879–1882*, New York: Palgrave Macmillan.

King, J. (2005), *Budweisers into Czechs and Germans. A Local History of Bohemian Politics, 1848–1948*, Princeton, NJ: Princeton UP.

Koll, A.-M. (2006), "Agrarianism and Ethnicity", in H. Schultz & E. Kubu (eds.), *History and Culture of Economic Nationalism in East Central Europe*, Berlin: BWV, pp. 141–160.

Kumar, K. (2003), *The Making of English National Identity*, Cambridge: Cambridge UP.

Levinger M., & P.F. Lytle (2001), "Myth and Mobilisation. The triadic structure of nationalist rhetoric", *Nations and Nationalism*, 7:2, pp. 175–194.

Lorenz, T., ed. (2006), *Cooperatives in Ethnic Conflicts: Eastern Europe in the 19th and early 20th Century*, Berlin: BWV.

Lynch, E. (2006), "Les usages politiques du soldat laboureur. Paysannerie et nation dans la France et l'Europe agrariennes, 1880–1945", in J.-L. Mayaud & L. Raphael (eds.), *Histoire de l'Europe rurale contemporaine: du village à l'État*, Paris: Armand Colin, pp. 332–349.

Malatesta, M. (1989), *I signori della terra: L'organizzazione degli interessi agrari padani (1860–1914)*, Milan: Franco Angeli.

Mayer, A.J. (1981), *The Persistence of the Old Regime: Europe to the Great War*, New York: Pantheon Books.

Moore, B. (1977), *Social Origins of Dictatorship and Democracy: Lord and Peasant in the Making of the Modern World*, London, Penguin Books [1966].

Morales Moya, A., J.P. Fusi & A. de Blas Guerrero, eds. (2013), *Historia de la nación y del nacionalismo español*, Madrid, Galaxia Gutenberg.

Nairn, T. (1997), *Faces of Nationalism. Janus revisited* (London: Verso).

Østergård, U. (1992), "Peasants and Danes: The Danish National Identity and Political Culture", *Comparative Studies in Society and History*, 34, pp. 3–27.

Paniagua, X. (1982), *La sociedad libertaria. Agrarismo e industrialización en el anarquismo español. 1830–1939*, Barcelona: Crítica.

Paxton, R.O. (1996), *Le temps des chemises vertes. Révoltes paysannes et fascisme rural, 1923–1939*, Paris, Seuil.

Ponton, R. (1977), "Les images de la paysannerie dans le roman rural à la fin du dix-neuvième siècle", *Actes de la recherche en sciences sociales*, 17–18, pp. 62–77.

Puhle, H.-J. (1967), *Agrarische Interessenpolitik und preussischer Konservatismus im wilhelmnischen Reich (1893–1914)*, Hannover: Verlag für Literatur und Zeitgeschehen.

Putnam, R. (1993), *Making Democracy Work. Civic Traditions in Modern Italy*, Princeton, NJ: Princeton UP.

Putnam, R. (2000), *Bowling Alone: the Collapse and Revival of American Community*, New York: Simon & Schuster.

Readman, P. (2008), *Land and Nation in England*, Woodbridge: The Brydell Press.

Rommes, R. (2014), *Voor en door boeren? De opkomst van het coöperatiewezen in de Nederlandse landbouw vóór de Tweede Wereldoorlog*, Hilversum: Verloren.

Scott, J.C. (1984), *Everyday Forms of Peasant Resistance*, New Haven: Yale UP.

Scott, J.C. (1986), "Everyday Forms of Peasant Resistance", *Journal of Peasant Studies*, 13:2, pp. 5–35.

Skey, M. (2011), *National Belonging and Everyday Life*, Basingstoke: Palgrave Macmillan.

Smith, J.L. (2014), *Works in Progress: plans and realities on Soviet farms, 1930–1963*, New Haven: Yale UP.

Sobieraj, S. (2002), *Die nationale Politik des Bundes der Landwirte in der Ersten Tschechoslowakischen Republik. Möglichkeiten und Grenzen der Verständigung zwischen Tschechen und Deutschen (1918–1929)*, Bern: Peter Lang.

Soutelo, R. (1999), *Os intelectuais do agrarismo*, Vigo: Universidade de Vigo.

Sternhell, Z. (2006), *Les anti-Lumières. Du XVIII siècle à la guerre froide*, Paris: Fayard.

Stock, C.M. (1996), *Rural Radicals. Righteous Rage in the American Grain*, Ithaca: Cornell UP.

Struve, K. (2005), *Bauern und Nation in Galizien. Über Zugehörigkeit und soziale Emanzipation im 19.Jahrhundert*, Göttingen: Vandenhoeck & Ruprecht.

Tarrow, S. (1994), *Power in Movement: Social Movements, Collective Action and Politics*, Cambridge: Cambridge UP.

Tilly, Ch. (1978), *From Mobilization to Revolution*, New York, Random House.

Urwin, D. (1980), *From Ploughshare to Ballotbox. The Politics of Agrarian Defence in Europe*, Oslo: Universitetsforlaget.

Van Molle, L. (1990), *Chacun pour tous. Le Boerenbond Belge, 1890–1990*, Leuven: UP Leuven.

Van Molle, L. (2013), "Confusing categories: peasants, politics and national identities in a multilingual state, Belgium c.1880–1940", *Historia Agraria*, 60, pp. 91–118.

Varley, T. (2010), "On the Road to Extinction: Agrarian Parties in Twentieth-Century Ireland", *Irish Political Studies*, 25:4, pp. 581–601.

Villares, R. (1982), *La propiedad de la tierra en Galicia 1500–1936*, Madrid: Siglo XXI.

Weber, E. (1976), *Peasants into Frenchmen. The Modernization of Rural France, 1870–1914*, Stanford: Stanford UP.

Zangheri, R. (2000), "Contadini e politica nell'800. La storiografia italiana", in *La politisation des campagnes au XIX siècle, France, Italie, Espagne et Portugal*, Rome: École Française de Rome, pp. 13–27.

Index

A Coruña 17, 29–31, 173–77, 180, 185–86, 189, 191, 209, 266
A Nosa Terra 174, 179–80, 187–89
Abovyan, Xačatur 19
Ädelsward, Theodor 253, 255–58
Adler, Max 89, 91
Agrarian parties 270, 275, 282–285, 290
Agrarian question 11, 266–268, 277
Akçura, Yusuf 228
Albania 26
Albanian nationalism 22
All-Russian Congress of Soviets 70
Alsace-Lorraine 3, 49
Alsatian movement 160, 162, 165
Álvarez, Basilio 171, 193, 195
Ammende, Ewald 260, 262
Amsterdam 5, 11, 32
Aosta Valley 8, 45, 150–52
Armenia 48, 249
Austria-Hungary 4, 7, 43, 106, 247, 249, 252, 254
Autonomy
    Cultural Autonomy 47, 68, 71, 88, 109, 111, 126, 131, 154, 259
    Territorial Autonomy 7, 131, 136
    Non-territorial Autonomy 87, 111–12

Barcelona 22, 31–32, 55, 156, 159, 173, 184, 188, 210
Basque Country 6, 42, 51, 52, 170, 173, 184, 185, 187, 190, 192, 195, 213
Basque Nationalism 59, 167
Basque Nationalist Party 42
Bauer, Otto 7, 70, 71, 87, 89, 110–112, 119
Below, Georg von 233
Beneš, Edvard 49, 58
Bessarabia 239
Billig, Michael 281
Boer nationalism 40
Boerenbond 279, 280
Bohemia 49, 55, 104, 117, 122, 125–27, 130, 131, 133, 136, 239
Bolsheviks 4, 6, 49–51, 54, 65, 68–75, 85, 127, 235–36
Bovet, Ernest 258

Brañas, Alfredo 173, 187
Breton nationalism 161–62
British empire 11, 41, 54, 183, 193
Brittany 8, 11, 58, 161–63, 166, 187, 213
Bukharin, Nikolai 76
Bukovina 239, 254
Bulgaria 149, 234
Bulgarian language 27
Bund der Landwirte 278, 283
Butterfield, Herbert 230

Cabanillas, Ramón 176, 195
Cambó, Francesc 172, 174, 177, 182, 184–85, 189–190
Camproux, Charles 159
Carinthia 239
Carpathian basin 116
Carpatho-Ruthenians 136
Castelao, Alfonso R. 176, 185–86, 190, 192
Castilian language 180
Catalan home-rule 40, 55
Catalan language 157, 174, 210
Catalan nationalism 42, 156, 172
Catalan volunteers 53, 156, 183
Catalonia 6, 9, 40, 42, 51–55, 58, 146, 157, 170, 173, 183–84, 187, 190, 192, 195, 209–11, 267
Caucasus 3, 19, 44, 47, 67, 69, 78, 249
Celticism 30, 161–62, 187
Central Asia 3
Central Empires 3, 43, 47–48, 183
Central Organization for a Durable Peace 250
Cisleithania 104
Clemenceau, Georges 48
Coimbra, Leonardo 185
Collins, Michael 188
Colonial empires 62
Comité central des minorités nationales de France 162, 169
Communism 79, 113, 241
    and nationality question 34, 65–79, 127, 236–37
Communist Party 72, 73, 74, 76, 236
    of the Soviet Union 74

Conferences on Nationalities and Subject Races 39
Congress of European Nationalities 10, 259–62
Corsica 1, 38, 213
Croatia 11, 276
Cyprus 19
Czech/Czechoslovak Legion 127, 183, 228
Czech nationalism 137
Czechoslovakia 8, 116, 123, 126, 128, 131, 135–36, 138, 149, 212, 228, 231, 283

Darwinism 90, 92–93, 171, 227, 239
De Valera, Éamon 189
Demonstration effect 39, 155–56
Denmark 34, 281
Dickinson, Willoughby 258–59
Dualistic era 116
Dublin 2, 9, 17, 29–30, 178, 194, 227, 275

Easter Rising 17, 19, 29, 44, 161, 170, 187–88, 194
Edinburgh 32
Edwards, Robert D. 227
Eisner, Kurt 224
Émigrés 2, 7, 10, 40, 58, 59
Engels, Friedrich 94, 96
Entente 3, 6, 43–44, 48, 53, 122, 128, 135, 139, 156, 165, 252
Estelrich, Joan 190, 256, 258–59
Estonian nationalism 67, 249
Ethnography 239

Faroe islands 41
Fascism 12, 87, 152, 232, 241, 288
Fayle, C. Ernest 123
Federalism 53, 87, 97, 119, 140, 148, 154, 162–63, 166–67, 283
  Multinational federalism 106–11
Fédération Régionaliste Française 41, 147
Félibrige 41, 158, 159
Fichte, Johann G. 38, 91, 100–01, 106
Finland 37, 47, 72, 226
Fischhof, Adolf 117
Flanders 12, 38, 42, 44, 58, 154, 163–65
Flemish movement 14, 153, 169
  in France 163–65

Floral Games 22, 32, 157
Foreign Legion 53, 156
Foreign Office 57, 224–25, 250, 254, 257
Forel, Albert 251
Fourteen Points 2, 4, 6, 49–50, 53–54, 63, 130, 145, 152, 156, 172
France 8, 30, 37–38, 41–42, 49, 53, 57, 67, 123, 146–47, 154, 156–57, 159–60, 162–64, 178, 186, 209, 212–13
Frank, Walter 232–33
French revolution 96, 97, 207–08, 213, 230
Frisia 1
Frisian movement 45
Frontpartij 12

Gabrys, Jean 47–48, 150, 249–50, 253, 262
Gaelic language 31
Gaelic League 17, 29–30, 175, 177–178
Galicia 2, 5–6, 8, 9, 11, 22, 29, 31, 37, 53, 170, 173–78, 180–90, 193–95, 199, 202, 208–11, 214–16, 258, 266, 267, 275–77, 284
Galician Land-reform movement 171, 173–74, 182, 192–95, 270, 275–76
Galician language 1, 12, 31, 170, 173–74, 199, 200–03, 205, 208, 210, 214–15, 266
Galician diaspora 174
Galician nationalism 8, 9, 12–13, 170–71, 174–75, 180–84, 186, 189–90, 194, 196
Galician regionalism 17, 36, 173, 187, 193
Gantois, Jean-Marie 163–65
Garibaldi, Giuseppe 67
Geneva 2, 58, 212, 231
George, Lloyd 50, 127, 251
Georgia 48
German minorities 42
Germany 17, 34, 38, 53, 91–92, 98, 123–24, 128, 136, 152, 163, 183, 212–13, 223–26, 230–34, 238, 240, 257, 262, 279–80
  German empire 67
  Weimar Republic 57, 224
Giles, A. F. 124
Goetz, Walter 233
Goll, Jaroslav 232
Gooch, George P. 225
Great Britain 51, 123–24, 194, 337, 230
Greece 149, 249
Greek nationalism 3, 19, 22, 43

INDEX

Griffith, Arthur   40, 179
Grimm, Jacob   24–26

Habsburg dynasty   116, 133
Hegel, Wilhelm F.H.   91, 96, 100
Herder, Johann G.   100, 106, 124, 207, 212
Hersart de La Villemarqué, Théodore   26
Hildebrand, Karl   251
Hò-Chi-Minh   46
Hobsbawm, Eric J.   12, 273
House, colonel   50
Hroch, Miroslav   26, 29, 32, 34–35, 208, 282
Humboldt, Wilehlm von   102, 207–08
Hungary   8, 40–41, 57, 104, 115–16, 118, 120–21, 125, 128–32, 134–35, 137–39, 149, 233–34, 248

Indigenization   65, 72, 74
Indian nationalism   46, 58
Inter-Parliamentary Union   247–48, 250, 255–56
International Agrarian Bureau   284
International Federation of League of Nations' Societies   10
Ireland   17, 19, 29–30, 34, 37, 40, 42, 53, 172, 175, 178–80, 183–84, 186–90, 192–95, 213, 227–28, 256, 277
Irish Free State   11, 213, 227
Irish Nationalism   9, 17, 19, 155, 187
Irish Parliamentary Party   40, 188, 193
Irish Republican Brotherhood   29, 175
Irmandades da Fala   1, 17, 29, 36, 195–97, 201, 214, 216–17, 276
Irmandade Nazonalista Galega   177
Irving, Washington   21

Jaakkola, Jalmari   226
Janowsky, Oscar   262
Jászi, Oszkár   7–8, 115–16, 119–21, 128–32, 134–39, 251
Jews   68, 249, 254, 259
Joffre, Joseph   157, 183

Kaganovich, Lasar   69
Kálal, Karel   122
Kautsky, Karl   70, 87, 93–94, 110, 224
Kohn, Hans   275

Koht, Halvdan   231, 253
Krakow   229

Lange, Christian   256, 255
Language
   Language policy   83, 207, 213, 217
   Minority language   2, 9, 34, 152, 199, 211, 213
   Language revival   29
Lansing, Robert   57, 145, 148
Latvia   34, 40, 111, 127
Laun, Rudolf   251–55, 257–58
Lausanne   10, 47, 200, 249
League of Allophone Peoples   47
League of Nations   10, 51, 55, 58–59, 145, 148–50, 157, 169, 183, 212, 231, 245, 250, 256–58, 262
Lebesgue, Philéas   186, 189
Lenin, Vladimir I.   54, 65, 68–70, 73–74, 87, 94, 127, 172, 206, 236
Ligue Valdôtaine   45, 151–52
Literary renaissance   203
   in Catalonia   32, 209
   in Galicia   179, 191, 203, 209
   in Occitania   158
Lithuania   40, 47
Lliga Regionalista   40, 184, 210
London   2, 11, 39, 44, 46, 58, 122, 227, 248–49, 276
Lower Styria   239
Lugo   170, 176–77, 180, 184–85
Lviv   229

Macedonia   37
Macedonian language   27
Macedonian movement   42
MacSwiney, Terence   188
Magyar minorities   283
Magyarization   118, 131, 212
Mann, Thomas   92
Marx, Karl   88, 90, 93–95, 100
Marxism   69, 75, 88, 93–94, 96, 101, 267
   Austro-Marxism: 88–89, 108, 112, 121, 126, 191
   and national question   7, 50, 89, 93–98
   Marxism-Leninism   235–36
Masaryk, Thomáš G.   7, 8, 49, 58, 115–16, 119–128, 131–32, 135–39, 212, 231

Maspons i Anglasell, Francesc 259
Mayer, Arno J. 270
Mazzini, Giuseppe 19, 38
Mérimée, Prosper 25–26
Michels, Robert 254
Mickiewicz, Adam 19
Minority Treaties 149, 256–57, 261
Moody, Theodore W. 227
Moravia 97, 104, 117, 125, 239
Moscow 70, 72, 74–78
Munich 32
Murguía, Manuel 30, 173, 186–87, 191
Murray, Gilbert 262

Namier, Lewis 230
Napoleon Third 3
National culture 5, 71, 75–76, 92–93, 102, 104
National history 2, 22, 28, 223, 229–36, 238–40
National minorities 8, 10, 13, 58, 61, 97, 105, 108, 111, 125–26, 141, 149–50, 168, 171, 189, 247–48, 251–53, 255, 257, 260–62, 264–65
Nationalism 5, 8, 9, 12–14, 17–18, 20, 26–27, 29, 31–39, 42–43, 52–53, 59–64, 69, 81–83, 85, 87–89, 91, 95, 103, 119, 124–25, 134, 137, 140–41, 147, 153, 155–56, 161–62, 166, 175, 179–97, 211, 216, 219, 223, 226–27, 229–30, 234, 236, 238, 240–41, 243, 246, 262, 266–67, 272–73, 275–76, 279, 287–89
Nationality Law (1868) 118
Nationality principle 3, 6, 9, 43–47, 49–51, 53, 57–58, 119, 250
Netherlands 165
Noli, Fan 19
Nós 30, 172, 175, 180, 186, 188–89

Occitania 1, 8, 159
Ordzhonikidze, Grigori 69
Orlando, Vittorio 151
Oslo 238, 252
Otero Pedrayo, Ramón 170, 179, 190–91
Otlet, Paul 47, 249
Ourense 173, 175–77, 194

Painlevé, Paul 48
Pan-nationalism(s) 160
  Pan-celtism 161
  Pan-germanism 240

Pan-netherlandism 165
Pan-slavism (Slavic) 32
Paris 2, 8, 11, 22, 38, 44, 46–48, 58, 145, 150, 179, 200, 208, 249, 254–55, 260–61
Parti autonomiste bréton 162–63
Parti national bréton 42, 182, 276
Partido Galeguista 1, 182, 276
Partito Sardo d'Azione 12, 60, 213
Peace Conference 5, 8, 48, 57–58, 145, 150, 152, 160, 238, 254, 260
Peace movement 10, 39, 44–45, 47, 255
Peace Treaties 10, 149, 158, 172, 223, 233, 265
Peasant parties 11, 283
  Croatian 276, 283
  Czechoslovak 283
  Serbian 283
Pélissier, Jean 47, 48, 150, 249, 262
Peña Novo, Lois 177, 187, 190, 192
Pi i Margall, Francesc 41, 55
Plechanov, Georgij 235
Poland 22, 47, 49, 55, 57, 67, 69, 111, 123, 131, 149, 187, 211, 229, 234–35, 239, 247, 258, 261
Polish Legion 183
Porteiro Garea, Lois 175–76, 190–91
Portugal 172, 183–86, 199, 210, 626
  First Portuguese Republic 185
Portuguese language 185
Prague 4, 32, 119, 214, 284
Pokrovskij, Michail 236–37
Protection of Minorities 58–59, 112, 148, 247–48, 252–53, 256, 258–59
Provence 22, 47, 164
Public opinion 40–41, 43, 47, 58, 132, 140, 156, 158, 165

Radić, Stjepan 276
Ranger, Terence 273
Rapant, Daniel 228
Redmond, John 40
Regionalism 17–18, 27, 29, 31–32, 35–36, 147, 152, 157, 164, 166, 171–74, 177, 179, 182, 187, 189, 193–94, 209
Renner, Karl 70–71, 89, 96, 104–05, 107, 109, 119
Roden-Buxton, Charles 251
Ribalta, Aurelio 174, 209–10, 214
Ricklin, Eugène 160
Riga 4, 78, 227

INDEX

Risco, Vicente   173, 175–77, 180, 184, 186–87, 189–93, 195
Romania   38, 97, 119, 135, 149, 234, 239
Romanian nationalism   22, 47, 239, 247–48
Romansh language   45
Romanticism   90, 191, 207
Roussillon   8
Rovira i Virgili, Antoni   41, 54, 183
Ruralism   11, 267–69, 271, 272, 285
Russia   19, 43, 47, 49, 65–72, 123–24, 130, 172, 224, 227, 234–37, 249, 250, 284
  Tsarist Empire   3, 6, 42, 47–48, 66, 68
  Russian nationalism   81, 236
  Great Russian chauvinism   6, 69, 75
  Russian revolution   81, 84, 130, 230, 287
Ruyssen, Théodore   250, 258

Saami   27
Sáinz Rodríguez, Pedro   235
Santiago de Compostela   1, 6–8, 10, 31, 174, 176
Sardinia   12, 45, 213
Saussure, Ferdinand de   200–01, 214
Scotland   34, 42, 58, 162
Schleswig   5, 46, 281
Scott, Walter   21, 25–26
Seignobos, Charles   40, 249
Self-Determination   1, 2, 4–8, 11–12, 43–44, 46, 49–50, 126–27, 146–50, 152–55, 160–61, 165, 257, 262
  National Self-Determination   2, 4, 5, 7–8, 50–52, 54–55, 57–58, 68–72, 87–88, 90–92, 106, 109–11, 129–30, 136–38, 238
Serbia   11, 123, 135
Šestakov, Andrej V.   237
Seton-Watson, Robert W.   44, 121–22, 124–25, 248
Sinn Féin   29, 40, 53, 155, 179, 187, 188
Sjögren, Anders   26
Slovak nationalism   121, 134–35
Slovakia   228
Slovenia   104, 283
Social Democracy   111–12, 231
Socialism   7, 49, 71, 79, 83, 85, 95, 103, 108, 233, 237, 279
South Tyrol   46, 151–52, 239
Soviet Union   7, 65, 72–74, 77–78, 111, 225, 235–36, 238, 241

Spain   1, 20, 29, 54, 146, 170, 172–74, 176, 181–83, 189, 193, 235, 238, 256, 258–60, 262
St. Petersburg   22
Stalin, Joseph   65, 69, 71, 74–76, 87, 236–37
'State rights'   117, 121, 128
Strauss, Johann   20
Swiss German   9, 214
Switzerland   44, 48, 135, 213

Tbilisi   78
Teixeira de Pascoaes   186
The New Europe   122–27, 138
Thimme, Friedrich   224
Tisza, István   134
Toulouse   22, 158
Toynbee, Arnold J.   238
Transilvania   5
Transleithania   42, 116
Transnational Networks
  of language activists   17, 20–21, 27
  of minority groups   58–59, 76, 245–46, 249–50, 253–55, 257, 259–62
  of nationalist activists   30–33, 37–39, 47–48, 146, 155–60
Trevelyan, George   229
Trianon Treaty   234
Turku University   226
Tyrol   34, 46, 151–52, 239

Ukraine   40, 47, 69, 111, 249
Ulster   17, 19–20, 183, 227
Unió Catalanista   156
Union des Nationalités   2, 10, 47–48, 150, 169, 183, 248–49, 250
Union régionaliste bretonne   42, 160
Upper Silesia   5, 46, 239
Usteri, Paul   255

Valencia   22, 31
Versailles Treaty   188, 224, 239
Vicetto, Benito   30
Vienna   22, 50, 112, 246, 248, 252
Villanueva, Joaquín de   30
Villar Ponte, Antón   30, 170, 174, 180, 185, 187–88, 190–92, 203, 209–10, 215–16
Vilnius   22, 229, 239
Volksgeschichte   233, 238

Wagner, Richard   21
Wales   1, 24, 34, 161–62
Wallonia   8, 154
Walloon movement   19, 20, 153–55, 166
War
   Balkan Wars   3, 43
   First World War   1, 4, 5, 7–9, 11–15, 20, 26, 37–40, 42, 59, 62–63, 115–16, 121–23, 126–29, 131–32, 135–36, 139–40, 145, 147–48, 155–56, 160, 163, 168–69, 199, 211, 215, 218, 221, 223, 225–26, 228, 231, 233–34, 238–40, 243, 263, 265
   Russian civil war   4, 65, 71–72, 75

War guilty debate   223
Warsaw   229, 258
Wilfan, Josip   260
Wilson, Woodrow   4, 6, 48–51, 54–57, 127, 136, 146, 148–49, 172, 231
   ideas on self-determination   2, 4, 8–9, 45, 48–51, 130, 134, 136, 148–49, 172, 1
   myth of   53–58, 94, 141, 171, 183
Winter, Ernst K.   240

Yeats, W. B.   188, 190, 195, 215
Yerevan   78
Yugoslavia   149, 152, 261, 283

Printed in the United States
By Bookmasters